Social Forces and Schooling

EDUCATIONAL POLICY, PLANNING, AND THEORY
Series Editor: Don Adams, University of Pittsburgh

Analytical Models in Educational Planning and Administration
HECTOR CORREA

Contemporary Educational Theory
ROBERT E. MASON

Education and Emigration: Study Abroad and the Migration of Human Resources
ROBERT G. MYERS

Eucation as Cultural Imperialism
MARTIN CARNOY

Education in National Politics
NORMAN C. THOMAS

The Possibilities of Error: An Approach to Education
HENRY J. PERKINSON

The Public School Movement: A Critical Study
RICHARD PRATTE

Schooling and Social Change in Modern America
DON ADAMS WITH GERALD M. REAGAN

Schooling in a Corporate Society: The Political Economy of Education in America
MARTIN CARNOY

Social Forces and Schooling: An Anthropological and Sociological Perspective
NOBUO KENNETH SHIMAHARA AND ADAM SCRUPSKI

Social Forces and Schooling

An anthropological and sociological perspective

Nobuo Kenneth Shimahara
AND **Adam Scrupski**
Rutgers University

WITH CONTRIBUTIONS BY
Michael W. Apple, Elise Boulding, Yehudi A. Cohen,
Maxine Greene, Donald Oliver, Charles A. Reich,
and Gerry Rosenfeld

David McKay Company, Inc.   New York

SOCIAL FORCES AND SCHOOLING
An Anthropological and Sociological Perspective

COPYRIGHT © 1975 BY David McKay Company, Inc.

INTERNATIONAL STANDARD BOOK NUMBER: 0–679–30271–9

LIBRARY OF CONGRESS CATALOG CARD NUMBER: 74–24788

MANUFACTURED IN THE UNITED STATES OF AMERICA

Designed by Angela Foote

To Joan and Yasuko

PREFACE

Extensive schooling is central to the development of highly advanced industrial societies. Indeed, schooling in America is one of the most extensive institutional spheres of activity, requiring enormous social cost. Our intention here is to draw largely upon anthropology and sociology so that we may examine fundamental cultural and social processes, on the one hand, and the nature of schooling, on the other, from a viewpoint of these twin disciplines directly engaged in the study of culture and social system. In chapters where these disciplines are not explicitly involved, we attempt to explore schooling as systematically as possible in relation to its larger cultural and social matrix. Our approach, suggested by the subtitle of this book, "An Anthropological and Sociological Perspective" allows for a wide latitude of discussion in which anthropologically and sociologically relevant concepts, theories, and findings are used.

Our focus is on schooling in American society. It is discussed by eight co-authors. Since this is a collaborative volume, we have given special heed to its overall conceptual framework in order to provide a maximal unity and continuity among different chapters. As always, it is difficult to edit a collaborative work consisting of original essays even though careful plans were made at the stage of designing it. While admitting to some disjunctions among them, we hope that they are by no means detrimental to the pursuit of the central theme and the integrity of our volume.

Finally we would like to express our appreciation to Mr. Edward Artinian, director of the College Department, David McKay Company, for his efficient administrative cooperation.

Nobuo Kenneth Shimahara
Adam Scrupski

CONTRIBUTORS

Michael W. Apple is an associate professor of curriculum and instruction at the University of Wisconsin at Madison. He has written articles and monographs in curriculum theory and development on such topics as ideology and curriculum thought, the hidden curriculum, and student rights. Among his recent publications are *Educational Evaluation: Analysis and Responsibility* and the forthcoming *Schooling and the Rights of Children.*

Elise Boulding is a professor of sociology and project director of the Institute of Behavioral Science, University of Colorado. She is chairperson of the Consortium on Peace Research, Education and Development, and a member of the Board of Directors of the Institute for World Order. Professor Boulding translated Fred Polak's two-volume *The Image of the Future.* Her publications include articles published in professional journals. She is currently working on a book on the effects of modernization on women's roles in countries at all levels of industrialization and is also doing research on transactional religious networks.

Yehudi A. Cohen is a professor of anthropology at Livingston College, Rutgers University. He has conducted field work in Jamaica, Okinawa, and Israel, has taught at the University of California at Davis and at Columbia, Stanford, Northwestern, and Pennsylvania. His principal interests are political anthropology, cultural evolution, education, culture and personality, religion, and cross-cultural research. He is the author of *The Transition from Childhood to Adolescence*, author and editor of *Social Structure and Personality: A Casebook*, and editor of *Man in Adaptation* (in three volumes).

Maxine Greene is a professor of philosophy and education at Teachers College, Columbia University. Professor Greene, who was editor of the *Teachers College Record* (1965–70) and past president of the Philosophy of Education Society and the American Educational Studies Association, is currently editor of *Review of Research in Education*. She is the author of numerous journal articles and chapters in anthologies; her books include *The Public School and The Private Vision, Existential Encounters for Teachers*, and most recently, *Teacher as Stranger*.

Donald Oliver is a professor of education at Harvard University's Graduate School of Education. He has been instrumental in the development of experimental curricula and curriculum materials, having participated in the creation of the Cambridge Pilot School and authored the *Public Issues Series*, a social science curriculum program focusing on the analysis of controversial public issues. Professor Oliver has contributed many articles to such journals as the *Harvard Educational Review* and *Social Education* and is a coauthor of *Teaching Public Issues in the High School* and *Clarifying Public Controversy*. Currently he is working on a research project investigating the antecedents of the political and economic ideology of youth.

Charles A. Reich has been a professor of law (1964–74) and is currently a Senior Fellow at Yale Law School. His major interests include constitutional law, the American corporate state, and American social history. He is the author of *The Greening of America* and a number of articles published in such journals as the *Yale Law Journal, Harvard Law Review*, and *California Law Review*.

Gerry Rosenfeld was formerly chairman of the Department of Anthropology at Hofstra University and is now the director of the Graduate Program in the Teaching of Anthropology at the State University of New York at Buffalo. His interests include applied anthropology, educational anthropology, urban anthropology, and African/American cultures. Professor Rosenfeld has written *"Shut Those Thick Lips": A Study in Slum School Failure* and is currently working on another book, *Anthropology for Teachers.*

Adam Scrupski is an associate professor at the Graduate School of Education, Rutgers University, where he teaches the sociology of education. He has been active in projects designed for the education of pre-service and in-service teachers, having been a coordinator of the Rutgers Experiment in Teacher Education, and has taught in similar programs at Rutgers and Princeton Universities. Professor Scrupski has coauthored an article describing the Rutgers experimental program. Currently he is the director of the Center for Experimentation in Teacher Education at Rutgers.

Nobuo Kenneth Shimahara is an associate professor at the Graduate School of Education, Rutgers University, where he teaches the anthropology of education. He has taught at Rhode Island College, Michigan State University, and the University of Alberta. His publications include *Burakumin—A Japanese Minority and Education* (published in The Hague), *Educational Reconstruction: Promise and Challenge* (as editor), and articles which have appeared in professional journals. He is currently working on a new book that presents a critical analysis of social and educational policies of contemporary American society. His interests include the anthropology of education and urban anthropology.

CONTENTS

**PART ONE: CONTEMPORARY SOCIAL AND
CULTURAL PERSPECTIVE**   1

    1. NOBUO KENNETH SHIMAHARA
       Theoretical Framework: Introduction   *3*

    2. NOBUO KENNETH SHIMAHARA
       Cultural Evolution: Technology as a Converging Force   *15*

    3. NOBUO KENNETH SHIMAHARA
       American Society, Culture, and Socialization   *49*

    4. CHARLES A. REICH
       *Countercultural Forces: Emerging Divergence in
       American Culture*   *82*

PART TWO: THE ESTABLISHMENT SCHOOL —SYSTEM AND SENTIMENT 101

5. YEHUDI A. COHEN
   The State System, Schooling, and Cognitive and Motivational Patterns 103

6. ADAM SCRUPSKI
   The Social System of the School 141

7. ELISE BOULDING
   Adolescent Culture: Reflections of Divergence 187

PART THREE: INNOVATION OF THE ESTABLISHMENT 221

8. ADAM SCRUPSKI
   Educational Management: Promise and Failure 223

9. DONALD OLIVER
   Utilitarian Perfectionism and Education: A Critique of Underlying Forces of Innovative Education 250

10. GERRY ROSENFELD
    Urban Education: The Establishment's Last Stand 282

PART FOUR: DIVERGENCE AND ITS REFLECTION IN SCHOOLING 311

11. MAXINE GREENE
    Paul Goodman and Anarchistic Education 313

12. MICHAEL W. APPLE
    Ivan Illich and Deschooling Society: The Politics of Slogan Systems 337

13. ADAM SCRUPSKI
    Educational Horizon: Promise, Challenge, Vulnerability 361

Contemporary Social
and
Cultural Perspective

1

Theoretical Framework: Introduction

Nobuo Kenneth Shimahara

This book examines the relationship between "social forces" and schooling in American society. In general, schooling in America as an institutional function has evolved as a response to the structural differentiation of American society in which schooling is required. An extensive development of schooling since the last half of the nineteenth century is largely a function of the progressive extension of industrialism and its political system. In this sense schooling can be viewed as a positive response to societal adaptation to the needs of industrialism as well as to the needs of a societal integrative system at the industrial level of cultural evolution.

Schools reflect and reinforce the needs and order of social institutions in one way or another. But not all schools fulfill the same functions to the same degree. Critical observation suggests that they diverge in terms of their orientations relative to their responses to social forces. From a qualitative point of view this divergence deserves careful attention though, quantitatively speaking, it may not be highly significant. It suggests the existence of pressure for change in the institutional function of schooling. The essays in this volume contend that the existence of such pressure for change is *not* a phenomenon sui generis but a response to divergent social forces. We attempt to view the relationship of schooling with the society in a dialectical frame of reference.

Convergent and Divergent Forces

We define social forces in terms of two concepts: convergence and divergence. These concepts are not commonly used in the social sciences, but they can serve as analytical concepts by which to study the dialectics of culture. These two terms are in part derived from Herbert Marcuse's critical examination of "one-dimensional" society.[1] Convergence refers to one-dimensionality and domination. More concretely, it means the domination of technological rationality and its underlying political orientation over other forms of rationality and cultural life in societies of advanced industrialism in general, and American society in particular. When such domination is extensive and persists, society becomes one-dimensional in its orientation and institutional operation. Divergence, on the other hand, suggests the forces opposed to domination: the forces of "negation." Its more concrete forms are counter movements, a counter-culture, and institutional changes running counter to the essence of technological rationality.

Let us explore a social and cultural framework in which these two concepts are defined. One major aspect of our particular interest, as suggested by reference made to the notion of convergence, is the technological sphere which imposes its constraints and imperatives upon the contemporary pattern of American life. Technology, defined broadly as the socially organized capacity for controlling objects of the physical environment, has played an axial role in the development of human society and culture. It is one of the foci of attention for students of culture and society in their study of the development of social organizations. Technology constitutes a central feature relative to the contemporary institutions of American society including the political, economic, military, educational, and social spheres. Irving Kristol's commentary is apt testimony to this fact:

> It is very hard to articulate the premises beneath the religion of technology. The idea of progress is essential to it, of course. But it is not exactly the Enlightenment idea of progress, as expounded by Condorcet for instance. For though this assumed that, with the accumulation of knowledge, men would become superior creatures, it also assumed that this knowledge would be moral and philosophical, not merely technological. In contrast, we do not assert man's necessary goodness but locate the necessity in man's power. We are

therefore opposed to any authority, moral, philosophical or political, that would set "arbitrary" limits to the way in which the increase of technological knowledge shapes our world. We are against a "closed society," for an "open" one. Open to what? Well, to perfection perhaps, but to the future certainly. The justification for modernity is to be found in the modern adventure itself.[2]

Modern technology imposes upon society a new definition of rationality and a new mode of thought with emphasis on functional relations and quantitative capacity. It employs as its criteria of performance efficiency and optimization. The functional rationality, the axial principle of technology, is incorporated into new modes of education in varying degrees. Technology has contributed to the emergence of new economic interdependencies and new social interactions created by the developments in transportation and communication that are consequences of technology. It is also responsible to a considerable extent for new social relations based upon professional and occupational ties.[3]

Meanwhile, modern technology has replaced the preeminence of the primary industry that consisted of agriculture, fishery, and forestry by the secondary industry (manufacturing) and the tertiary industry (service). As economist Colin Clark, who originally used these terms, says:

A wide, simple and far-reaching generalization in this field is to the effect that, as time goes on and communities become more economically advanced, the numbers engaged in agriculture tend to decline relative to the numbers in manufacture, which in their turn decline relative to the numbers engaged in services.[4]

Among advanced industrial nations the United States is the only society that allocates more than half its total work force to the tertiary industry.[5] The characteristics exhibited by the predominance of the tertiary industry in America include: a radical shift from a goods-producing to a service economy, the preeminence of the professional and technical class, the centrality of theoretical knowledge in the performance of roles and policy formulation, utilization of technology, and decision making by "intellectual technology." [6]

While the technological extension of American society is continuously encouraged at various levels of the institutional order, its function and impact have been also brought to critical attention. For example, Marcuse contends that our society is one-dimensional where social dialectics have nearly ceased to exist, since the oppositions to the dominance of technological rationality are contained and neutralized within the dominant structure without establishing significant alternatives to domination.[7] Theodore Roszak calls this society a technocracy whose foundation is based on the monistic concept of human collectivity with technology and its administration as the most influential determining force of social life.[8] "Objective consciousness," according to Roszak, penetrates every major aspect of the social fabric. Great human problems are often considered primarily technical and therefore technically solvable; technical experts are called for as the source of salvation.

Peter Berger's observation is also relevant. He states that three cardinal principles of technological production, "mechanisticity," "reproducibility," "measurability," require the development of a particular cognitive style.[9] It is characterized by such traits as: componentiality, separation of means and ends, pervasive quality of abstraction, anonymous social relations leading to self-anonymization and componential self. What is strikingly significant is the fact that through the development of this cognitive style the individual in a technological society sees his social and cultural reality in terms of components, abstraction, and the anonymity of his own identity.

Marcuse's observation of the one-dimensionality of the contemporary industrial mode of life is cogent in many respects. The pervasiveness of objective consciousness of which Roszak speaks reinforces this one-dimensionality. Yet we have witnessed social forces that have given rise not only to cultural convergence but also to cultural divergence. For example, while our society has a tendency to create deliberately "dynamic obsolescence" and a sense of imbalance which promote greater consumption, production, and insecurity in a linear direction, the reactions to this linearity cannot be ignored. We have seen youth's disaffection toward their society, oppositions to dehumanization accelerated by technology, criticisms of the prevailing consumption pattern, the rising ecological movement, varying degrees of disloyalty toward the government, and the like. These reactions may constitute only minor forces in a quantitative sense, but they may form a significant frontier in a qualitative sense in transforming a qualitative state of human experience and consciousness.

At any rate, that social change involves "containment" of oppositions as well as conflict and polarization is undeniable. Without entirely refuting Marcuse's overall thesis, we emphasize comparatively dynamic processes of social change mediated by the forces of both convergence and divergence.

Diverging forces are not as powerful as the other in shaping the direction of the society, but they are significant and deserve critical attention. In terms of divergence we are interested in examining counter-cultural forces as one of the social oppositions. Our exploration of convergence, on the other hand, focuses on the technological network of cultural development upon which most people in America inevitably depend in order to live in the contemporary structure of our society, symbiotic in relation to the techno-network. Thus, our life is inseparable from modern technology. In large measure, the latter shapes the former in terms of its styles and context. It determines the direction of the society. Here Roszak's observation also becomes relevant.

Divergence and convergence, however, are not totally alienable from each other. For cultural divergence is in many cases a by-product of, or a reaction to, the forces of cultural convergence. The countercultural movement, for example, was initiated and has been advanced by the beneficiaries of the affluent technological society, rather than by those deprived. Nevertheless, convergence and divergence are by no means the phenomena differentiating one from another merely in terms of the degrees of contrast, but the phenomena qualitatively different from each other in terms of orientations of experience.

Schooling and Its Response to Social Forces

We believe that the theories and practices of formal education reflect, in variable degrees, these forces of convergence and divergence no less than the contemporary political modes of life. This assumption may be conceptualized in the framework of sociology of knowledge as it applies to the educational sphere of society.

Let us envisage a continuum of educational orientations in America. At one end of this continuum is the orientation of the educational establishment conforming to the social order of domination. Next to it is the orientation of educational innovation whose fundamental assumption is not significantly different from the former, but it is infused with enthusiasm for the application of advanced technology and also with a sense of what is now often called "accountability." Then, at the other end of the continuum, we find a radical orientation—"radical" in the sense that it consists, in part, of questioning the fundamental assumptions of the other orientations. It is opposed to the ideologies of the educational establishment and educational innovation. What is often called the New School Movement (or Free School Movement) is one example of this orientation.

For the sake of convenience let us call the common, central thrust of the positions of educational establishment and educational innovation an *adaptation* orientation; the position of the New School Movement a *personalistic* orientation. These two orientations are antithetical to each other.

The adaptation orientation is the predominant orientation that penetrates the theories and practice of public education in America. Within this framework, schools are seen as a powerful agent of education, compelling social members to learn knowledge, skills, values, and attitudes central to the survival of the ongoing society. The process of schooling is highly systematized; learning experience is carefully designed so as to make the young internalize the cognitive and motivational patterns of the functional structure of society. Schooling is a vital functional part of the social system in that its sociological role is evaluated in terms of the effectiveness of reinforcing individual fitness through socialization. The adaptation orientation was succinctly stated by Emile Durkheim in *Education and Sociology*:

> [The social being] is a system of ideas, sentiments, and practices which express in us, not only personality, but the group or different groups of which we are part; these are religious beliefs, moral beliefs, and practices, national or occupational traditions, collective opinions, of every kind. Their totality forms the social being. To constitute this being in each of us is the end of education.[10]

In contrast to the stress on transmissive cultural process found in the adaptive orientation, the personalistic orientation of the New School Movement is characterized by concern with personal needs and values. It reflects contemporary counterculture themes in a number of ways. Self, for example, assumes the ultimate reality of experience both in the New School Movement and the contemporary counterculture. The restoration of self and its development is the focal concern of counterculture advocates. Related to this theme is the stress upon the immediacy of experience and experiential relevance which appear in both movements. Every experience and educational event is valued for its own sake, not as preparation for remote goals.

Anarchism is also a common theme. As defined by the late Paul Goodman, anarchism is a social process where individuals' participation in communities of people, such as neighbors, professionals, and school-children, is maximized.[11] It means a breakdown of bureaucracy (where corporate needs take precedence over individual needs and where life is organized in terms of organizational imperatives). Both the New School Movement and the countercultural movement are concerned with the integrity of experience and the unity of life. The wholeness of life emerges as a theme, as in *The Making of a Counter Culture* by Theodore Roszak.

By the New School Movement we mean an emerging educational

movement advanced by neoromantic anarchists, counterculture advocates and their followers, and antitraditionalists such as those educators involved in free schools. No unified ideology or organization coordinates the movement. It is a convergence of educational ideas and practices that share common commitments. Influential among the theorists, critics, and practitioners who are spokesmen of the movement are Jonathan Kozol,[12] John Holt, Paul Goodman, Edgar Friedenberg, A. S. Neill, and Ivan Illich.

The New School Movement is also antitraditional in that it rejects the values of established schooling. Above all, Goodman, Friedenberg, and Illich are prominent spearheads of this antitraditionalism.[13] "The schools," says Goodman, "less and less represent *any* human values, but simply adjustment to a mechanical system." [14] Goodman is especially critical of the standardization of pupils' behavior and the banning of spontaneous interest and activity which the schools, he believes, impose upon children. He finds in the schools no place for spontaneity, "open sexuality," and free spirit; schools are interested only in aptitude and conformity, not in initiative. Such schooling, according to him, has lost all moral meaning. He believes that education must be entirely voluntary; that no personal growth takes place except by intrinsic motivation.

Those involved in the New School Movement believe that spontaneous growth is the objective of pedagogy and that the child has the intrinsic power to learn better when he is free from external pressures for learning. Illich, the proponent of educational anarchism, insists that most learning happens casually and that even intentional learning is not substantially the result of programmed instruction.[15] The demand for manufactured maturity which the schools make, he says, is an unpardonable negation of spontaneous activity also inflicted upon children by schools.[16]

Let us imagine a bifocal vision of a culture-and-personality continuum used in cultural anthropology.[17] Individuals are at the one end of this continuum and culture is at the other. These two poles are not separate entities but are only analytically distinguishable units on the same continuum. While the development of personality depends on culture, which provides a context of experience, the existence of culture requires the patterning of individual personalities congenial to the cultural structure. The continuum consists of a series of transactional interplay between individuals and culture with reciprocal influence. The continuum of our bifocal vision is useful to understanding the polarization that exists between the adaptation orientation and the personalistic orientation.

In reaction to the subjugation of the individual to culture which tends to be reinforced by the adaptation orientation, the New School Movement is moving to the other end of the culture-and-personality continuum. This pendulum now swings to personality. The adaptation orientation and the personalistic orientation are mutually exclusive. While the adaptation orientation of establishment and innovative education is primarily concerned with cultural internalization and universalism, with less regard for individual idiosyncrasies and interests as they relate to personal development, the New School Movement is largely interested in immediate experience, immediate relevance of education, and the unique character of each person's life-world. But the movement can also be criticized for its crass inattention to the cultural context and continuity that bind the individual life-world. Also notable is the contrast between two notions of education. The movement assumes that education is more a personal matter than a social one in that it is initiated and developed by intrinsic motivation. Establishment and innovative education sees schooling in reference to the functional prerequisites of social process. Thus, our continuum of culture-and-personality is polarized.

This is not to say that these two positions have no concern at all with reciprocal relationships between culture and personality, i.e., bifocalism. Nevertheless, their antagonism toward each other is unambiguous. What should be emphasized is the fact that the needed reciprocity between culture and personality is absent in both positions. No individuals can survive without culture, nor can culture exist without its constituents contributing to the culture's continuity.

We are interested in inquiring into the positions briefly delineated here—educational establishment, educational innovation, and the New School Movement—as they relate to the social forces of convergence and divergence.

Plan of the Book

PART 1: CONTEMPORARY SOCIAL AND CULTURAL PERSPECTIVE–Chapter 1 presents the overall conceptual framework.

Chapter 2 explores the evolutionary process of culture which has led to advanced industrialism, the contemporary level of complex cultural adaptation of American society. Particular attention is given to the role that technology has played in the evolution of culture. This chapter also examines various patterns of cultural adaptation based on technology, the function of technology vis-à-vis the development of social organizations, and industrialism. Implications of industrialism as a pattern of cultural adaptation for contemporary life of men are explored. The approach adopted is fundamentally theoretical. This chapter also outlines the nature of what we have called convergent or dominant trends in contemporary

American society. The technocratic, organizational, objective perception of reality characteristic of participants in such a social structure is examined.

Chapter 3 focuses on American society and attempts to provide a structural interpretation of the society. The structure and process of American society is discussed in terms of structural differentiation and adaptive upgrading. Major emphasis is placed on broad economic, technological, organizational, political, belief systems, and other social phenomena resulting from structural differentiation with attention to family structure and socialization practices. The main aim of this chapter is to provide a theoretical exposition of American society and culture.

Chapter 4 deals with the emergence of what Roszak, Reich, and Revel refer to respectively as counterculture, Consciousness III, and the new American revolution—what we have termed divergence. The roots of this divergence are explored. Thus, the relationship of convergent and divergent phenomena in a new kind of dialectic are demonstrated.

PART 2: THE ESTABLISHMENT SCHOOL—SYSTEM AND SENTIMENT–Chapter 5 explores interrelationships among state systems, schooling, and cognitive and motivational patterning. The author examines an evolutionary process of society in which schools have been developed as an aspect of states' adaptations to pressures engendered by their participation in civilizational networks. Schooling is seen as fulfilling a function of social-boundary maintenance. Particular attention is given to the structure and process of various institutional spheres determining the function of schooling in complex industrialism and to the contribution schooling makes to the patterning of cognitive and motivational bases for the maintenance of the state system.

In chapter 6 the author examines the social system of the traditional school as it supports and extends the structure and sentiments that characterize the established classroom situation. The conventional school organization, composed of administration, faculty, guidance counselors, and other support personnel, with its accompanying pattern of relationships and sentiments is viewed in a systemic relationship to the classroom group, supporting and strengthening the basic orientations and patterns of interaction developed therein. Thus, when convergent forces make themselves felt in the school today, it is not surprising that conflict and discord involve the entire school.

Moving to chapter 7, the adolescent subcultures are treated as they are related to the convergent and divergent forces of the society. They are viewed in a historical perspective. The central thrust of this chapter is to develop a typology of adolescent subcultures as various modes of adaptation of the adolescents. Social class enters as a major variable in the typology. Particular attention is given to social-system orientations and sociah charactaristics of different adolescent subcultures.

PART 3: INNOVATION OF THE ESTABLISHMENT–In part 3 what we have called the "educational innovation" of the establishment may be seen as the attempt on the part of representatives of the established order in education to contend with emerging forces through an extension of convergent method. Thus, chapter 8 reviews the characteristics of educational administration as a discrete enterprise whose concern roughly parallels and reflects the development of the technostructure in American society. The structure and process of educational administration is explored extensively from a sociological point of view.

Turning to chapter 9, a critical examination is made of an ideology that underlies the contemporary social and cultural conditions in which innovative education is operating. Utilitarianism, the central orientation of this ideology, is seen as a dominant philosophical foundation for innovative education.

In chapter 10 the great failure of American education—mid-century urban schools—is seen in the context of extending bureaucratization. Accountability as a bureaucratic notion in a technocratic society is employed in an attempt to ensure service in an educational system that bureaucracy itself seems to have brought to the point of breakdown.

PART 4: DIVERGENCE AND ITS REFLECTION IN SCHOOLING–Chapter 11 and 12 return to an examination of divergent forces with a critical treatment of significant representative aspects of the New School Movement. The treatments of education by Paul Goodman and Ivan Illich reflect better than any others current dissatisfaction with present-day schools. Both Goodman and Illich, unlike other contemporary critics of education, propose alternative forms of education which seem consistent with many of what we consider divergent trends. In addition, their general sensitivity to the position of youth in contemporary society offers the possibility of relating their proposals to the earlier treatment of the adolescent culture as a divergent phenomenon.

Thus chapter 11 focuses attention upon the late Paul Goodman, a spokesman of the divergent forces who critically examined the function of schooling and, in turn, offered a proposal to make education more conducive to personal growth. The author of this chapter discusses also Goodman's vision of anarchism which is, for him, a better form of social relations.

Chapters 11 and 12 complement each other in the sense that while the former explores a microcosmic aspect of deschooling and education as a process of personal growth, the latter examines a macrocosmic dimension of deschooling. Ivan Illich, another powerful spokesman of the divergent forces, contends that society must be deschooled if the individual and community are to foster authentic qualities of life. Illich offers a sociological critique of contemporary schooling as its principal function is oriented toward meeting the needs of the corporate order of society. Chapter 12 looks at these aspects of Illich's vision.

Following the essays on Illich and Goodman, chapter 13 examines the promise and vulnerability exhibited by the New School Movement which is reflected in the general orientation toward education promoted by Goodman and Illich.

NOTES

1. See Herbert Marcuse, *One-Dimensional Man* (Boston: Beacon Press, 1968).
2. Irving Kristol, "Keeping Up With Ourselves," in *The End of Ideology Debate*, ed. Chaim I. Waxman (New York: A Clarion Book, 1968), p. 107.
3. For a further discussion, see Daniel Bell, *The Coming of Post-Industrial Society* (New York: Basic Books, 1973), p. 189.
4. Colin Clark, *The Conditions of Economic Progress* (London: Macmillan, 1960), p. 492.
5. Bell, *The Coming of Post-Industrial Society*, p. 15.
6. Ibid., p. 14.
7. See Marcuse, *One-Dimensional Man*, pp. 1–120.
8. Theodore Roszak, *The Making of a Counter Culture* (New York: Anchor Books, 1968), pp. 1–41.
9. See Peter Berger, Brigitte Berger, Hansfield Kellner, *The Homeless Mind: Modernization and Consciousness* (New York: Vintage Books, 1973), pp. 24–40.
10. Emile Durkheim, *Education and Sociology* (Glencoe, Ill.: Free Press, 1956), p. 124.
11. Paul Goodman, *The New Reformation* (New York: Random House, 1970), pp. 143–64.
12. Kozol's position has recently changed toward political radicalization. See Jonathan Kozol, *Free Schools* (Boston: Houghton Mifflin, 1972).
13. See Paul Goodman, *Compulsory Mis-education and the Community of Scholars* (New York: Vintage Books, 1964); Edgar Friedenberg, *Coming of Age in America* (New York: Vintage Books, 1965); Ivan Illich, *Deschooling Society* (New York: Harper & Row, 1971).
14. Goodman, *Compulsory Mis-education*, p. 21.
15. Illich, *Deschooling Society*, p. 12.

16. Ibid., p. 60.

17. See standard texts on culture and personality. For example, Anthony Wallace, *Culture and Personality* (New York: Random House, 1970); John Honigmann, *Personality in Culture* (New York: Harper & Row, 1967).

2

CULTURAL EVOLUTION: TECHNOLOGY AS A CONVERGING FORCE

Nobuo Kenneth Shimahara

This chapter explores the evolutionary process of culture that has led to advanced industrialism, the contemporary level of cultural adaptation of American and other equivalent societies in terms of technological development. Of particular interest is the role that technology has played in the evolution of culture. Attention is given to various patterns of cultural adaptation based on technology, the function of technology vis-à-vis culture, the effect of technology upon the development of social organizations, and industrialism and its social organizations. Implications of modern industrialism as a pattern of cultural adaptation for contemporary men are also discussed. This chapter does not focus on American culture per se but it is discussed in the general context of our inquiry into the process of cultural evolution in which American culture has demonstrated the most advanced form of industrialism, capable of employing highly complex and sophisticated technology.

In order to survive and perpetuate, man not only adapted to a habitat that imposed particular physical conditions upon him, but he also actively attempted to utilize it. Energy is the source of man's life, process, and organization, just as it is the source of the movement of extrasomatic objects and constitutes the physical universe of which man's environment is a part. In this sense human life is understood as a mode of adaptation involving a process of capturing and utilizing free energy to put it to work in the service of man. Thus, culture as the self-expression of man and his activities is the same process that constitutes the most vital basis for his biological perpetuation as well as his social life and its extension.

As Leslie White says, "Culture is an organization of things in motion, a process of energy transformations." [1] When culture is viewed as a process of energy transformations, its foundation is identified as a system of human activities employed to harness free energy. In this sense, every culture is an organization of activities intended to produce need-serving goods and services. What this means is that these human activities are organized to harness and transform free energy to meet the needs of people as they are culturally and biologically defined. Culture captures energy from nature and transforms it into people and their social and political systems. The level of cultural development seen from both qualitative and quantitative aspects, therefore, is determined by the extent to which the energy system of culture is advanced. The question of how the harnessing of energy is implemented is a problem that various cultures have had to solve in one form or another.

Technology has its locus in the context of this problem of man's cultural evolution. [2] Technology must be understood here broadly as a structure of human behavior and its product by means of which man's adaptation to the external world is achieved and maintained. It is "the socially organized capacity for actively controlling and altering objects of the physical environment in the interest of some human want or need." [3] For the survival and extension of man's society culture must secure food, protection from enemies, and internal solidarity and continuity. Life-sustaining and life-extending processes are technological in an inclusive sense; they involve the interaction between man and the environment which requires the utilization of energy. [4]

Inception of Civilization

Let us look first at the earliest stages of the evolution of culture in order to appreciate the general relationship between technological development and the growth of the energy system of culture.

Archaeologist Gordon Childe points out that man's organic evolution came to a standstill about 25,000 years ago. [5] Yet man's post-organic, cultural evolution did not exhibit its dramatic development until the beginning of the last one-third of the history of the biologically matured *Homo sapiens*. The Neolithic times of the prehistoric period first started to stimulate drastic cultural evolution approximately 7,000 to 8,000 years ago in Egypt and Mesopotamia—a period archaeologically identified as the New Stone Age.

Archaeologists divide the prehistoric period into Stone, Bronze, and Iron Ages by the criteria pertaining to the technological materials used for production, particularly cutting instruments such as axes. These divisions, however, do not only represent different stages of the development of technological instruments but also their significance in the growth of complex social relations, division of labor, and economic and political structure. The Stone Age is further divided into the Paleolithic period (the Old Stone Age) and the Neolithic period (the New Stone Age). Men of the Paleolithic period possessed the lowest level of technology to harness energy, as seen in the fact that they relied for a living entirely upon hunting, gathering, fishing. Their adaptive pattern was purely primeval nomadism. But from a point of view of their ability to appropriate energy, a few things must be said about them. They were able to use fire. Certainly man's control of fire contributed to his emancipation from the total dependence upon his environment. It enabled man to endure cold weather and subsequently to penetrate into temperate and even cold regions. It enabled him to cook substances indigestible if not cooked. Men of the Upper Paleolithic groups also learned to make certain tools adapted to special purposes, such as highly simple bows and spearthrowers.

The Paleolithic period was followed by the Neolithic revolution, the duration of which extends from about 7000 B.C. to 1800 B.C. depending upon cultural groups.[6] The Neolithic revolution brought about the first dramatic change in the energy system of culture by providing man with a higher level of technological control over food supply. It involved a system of energy transformation in the form of cultivation and stock-breeding which were developed as a result of the domestication of wild grasses and plants and wild animals. It should be noted that the production of wheat and barley constituted the foundation of early Neolithic economy. But this economy evolved in the form of nomadic horticulture largely due to men's inability to solve the problem of soil exhaustion. In the central regions of the Neolithic "civilization" such as settlements in North Africa, however, horticulture became more stabilized and was combined with stock-breeding. This mixed-farming economy provided man with not only greater control over human food supply but also a motivation for the accumulation of food surplus which was indispensable for the development of urban states. Tools used by Neolithic men became more sophisticated. They learned to sharpen the edge of the Neolithic tool by grinding. Attention should also be paid to the fact that the Neolithic economy stimulated the increase of population.[7]

Thus, the preparation for higher levels of social organizations had been made. Here arrived now the post-Neolithic period (the Bronze Age) which set a preliminary stage for the growth of urban cultural life. This was a new energy system harnessed by new tools; efficient means of transportation; collectivities of men; improved efficiency of farming economy; the development of the division of labor and political systems; and the invention of new symbolic systems which include writing, measurement, and calendrical systems. This period had its inception sometime between 6000 and 3000 B.C.[8] It began to transform advanced Neolithic communities of self-sufficing farmers into populous, sedentary settlements which may be called cities; and as this transformation further developed, these cities constituted politically regulated states based upon primary industries as well as secondary industries.[9] It represented a greater degree of technological sophistication. This was the beginning of movement from what Lewis Morgan called *societas* (society) to *civitas* (state). The following paragraph in his *Ancient Society* expounds this point:

It may be here premised that all forms of government are reducible to two general plans, using the word plan in its scientific sense. In their bases the two are fundamentally distinct. The first, in the order of time, is founded upon persons, and upon relations purely personal, and may be distinguished as a society (societas). . . . The second is founded upon territory and upon property, and may be distinguished as a state (civitas). The township or ward, circumscribed by metes and bounds, with the property it contains, is the basis or unit of the latter, and political society is the result. Political society is organized upon territorial areas, and deals with property as well as with persons through territorial relations.[10]

The formative stage of political organizations and technological instruments deserves brief attention here. Permanent and collective settlement was not accidental but was required by the geographical and economic conditions of Neolithic communities in North Africa and the Middle East. Irrigation was needed to supply constant water; related to it was the need for collective work to restrain the violence of floodwaters by creating banks and also to create drainage channels to dry swamps. Large-scale irrigation required the collective mobilization of stupendous human labor which, in turn, necessitated a certain pattern of political coordination. Coupled with such new developments was reclamation. Land for the great cities of Babylonia, for example, had to be virtually reclaimed, an undertaking beyond the power of individuals or small groups. It demanded an organization of labor, a capital of labor freed from farming, a stock of surplus foodstuffs consumed by men engaged in draining, embanking, and reclamation. While these conditions facilitated the stabilization of settlement, the enlargement of farming products and the improvement of housing accommodation and architecture made further contributions to it.

Meanwhile, stone implements began to be replaced by metal ones—copper implements. This marked a great scientific and technological advance. Men learned to smelt copper ores, transforming them into copper. The fusibility of copper provided its superiority over stone. Intelligent metallurgy had already developed between 4000 and 3000 B.C., but in the technological developments of this period we must include the use of plows drawn by oxen, wheeled vehicles, the use of domesticated camels, and the improvement of navigation with the invention of dugout canoes and skinboats. They contributed to a revolutionary change in agricultural production and transportation. Thus, men acquired more control over the harnessing of energy, and in so doing they ushered in the dawn of politically regulated societies, that is, pristine-nation-states (entering the Iron Age).

By 3000 B.C. the evolutionary cultural focus shifted to states based upon urbanization, social stratification, and more intensified division of labor. The political foreground of these stages was composed of a theocratic elite including priests, princes, scribes, officials, specialized craftsmen, and professional soldiers. The formation of states enabled them to implement enormous networks of large-scale irrigation. As Yehudi Cohen contends, "the construction of these networks [large-scale irrigation networks] has always followed the integration of a society into a nation state by centrally unifying political institutions." [11] From a political point of view, the construction of such irrigation networks conferred upon the political elite effective power to control people, not only because the latter depended upon them for the indispensable water supply, but also because the construction required an exceptionally effective means of imposing sustained effort and discipline upon communities that benefited by it. States also need to mobilize men in the area of trade to import the most vital materials for growing urban life such as timber, freestone, and ores, since the Nile Valley and Sumer were short of them.

As metallurgy advanced further, metallurgical specialization occurred. This is demonstrated by the evidence that goldsmiths made wire and solder; coppersmiths could probably employ the *cire perdue* process—a highly sophisticated process of molding smelted copper by pouring it into a model made of clay. The industrial use of iron did not appear until about 1300 B.C., however, and it was first introduced in Asia Minor, not in Mesopotamia or Egypt.

What we have seen here is a progressive extension of men's capability to transform energy more effectively: greater technological control over water supplies, rivers, geographical conditions; greater command of food supply; and formation of states where labor, settlements, housing accommodation, trades, irrigation, and specializations were politically controlled by centralized authorities. "The urban revolution" was accomplished in Egypt, Mesopotamia, and the Indus Valley.[12]

Our discussion at the start of this chapter revolved around the proposition that a culture is an energy-transforming system, a system which attempts to put free energy to work in the service of cultural needs. We have illuminated this proposition by referring to the development of energy systems of culture, focusing attention on Neolithic times and the pre-Neolithic period as well as the post-Neolithic. The reader must be aware, however, that the demarcations among these periods are highly arbitrary and that they overlap each other in actuality, depending upon cultural groups. Yet central technological strategies of cultural adaptation in these periods are clearly distinguishable from one another. We have shown how technological levels contributed to differential digress of the utilization of free energy.

In summary, hunting-gathering is the first energy system of culture. It represents a highly primordial technological level in that it is totally dependent upon men's use of muscular energy and the conditions of natural forces. The horticultural strategy advanced through techniques involved in energy transformation; it acquired greater control over human food supply through farming. Pastoralism was soon added to farming in order to increase energy supply. Agriculture, which came into operation later, produced a higher technological order. It involved a complex organization of manipulation of natural forces including the plowing of agricultural land by draft animals, irrigation, and reclamation. Population growth, permanent settlements, an urbanized mode of life, and the rise of political societies were concomitant phenomena.

Cultural Evolution and the Role of Technology

The function of technology is discussed here in an evolutionary perspective of culture. Brief attention is first given to the historical background of evolutionism and, in turn, the role of technology is discussed. Cultural evolutionism has been a highly controversial issue since evolutionary theories were advanced in the nineteenth century; in fact, the evolutionary approach to studies of culture has been severely curtailed in the twentieth century, particularly in anthropology. When Franz Boas, the dean of anthropology in the first half of this century, started to attack evolutionism, the evolutionary approach was all but abandoned by anthropologists, at least until the 1940s. As Elman Service points out, "Leslie A. White, Julian Steward, and V. Gordon Childe[13] were virtually alone in opposing the antievolutionary temper of the times." [14] Not until after the mid-century was an evolutionary outlook received with little hostility (if not favorably) in American anthropology. Anthropologists' interests in evolution are now reviving gradually.

The evolutionary interpretation of culture was promoted by Lewis Morgan and Edward Tylor in America and England respectively. They viewed cultures as evolving according to the universal scheme of progressive development, but they were not concerned about the process of systemic change of particular societies.[15] Morgan, for example, divided it into what he called "ethnical periods" designated as savagery, barbarism, and civilization. The former two ethnical periods were in turn broken down respectively into lower status, middle status, and upper status. In Morgan's scheme the energy system developed by hunting and gathering belongs to the level of savagery while the period of the Neolithic revolution represents the middle status of barbarism and the upper status is characterized by the invention of the process of smelting iron ores. Civilization begins when nation-states come into existence along with a sophisticated phonetic alphabet and writing systems. In both Morgan and Tylor's framework of evolution, technology and material culture are regarded as achieving a cumulative evolution independent from other aspects of culture such as religion and intellectual progress.

Meanwhile, influential nineteenth-century sociologists such as Herbert Spencer and Emile Durkheim also interpreted social development in an evolutionary framework. In Spencer's view social evolution consists of a universal social process in which cultural progress is determined by the extent to which society undergoes complexity and heterogeneity.[16] For Durkheim the division of labor is the key to the progress of society (as will be discussed later in detail).[17] Marx and Engels, too, developed about the same time what they termed "historical materialism," in essence an evolutionary interpretation of society in which technology and economic mode of production play key roles.

The evolutionary approach is different from a historical one. The fundamental question here is to determine how evolution differs from history. According to Leslie White, the most influential contemporary spokesman of evolution in anthropology, evolution is a progressive sequence of forms which are identified and studied without reference to particular times and locations of cultures; history, on the other hand, is a developmental process of unique events whose relevance is determined in terms of particular times and places. As White states, evolution is "a temporal sequence of forms: one form grows out of another; culture advances from one stage to another." [18] While White's position has been disputed by Alfred Kroeber,[19] George Murdock,[20] and others, it has received a conceptual elaboration undertaken by Marshal Sahlins and Elman Service.

Sahlins argues that evolution is a bifocal process or phenomenon.[21] The first is what he terms "specific evolution," which means that a specific culture improves its chances for survival by increasing its adaptability. Specific evolution consists in a particular system's progress in the efficiency of energy capture and its adaptation to an environment. It demonstrates, therefore, the phylogenesis of a given cultural system. The second is general evolution. It is a directional process of cultural progress stage by stage, a development of cultural forms measured by universal and absolute criteria without reference to adaptive specializations of individual cultures. Sahlins states:

> Specific evolution is not the whole of cultural evolution. Culture not only produces adaptive sequences of forms, but sequence of higher forms; it has not only undergone phylogenetic development, but over-all progress. In brief, culture has evolved in a general respect as well as a specific one.[22]

It is assumed that culture in a generic sense of the term evolves from lower to higher levels of energy capturing, integration, and all-round adaptability. On the other hand, specific evolution is assumed to be a ramifying, specifying process of culture, that is, "adaptive modifications of particular cultures."

These polaristic types of evolution, according to Service, are inversely related to each other.[23] The more specialized a given culture is in its adaptation, the less potential it has for advancing to a next stage of all-round cultural development in general evolution. This means that new advances in the sense of overall progress are more likely to take place in less specialized individual cultures where there is not a high degree of stabilization of adaptive specializations than in highly specialized cultures. Service calls this relationship obtaining in evolution "the Law of Evolutionary Potential." [24]

The conceptual elaboration undertaken by Sahlins and Service has contributed to the clarification of White's position. White is primarily concerned with one aspect of evolution, i.e., general evolution rather than specific evolution. On the other hand, anthropologists like Krober and Julian Steward are interested in specific evolution, as exemplified by Steward's theory of multilinear evolution.[25]

Let us now discuss the function of technology within the framework of evolution examined above. As we have seen, technology constitutes a vital force in the systemic development of culture affecting particularly political, economic, and social structures. If man and culture are defined as thermodynamic systems of energy capture contributing to each other, facilitators of energy transformation become an important factor in cultural evolution. Man seeks to capture the free energy available in nature and transform it into various forms of socially shared expressions and organizations whose integrated system is called culture. Culture in turn seeks to ensure man's biological function by providing food, protecting and defending him against external forces, and maintaining the integration of people. The function of culture, in other words, is to harness free energy and its expenditure. Technology is a prime facilitator for the utilization of cosmic energy.

In pursuing the function of technology an important question is posed. Because technology is crucial to the development of an energy system of culture, some evolutionists, such as Marx, Engels, and White, identify technology as the prime determinant of culture, the other systems of culture being secondary to and subjugated to the influence of technological forces. Among contemporary evolutionists White has best articulated a theory of technological determinism. But not all evolutionists subscribe to this position, although they, too, regard technology as a vital factor in the evolution of culture. According to the determinist position, technology determines not only the direction of progressive cultural development but also the structural basis of society. Various criticisms have been raised against it including the following by Frank Miller:

> . . . the role of technology in social cultural change has long been the focus of scholarly dispute. . . . Determinism, in simple language, is the doctrine that things or events are determined; that is, they have to be the way they are because certain laws or forces make them that way. . . . I deliberately use the term "doctrine" rather than "theory" because I consider these arguments to be philosophical disputes about basic assumptions, not debates about scientific theories that can be verified or rejected by empirical evidence.[26]

We do not argue, however, that the technological determinism espoused by White is merely an ontological belief. It is not a doctrine as defined by Miller but a theory which can be subjected to empirical analysis. We wish to treat White's position as a hypothesis rather than a doctrine, to be examined further. Let us take a closer look at it.

In his article titled "Energy and the Evolution of Culture" published in 1943 which became a basis of his later works, White contends:

> *The social organization* (*E* excluded [*E* refers to ends of a social system such as solidarity and integration as compared with means such as mechanisms for food getting, defense from enemies]) *of a people is dependent upon and determined by the mechanical means with which food is secured, shelter provided, and defense maintained.* In the process of cultural development, *social evolution is a consequence of technological evolution.*[27]

In *The Science of Culture* he states: "Social systems are in a very real sense secondary and subsidiary to technological systems. . . . The technology is the independent variable, the social system the dependent variable." [28] He distinguishes three or sometimes four subsystems of culture put in the order of functional relationships: technological, sociological, ideological systems.[29] He posits that the social organization or sociological system of culture is a function of the technological system, and in turn that the ideological system is a function of the sociological system. Thus the three-level system composes an order of functionally deterministic relationships underlying a culture.

Nevertheless, White recognizes clearly that the sociological system is capable of conditioning the operation of technology, and that ideology can also affect social organizations. The relationship among them, he admits, is one of mutual interaction and influence, "though not necessarily equal." A given social system may arrest the development of technology by generating restraints imposed upon a culture or it may encourage its operation. One example of the latter may be the American and Russian social systems which helped accelerate the development of military technology involving nuclear physics, space exploration, biochemistry, and sophisticated engineering during and after the cold-war period; an example of the former would be the political and social systems of the Middle Ages which restrained technological growth. In White's words,

> When the expanding technology comes into conflict with the social system, one of two things will happen, either the social system will give way, or technological advance will be arrested. If the latter occurs, cultural evolution will, of course, cease.[30]

White's argument does not stop here, however. These systems, he insists, do condition each other but "to condition is one thing; to determine, quite another.[31] He then presents his evolutionary formula that two factors determine the level of cultural evolution, i.e., the level of the magnitude of human need-serving goods and services produced and expended: the first is the total amount of energy harnessed by man per capita per year; the second, the development of technology or the efficiency of the technological means with which energy is transformed.

Though he does not reject White's general theory of cultural evolution, Sahlins takes a more critical and cautious stand. He emphasizes local selective circumstances as crucial to the total transformation of free energy into cultural forms and organizations.[32] Whereas technological efficiency is the key determinant in White's theory, Sahlins points out that it cannot be an absolute determinant of cultural progress. Increased technological efficiency, argues Sahlins, may be counterbalanced by a local selective circumstance in which a people may decrease their labor input when technical efficiency increases. In this case the total amount of cultural expansion is not in proportion to the rate of technological efficiency. This phenomenon is often seen in less advanced societies of energy system upon which Western technology is imposed. Sahlins also argues that cultural progress is the *total transformation* involved in the maintenance and development of a cultural organization.[33] Progress thus is not entirely equated with technological advancement. It involves a higher energy level of culture characterized by increased systemic complexity and differentiation. In other words, it is manifested in the proliferation of material elements; a multiplication of social groups; an increase in the division of labor; and more effective means of social integration such as clan, tribe, nation-state.

Here we are primarily interested in exploring the relationships between technology and other systems of culture. We have seen that the technological, sociological, and ideological systems of culture interact with one another, constituting functional relationships. Along with the evolutionists' position, we hypothesize that the technological system has greater conditioning effect on the total organization of culture than the other systems in the process of interaction among the three systems.

In this connection, it may be relevant to make reference to another view. Yehudi Cohen, whose anthropological disposition is evolutionary, contends:

. . . it appears to me that technological change underlies institutional change in stateless societies; conversely, changes in nontechnological (especially political) institutions underlie technological change in nation-states. In the latter case, institutional changes stimulate technological development, and the latter in turn lead to accommodations in family and kinship systems, in many aspects of law and social control, in religion and values and ideologies.[34]

Here Cohen does not speak of determinism but of the dominance of particular institutions over other institutions. His inquiry into the relationships between the technological sector and the nontechnological one is highly relevant and feasible. Cohen does not sufficiently explain, however, why the sequence of institutional domination is radically reversed as cultural evolution passes from the level of stateless society to the level of nation-state. He simply presents a point of debate that at the stateless level cultural organizations based primarily on kinship systems are largely related to, and function in connection with, the demands of technology; but that when these organizations are politically integrated into a state, it is the political institutions to which other institutions including the technological respond. To him, political integration therefore constitutes the key in the transition of relationships between technology and nontechnological institutions. And "the political institutions of a state," insists Cohen, "embody only the potentials for technological advance and do not guarantee that it will occur, but technological advance is always severely limited in the absence of a unifying state." [35]

In relation to Cohen's position, it is hypothesized that political integration is a necessary condition for the embodiment of technological potentials but not a sufficient one. This hypothesis becomes particularly significant when it is applied to a gamut of nation-states with different degrees of technological advancement which passed the stage of statelessness many centuries ago. In examining highly industrialized societies like the United States, is it a feasible proposition to assume that the political structure is more influential than advanced technology in the development of social organizations and ideology? This question remains unanswered and requires further inquiry.

Social Organizations and Technology

We turn now to the development of organizations of culture that come into play with technology. Our thesis has been that technology is a major evolutionary factor in the total transformation of energy into need-serving goods and services expended by men; that is, into the social organizations developed to meet their needs and extend their culture effectively. A social organization is a relatively stable pattern of social relations of individuals within a society; it involves the definitions of roles and statuses of the members of an organization and, therefore, refers to a social structure. From an anthropological point of view, its rudimentary function is to promote a society in which its structural features are defined. It consists in a threefold role. It involves an organization of human activities to secure shelter and food; an organization of mechanisms and regulations by which the constituent members are protected from both internal and external forces of hostility and aggression; an organization to promote the extension of a society through successful biological reproduction.

The effectiveness and development of social organization depends upon technology since technology conditions its functions. When, for example, the energy system of a social organization must depend solely on the energy of human organism, its efficiency and capacity are minimal. At this level men are primarily engaged in the appropriation of natural energy made available by hunting and gathering. The capability of social organization expanded significantly when men learned to harness free energy by the domestication of wild animals and cereals. The distinction between the appropriation of natural resources and their harnessing consists in the improvement of men's mastery of technology to control extrapersonal energy. When they domesticated animals and cultivated the cereals, men put a part of nature under their control. The energy resources for culture building were greatly increased as a consequence of this increase in control over the forces of nature. Technology conditions the capacity of social organization to function; and it can also significantly affect the level of social differentiation and complexity—the degree of division of labor and economic development, and the level of political integration. We look next at the relations between these aspects of social organization and technology.

SOCIAL DIFFERENTIATION AND COMPLEXITY–Differentiation and complexity are two functional dimensions of cultural evolution by means of which the degree of cultural development can be determined. Differentiation refers to a proliferation of groups of individuals, an increase in the division of labor, and the development of social stratification. Complexity indicates levels of social and political integration.[36] The more culture evolves, the greater the degree of differentiation becomes, and the more complex culture grows, the higher level of integration it requires. The division of labor and the level of political integration are specific dimensions of a general evolutionary process of differentiation.

Morton Fried has developed a useful taxonomy of society which we can apply to the discussion of our problem.[37] Fried categorizes societies in an order of evolutionary process: (1) egalitarian society, (2) rank society, (3) stratified society, (4) state society.

The minimal level of differentiation and complexity is found in simple egalitarian societies.[38] While egalitarian society is characterized by an absence of institutions and their related features, it provides all individuals with relatively equal social recognition and positions of valued status as long as they are capable of filling such positions. This type of society depends upon a hunting-and-gathering technology whose operation is made possible by the use of men's muscular energy. It corresponds to the technology of the Paleolithic period. This technology does not allow the development of large political units and food surpluses; nor does it make possible the differentiation of roles except in terms of sex and age. Egalitarian society is generally based on the social structure of a small band composed of a small number of families. Its foundation is a network of kinship system and its social order is characterized by the equal distribution of prestige and a system of reciprocal economy. These simple societies are marginal in terms of the potentials of energy system to be captured and far from civilizational centers. Some examples of such societies are the Eskimo, African Bushman, Australian Bushman, and Pygmy.[39]

Rank societies[40] represent the next development of social differentiation and complexity. Technology is not yet developed enough to introduce a complex division of labor in a rank society; nor does it require the extensive development of social stratification. The division of labor of a rank society is still inarticulate and primarily based on the criteria of age and sex as in the case of an egalitarian society. However, a rank society is a social structure in which positions of valued status are established to which a limited number of persons can have access, but it does not limit the access of individuals to the basic natural and social resources.[41] The introduction of this elementary hierarchy of prestige becomes necessary as kinship systems and the size of society grow larger. A rank society no longer depends greatly upon hunting-and-gathering technology; it is based on horticultural and even rudimentary agricultural technology. Relatively large villages and permanent settlements come into existence as a consequence of this new technology; egalitarian societies, in contrast, are small nomadic bands and have less population density. These features of the society allude to the dawn of the Neolithic agricultural revolution. Another emerging feature of a rank society is its economic system. Though the form of economic circulation is the reciprocal exchange as seen in an egalitarian society, the exchange is more systematized in a rank society to achieve an integration of economic system. There is a center of exchange to and from which goods flow. Fried points out, "invariably that center is the pinnacle of the rank hierarchy or, as complexity mounts, the pinnacle of a smaller component network within a larger structure." [42] Individuals who administer the distribution of goods at the center receive high prestige.

Another important aspect of social complexity is the social relations in a rank society articulated by the kinship system which is paramount to the life of people. In regulating people's interpersonal relations and activities, the kinship system is far more important in rank society than in egalitarian society. While the web of kinship of the latter society is determined by ecologically favored residential rules, the focus of the former society is upon "the ideology of kinship," i.e., the functional and social significance of kin relationships which affect the framework of kinship.[43] The development of the ideology of kinship is in part a consequence of the growth of sedentary settlement, which in turn contributes to the greater stabilization of social structure.

Another significant aspect of differentiation and complexity lies in the fact that rank society introduces formative stages of political authority. As Fried points out, there are no effective commands and sanctions which enforce people's compliance to authority.[44] Because of the unstable nature of the social structure of egalitarian society where social relations are not firmly sedimented, there is no consistent pattern of authority and leadership. In rank society, on the other hand, a regular form of authority emerges which is consistently reinforced and extends to various aspects of social life. Authority is the religious and ritual expression of leadership stemming from the great influence a person of high rank exercises upon the productivity of his society. He directs and schedules productive activities.

There is a large group of rank societies, among which one good example is Tikopia which has been studied extensively by Raymond Firth. Another example is Yatenga of the West African Voltaic Republic which has some elements of stratification. As reported by Peter Hammond, Yatenga is based on subsistence technology, and its economy is regulated according to the exchange of goods and the reallocation of valued materials:

> The inherited right to the individual proprietorship of productive goods other than land is also always limited by need. A man who inherits the use of a house or granaries he does not need is morally obligated to initiate their reallocation. Because he cannot use them for production and because they are not a negotiable form of wealth, it is to his advantage to do so. His economic interest is best served not by keeping them, but by accumulating good will in redistributing them. . . . Handtools such as hoes and knives are the only productive goods privately owned by the Mossi [people of Yatenga].[45]

According to Hammond, the technology of Yatenga has impeded social transformation since it is capable of sustaining the indigenous social system based on kinship and the division of labor based on age and sex. This has led to the perpetuation of powerful ancestor worship keeping the natives from separating themselves from the land. If, on the other hand, the Mossi technology could not sustain their social system, Hammond contends that they would be forced to leave the land to market their labor in order to purchase the goods they need to live.[46] This is a case in which technology imposes constraints on the modification of social organization.

A further development of differentiation and complexity leads to the formation of stratified society.[47] Technology requires a more functional social structure not regulated by the kinship system, inarticulate political authority, or the rudimentary division of labor, but by an entirely new system of control and a complex division of labor. Stratified society creates pressures for a higher level of social integration and differentiation of specialized groups. This means the attenuation and even the destruction of the kin relationships that dominate rank society. Thus, kinship is no longer a means of social control and adjudication in stratified society. The individuals of the same sex and equivalent age status do not have equal access to the basic resources of society.

The inception of stratified society, as discussed earlier, is found in Neolithic communities of agriculturalists. Stratified society is based upon a structure of differential access to the natural and social resources leading to the establishment of stratification as a mechanism of social control.

The economic mode of production and distribution is to a significant extent determined by the technological processes of society. In the rank society the economic organization is virtually identical with its kinship organization. It is harmonious with the social system in that both are based upon cooperation and mutual aid. Economic transaction assumes the form of personal exchange of goods. Equality and fraternity character- izes the mode of life in rank and egalitarian societies. In many of these societies the right to use and exploit may be private, but ownership is communal and public. This economic pattern is superseded by a new mode of production and distribution in the stratified society; the latter is based on a new division of labor incorporating differential types of power, control, and prestige. Economic transaction is conducted in terms of the objects to be distributed without special reference to interpersonal relations which are highly important in the exchange of goods in rank society. A system emerges here in which property relations constitute the basis of social relations, rather than the reverse. The core of the technological processes mentioned above is exemplified by the agricultural revolution seen in Neolithic and post-Neolithic times which introduced new techniques of cultivation, irrigation, drainage, rotation of crops, fertilization, and so on.[48]

A high level of political integration is attained in stratified society in terms of two kinds of social process. The first is a great increase in the size of the political unit. Under the impetus of a developing agricultural technology and an increasing food supply, clan and tribal units grow to huge size and are gradually integrated into a much larger political system. Another process is a growth of social stratification differentiating people and occupational groups in terms of the differential rights and access to social and political positions of high prestige and power and to the natural and social resources. This process has to do with the emergence of complex socioeconomic classes associated with differential levels of living, security, wealth, and property. The growth of social differentiation and complexity is simultaneously accompanied by a rapid increase of population, a crucial condition for the establishment of a state.

As Fried says, "societies that are stratified but lack state institutions are not known to the ethnographer." [49] This means that stratified societies are embryonic states in transition from highly developed rank societies to the least stable but formative system of the state. Lewis Morgan's description of this process is apt:

> The localization of tribes in fixed areas and in fortified cities, with the increase of the numbers of the people, intensified the struggle for the possession of the most desirable territories. It tended to advance the art of war, and to increase the rewards of individual prowess. These changes of condition and of the plan of life indicate the approach of civilization, which was to overthrow gentile and establish political society.[50]

We now arrive at the highest form of differentiation and complexity: the state. The state is the system of an integrated political unit in which complex institutions, both formal and informal, are developed to maintain an order of stratification. Its main concern is the perpetuation of its boundary system which is made possible by the reinforcement of organizational principles associated with hierarchy, differential degrees of access to the natural and social resources, compliance with the state's imperatives related to defense, territoriality, and official policies. It has specialized institutions of coercion employing physical force in the forms of an army and a police force. As Ferdinand Tönnies said in *Community and Society*,

> . . . the state, especially by legal definition, is nothing but force, the holder and representative of all natural rights of coercion. The state makes the natural law an instrument and part of its own will; it interprets that law. But the state can also alter what is thus under its

control. It must be able to do so not only *de facto* but also *de lege*. For it can make the regulations of its interpretation of law legally binding for its subjects. Interpreting what is law amounts, for them, to announcing what shall be law, with all the ensuing legal consequences.[51]

At the level of the state, the kinship system has little to do with social control, and the complex institutions built on the functional needs to defend the central order of social stratification replaces the mechanisms of exercising power and control seen in the earlier types of society.

The underlying technology of stratified and preindustrial state societies is agriculture. The energy system of such societies is enormously expanded as demonstrated by a rapid growth in population, great architectural edifices, and the development of large political units and cities and the refinement of engineering works, all of which contribute in one way or another to the greater transformation of unharnessed energy. All these aspects of cultural progress are fundamentally dependent upon agricultural technology. As Lynn White, Jr., says:

> From the Neolithic Age until about two centuries ago, agriculture was fundamental to . . . human concerns. Before the late 1700's there was probably no settled community in which at least nine-tenths of the population were not directly engaged in tillage.[52]

Thus, every significant improvement in the processes of agricultural technology affects the other organizational sectors of society.

We look at a historical case relevant to our discussion studied by Lynn White, Jr. It is his contention that a causal connection exists between the innovation of the plow and the formation of the manorial system in northern Europe during the early Middle Ages.[53] The heavy plow drawn by a team of eight oxen was introduced in northern Europe to till the dense, rich, alluvial bottomlands which could yield greater crops than the light soils of the uplands. This was an agricultural "engine" significantly substituting for human energy and time which was not seen in southern Europe where the scratchplow was used. This efficient heavy plow enabled the farmer to enlarge the area of land he could cultivate, and its most productive use required changing the shape of fields from squarish to long and narrow for each stripfield. It made possible the cultivation of the most fertile soils and the greater production of crops. The introduction of the heavy plow resulted in a decisive change in the peasant society of the north; the manor as a cooperative agricultural community consequently came into existence. It was profitable as well as necessary for farmers to organize a cooperative team. It was not possible for an individual farmer to operate such a plow drawn by eight oxen; also, to use it effectively the land of a village had to be reorganized into vast, fenceless fields plowed in long, narrow strips. The formation of these organized activities in turn required a powerful village council of peasants which made agricultural plans and aimed to settle disputes among the peasants. These social organizations were the essence of the manorial economy and a consequence of the heavy plow.

Related to this is the innovative utilization of horsepower. The agricultural revolution was further advanced when the horse replaced the ox. Such replacement necessitated the development of a harness and nailed horseshoes; and, by the end of the eleventh century, the horse used for plowing and transportation was commonly seen on the plains of northern Europe. The efficiency of plowing and land exploitation, and the speed and expense of land transportation, was significantly changed by the widespread employment of the horse equipped with the new harness and nailed shoes. Such efficiency and speed, accelerated by extrapersonal energy in the technological process, led to the development of the urbanization of the agricultural workers in the late Middle Ages when tiny hamlets of farmers were replaced by huge villages.[54] The harnessing of energy yielded by the horses made it possible for farmers to settle in large villages separated from their agricultural lands. According to Lynn White, Jr.:

> Thus extensive regions once scattered with tiny hamlets came to be cultivated wildernesses dominated by huge villages which remained economically agrarian, for the most part, but which in architecture and even in mode of life became astonishingly urban.[55]

Despite many other changes in agricultural techniques, the fundamental mode of agricultural energy transformation changed little between the Bronze Age and the eighteenth century A.D. Leslie White suggests that technological development was arrested by the social and political systems in preindustrial state societies where the ruling class, the pinnacle of stratification, failed to provide sufficient incentives for greater energy systems.[56] Because of this, the ancient Oriental civilizations are superior in many respects (such as architecture, engineering works) to the cultures of Europe between the fall of the Roman Empire and the rise of the Power Age.[57] The revolutionary extension of energy transformation had to await the arrival of the industrial revolution begun about 1760 during which fuel energy, an entirely new form of energy source, was made available. Coal and oil now constituted a basis of the Power Age. The industrial revolution led to a form of social differentiation and complexity characterized by the tremendous development of secondary and tertiary industries, a geometric growth in the division of labor, an increase in population, larger political systems, bigger cities, an accumulation of wealth, and a rapid development of the arts and sciences.

Industrialism

Industrialism is the most contemporary mode of cultural adaptation and the frontier of cultural evolution. It represents a higher level of energy system based upon entirely different sources of energy and an entirely different kind of technology. The new technology is no longer agriculture but a different and much more efficient mode of energy transformation which has commonly been called industry. The discovery of energy generated by fuel prepared a technological foreground which made possible the introduction of steam and combustion engines. The era of industrialism was set in motion. But industrialism involves not only the new machine technology but also new organizations of social relations evolving around a network of men's relationships with technology.

These social relations are discussed briefly here. In preindustrial societies (such as rank societies) the nature of social relations was more or less characterized by what Ferdinand Tönnies called *Gemeinschaft* (community).[58] Though social relations of *Gemeinschaft* vary greatly depending upon the degree to which societies are developed, they are based fundamentally upon the assumption of a perfect unity among men as a natural condition and of the common root of this natural condition. It is assumed that this condition is the source of coherence in social and reproductive life. *Gemeinschaft* involves social relations beginning with dyadic relations obtaining in a family and extending to relatively large-scale networks of kinship system, neighborhood, and friendship. Inequalities in these social relations can be increased only to a limited extent, since the excessive development of inequalities dissolve the essence of *Gemeinschaft*. Another important characteristic of social relations is that the fabric of *Gemeinschaft* is based on reciprocal, binding sentiments which Tönnies called "understanding";[59] thus, the relationships between the community and its constituents rest upon "understanding" rather than contract.

With the transition from preindustrial society to industrial society, i.e., from the predominance of agriculture to the predominance of industry, the nature of social relations is radically modified. There is no longer an a priori unity as seen in *Gemeinschaft;* instead, individual men are separated from one another and a condition of tension exists against one another. Individuals' spheres of activity and power are sharply separated and defined, so that the attenuation of close interpersonal relations characteristic of a primary, communal group occurs. Social relations based on these conditions of society constitute what Tönnies termed *Gesellschaft* (society).[60] Activities in *Gesellschaft* are restricted to definite ends and means and constitute a highly specialized division of labor. Not "understanding" but contract becomes the basis of social relations. The advance of *Gesellschaft* leads to the development of extensive world markets and the accumulation of capital. It also makes the workers mere possessors of working power, deprived of property, and enables free merchants and capitalists to acquire domination over the workers.

Tönnies' notion of *Gesellschaft* essentially corresponds to Emile Durkheim's social category based upon "organic solidarity." [61] Where organic solidarity is preponderant, according to Durkheim:

[Societies] are constituted, not by a repetition of similar, homogeneous segments, but by a system of different organs each of which has a special role, and which are themselves formed of differentiated parts. Not only are social elements not of the same nature, but they are not arranged in the same manner. They are . . . co-ordinated and subordinated one to another around the same central organ which exercises a moderating action over the rest of the organism.[62] . . . In effect, individuals are here grouped, no longer according to their relations of lineage, but according to the particular nature of the social activity to which they consecrate themselves.[63]

As is clear from the above, organic solidarity obtains when there is an advanced division of labor in which, while each role player performs and monopolizes the sphere of his role, his sphere expresses not only his individuality as a role player but also the relation in which it is a part related to a whole social structure. Durkheim introduced the notion of organic solidarity as an advanced state of social cohesion vis-à-vis "mechanical solidarity." The latter refers to a pattern of solidarity established by virtue of the fact that a society is basically homogeneous, devoid of a clearly defined division of labor.[64] Thus, the extent to which the division of labor develops indicates the degree of transformation of a society from a social structure of mechanical solidarity to that of organic solidarity.

Let us expand Durkheim's thesis and apply it particularly to industrialism. Durkheim spoke of social "concentration" and "condensation," by which he meant the organic unification of societal segments and the extension of intrasocietal relations. He identified three principal "causes" which promote the progressive condensation of societies in historical development. The first is the progressive concentration of population which, second, leads to the development of large cities; the third cause is the development of an efficient network of communication and transportation.[65] Durkheim contended that evolutionary development results from a break in the equilibrium of the social structure creating intra- as well as intersocietal conflicts and that these conflicts can be resolved by a more developed division of labor.[66] The development of the division of labor is considered a function of the need to struggle for existence.

The first and second "causes" referred to above have definite relations with the energy system of industrialism that needs manpower in the form of labor sold by the free workers, as discussed in reference to *Gesellschaft*, and that stimulates a further growth of population and cities. Particularly the third "cause" is important to the advance of industrialism. The new technology not only transformed iron ores into machines and tools but also enormously extended the spheres of intersocietal relations by the efficient methods of communication and transportation resulting from the invention and improvement of steam and fuel combustion engines, the utilization of electric power, telecommunication, and the like. Industrialism stimulates intersocietal trade and exchange of knowledge and techniques as well as manpower. It results in the multidimensional extension of political, economic, and technological spheres of the nation-state. The more such social extension advances, the more the energy system of the nation-state depends upon intersocietal relations. At the same time, industrialism requires both the "condensation" of a societal boundary system and its firm structure.[67]

As we saw in the development of *Gesellschaft*, contract serves as the basis of industrialism upon which the division of labor operates. In contrast to "understanding," contract is a rational principle in that it aims to achieve definite ends with definite means, both of which are clearly spelled out. The progressive development of industrialism seeks further condensation and greater efficiency.

Industrialism, as suggested above, develops and requires a particular pattern of orientation which guides the social action of individual members in social organizations. It is suggested here that the more industrialism advances, the more articulated this pattern of orientation becomes. To demonstrate this point, we shall arbitrarily select for discussion orientational "pattern variables." The notion of pattern variables has been introduced by Talcott Parsons in *The Social System*.[68] His original pattern variables constituting the value-orientation of social action consists of five pairs of variables: affectivity vs. affective neutrality, self-orientation vs. collectivity-orientation, universalism vs. particularism, achievement vs. ascription, and specificity vs. diffuseness. These pattern variables enter in several levels: the concrete and empirical level where the *individual* role player must make five discrete choices; the collectivity level at which role definitions are made in terms of the pattern variables; the *cultural* level as aspects of value-standards which are determined in terms of these variables.

From these pattern variables, the three most relevant pairs will be chosen for discussion: achievement vs. ascription, universalism vs. particularism, and specificity vs. diffuseness. To these are added two other variable pairs, rationalism vs. traditionalism[69] and contractualism vs. familisticism.[70] These five variable pairs are treated here as five different continua, each of which consists of a continuum with two orientational poles. We will also be concerned with only the cultural level where these continua enter.[71] It is assumed that societies with different degrees of evolutionary development, including societies with differential stages of industrialism, make a movement from one polarity on each continuum toward another. Therefore, if a society develops industrialism progressively, it is suggested that it will move on each continuum toward the maximization of value-orientations conducive to the most efficient form of industrialism as an energy system.

The first continuum is achievement-ascription. Achievement is an orientation with its focus on the commitment to achievement, success, effectiveness; and the goals to be achieved are defined explicitly. On the other hand, ascription refers to the emphasis on given attributes such as sex, age, intelligence, and status, which are conditions of role performance. Hindu society is one example that demonstrates the correlation between its relative absence of industrialism and its value orientation on the achievement-ascription continuum.[72] That is, the energy system of Hindu society, still considerably based on the caste system, depends upon the ascriptive orientation; correlatively, industrialism is developed very little. American society, by contrast, stresses the achievement orientation; its correlate is the extensive development of industrialism.

Universalism vs. particularism is our second continuum. Universalism refers to the generalization of a relational system that is cognitively validated. That is, it assumes that there are universalistic, cognitive orientations which are emphasized in role performance—such as universally valid moral standards and the obligation to fulfill contractual agreements. Particularism is an orientation based on a cathectic, particularistic frame of reference. It involves no universal criteria applied to the evaluation of various relational situations of social action. Paternalism is one example of particularism. "Developing nations" such as Zambia and

Tanzania[73] are in a gradual transition from a *Gemeinschaft* to a *Gesellschaft* and are replete with residues of rank society centering on the particularistic orientation. Highly industrialized nations, on the other hand, usually adopt the universalistic orientation as a principle on which the operation of the division of labor of industrialism depends.

Let us move to the specificity-diffuseness continuum. Japanese society provides an example of the orientation of diffuseness. Despite the fact that Japan is a highly industrialized society, its social system operates to a considerable degree on this orientational variable. An example of the specificity orientation is provided by American society. Specificity is a mode of orientation that clearly defines the limits of interest and instrumental (functional) relations of an individual vis-à-vis other role players. He is related to others in specific terms of his interest. Opposite to this orientation is diffuseness. The individual role player is regarded as significant in an infinite multitude of relational systems. For example, while an American corporate executive is not treated by his subordinates as their official superior outside the realm of their work, a Japanese executive is treated as an executive by his subordinates in a variety of social situations (e.g., in a bar and a party) that have nothing to do with role responsibilities in their corporation.[74]

In the case of the universalism-particularism continuum, the progressive development of industrialism serves as an index of movement from the particularistic orientation toward the universalistic. But our Japanese case does not seem to demonstrate clearly the correlation between industrialism and the movement in the continuum of specificity-diffuseness. Nevertheless, a more scrupulous analysis of Japanese social relations in various organizations reveals that the progressive articulation of Japanese industrialism demands a progressive movement toward specificity.[75] Technology in Japan has not radically modified social relations as seen in many Western societies. But it is hypothesized that it will require significant modification in the Japanese social relations if Japanese society is to avoid great intra- and intersocietal conflicts that will be brought about by its expanding energy system.

As already touched upon, societies advancing in terms of the magnitude of total energy transformation also exhibit a movement in the continuum of contractual-familistic polarities. We find a correlation here also between this movement and the growth of industrialism. Whereas American society is based on the principle of contractual *Gesellschaft* as a condition of industrialism, traditional Chinese society (precommunist) built on the agriculture-based clan system stressed the familistic orientation.

Our last orientation is the rational-traditional continuum. While the traditional orientation puts the focus on the automatic reaction and conformity of an individual to a course of action expected to be taken within the framework of social organization, the rational orientation emphasizes a mode of action in which the actor weighs ends and means and selects alternative means to accomplish ends. The former is seen in the *Gemeinschaft* with the inarticulate division of labor; the latter, meanwhile, is a functional principle of societies of industrialism. Robert K. Merton, in his study of the influence of Puritanism upon the development of science and, by implication, its application (i.e., modern technology), states: "The deep-rooted religious *interests* of the day [in 17th century England] demanded in their forceful implications the systematic, rational, and empirical study of Nature for the glorification of God in His Works and for the control of the corrupt world." [76] He goes on to say: "the combination of *rationalism* and *empiricism* which is so pronounced in the Puritan ethic forms the essence of the spirit of modern science." [77] Like modern science, industrialism and its development require rationalism. It is contended here also that as the basis of the energy system of a society changes to industrialism and its further growth, the society demonstrates a movement toward the rational pole on the traditional-rational continuum. If, on the other hand, it is far removed from industrialism, it rests more on a traditional orientation than a rational.

In conclusion, as societies increase the level of their energy system based on industrialism, the basis of their orientations changes progressively toward the maximization of achievement, universalism, specificity, and rationalism.

Implications

What is suggested above is that an advanced industrial society organizes its social structure to adapt to its technological efficiency. American society rests on the infrastructure of advanced technology and articulates its technological rationality—the orientation of achievement, universalism, specificity, contractualism, and rationalism. But whether technology advances in special areas of war, industry, and/or other areas depends to a considerable degree upon social stimulations like rewards, inducements, and incentives. American society is capable of offering the most conducive stimulations for technological development in general. There must be compatibility between advanced technology and the political, economic, and other institutions of society. The technology of American industrialism is capable of developing further necessary compatibility with major social institutions by virtue of the fact that the latter continue to stimulate social and individual sensitivity toward the vital orientation for the advancement of technology.

While this compatibility exists, we contend that industrial technology imposes definite social, economic, and political characteristics upon the American society in which it is established.[78] As Robert L. Heilbroner says, "the prevailing level of technology imposes itself powerfully on the structural organization of the productive side of society." [79] This creates unavoidable conflicts between the technological processes and certain institutions of society, which pose a contradiction to the notion of compatibility referred to above. Robert and Helen Lynd provided an example of such conflicts in their classic study of Middletown.[80] American industrialism (please remember that industrialism refers to industrial technology and social relations centering upon men's relations with technology), however, is capable of putting these conflicts under control; this leads to one form of compatibility or another, though it contains conflicts—the conflicts which are containable in the sense that these conflicts are not uncontrollable obstacles to the imperatives of technological development.

Technology displays "a 'structured' history," in Heilbroner's words.[81] Technological evolution is a sequential and determinate process. That is, it is essentially incremental and absent of technological leaps. This makes technology a powerful force in a society upon which it imposes certain constraints and new alternatives.

The controversial philosopher and political scientist Herbert Marcuse looks at the determinate force of technology:

> The prevailing forms of social control are technological in a new sense. To be sure, the technical structure and efficacy of the productive and destructive apparatus has been a major instrumentality for subjecting the population to the established social division of labor throughout the modern period. . . . The technological controls appear to be the very embodiment of Reason for the benefit of all social groups and interests—to such an extent that all contradiction seems irrational and all counteraction impossible.[82]

Marcuse continues:

> The most advanced areas of industrial society exhibit throughout these two features: a trend toward consummation of technological rationality, and intensive efforts to contain this trend within the established institutions.[83]

Marcuse concludes that the political imposition of forceful technological rationality upon people and their social organizations creates a one-dimensional society where other rationalities and alternative values and oppositions are impossible. Opposition to, and conflict with, technological domination are effectively contained and dissolved within the framework of political and economic institutions conforming to technological rationality.

The French philosopher Jacques Ellul, who widely stimulated studies of the effect of technology upon social life by the publication of *The Technological Society*,[84] reinforces the notion of technological containment. "Technique," he says, "constitutes a closed circle." [85] "We must remember the autonomous character of Technique. We must likewise not lose sight of the fact that the human individual himself is to an ever greater degree the object of certain techniques and their procedures." [86]

Meanwhile, American industrial technology intensified certain aspects of the infrastructure of society.[87] One such aspect is the abstraction of social relations. Social relations are increasingly impersonal and categorized into functional, instrumental relations of one kind or another. A sense of immediacy and a community of face-to-face relations are irrelevant to abstract values of technology. Related to this is the generalization of social relations. This refers to a social process in which local groups and communities are being subverted and eliminated by the political and economic forces of the national order of institutions to increase the efficiency of industrialism. Various communities and institutions that are often spoken of are not communities and institutions with technological, economic, and political autonomy; instead, they are largely physically distinguishable parts of the national order. They are forced to conform to the imperatives of national institutions. The technological structures of our society have also exerted individuating and fragmenting effects upon the traditional patterns of social relations. As Robert Nisbet says, "By virtue of the abstract and impersonal character of the technological system, the individual is able to perceive himself more vividly as a separate being rather than as an organic member of a community." [88] Individuation results from the functional necessity of industrial technology and contributes to the subversion of local communities.

Added to these aspects of social relations is the rationalization of individual and informal decision making. Such decision making is now subjected to a formal, hierarchical procedure of administration operating under the control of experts. The development of contemporary formal organizations is an example of this rationalization. To give another example, John Kenneth Galbraith speaks of the development of an industrial state in terms of the transition of the locus of decision making.[89] Until the emergence of industrialism, land ownership was the most important source of social prestige and political power. When industrialism came into being, capital replaced land as the source of technological operation. Both landowners and capitalists with great social prestige and power made individual decisions to manage their enterprises. The new industrial state, however, replaced such a method of management in favor of a rationalized system of management, which Galbraith calls a "technostructure," composed of various groups of experts, but not capitalists, by whom decision making is exercised.

Abstraction, generalization, individuation, and rationalism, as suggested earlier, are indeed distinct features of the social relations of American culture. American society intensifies these features of personal and institutional life more than any other society adopting industrialism as the energy system because it has the most advanced form of industrial technology.

Related to these aspects of industrialism is a "bifurcation of role and person" [90] which becomes a strain for individuals in America. Technological industry has been accelerating the bifurcation of social relations into two rather incompatible realms. One is the realm of role, which is increasingly specialized and functionally defined regardless of the personal characteristics of the individuals who are assigned roles. This realm is characterized by hierarchies, job specifications, minute definition of responsibilities, rating systems, escalator promotions, and other dimensions of rationalism. The other is the realm of person, which does not define persons in terms of abstract and generalized criteria of social relations but in terms of individual personalities and private worlds. As the bifurcation grows wider and wider as a function of industrialism, individuals tend to suffer from the fragmentation of self.

This also relates to another important dimension of the social structure of technological industry. As functional individuation or specialization becomes a predominant feature in society (as it has in American society), individuals lose the common symbols of meaning upon which a human bond relating one person to another is based. The common symbols of meaning are often seen as of secondary importance vis-à-vis the functional values underlying social organizations. In other words, organization tends to take precedence over person. This results in the development of various psychological phenomena which are often called "alienation," "depersonalization," and the like. In the face of this problem, the national political institutions have the responsibility of developing an individual sense of unity and boundariness, not at the personal level but at the national. This responsibility involves the imposition upon people of standard universal education, a common language, ideological indoctrination, control of the economic and political structure at the national level, control of the communication networks by national centers, extensive armed forces, and the heavy reliance of individuals upon national policies. This point leads us back to Marcuse's contention, that is, intensive efforts are made to maximize a trend toward consummation of technological rationality within the boundary of existing political institutions. This boundary system of political institutions is, in turn, modified by technological processes.

The fabric of contemporary American social relations is affected by the bifurcation of role and person, and by the replacement of the common symbols of meaning operative at the personal level by the organizational values and the common symbols of meaning controlled by the national order of political institutions.

Another relevant dimension of American technological society is an absolute faith in technology and its capability.[91] Thus, if something is technologically possible, it is assumed that it must be done. This faith in technology has led to frontiers of space exploration, military technology, and communication-transportation networks. It is a cultural expression of energy expansion and demands maximal efficiency and output. "The requirement of maximal efficiency," contends Erich Fromm, "leads as a consequence to the requirement of minimal individuality." [92] Whether this is the case or not, advanced industrialism requires the redefinition of the individual and his relation to other individuals (see chapter 3).

The late Jules Henry's observation is also relevant. He characterized American culture as the one driven by a set of cultural imperatives resulting from the relative absence of what he called "production-needs complementarity," common to various societies of industrial technology but most typical of American society.[93] The absence of production-needs complementarity means the lack of equilibrium between needs and production; production exceeds needs, and new needs are always created to consume the produced goods and services which are put in market not to meet the existing needs but to meet needs created a priori (see chapter 3 for the underlying orientation).

The deliberate creation of such a priori needs by economic institutions is one of the cultural imperatives mentioned above. Indeed, billions of dollars are spent just for this purpose. Another cultural imperative is a social phenomenon of dynamic obsolescence. Americans are unusually afraid of being out of fashion and consequently often change cars, houses, residence, clothes, TV sets, and the like to feel that they are not behind the times. A sense of continuous imbalance and asymmetry is deliberately fostered so as to produce more goods and services which can replace the old ones. Stability is considered a great threat to American industries. This is a deep-seated cultural imperative. It is an essential ingredient of the American value system as will be discussed in the following chapter.

These phenomena are a function of the assumption that the unlimited expansion and integration of industrialism is vital to Americans and their society. This assumption appears to be an isolated psychological phenomenon indigenous to American culture, but it is rooted in the evolution of industrialism moving toward further expansion and greater integration. This, therefore, is not uniquely an American cultural emphasis but rather suggests an evolving direction common to other societies of advancing industrialism.

The following chapter looks extensively at positive implications of advanced industrialism for contemporary life in American society. Therefore we shall not spare space for a discussion of positive effects of industrialism in this chapter.

Postscript

This chapter developed a theoretical perspective on cultural evolution. In this effort sweeping generalizations have been made here and there. Their validation requires empirical support and the presentation of relevant data which have not been sufficiently offered. However, the central thrust of this chapter has been to present an interpretation of the evolutionary course of culture leading to the contemporary scene with specific regard for the role that technology, defined broadly, has played.

Schooling is a major institution in societies of advanced industrialism. It has not, however, been discussed here; it will be explored in later chapters where it is the main subject. This chapter analyzed a technological dimension of culture and its related aspects which affect schooling.

NOTES

1. Leslie White, *The Evolution of Culture* (New York: McGraw-Hill, 1959), p. 38.

2. For a further discussion, see chapter 2, "Energy and Tools," in White, *The Evolution of Culture*, pp. 33–57.

3. Talcott Parsons, *Societies* (Englewood Cliffs, N.J.: Prentice-Hall, 1966), p. 15.

4. White, *The Evolution of Culture*, p. 19; also see Yehudi Cohen, ed., *Man in Adaptation: The Institutional Framework* (Chicago: Aldine-Atherton, 1971), pp. 6–10.

5. Gordon Childe, *Man Makes Himself* (New York: Mentor Books, 1951), p.

34. As Childe points out, "Dates in years before 3000 B.C. are just guessed, and are rarely given. For the next thousand years several systems of chronology are vague both for Egypt and Mesopotamia" (p. 189).

6. Ibid., p. 75. This period extends from about 7000 B.C. to 1800 B.C. depending upon Neolithic communities. Childe notes, however, "Neolithic civilization is a dangerous term applicable to a huge variety of cultural groups." In fact, during this time the post-Neolithic period began in various communities.

7. There are two different views on the relationship between technology and population growth. The first stresses that population growth is a result of increasing technology and productivity; the second contends that the development of technology and productivity are a function of population increase. The former view is represented by Gordon Childe and others whereas the latter view is espoused by Ester Boserup. For further details, see Philip E. L. Smith and T. Cuyler Young, Jr., "The Evolution of Early Agriculture and Culture in Greater Mesopotamia: Trial Model," in *Population Growth*, ed. Brian Spooner (Cambridge, Mass.: MIT Press, 1972), pp. 1–59.

8. See note 5.

9. Childe, *Man Makes Himself*, p. 87.

10. Lewis Morgan, *Ancient Society*, ed. Leslie White (Cambridge, Mass.: Belknap Press of Harvard University Press, 1964), p. 14.

11. Cohen, *Man in Adaptation*, p. 18.

12. For a further exposition of the theme explored here, the reader is referred to Childe's excellent work, *Man Makes Himself* from which several quotations have been made here. Also see White, *The Evolution of Culture*, chap. 12, "The Agricultural Revolution," pp. 281–302; Morton Fried, *The Evolution of Political Society* (New York: Random House, 1967).

13. See Childe, *Man Makes Himself*; Julian Steward, *Theory of Culture Change* (Urbana, Ill.: University of Illinois Press, 1955); Leslie White, *The Science of Culture* (New York: Grove Press, 1949).

14. Elman Service, *Cultural Evolutionism* (New York: Holt, 1971), p. 9.

15. Morgan, *Ancient Society*, pp. 11–23.

16. See Herbert Spencer, *On Social Evolution*, ed. J. D. Y. Peel, (Chicago: University of Chicago Press, 1972), pp. 38–52.

17. Emile Durkheim, *The Division of Labor in Society* (New York: Free Press, 1964).

18. White, *The Evolution of Culture*, p. 30.

19. See Alfred Kroeber, "History and Evolution," *Southwestern Journal of Anthropology* 2, no. 1 (1946): 1–15.

20. See George Peter Murdock, *Social Structure* (New York: Macmillan, 1949), p. 116.

21. Marshal Sahlins and Elman Service, ed., *Evolution and Culture* (Ann Arbor: University of Michigan Press, 1970), pp. 12–13.

22. Marshal Sahlins, "Evolution: Specific and General," in Sahlins and Service, *Evolution and Culture*, p. 28.

23. Elman Service, "The Law of Evolutionary Potential," in Sahlins and Service, *Evolution and Culture*, p. 97.

24. Ibid.

25. See Steward, *Theory of Culture Change*.

26. Frank Miller, *Old Villages and a New Town: Industrialization in Mexico* (Menlo Park, Calif.: Cummings Publishing, 1973), p. 14.

27. Leslie White, "Energy and the Evolution of Culture," *American Anthropologist* 45, no. 3 (July–September 1943): 347.

28. Leslie White, *The Science of Culture* (New York: Grove Press, 1949), p. 365.

29. Ibid., pp. 364–65.

30. White, "Energy and the Evolution of Culture," p. 349.

31. White, *The Science of Culture*, p. 366.

32. Sahlins, "Evolution: Specific and General," p. 34.

33. Ibid., p. 35.

34. Cohen, *Man in Adaptation*, pp. 15–16.

35. Ibid., p. 17.

36. Social differentiation and complexity are often identified as similar processes. For example, Yehudi Cohen states: "*Differentiation* refers to the degree to which institutions or roles are separated from each other. . . . [On the other hand] *Complexity* refers to the degree to which a society is composed of different groups" (Cohen, *Man in Adaptation*, p. 11). In this chapter, however, differentiation refers to the process by which statuses, roles, groups, and institutions differentiate in a society with the result that it leads to different role behavior of people and to the development of functional division of labor. Meanwhile the concept of complexity is used here to mean that, while it implies the extent to which "a society is composed of different groups" it specifically refers to the extensity and level of social integration of these differentiated groups.

37. See Fried, *The Evolution of Political Society*.

38. Ibid., pp. 51–52.

39. For further details, see Wendell Oswalt, *Habitat and Technology* (New York: Holt, 1963) in which he develops a taxonomy of technoculture as it applies to the evolution of hunting.

40. Fried, *The Evolution of Political Society*, p. 109.

41. Ibid.

42. Ibid., p. 117.

43. Ibid., pp. 120–21.

44. Ibid., p. 133.

45. Peter Hammond, *Yatenga* (New York: Free Press, 1966), p. 78.

46. Ibid., p. 107.

47. Fried, *The Evolution of Political Society*, p. 186; see White, *The Evolution of Culture*, chap. 9, "Economic Organization of Primitive Society," pp. 237–60.

48. See White, *The Evolution of Culture*, pp. 329–53.

49. Fried, *The Evolution of Political Society*, p. 224.

50. Morgan, *Ancient Society*, p. 458.

51. Ferdinand Tönnies, *Community and Society*, trans. and ed. Charles P. Loomis (New York: Harper Torchbooks, 1963), p. 216.

52. Lynn White, Jr., *Medieval Technology and Social Change* (Oxford: Clarendon Press, 1962), p. 39.

53. Ibid., pp. 39–56.

54. Ibid., pp. 57–76.

55. Ibid., p. 67. In connection with our discussion of the relationships between technology and culture, the reader is encouraged to pay attention to such

case studies as the ones conducted by Pertti J. Pelto and Ludger Muller-Wille on the technological revolution in the Arctic brought about by the introduction of snowmobiles; also a case study conducted by John J. Poggie, Jr., on the transformation of Mexican villages into a new city brought about through the industrialization of these villages. These case studies are included in H. Russell Bernard and Pertti Pelto, eds., *Technology and Social Change* (New York: Macmillan, 1972). Particularly relevant to our discussion is Pelto's conclusion: "Date on the relationship of snowmobile ownership to economic position in Lapland [in Finland] suggest that social differentiation between the 'haves' and the 'have-nots' is likely to be intensified by the economic effects of snowmobiles. A number of the middle-range reindeer herders told us that the mechanization of herding is forcing all except the wealthiest owners out of the reindeer business. There were already some clear differentiations between the 'rich' and the 'poor,' but until now the poorer Lapps were not significantly handicapped in their participation in herding activities. Every man had sufficient sled reindeer to travel to the roundups, to his herds, and to carry out his other hauling and transporting. . . . Now the picture is different. The wealthier half of the population can afford snowmobiles, while many of their kinsmen and neighbors cannot. Because of the far-reaching significance of snowmobiles for economic activity, the relative disadvantages of the poorer people have been increased, making it very likely that there will be a push toward greater socioeconomic stratification" (pp. 194–95).

56. White, "Energy and the Evolution of Culture," pp. 347–48.

57. White, *The Science of Culture*, p. 373.

58. See Tönnies, *Community and Society*, sec. 1, "Theory of Gemeinschaft," pp. 37–64.

59. Ibid., p. 47.

60. Ibid., see sec. 2, "Theory of Gesellschaft," pp. 64–102.

61. See Durkheim, *The Division of Labor in Society*, chap. 3, "Organic Solidarity Due to the Division of Labor," pp. 111–32.

62. Durkheim referred to a social organism which has different independent parts; but each part is simultaneously related to other parts and a whole structure composed of these parts.

63. Durkheim, *The Division of Labor*, pp. 182–83.

64. Ibid., see chap. 2, "Mechanical Solidarity Through Likeness," 1:70–110.

65. Ibid., p. 257.

66. Ibid., p. 270.

67. See Yehudi Cohen, "Social Boundary Systems," *Current Anthropology* 10, no. 1 (February 1969): 103–19.

68. Talcott Parsons, *The Social System* (Glencoe, Ill.: Free Press, 1959), pp. 58–67.

69. This is a continuum of variables by Max Weber. See Max Weber, *The Theory of Social and Economic Organization*, trans. A. M. Henderson and Talcott Parsons (Glencoe, Ill.: Free Press, 1947), p. 115.

70. Pitirim Sorokin, *Social and Cultural Dynamics* (New York: American Book, 1937), 3:23–41. See also Pitirim Sorokin, *Society, Culture, and Personality* (New York: Harper & Row, 1947), pp. 93–118.

71. See John McKinney and Charles Loomis, "The Application of Gemeinschaft and Gesellschaft as Related to Other Typologies," in Ferdinand Tönnies,

Community and Society, trans. Charles Loomis (New York: Harper Torchbooks, 1963), pp. 22–23.

72. For an examination of ascriptive value orientations in the Hindu society, see Milton Singer and Bernard Cohen, eds., *Structure and Change in Indian Society* (Chicago: Aldine, 1968).

73. For example, this point is discussed in parts of the following works: J. G. Lieberman, *Colonial Rule and Political Development in Tanzania* (Evanston: Northwestern University Press, 1971); P. Smith, ed., *Africa in Transition* (London: M. Reinhardt, 1958); Norman Long, *Social Change and the Individual* (Manchester: Manchester University Press, 1968).

74. See Chie Nakane, *Japanese Society* (Berkeley: University of California Press, 1972).

75. See Robert Cole, *Japanese Blue Collar* (Berkeley: University of California Press, 1971).

76. Robert K. Merton, *Social Theory and Social Structure* (New York: Free Press, 1968), pp. 628–29.

77. Ibid., p. 633.

78. See Robert Heilbroner, "Do Machines Make History?", *Technology and Culture* 8 (July 1967): 340.

79. Ibid., p. 342.

80. See Robert Lynd and Helen Lynd, *Middletown in Transition* (New York: Harcourt Brace, 1937).

81. Heilbroner, "Do Machines Make History?", p. 338.

82. Herbert Marcuse, *One-Dimensional Man* (Boston: Beacon Press, 1964), p. 9.

83. Ibid., p. 17.

84. See Jacques Ellul, *The Technological Society*, trans. John Wilkinson (New York: Vintage Books, 1964).

85. Jacques Ellul, "Ideas of Technology: The Technological Order," trans. John Wilkinson, *Technology and Culture* 3 (Fall 1962): 395.

86. Ibid., p. 398.

87. See Robert Nisbet, "The Impact of Technology on Ethical Decision-Making," in *The Technological Threat*, ed. Jack Douglas (Englewood Cliffs, N.J.: Prentice-Hall, 1971), pp. 39–54.

88. Ibid., pp. 50–51.

89. John Kenneth Galbraith, *The New Industrial State* (2nd ed.; Boston: Houghton Mifflin, 1971), pp. 45–58.

90. Daniel Bell, "The Disjunction of Culture and Social Structure: Some Notes on the Meaning of Social Reality," in Douglas, *The Technological Threat*, p. 114.

91. Erich Fromm, *The Evolution of Hope* (New York: Bantam Books, 1968), pp. 33–34.

92. Ibid., p. 34.

93. Jules Henry, *Culture Against Man* (New York: Vintage Books, 1963), pp. 3–44.

3

AMERICAN SOCIETY, CULTURE, AND SOCIALIZATION

Nobuo Kenneth Shimahara

In the foregoing chapter we discussed the evolutionary process of culture in which technology has played a major role. We have seen the development of technological systems beginning with a highly rudimentary form of hunting-gathering and leading to a very sophisticated form of industrialism. Industrialism is a particular type of energy system conducive to the most efficient transformation of free energy and requires the development of a particular pattern of social system.

This chapter is an extension of chapter 2 but it is primarily concerned with the structural aspects of contemporary American society as well as with the patterns of American family and socialization. While American society has been seen in a macrocosmic perspective of social evolution earlier, it is discussed here with a macrocosmic focus upon its particular aspects.

A Structural Interpretation of American Society

There are a number of ways of interpreting American society, but we will employ an approach consistent with the evolutionary perspective discussed earlier. What characterizes contemporary American society as well as other societies of highly developed industrialism are two related developmental processes. One is a phenomenal development of structural differentiation and the other is adaptive upgrading which is a function of structural differentiation.[1] These analytical concepts, which are often used by structurally oriented sociologists such as Talcott Parsons and Winston White, are introduced here because they contribute to a fruitful interpretation of the development of American social structure.

Structural differentiation[2] is an essential index of the development of American institutions of major spheres of activity. It results from the differentiation of specialization and role structure in the economic sphere and from the development of social stratification in the political and social spheres. An increase in structural differentiation leads to an increase in social organizations resulting in the creation of a greater number of opportunities for individual roles in the occupational sphere as well as the other. That is to say, the process of structural differentiation yields a decrease in ascription, i.e., emancipation of individuals from ascription of means to ends by virtue of the fact that it dissolves ascriptive constraints and boundaries imposed upon them. The loosening of ascriptive ties, in turn, leads to an increase in adaptive capacity of individuals and society. As Winston White says,

> In a society with a high degree of ascription (which is another way of saying a low degree of structural differentiation), the resources required for different functions cannot be generated independently of one another. Thus, in the classical peasant society, the labor force available to work the fields depends largely on the number of children born and reared in the family.
>
> As structural differentiation occurs within a society, functional specialization also occurs. When two functions, previously performed by the same structure, are subsequently performed by two newly differentiated structures, each function, under favorable conditions, can be fulfilled more effectively than before.[3]

An example from American society illustrates the above point. In the nineteenth century there were many family firms where both economic and familial functions were carried out by the same structure. But the structural differentiation of firms from families liberated individuals from diffuse structures of roles and consequently increased their adaptive capacity. For example, the family no longer had to be run like a business; in turn, the business could dissociate itself from various familial problems little concerned with business operation. Decisions made for the firm on, say, financing were treated independently of familial decisions on similar matters. Moreover, the employment of labor for the firm was no longer ascribed to familial membership; the recruitment of qualified and able men was made possible. Resources were mobilized more efficiently by such means of differentiation. This example can be extended further to include modern corporations where the division of labor, i.e., structural differentiation, is articulated so highly that the roles and responsibilities of individual employees are entirely free from ascription to the other domains of their life. Their employment and evaluations for promotion are based largely on the criteria of achievement and universalism as opposed to ascription and particularism which are characteristic elements of undifferentiated family firms. The progressive differentiation of organizations and the efficient mobilization led to the growth of what Robert Presthus terms the organizational society.[4]

Structural differentiation, according to Winston White, has two related dimensions: extensity and upgrading.[5] Extensity refers to the extent to which structural differentiation *"permeates all structures of the same class."* [6] If, for example, many family businesses coexist with corporative businesses in America, it is understood that structural differentiation, i.e., extensity in this given special field, is limited to the extent to which these family businesses resist the degree of differentiation found in large corporations. The extensity of structural differentiation thus serves as an indicator of the adaptive capacity of society.

Let us turn now to the concept of adaptive upgrading. As mentioned earlier, it is a function of structural differentiation. As the differentiation of society progresses, it requires an increase in demands for performance. Upgrading refers to an increase in the capability to perform roles required by virtue of the fact that the differentiation of specialization demands structural efficiency. Two interrelated dimensions are involved in adaptive upgrading. The first is an increase in demands for the training of individuals for differentiated tasks, leading to the formation and subsequent upgrading of systematic preparation, i.e., formal education. The second is the structure of roles requiring more specialized skills and knowledge as well as a higher degree of general competence in the area in which individuals work.

Going back to our example of the family firm, as the firm is separated from the family the former is controlled by more rationalistic principles in the sense that specific means to specific ends are articulated and put in operation. And as such a firm becomes a mature modern corporation, this growth in structural differentiation demands changes in the criteria for employment as well as in the evaluation of competence toward an increasingly greater degree of specificity and achievement. These changes directly affect the structure and process of formal preparation so as to meet higher expectations for competence and efficiency created by differentiation—more precisely by extensity. Therefore the extent to which the upgrading of formal education is demanded in American society reflects the degree of structural extensity achieved in the American social structure. In the past two decades or so, college degrees have been seen as the passport to attain skilled work in big corporations; moreover, during this period graduate degrees have also been demanded by mature corporations as well as governmental institutions. Upgrading in formal training is responding to a progressive increase in structural differentiation in a gamut of American institutions and bureaucratic structures.

Thus far we have spoken of differentiation and upgrading. Meanwhile, differentiation processes pose a new problem of integration for a given system. When economic production is separated from a kinship group and constitutes a separate unit which we called a firm, these two categories of subsystems must be coordinated within a framework of a broader system if social integration is to be maintained. This problem of integration can be applied to higher levels of differentiation at which large corporations and other bureaucratic organizations operate. The coordination and integration of these subsystems in American society can no longer depend upon local integrative mechanisms such as a community boundary system of political organization but, increasingly, must depend upon a national integrative structure which may be called a national boundary system.

This boundary system consists of a network of national orders of institutions. On the one hand, structural differentiation has eroded local peculiarities and ascriptive boundaries; on the other, it has elevated the level of societal integration. Despite the fact that different racial and ethnic groups in America demand local control and boundaries favorable to them, their effective resistance toward national control and integration has decreased as each of them has had to depend on the national orders of American social structure.[7] One example is a relative decrease of overt discrimination against racial and ethnic elements in various spheres of institutions including the political, economic, educational. Such decrease in discrimination has required and will require national intervention in the interest of national integration.

Related to the widening of the integrative scope of American society is the sedimentation of the value system of the society. Variable value orientations peculiar to different collectivities developed in less differentiated stages of American society have been subjected to integrative pressures which require these collectivities to make not a reinforcement of such orientations but "an adjusted, specialized 'application' " of the general system of the society.[8] This often poses a problem, as Talcott Parsons states:

> A system or sub-system undergoing a process of differentiation, however, encounters a functional problem which is the opposite of specification: the establishment of a version of the value pattern appropriate to the new types of system which is emerging. Since this type is generally more complex than its predecessor, its value pattern must be couched at a higher level of *generality* in order to legitimize the wider variety of goals and functions of its sub-units. The process of generalization, however, often encounters severe resistance because commitment to the value pattern is often experienced by various groups as commitment to its particular content at the previous, lower level of generality. Such resistance may be called "fundamentalism." To the fundamentalist, the demand for greater generality in evaluative standards appears to be a demand to abandon the "real" commitments. Very severe conflicts often crystallize about such issues.[9]

The process of generalization of values at a high level of valuational integration has developed in American society as it has accommodated an increasingly greater degree of structural differentiation so that differentiated subsystems or collectivities could be bound by certain common sources of social integration. For example, the desirability of equality as a value concept has been generalized to the extent that it is applied to a national range of various institutions. These institutions are expected to incorporate the desirability of equality into their employment practices regardless of certain ascriptive elements they may have such as localities, ethnic affiliations, and the like. Such expectation, however, is often met by resistance dysfunctional to the promotion of the adaptive capacity of American society.

To summarize our discussion thus far, the functional capacity of American society has been increased in terms of two major aspects: (1) its horizontal aspect, namely extensity—permeation of structural differentiation; (2) its vertical aspect, i.e., adaptive upgrading. An increase in the horizontal dimension of functional capacity requires an increase in the vertical dimension—upgrading the level of performance in special areas and greater demands to achieve a higher level of social integration, extension of value at a general level, and functional specialization. Furthermore, it requires other qualities of the vertical dimension related to personality aspects. Upgrading the level of performance relates to intensive as well as extensive formal education received by most Americans, which is intended to increase both cognitive and affective capacities of individuals. The increase of such capacities means not only the growth of capability to perform occupational roles but also the attainment of a personality that can maintain personality integration in a highly differentiated structure of life and also upgrading the ability to choose and explore.

To highlight a development of extensity and upgrading in American society further, a brief observation of social change in the mid-twentieth century can be made. Social change in America between 1940 and 1970 has been characterized by a phenomenal increase of social interdependence and the complexity of role relationships. The notion of the new industrial society which John Kenneth Galbraith advances, for example, suggests a frontier of this social change.[10] The heart of a mature industrial organization, he observes, is what is called the technostructure (see chapter 2).[11] The technostructure is an organization of groups of experts in various fields by which important decisions related to organizational activities are made. Galbraith states: "modern economic society can only be understood as an effort, wholly successful, to synthesize by organization a group personality far superior for its purposes to a natural person and with the added advantage of immortality." [12] What is referred to here as a group personality constitutes a technostructure, a central structure of decision making in the advanced system of American industrialism.[13] The technostructure has three functions as defined by Galbraith. The first is to draw on and appraise information available in different fields of specialization in order to reach the best decisions at a given point in the technological development of modern industry. The second function, directly derived from the advancement of technology, is the necessity for efficient planning. The third function is to coordinate a variety of specialized talent to bring it to bear upon the common purpose. These functions are requirements of highly advanced industrialism where the frontier of modern technology is based upon organized intelligence.

Indeed the technostructure is a result of the structural differentiation of an organization. Until about three decades ago, important decisions of industrial organizations involved not organized intelligence but individual entrepreneurs—natural persons in Galbraith's phrase—as heads of these organizations. On the other hand, the operation of a technostructure requires an upgrading of personnel in terms of their training and performance as experts constituting a group of organized intelligence. These two processes of differentiation and upgrading simultaneously require interdependence and a complex system of role relationships as demonstrated in the case of a technostructure. The higher the level of social differentiation, the greater the social interdependence. To quote again from Galbraith:

> Qualified manpower is decisive for the success of the industrial system. The education on which it depends is provided mostly in the public sector of the economy. By contrast, capital, which was once decisive, comes mostly from the private economy. The market for the most advanced technology and that which best allows of planning is also in the public sector. Much scientific and technical innovation comes from, or is sponsored by, the state or by publicly supported universities and research institutions. The state regulates the aggregate demand for the products of the industrial system. This is indispensable for its planning.[14]

Let us also take a brief retrospective look at historical processes of differentiation and upgrading. The predominant impact of structural differentiation on individuals in America is in their occupational roles. Today the American occupational structure is by and large independent from households. The differentiation of the former from the latter has subsequently led to the employment of a major portion of Americans of working-force age in large organizations. This change was precipitated by the decline of agricultural population which took place in an early part of this century. Concomitant with a phenomenal increase of workers in the secondary and tertiary industries is the growth of a labor force consisting of women. Furthermore, the proliferation of governmental regulatory agencies, especially since the days of the New Deal, has contributed to an enlargement of public-sector employment. About 20 percent of the working force are currently employed by different levels of government.

In the meantime a rapid expansion of population (from 123 million in 1930 to 200 million in 1970) has created pressures for social interdependence and organic solidarity in Durkheim's terms. For example, the federal government, large corporations, and institutions of higher education must have an appreciable degree of coordination, i.e., interdependence upon one another, in order to allocate the labor force, to train manpower, and to guarantee employment for a majority of trained manpower. On the other hand, urbanization in the 1950s and '60s intensified social interdependence while the rise of suburban population necessitated a rapid increase of social organizations in new communities.

Turning to the process of upgrading, the proportion of persons in professional and technical occupations that require training at higher education levels has been increasing steadily. Even during the relatively short period of thirty years between 1930 and 1960 it has nearly doubled. A similar proportion of growth can be applied to managerial, official, entrepreneurial occupations. The percentage of semiskilled labor has been inversely decreasing since it reached the highest point in 1948. Meanwhile, the 1950s and '60s witnessed a rapid increase in need, and heavy demands for the training, of scientists, engineers, and technicians in industry. This process of upgrading, if it is viewed in a relatively long-range perspective of time, will be continued in the future, demanding higher levels of educational preparation for practically all jobs. Upgrading necessitated by higher demands for performance thus exerts its pressures on educational and occupational areas, intensifying interdependence in the two areas.

Finally it should be pointed out that structural differentiation and upgrading is directly influenced by the extension of technology.[15] For a discussion on technology's role in American society, I refer the reader to chapter 2, particularly the sections on "Industrialism" and "Implications." One point, however, needs to be repeated here as it relates our present discussion to the next section. American society rests on the infrastructure of advanced technology and articulates its technological rationality—the orientation of achievement, universalism, specificity, contractualism, and rationalism. Abstraction, generalization, individuation, and rationalism are distinct features of the social relations of American culture. American society intensifies these features of personal and institutional life more than other societies adopting industrialism as the energy system because it has the most advanced form of industrial technology.

A Structural Interpretation of Effects of Differentiation and Upgrading

The impact of differentiation upon individuals can be seen as an increase of freedom from ascriptive ties with kinship groups and boundaries of traditional communities and from the diffuse structures of their relationships with members of these collectivities. More positively, they have attained more freedom to explore and choose various alternatives made possible by structural differentiation. Structural differentiation, however, has imposed upon individuals greater responsibility and expectations for performance. Individuals in the current state of structural differentiation in America must act without ascriptive directives and take personal responsibilities for their performance, whereas in earlier stages of differentiation they were guided by ascriptive ties and the norms of their groups.

The impact of differentiation upon American society is seen in a phenomenal development of social interdependence and the formation of an organizational society. While differentiation has resulted in a proliferation of organizations, it has led to the expansion of many if not most of these organizations. Organization thus has become the most salient as well as predominant dimension of individual life and society, as Robert Presthus and William H. Whyte have critically suggested in their books *The Organizational Society* and *The Organization Man.*[16]

In studying the effect of differentiation and upgrading, we shall look at some observations of critics of the organizational society. Charles Reich identifies the fundamental premises on which the organizational society is built with what he calls Consciousness II—a mentality reflecting these premises. Reich observes:

> At the heart of Consciousness II is the insistence that what man produces by means of reason—the state, laws, technology, manufactured goods—constitutes the true real.[17] . . . One of the central beliefs of Consciousness II concerns work. The belief is that the individual should do his best to fit himself into a function that is needed by society, subordinating himself to the requirements of the occupation or institution that he has chosen. He feels that as a duty, and is willing to make "sacrifices" for it.[18] . . . Because of his lack of wholeness [caused by the split between his private life and organizational demands], because of his enforced playing of roles and subjection to outside standards, the consciousness of a Consciousness II person becomes vulnerable to outside manipulation. The individual has no inner reality against which to test what the outside world tells him is real.[19]

Here an individual who lives and works in the organizational society of America is depicted as an automaton critically deficient in freedom and a sense of what his life is all about. Reich goes on to argue that Consciousness II has destroyed man's authenticity and liberty and that the restoration of these qualities of life requires the birth of a new consciousness which he calls Consciousness III. "Consciousness III," says Reich, "starts with self [and it] declares that the individual self is the only true reality." [20] We are given here a romantic and "countercultural" interpretation[21] of what man's reality ought to be in negative response to the organizational society in which the organizational rationality of society is seen to have constituted formidable constraints for individuals.

Another critic, Herbert Marcuse, sees the "shrinkage of the ego" and "collectivization of the ego ideal" as a result of forces of the organizational society affecting individual life. Marcuse argues:

The sweeping changes in advanced industrial society are accompanied by equally basic changes in the primary mental structure. In the society at large, technical progress and the global coexistence of opposed social systems lead to an obsolescence of the role and autonomy of the economic and political subject.[22] The result is ego formation in and by masses, which depend on the objective, reified leadership of the technical and political administration. In the mental structure, this process is supported by the decline of the father image, the separation of the ego ideal from the ego and its transference to a collective ideal.[23]

He goes on:

The more the autonomous ego becomes superfluous, even retarding and disturbing in the functioning of the administered, technified world, the more does the development of the ego depend on its "power of negation," that is to say, on its ability to build and protect a personal, private realm with its own individual needs and faculties. Yet this ability is impaired on two grounds: the immediate, external socialization of the ego, and the control and management of free time—the massification of privacy.[24]

Marcuse's argument is based upon several assumptions which may be partially or entirely supported by evidence. As pointed out in the previous chapter, Marcuse contends that the external forces of an organizational society based upon technological rationality produces a one-dimensional life, i.e., a unilinearity of life that does not permit effective oppositions to one-dimensionality. In such a society, assumes Marcuse, "the power of negation"—individuals' power to form counter forces—is contained and neutralized. Thus the formation of the ego and individuality takes place within, and is subjected to, one-dimensional forces. This is what he calls "external socialization of the ego." Marcuse also believes that this results in the diminution of the ego.

What is common between the two arguments discussed above is the belief that the development of structural differentiation (which produces social interdependence) and adaptive upgrading as we see it in American society runs counter to the growth of individuality, individuals' abilities to guide themselves and to form a sense of their own life. On the other hand, there is an idealization of less differentiated societies where individuals are assumed to be able to grow as unique individuals and to exercise their power of negation possibly leading to a greater degree of dialectical process of society.

We shall cite another critic, the author of *The Organizational Society*, who has made a sociologically important, critical analysis of American organizations. Robert Presthus states:

> The specialization and discipline of big organizations have both functional and dysfunctional consequences. Their gains in material rewards, industrial efficiency, and military power are clear enough. Their dysfunctions are more subtle and pervasive, raising problems of individual autonomy, integrity, and self-realization. Prominent among them today is a *displacement of value* from the intrinsic quality of work to its byproducts of income, security, prestige, and leisure [footnote deleted]. This displacement stems from the impersonality, the specialization, and the group character of work in the typical big organization. Its larger significance may appear in an alienation from work, resulting from such factors as the economy's frequent concern with essentially trivial products. The organization's capacity to meet the demands of change may suffer, since criticism and innovation tend to be muffled by its demands for conformity.[25]

Here Presthus identifies a major "dysfunction" of the organizational society as "a displacement of value from the intrinsic quality of work to its byproducts of income, security, prestige, and leisure." He further attributes it to interpersonal relations characterized by impersonality and competition as well as to a highly specialized division of labor. Compared to the former critics' observation, Presthus seems also to assume that the intrinsic quality of work obtains in less differentiated organizations. But the domination of the extrinsic nature of work leads to an organizational person's alienation from his work.

All these critics (a countercultural advocate, a Marxist philosopher, and a sociologist) agree that the organizational society generally works against individual growth. From the point of view of an evolutionary framework in which the present state of American society is a result of the processes of structural differentiation and adaptive upgrading, however, these critics' observations are one-sided. Though their contentions are feasible and empirically supportable in parts (as pointed out in the foregoing chapter), they do not provide sufficient accounts of the organizational society in which differentiation and upgrading have not only resulted to some extent in what they see as negative and dysfunctional but significantly in the promotion of individuals' freedom in important areas. We have noted that the functional capacity of society is determined by the extent to which the processes of differentiation and upgrading have developed and also that structural differentiation (as in the case of a family firm) has contributed to the emancipation of individuals in many respects.

Let us point out, from our evolutionary point of view, some of the attributes constituting the emancipation of individuals. In the contemporary state of American society, individuals have acquired a much greater structural range of freedom: structurally determined freedom, from ascription and diffused structures of life to alternatives of choice. Subsequently this means that they must assume greater personal responsibility for their performance; they are their own agents in many respects, not bound by the elements of traditionalism.[26] Reich's contention that individuals are forced to play roles and accept subjection to outside standards is overstated.

The second point to be made is related to the notions of competition and autonomy. As Durkheim pointed out, generally an increase in the division of labor, i.e., specialization, reduces competition. The more specialized jobs exist, the less competition obtains. Competition, however, becomes a vital element at a considerably high level of expectations and rewards allocated to particular roles of specialization. At the same time it should be pointed out that upgrading, particularly at the level of professional and technical specialties, provides more autonomy for individuals by freeing them from automatic subjection to external forces and from restraints toward assuming greater authority. This is evident in the technostructure. It must be noted here that the gains derived from differentiation are not merely material rewards, industrial efficiency, and military power of which Presthus speaks.

Third, the high level of differentiation at which our society exists requires an equally high level of personality organization that can integrate motivational resources. While individuals are expected to master complex cognitive competence and skills, they also confront the demand for upgrading the consciousness of human relations to deal with personality problems and social complexity. As contended by Marcuse, the collectivization of the ego ideal takes place here, but the shrinkage of the ego is not a necessary correlation. The autonomous ego to which Marcuse refers is an ideal conception, not a real one, whether in less or highly differentiated societies. On the other hand, it is an entirely empirical question whether the "power of negation" he speaks of has diminished as our society has developed from earlier stages of complexity to the present. At least from a theoretical point of view, it is feasible to hypothesize that the power of negation has not decreased but that its application and the modes of this application have changed due to structural changes of the society. The current level of differentiation of American society thus expects its members to develop greater adaptive capacities, which were not necessary at earlier times when the adaptive mechanism was simpler.[27]

Now we turn to the effect of differentiation and upgrading upon the American value system. Interpretations of the effect vary rather widely. Talcott Parsons and Winston White maintain that structural differentiation has not significantly affected basic American values at the high level of generality and abstraction.[28] It is necessary here to distinguish between values and norms. As defined by Clyde Kluckhohn,[29] values are conceptions of the desirable and therefore conceptions of the highest generality as applied to the system of action. Norms, meanwhile, are regulative principles at a specific and concrete level involving institutional processes and structures. This distinction suggests that structural change directly affects norms whereas the modification of values may not be caused by it. Thus in our discussion of differentiation it is important not to confuse values with institutional norms and goals.

According to Parsons and White, what they call "instrumental activism" is central to the American value system.[30] It has its origin in the New England Puritanism that views an individual as an instrumentality of God's will and thus encourages him to become an active agent achieving mastery over nature. Society is conceived as instrumental to the individual and has a moral mission to which he is obligated to contribute. As James Peacock and A. Thomas Kirsch interpret the notion of instrumental activism:

> American values of instrumental activism are most clearly expressed in the drive to produce *generalized resources,* i.e., resources (human as well as material) potentially mobilizable to achieve a wide variety of goals. Americans frantically produce anything and everything, from hula hoops to electronic computers, without much concern about the way these resources will ultimately serve society.[31]

That Puritan beliefs are disappearing rapidly from the scene in contemporary America is evident, but the secular version of our Puritan roots remains relatively unchanged as illustrated by the fact that the drive to produce and achieve and to utilize society as an instrument toward production still remains relatively active. This secular version is called "instrumental or institutionalized individualism." [32]

The question arises as to how the process of structural differentiation incorporates the values of instrumental activism at its different stages. This question is treated extensively by Parsons' and White's essay "The Link Between Character and Society" [33] and White's *Beyond Conformity.*[34] As discussed earlier, individual responsibility has increased to respond to a greater degree of generalized criteria resulting from the development of differentiation. Parallel with this, differentiation has produced greater generality of the form of success and achievement. In other words, as the earlier bases of institutionalized prescription have diminished, very general goals of success have become predominant. For example, the direct involvement of a person in productive activities in a family firm and the accumulation of profit resulting from it determined his success in the early years of American industrialism. Today recognition of approval and success in, for example, management, interpersonal relations, and a number of other areas is considered the equivalent of profit in earlier years. At present an organization, but not the individual, typically takes the burden of responsibility for producing a marketable product. Individuals make decisions, but in their capacities as members of their organization.

What is seen here is the fact that a complex organization now assumes the profit orientation that was once primarily attributable to individuals. Both personal and organizational goals relevant to primary social functions have undergone transformation as primary economic organizations have become more complex as a result of organizational expansion and an increase in the division of labor. Thus the personal goals pertinent to an earlier structure of economic activities no longer challenge individuals in the contemporary structure of society. Differentiation in the organizational structure is a causative factor in the modification of role expectations. In conclusion, Parsons and White suggest that these changes in personal and organizational *goals* caused by differentiation have taken place more or less independently of fundamental American *values* and have not therefore required significant change in instrumental activism. Goals, personal and institutional, at concrete, specific levels undergo and can undergo transformation without involving the simultaneous change of values conceived at a high level of generality when the former is structurally affected.

This conclusion can be extended not only to the occupational-economic sphere but also to other institutional spheres including family and socialization which we will discuss later.

The above view has been presented as an alternative interpretation of value and social change in response to David Riesman's analysis of this subject in *The Lonely Crowd*.[35] Though Riesman's analysis is carried largely in the evolutionary framework of institutional development which we have employed, he differs sharply from Parsons and White in his insistence that American character and values have significantly changed in response to the historical development of social and economic conditions in society.[36]

(Assuming that the reader is acquainted with Riesman's work, I shall avoid a presentation of details of his work.)

Riesman presents three patterns of character or sources of direction reflecting different stages of structural changes of society: tradition-direction, inner-direction, other-direction. Briefly stated, ascriptive conditions and structures of society provide goals and their means for tradition-direction. Fixed goals are internalized in the structure of each personality. As the decline of these ascriptive conditions, the process of social mobility and extension, and the conditions of *Gesellschaft* begin to affect social life, inner-direction becomes a predominant orientation. Here personal goals are clearly fixed and are transmitted through socialization. In the last stage, other-direction, the source of direction tends to become indeterminant as a result of increasing social differentiation and interdependence, the conditions of which make it highly difficult for individuals to act according to fixed goals which serve as the source of direction for inner-directed persons. Thus goals are not present a priori but externally and "situationally" determined.

Let us focus upon inner-direction and other-direction which are most relevant to our concern with social change and values. These two patterns of direction, according to Riesman, not only represent two distinct types of social character but also express two different systems of values. As a highly developed form of industrialism has become predominant in America in this century, a radical shift has taken place from inner-direction to other-direction; also a corresponding shift in American values and character structures.

As recalled, Parsons and White do not accept this thesis. They contend that the development of organizational structures and social conditions in the system of industrialism requires little change in fundamental values. Seymour Martin Lipset supports the view advanced by Parsons and White:

> Many American sociologists have documented changes in work habits, leisure, personality, family patterns, and so forth. But this very concentration on the obvious social changes in a society that has spanned a continent in a century, that has moved from a predominantly rural culture as recently as 1870 to a metropolitan culture in the 1950's, has introduced a fundamental bias against looking at what has been relatively constant and unchanging.
>
> Basic alterations of social character or values are rarely produced by change in the means of production, distribution, and exchange alone. Rather, as a society becomes more complex, its institutional arrangements make adjustments to new conditions within the frame-

work of a dominant value system. In turn, the new institutional patterns may affect the socialization process which, from infancy upward, instills fundamental character traits. Through such a process, changes in the dominant value system develop slowly—or not at all. There are constant efforts to fit the "new" technological world into the social patterns of the old, familiar world.[37]

Lipset maintains that equality in social relations and achievement in one's career are two basic "value orientations" of Americans that have not changed in the past one and a half centuries.[38] American emphasis on equalitarianism contributes to salient, widespread phenomena of competition, on the one hand, and to status uncertainty on the other. A combination of the values of equality and achievement tends to produce a social structure where individuals are uncertain about their social statuses; this, in turn, leads to a typical American tendency for conformity.[39]

This last point of conformity relates to Lipset's assertion that Americans have been conformists historically. To support it he presents documents left by noted European visitors to America in the nineteenth century including James Bryce, Harriet Martineau, and Alexis de Tocqueville.[40]

The subject we are discussing has evoked widespread attention. Two additional sources lend support to Riesman as opposed to Lipset, Parsons, and White. The first is William H. Whyte's contention that the Protestant ethic has been replaced by what he calls "the social ethic." He says:

> [Social ethic] mean[s] that contemporary body of thought which makes morally legitimate the pressures of society against the individual. Its major propositions are three: a belief in the group as the source of creativity; a belief in "belongingness" as the ultimate need of the individual; and a belief in the application of science to achieve the belongingness.[41]

Whyte attributes the decline of the Protestant ethic and a subsequent rise of the social ethic to organization. It is his thesis that the social ethic has permeated all spheres of contemporary life including ideology, education, formal organization, styles of life, residential patterns, and the like.

Clyde Kluckhohn has produced a careful analysis of a shift in American values. He suggests cautiously that American values, which had been stable over a period of one and a half centuries, may have undergone certain modifications over the past generation. He sums up his study by saying that he has made "no pretense of discerning a final common path":

1. Strictly personal values have receded in importance at the expense of more publicly standardized "group values" whether those of an organization, a community, a social class, a profession, a minority, or an interest group. "Conservatism" has increased. It is possible that the machine is coming to be taken as the implicit model for human behavior.

2. But there has been a concomitant rise in the "psychological values" related to mental health, the education and training of children, and the like. However, as DuBois puts it, "Self-cultivation in America has as its goal less the achievement of uniqueness and more the achievement of similarity."

3. The value placed upon "future success" has receded in favor of "respectable and stable security" seen in shorter time range.

4. Aesthetic values have notably risen in the hierarchy.

5. The value of institutionalized religion is greater but primarily in terms of changes No. 1 and No. 3 above . . . rather than in terms of intensified personal religious life.

6. "Heterogeneity" is becoming one of the organizing principles of the dominant American value system.

7. The ideal for American woman and her place in the society has altered as have our sexual codes.

8. There is an increased overt concern for abstract standards; greater value is placed upon explicit values.[42]

Four analytically different lines of inquiry are presented here. The first is the position represented by Parsons and White that instrumental activism is basically intact. But they emphasize that the form of instrumental activism has been extensively generalized due to structural changes of society. The second is Kluckhohn's view that fundamental values expressed by instrumental activism, stable for 150 years, may have been changed in the past few decades leaning toward other-direction.[43] This reinforces the third line of inquiry discussed by Riesman who insists that the trend of change from inner-direction to other-direction produced by structural changes is clearly evident. Lipset represents the last position. His analysis begins with the assumption that other-direction was prevalent in nineteenth-century America, an opposite view to that of Parsons, White, Riesman, and Whyte. Nevertheless, Lipset makes it clear that the pivotal values of equality and achievement have persisted and that because of these values inducing individuals' competitiveness and status uncertainty, other-direction has been "an epiphenomenon of American equalitarian ethos." [44] But along with Parsons and White who see other-direction as an extension of the generality of instrumental activism, [45] Lipset states:

> There can be little question that Riesman and Whyte are right also in showing how bureaucratization and urbanization *reinforce* those social mechanisms which breed other-direction. Success in a bureaucracy, and in the proliferating service occupations of modern society, depends primarily on the ability to get along well with others. [46]

And Lipset concludes:

> An increase in other-directedness helps facilitate economic development by making individuals more receptive to "the opinion of the 'generalized other.' " It creates greater willingness to accept new norms or techniques, and it helps reduce particularistic ties, thus facilitating the operation of pure market criteria. [47]

This conclusion is supported by White, [48] Parsons, [49] and by anthropologist Francis Hsu. [50]

The Structure of the American Family

In this section our primary concern is to examine the structure of the American family and to relate it to the process of structural differentiation. At the outset of his classical work *Social Structure*, George Peter Murdock defines the family as "a social group characterized by common residence, economic cooperation, and reproduction." [51] Unfortunately this definition fails to include socialization as a vital element in the function of a family. We shall first look at salient structural features of the American family as they relate to the definition of family.

The American family is typified by a nuclear family structure which includes only a married couple and their children. It is a biological or conjugal family constituting functional relations among husband, wife, and their children, excluding other members of kinship. In terms of rules of residence it is neolocal; [52] i.e., upon marriage husband and wife establish a separate residence from their parents and other relatives. This residential independence establishes a family of procreation [53] where a couple perform the function of reproduction; prior to marriage, they were formally associated with families of orientation [54] in which they were born and socialized by their parents. Thus every married person in American society normally belongs to two nuclear families though he is primarily obligated to his family of procreation.

With respect to rules of descent (as related to reproductive process in an inclusive sense), the typical pattern of descent of the American family is anthropologically defined as bilateral descent which "associates [an individual] with a group of very close relatives irrespective of their particular genealogical connection to him." [55] Bilateral descent permits the individual to have equal affiliation with his four grandparents—the parents of his parents of the family of orientation—and no unilinear emphasis which is found in a great number of societies. Bilateral descent can be appreciated more when it is contrasted with other patterns of descent such as patrilineal descent practiced in the traditional Chinese society where one's lineage is reckoned exclusively in terms of male relatives; matrilineal descent of the Hopi which assigns an individual to a kinship group consisting of females allowing the continuity of lineage along the line of female descent.

The structural prominence of the American family thus consists in neolocal residence, bilateral descent, and a pattern of conjugal family identified as the nuclear family. It leads to the relative isolation of the family from kinship, and, on the other hand, to a great emphasis on the establishment of one's own family of procreation. These structural features that emphasize the establishment of the individual's conjugal family as the center of life and that conversely deemphasize kinship ascription provide Americans with great individual freedom. The marriage bond between two individuals constitutes the key to both the establishment of a family and its continuity and, thus, the choice of one's partner based upon romantic love is a highly crucial matter.[56] As Francis Hsu points out, "The structural relationship most elevated in the American family is that between the husband and wife." [57] All other relationships are either subordinated to this central relational axis or subjected to modification by it. Romantic love is a reflection of this structural emphasis on the relationship between husband and wife. The unique accent placed on romantic love articulates the assumption that an individual has the freedom to make an exclusive choice of partner and that the relationship with this partner based on love is, at least from an ideal point of view, unaccountable to any ascriptive ties and external interpersonal constraints.

The most fundamental attributes of the husband-wife relationship are exclusiveness and discontinuity which reinforce each other.[58] Exclusiveness refers to a particular type of content of interpersonal interaction which claims the exclusion of external elements, whether they may be relatives or children, interfering with the integrity and privacy of the husband-wife relationship.[59] This also involves a structural feature which establishes the complete independence of a nuclear family. The dominant dyad of this type of family consisting of husband and wife subordinates other dyads (e.g., father-son, mother-son, etc.) to its primary needs. Discontinuity, another attribute, is largely a function of exclusiveness. The primary interest of this dominant dyad is to establish a family of procreation which lasts as long as husband and wife live. Upon their death it is discontinued. Meanwhile, when their children become mature and independent from their family of orientation, they respectively establish families of procreation. It should be noted here as a unique element that these two different types of families are mutually exclusive to a great extent in that they do not exist in most cases on the basis of common interest of the continuity and interdependence of families of different generations. For example, a mother's involvement with the child rearing of a family of procreation established by her daughter or a father's interference with his independent son's work is normally treated as an infringement upon personal matters. American emphasis is clearly upon the singularity of an individual as well as of a family which produces the structural characteristic of discontinuity. In kinship-oriented societies, this element of singularity is maintained at a minimum level in order to permit the domination of a kinship group over individuals and its continuity. Socialization, for example, is a common matter, the responsibility of which is mutually borne by a family of procreation and a kin group.[60]

Exclusiveness, discontinuity, and singularity attributable to American families and individuals have a vital psychological implication particularly in terms of socialization.[61] They operate in two interrelated ways. First, they tend to determine a structural frame which provides an individual child with a particular orientation toward interpersonal relations. Second, they tend to determine the content of interaction to promote such orientation. This orientation is self-reliance.[62]

From the time of birth an American child is placed in a separate room alone for his own benefit as well as for others'. While he is expected to maintain this relative physical distance from the parents, he develops intense relationships with his mother, which are often characterized by such Freudian terms as identification and object-cathexis through which he begins to learn a world outside his own ego. As he grows, he commences to recognize his father and siblings of different sexes. He is now at a stage of internalization where his psychological growth involves the development of a superego. His primary social anchorage has been confined to a family of orientation in the very early years of his life and will be largely so throughout childhood. It is extended variably to wider spheres of interpersonal relations as he reaches adolescence and, then, post-adolescence. Through this process of growth, he learns that he is expected to be self-reliant despite his early intense attachment to his mother and later intense association with peers. He becomes aware that the intensity and duration of these relations (content of interaction) are temporary and instrumental, and are therefore absent of permanency, contrary to kinship-oriented societies where they are not.

In other words, he finds that his world lacks considerably ascriptive and permanent relations either of the kinship or the nonkinship categories (structural frame) on which he can depend. This sense of his world is gradually fostered and reinforced as he learns that the dominant dyad in the family (structural frame) is the father-mother relationship from which he has to depart; it is exclusive and discontinuous. His world does not provide relatively permanent protection for him‾ unless he earns it not based on ascription but by virtue of achievement and competition. Thus he is conditioned to think in terms of the first-person singular, here and now, as it relates to his rights, pleasure, privacy, social status, and chances for advancement.

Self-reliance, however, has to be understood in a relative sense. As noted earlier, the bureaucratization, urbanization, and other structural changes of contemporary life in America demand a greater degree of interdependence to which individual Americans have to make relational adjustment. Self-reliance is directly related to the values of equality and achievement emphasized in America, the realization of which tends to accompany status uncertainty and subsequently conformity. The psychological cost of self-reliance is high, for while he clings to the ideal of equality and achievement, he is not "psychologically" protected well by people with whom he is directly concerned. Here is the need for protection which, according to Hsu, takes the form of conformity.[63]

While exclusiveness and self-reliance constitute an important concern in interpersonal relations in American family and society, they are also subjected to accommodation to the peculiarity of American familial structure. As Parsons observes:

> Since the effective kinship unit is normally the small conjugal family, the child's emotional attachments to kin are confined to relatively few persons instead of being distributed more widely. Especially important, perhaps, is the fact that no other adult woman has a role remotely similar to that of the mother. Hence the average intensity of affective involvement in family relations is likely to be high. Secondly, the child's relations outside the family are only to a small extent ascribed. Both in the play group and in the school he must to a large

extent "find his own level" in competition with others. Hence the psychological significance of his security within the family is heightened.[64]

Thus the high intensity of emotional attachment to the conjugal family, on the one hand, and the elements of exclusiveness and self-reliance, on the other, are not mutually exclusive. The former should be also pointed out as another salient aspect of American family. As will be discussed later, this poses a highly difficult problem for adolescents and youth in transition from a stage of childhood where an expressive (affective) orientation dominates, to adulthood in which an instrumental (cognitive, universalistic, achievement) orientation replaces the former orientation. In one respect, this transition constitutes gradual emancipation of an adolescent from his tie to the family; in another, it is a very agonizing process in that, while he still needs affective protection offered by his family, he is increasingly subjected to pressures of his external world which imposes upon him the instrumental orientation.

We now look briefly at the American family from a viewpoint of process. It has been observed that, in response to the generic process of structural differentiation, the American family has been undergoing structural changes. One significant feature is that it has become more differentiated than before, as noted in our discussion of the family structure. It is now a smaller unit. It has differentiated from a larger extended family, and it is also a more specialized agent resulting from the separation of the economic function now assumed by other organizations than the family. Consequently the abandonment of productive function within the scope of the family has enabled it to specialize in "the socialization of children and the psychological . . . 'tension-management' of its adult members." [65] Related to this process of differentiation, the American family has been structurally isolated more than before; it is not only isolated from its kinship group but also geographically due to social mobility. All these changes have entailed a significant consequence which more sharply differentiated the role of the father from that of the mother. Comparatively speaking, the father is largely concerned with extrafamilial activities while the mother concentrates in responsibilities concerned with socialization and tension-management in the family.

Finally we can relate the occupational system to the function of the family. As discussed earlier, contemporary American industrialism has been based upon the differentiation of the occupational system, on the one hand, and its upgrading, on the other. One frontier of the present occupational system is the proliferation of technical roles requiring the upgrading of the level of competence and responsibility. Contemporary industrialism needs a certain type of family which is most conducive to its function. A composite family or an extended family composed of biological families of the same kinship group is not a pattern of family conducive to American industrialism. It is primarily kinship-oriented and, furthermore, ascriptive forces are strong. In contrast, the American nuclear family is relatively free from kinship ascription; geographically, psychologically, and socially mobile; and can be effectively oriented toward occupational needs of the external world; it also emphasizes personal achievement. These are some traits of the American nuclear family conducive to the occupational system of our society.

The requirement imposed by the occupational system upon the family demands "a high incidence of technical competence, of rationality, of universalistic norms, and of functional specificity." [66] This constitutes external occupational pressures to which families, among other institutions, are expected to respond by fostering children's competence and attitudes which can meet occupational requirements. The level of the function of family in this particular aspect, in other words, is required to be upgraded by the occupational structure.

Socialization Process

The above point directly leads us to the aspect of socialization. We now examine some salient features of American socialization that have been affected by the process of structural change discussed in the earlier sections.

As Kenneth Keniston notes, "the keystone of bringing up middle-class American children is their intense dependence on their mothers." [67] In contrast, in kinship-oriented societies the initial dependence of a child upon his mother is attenuated by the fact that his kin group is also extensively involved in socialization. The combination of the intense dependence of a child upon his mother, in particular, and upon his nuclear family, in general, in American society with permissiveness, is closely correlated to the emphasis of this society upon independence, autonomy, achievement, and self-control. The intensity of expressive relations developed in his very early years between him and her enables her "to invoke the most powerful of all disciplinary sanctions—the withdrawal of love, variously expressed as 'disappointment' in him, or loving him when he is 'good' and disapproving of him when he is 'bad.' " [68]

In other words, the mother is in a position to employ the contingency of reward which is the basic source of leverage for motivating the process of learning. And she makes an exclusive use of this position to facilitate learning. In response to her sanctions, the child, in turn, develops a motivational organization; in gradual progression he proceeds to learn a role vis-à-vis her which involves a higher level of motivational and cognitive generalization and organization. The content of this organization is characterized by the mother's expectations for early autonomy and independence, early development of the capacity for self-control, and early mastery of cognitive competence. This intense relation thus produces the intense learning for particular kinds of experience. To cite another statement made by Keniston:

> From a very early age—often before he can talk—he begins to learn to postpone and delay instinctual behavior, to assess the consequences of his acts, to acquire conceptual skills, to subordinate feelings to the "realistic" needs of the situation. Without a strong mother-child bond and without the mother's willingness to "exploit" that bond to bring up her child, our culture's difficult first lessons cannot be learned.[69]

Hsu seems to interpret this intense affective attachment of the child with his mother as contradictory to the notion of self-reliance which Americans generally entertain.[70] But he errs here since he fails to take into account the functional significance of a high degree of attachment and dependency as it stimulates the motivation for acquiring the capability for self-reliance.

Thus training for achievement begins very early in life. A typical American family, i.e., a middle-class nuclear family, provides structural accommodation for this training for the structure of the nuclear family is conducive to the nearly exclusive control of socialization and tension-management by mothers in their own families. This training, as has been alluded to, is further associated with occupationally geared requirements. It is directly carried into schooling where learning experience is formalized, intensified, and broadened.[71]

American society at the contemporary level of differentiation assumes that it can function effectively in the context of collective organizations which require particular qualities of individuals' capabilities. And these qualities are specifically associated with the emphasis upon independence, responsibility, and competence. Children are brought up and trained through schooling in this context of society where they are constantly challenged by external expectations (as well as internal ones when internalized) for performance to achieve such qualities of capability.

The great expectation of the society for performance poses a special problem when the young enter the stage of adolescence and youth. This is a transitional period from a period of life during which the expressive orientation (the orientation toward affective attachment and its associated elements of diffuseness and ascription) has dominated, to an emerging horizon where the instrumental orientation (the orientation toward achievement, specificity, and universalism) assumes domination over the expressive orientation—the stage where they will be accepted as "fully initiated" members. During this transition American society imposes greater demands on adolescents and youth for a higher level of competence and responsibility, i.e., a higher level of the instrumental orientation. This produces strains for them since they are challenged simultaneously by bifurcating forces. One is an increased external demand for the instrumental orientation and the other an internal need for a still considerable degree of affective, particularistic, and ascriptive bases of life inherent in their earlier socialization. They are expected to dissolve this bifurcation by reducing the internal expressive needs.[72]

Let us analyze further details of this process of transition from a structural point of view. The family, in a general sense, can be regarded as a group of heterogeneous kinship relations based on particularism, diffuseness, and ascription. If it is a part of the structure of a society based on the same orientations of particularism, diffuseness, and ascription, i.e., a kinship-oriented society, the transition of pre-adult members of the society is comparatively smooth since it does not involve a radical alteration of orientation. It requires an extension of identification and solidarity which have been internalized and fostered in the family. Thus, from a point of view of societal integration, kinship-oriented societies employ the same integrative principles as those practiced in the family.

The integration of pre-adult members, however, becomes a more complex problem when a society is based upon specificity, achievement, and universalism. This problem challenges American adolescents and youth. Though these orientational bases are to an appreciable degree incorporated into typical American nuclear families, comparative emphasis is not upon them but upon the orientations of particularism, diffuseness, and ascription which are a basis for intensive affective relations and dependence. The integration of young people into the society, therefore, is not made possible on the ground of an extension of the integrative principles of the family since solidarity of the social system must be maintained by patterns of behavior different from those in the kinship unit.[73]

When these pre-adult members are being transferred from a structure of particularistic relations to one of universalistic relations, this transition puts a strain on the solidarity and stability of the social system.[74] First, the stability of the orientations of these members is upset by the broadening of the scope of purely instrumental relations and universalistic values. Second, a stronger element of contingency in the regulation of roles and the achievement of rewards and gratification enters. These emerging elements in life tend to lead to generational conflicts and the alienation of adolescents and youth—problems that tend to entail a strain on the integrative mechanism of society.

Meanwhile, the transition in question is peculiarly characterized by a pattern of need dispositions of adolescents and youth composed of ascriptive, solidary, collectivity-oriented elements. These need dispositions are heightened as a reaction to the upgraded requirement of generalized and universalistic standards imposed upon them in nonkinship member-ship. This tends to result in the formation of age-homogeneous groups of adolescents and youth in our society, which reflect strongly the expressive orientations indigeneous to the family—affective attachment, ascriptive ties, particularistic criteria for membership, collectivity orientation. When the bifurcating forces are operating upon them, these homogeneous groups serve as an intermediary step between the families of orientation dominated by expressive elements and the families of procreation that require the internalization of the instrumental orientations on the part of the parents. While social demands are present before adolescents and youth, these groups help them ameliorate strains by providing emotional protection such as solidarity and interaction among group members. They, in other words, contribute to psychological stability and maturity. Therefore, as S. N. Eisenstadt suggests, "allocation of roles and constitu-tion of groupings on the basis of homogeneous age is necessary from the point of view of the social system no less than for the personality integration of the individual." [75]

The structural position of American adolescents and youth vis-à-vis their society is characterized by segregation and the relative absence of harmony. In addition to their orientation toward the main values of their society which they confront, the lack of parallel development between the body and social maturity causes a stress contributing to the absence of harmony. Because adolescents' social maturity grows more slowly than their biological development, their bodily maturity is not usually given "a full cultural, normative meaning by the society." [76]

In American society pre-adult members and their age groups do not constitute a role structure as part of the basic institutional framework. They are treated as potential members of such institutional framework. Eisenstadt notes that in highly specialized societies in which "the basic integrative tasks of the society are performed within specialized, achieve-ment-oriented agencies . . . the scope of age groups diminishes." [77] In other words, they are structurally segregated and their contribution to "the integrative tasks of the society" is also reduced. This structural segregation legitimates itself on these assumptions: (1) adolescents and youth need longer and more systematic preparation for the upgraded occupational structure resulting from social differentiation; (2) their structural isolation is necessary to conduct extensive preparation for the performance of roles; (3) to motivate them to aspire to a society controlled by adults, presentation of the main values of their society with a strong idealistic emphasis in a highly selective way is necessary.

The fact that American youth composed of college students and adolescents organize groups with strong collective identification, cohesion, solidarity, loyalty as opposed to universalistic standards of the society is seen here as their adaptation to the structural segregation.[78] As noted by observers of student unrest on American campuses during the 1960s, many youth groups are based on an infrastructure of ideology which accentuates the discontinuity between youth and adulthood, and the unique mission of the youth to carry ultimate social and cultural values.

In this connection, it is relevant to mention a study conducted by Eisenstadt since it may provide an insight into American youth and adolescents. Speaking of youth movements in Israel, Eisenstadt remarks:

> . . . there is a negative correlation between strong aspirations to achievement roles (economic and occupational) and strong identification with youth movements. Those adolescents who set themselves ideals of occupational and vocational advancement either do not join a youth movement or are among the most indifferent members.[79]

It is hypothesized here that this negative correlation also obtains in American society. Research along this line of hypothesis will produce interesting results.

In the meantime, while American society imposes structural segregation upon its pre-adult members, it is a vital structural requirement of the society to implement their integration into the main social structure. Youth and adolescents are, therefore, given relative freedom to emancipate themselves from the social demands that beset them. They are offered three types of opportunities by which they would develop their identity and become gradually linked to adult society: (1) organized educational systems; (2) organizations operated with adult leadership such as YMCA, YWCA, the Boy Scouts, the Girl Scouts; (3) groups voluntarily organized by youth and adolescents such as organizations of student movements, conventional groups such as fraternities and sororities, various types of informal groups of adolescents. In varying degrees, these groups and organizations can provide youth and adolescents with opportunities to foster psychological needs for autonomy and to develop differentiated fields of activity; they also provide opportunities to incorporate them within organized groups (e.g., formal groupings in the educational system) in which they interact with adult members.

Nonetheless, the difficulties involved in structural segregation and a radical shift in the orientations of behavior make the transition of adolescents and youth an unusually painful process, both psychologically and socially. From a psychological point of view, they suffer from a loss of personal identity and emerging high demands to reestablish it. The reestablishment of personal identity involves a new definition of the self in the framework of universalistic and achievement-oriented criteria and of its relationship to others in a different setting of social relations. From a social point of view, they confront double demands—structural segregation and the internalization of the instrumental orientations to acquire cognitive competence and to be able to act at a high level of generality. As Erik Erikson says, "[ego identity] is a psychological process reflecting social processes; but with sociological means it can be seen as a social process reflecting psychological processes." [80] American society and other societies of advanced industrialism impose a combination of these two types of problems upon adolescents and youth, often causing alienation, deviation, indifference, and rebellion on the one hand, and pleasure seeking, hedonistic activities and peer-group-oriented behavior on the other. There is good reason why they present problems to the adult sector of society.

In contrast, within the range of simpler societies the transition from childhood to adulthood does not present acute problems; adolescents in these societies have both structural and psychological continuity. The value systems and integrative principles of their societies are *Gemeinschaft*-oriented and the scope of psychological process such as identity and gratification remains in the framework of collective orientation.

A question may be raised here as to whether all modern industrial societies make the transition equally difficult. Eisenstadt's study is relevant again.[81] He distinguishes between individualistically oriented modern societies such as American and Western European societies and collectively oriented modern societies which include Israeli and Russian societies. The different value orientations represented by these two types of societies entail different principles of identification and integration, and thus differential influence on the structures of age groups in these societies. He suggests that the extent of institutionalization and corporateness of age groups in a society corresponds to the degree of its collectivity orientation.[82] According to him:

The most organized and institutionalized age groups may be found in Soviet Russia and in the Israeli kibbutz (and formerly in Germany and Italy)—all of them societies with a very explicit community orientation in their value systems. . . . In comparison with them, the peer and adolescent groups of Western Europe and the United States, societies in which individualistic orientation is stronger, are looser in their composition and less institutionalized.[83]

In collectively oriented societies, formalized age groups are usually not limited to a particular locality but are often organized on a national scale; moreover, they are linked in various ways to different types of institutionalized adult agencies.[84] This close linkage between pre-adult members and adults, and the personal and collective anchorage provided by these corporate youth groups, can reduce the problems related to the transition in individualistically oriented industrial societies.

It is hypothesized here that the magnitude and intensity of the difficulty ensuing from the transition of American adolescents and youth will be reduced if the following two attempts are made: (1) age groups are organized on a more formal and extensive scale; and, thereby, (2) closer linkage is established between activities of those in the transitional stage and a variety of roles represented by main social institutions under the control of adults. In this connection, it would be relevant to make brief reference to the fact that various educational theories have been proposed in America to liberate particularly adolescents from the problem of transition. Though these theories neither have the same assumptions nor propose the same approaches to the problem, and theorists vary from James Coleman to Ivan Illich, from Paul Goodman to Margaret Mead,[85] there is one converging point in their proposals. It suggests participatory learning by the exposure of adolescents to, and their involvement in, a network of institutions controlled by the adult society in order to reduce structural segregation. Participatory learning can increase closer interaction between adults and pre-adults leading to the development of extensive linkage between adults and their institutionalized activities, on the one hand, and their counterpart, on the other.

Postscript

We have seen the development of American society in an evolutionary perspective. Our approach was to examine it in terms of the processes of structural differentiation and adaptive upgrading in order to provide a structural interpretation of American society. Attention has also been given to the effects of these processes upon the value system, the occupational system, socialization pattern, and family pattern.

The purpose of this chapter was not to present my critical view of

American society but rather to present *a* conceptual framework by which to look at the society. This evolutionary approach is only one angle from which to examine our society.

NOTES

1. See Talcott Parsons and Winston White, "The Link Between Character and Society," in *Culture and Social Character,* ed. Seymour Martin Lipset and Leo Lowenthal (New York: Free Press of Glencoe, 1961), pp. 89–135; Talcott Parsons, *Societies: Evolutionary and Comparative Perspective* (Englewood Cliffs, N.J.: Prentice-Hall, 1966), pp. 21–29; Winston White, *Beyond Conformity* (New York: Free Press of Glencoe, 1961), pp. 70–100.

2. For the definition of structural differentiation, see p. 27.

3. White, *Beyond Conformity,* p. 75.

4. Robert Presthus, *The Organizational Society* (New York: Vintage Books, 1962), pp. 3–26.

5. White, *Beyond Conformity,* p. 79.

6. Ibid.

7. See Parsons, *Societies,* p. 22.

8. Ibid., p. 23.

9. Ibid.

10. See John Kenneth Galbraith, *The New Industrial State* (2nd ed.; Boston: Houghton Mifflin, 1971).

11. Ibid., pp. 59–71.

12. Ibid., pp. 59–60.

13. For the definition of industrialism, see chap. 2.

14. Galbraith, *The New Industrial State,* p. 298.

15. See White, *Beyond Conformity,* p. 127.

16. See William H. Whyte, *The Organization Man* (Garden City, N.Y.: Anchor Books, 1956).

17. Charles Reich, *The Greening of America* (New York: Random House, 1970), p. 67.

18. Ibid., p. 72.

19. Ibid., p. 78.

20. Ibid., p. 225.

21. See Theodore Roszak, *The Making of a Counter Culture* (Garden City, N.Y.: Anchor Books, 1969).

22. Marcuse contends that a highly developed modern technological society is a one-dimensional one based upon technological rationality. It contains and reduces oppositions, whether they may be political and economic forces or other forces operating at different levels of society. As the social structure is determined more by technological rationality, the global coexistence of opposed social systems is possible to a greater extent. In other words, one-dimensional forces based on technological rationality are pervasive enough to lead to an obsolescence of the role and autonomy of the economic and political subject. See Herbert Marcuse, *One-Dimensional Man* (quotations made in chap. 2).

23. Herbert Marcuse, *Five Lectures* (Boston: Beacon Press, 1970), p. 59; also see Herbert Marcuse, *Eros and Civilization* (2nd ed.; Boston: Beacon Press, 1966).

24. Marcuse, *Five Lectures*, p. 23.

25. Presthus, *The Organizational Society*, pp. 8–9.

26. See chap. 2, pp. 50–51.

27. For a further exposition, see White, *Beyond Conformity*, pp. 101–25.

28. See Talcott Parsons, *Social Structure and Personality* (New York: Free Press, 1967), pp. 193–98.

29. Clyde Kluckhohn, "Values and Value Orientations," in *Toward a General Theory of Action*, ed. Talcott Parsons and Edward A. Shils (New York: Harper Torchbooks, 1962), p. 395.

30. Parsons, *Social Structure and Personality*, pp. 255–57; for a further exposition of Parsons' and White's view, see James L. Peacock and A. Thomas Kirsch, *The Human Direction* (New York: Appleton-Century-Crofts, 1970), pp. 255–57.

31. Peacock and Kirsch, *The Human Direction*, p. 256.

32. Parsons, *Social Structure and Personality*, p. 197.

33. See Talcott Parsons and Winston White, "The Link Between Character and Society" which first appeared in Lipset and Lowenthal, *Culture and Social Structure*; this was later reprinted in Parsons, *Social Structure and Personality*.

34. See White, *Beyond Conformity*.

35. David Riesman, *The Lonely Crowd* (New Haven, Conn.: Yale University Press, 1961).

36. In *The Lonely Crowd*, Riesman discusses three patterns of conformity and character orientation which are termed "tradition-direction," "inner-direction," and "other-direction." Speaking of changes in American character and values, a shift from "inner-direction" to "other-direction" becomes a crucial problem of analysis.

37. Seymour Martin Lipset, *The First New Nation* (New York: Basic Books, 1963), p. 102.

38. Seymour Martin Lipset, "A Changing American Character?", in Lipset and Lowenthal, *Culture and Social Character*, p. 145.

39. Ibid., p. 147.

40. See Lipset, *The First New Nation*, pp. 106–10; Lipset, "A Changing American Character?", pp. 145–56.

41. Whyte, *The Organization Man*, p. 7.

42. Clyde Kluckhohn, "Have There Been Discernible Shifts in American Values During the Past Generation?", in *The American Style*, ed. Elting Morison (New York: Harper, 1958), p. 204.

43. In reference to this, Parsons and White make the following remark in their "The Link Between Character and Society": "Most of the distinguished foreign observers of American Society emphasize patterns that are consistent with this statement" that at "[the] most general level the value-system has not undergone a fundamental change in recent times" in American society. . . . "Kluckhohn maintains the same thesis down to the decade of the 1930's; hence it is only for the most recent period that we are forced to differ with him." Parsons, *Social Structure and Personality*, p. 195.

44. Lipset, *The First New Nation*, p. 132.

45. See Parsons and White, "The Link Between Character and Society."

46. Lipset, *The First New Nation*, p. 132.

47. Ibid., p. 135.

48. See White, *Beyond Conformity*.

49. Parsons, *Societies*.

50. Francis Hsu also supports this conclusion in *Clan, Caste, and Club* (New York: Van Nostrand and Reinhold, 1963), p. 217.

51. George Peter Murdock, *Social Structure* (New York: Free Press, 1965), p. 46.

52. Ibid., p. 16.

53. Ibid., p. 13.

54. Ibid.

55. Ibid., p. 15.

56. For a further exploration, see Robin Williams, Jr., *American Society* (New York: Alfred Knopf, 1960), pp. 50–51.

57. Hsu, *Clan, Caste, and Club*, p. 194.

58. Ibid.

59. When the notion of exclusiveness applies to an individual, it refers to the exclusiveness of personal singularity such as the immutability of the worth of each person.

60. See Yehudi Cohen, *Transition from Childhood to Adolescence*, (Chicago: Aldine, 1964).

61. See the following three works by Hsu: *Clan, Caste, and Club*, pp. 192–231; *Americans and Chinese* (Garden City, N.Y.: Doubleday Natural History Press, 1970), pp. 15–120; "Kinship and Ways of Life: An Exploration," in *Psychological Anthropology*, ed. Hsu (Homewood, Ill.: Dorsey Press, 1961), pp. 400–456.

62. See *Clan, Caste, and Club*, pp. 192–231.

63. Ibid., pp. 204–13.

64. Talcott Parsons, "Kinship System of Contemporary United States," *American Anthropologist* 45, no. 1 (January–March 1943): 32. For a related discussion see Talcott Parsons and Robert Bales, eds. *Family, Socialization, and Interaction Process* (Glencoe, Ill.: Free Press, 1955), chaps. 1 and 2.

65. Parsons, *Social Structure and Personality*, p. 58. Kenneth Keniston calls it an "emotional center," in his *The Uncommitted* (New York: Delta Books, 1965), p. 273.

66. Parsons, "Kinship System of Contemporary United States," p. 34.

67. Keniston, *The Uncommitted*, p. 284.

68. Ibid., p. 285.

69. Ibid., pp. 285–86.

70. Hsu, *Clan, Caste, and Club*, pp. 196–98.

71. See Robert Dreeben, "The Contribution of Schooling to the Learning of Norms," *Harvard Educational Review* 37, no. 2 (Spring 1967): 23–49.

72. See Talcott Parsons, "Youth in the Context of American Society," *Daedalus* 91, no. 1 (Winter 1962): 97–123.

73. For a further discussion, see S. N. Eisenstadt, *From Generation to Generation* (New York: Free Press of Glencoe, 1956), p. 43.

74. Ibid., p. 47.

75. Ibid., p. 49.

76. S. N. Eisenstadt, "Archetypal Patterns of Youth," *Daedalus* 91, no. 1 (Winter 1962): 28–46.

77. Eisenstadt, *From Generation to Generation*, p. 207.

78. See Lewis Feuer, *The Conflict of Generations* (New York: Basic Books, 1969), pp. 318–436; James Coleman, *The Adolescent Society* (New York: Free Press of Glencoe, 1961).

79. Eisenstadt, *From Generation to Generation*, p. 235.

80. Erik Erikson, "Youth: Fidelity and Diversity," in *Daedalus* 91, no. 1 (Winter 1962): 15; also see pp. 5–27.

81. Eisenstadt, *From Generation to Generation*, pp. 240–47.

82. Ibid., p. 241.

83. Ibid.

84. Ibid., p. 242.

85. See James Coleman, *Adolescent and the Schools* (New York: Basic Books, 1965); Ivan Illich, *Deschooling Society* (New York: Harper & Row, 1971); Paul Goodman, *New Reformation* (New York: Random House, 1970); Margaret Mead, *Culture and Commitment* (Garden City, N.Y.: Doubleday, 1970).

4

COUNTERCULTURAL FORCES:
EMERGING DIVERGENCE IN
AMERICAN CULTURE*

Charles A. Reich

In the following, Charles A. Reich discusses the
emergence of a counterculture in American society; he terms it
Consciousness III in *The Greening of America*, from which this
chapter is excerpted. He identifies the social and cultural
conditions that have given rise to this counterculture at the
outset of this essay. Some of these conditions were also explored
in the preceding chapter. Reich then proceeds to analyze
extensively the character of Consciousness III. It will be noted
that this is the only chapter not specifically written for this
volume.—EDS.

The logic and necessity of the new generation—and what they are so
furiously opposed to—must be seen against a background of what has gone
wrong in America. It must be understood in light of the betrayal and loss
of the American dream, the rise of the Corporate State of the 1960s, and
the way in which that State dominates, exploits, and ultimately destroys
both nature and man. Its rationality must be measured against the
insanity of existing "reason"—reason that makes impoverishment, dehumanization, and even war appear to be logical and necessary. Its logic
must be read from the fact that Americans have lost control of the
machinery of their society, and only new values and a new culture can
restore control. Its emotions and spirit can be comprehended only by
seeing contemporary America through the eyes of the new generation.

The meaning and the future of the revolution emerge from this
historical perspective. The revolution is a movement to bring man's

---

* From *The Greening of America*, by Charles A. Reich. Copyright © 1970 by Charles A.
Reich. Reprinted by permission of Random House, Inc. A portion of this book originally
appeared in *The New Yorker* in somewhat different form.

thinking, his society, and his life to terms with the revolution of technology and science that has already taken place. Technology demands of man a new mind—a higher, transcendent reason—if it is to be controlled and guided rather than to become an unthinking monster. It demands a new individual responsibility for values, or it will dictate all values. And it promises a life that is more liberated and more beautiful than any man has known, if man has the courage and the imagination to seize that life.

The transformation that is coming invites us to reexamine our own lives. It confronts us with a personal and individual choice: are we satisfied with how we have lived; how would we live differently? It offers us a recovery of self. It faces us with the fact that this choice cannot be evaded, for as the freedom is already there, so must the responsibility be there.

At the heart of everything is what we shall call a change of consciousness. This means a "new head"—a new way of living—a new man. This is what the new generation has been searching for, and what it has started achieving. Industrialism produced a new man, too—one adapted to the demands of the machine. In contrast, today's emerging consciousness seeks a new knowledge of what it means to be human, in order that the machine, having been built, may now be turned to human ends; in order that man once more can become a creative force, renewing and creating his own life and thus giving life back to his society.

It is essential to place the American crisis and this change within individuals in a philosophic perspective, showing how we got to where we are, and where we are going. Current events are so overwhelming that we only see from day to day, merely responding to each crisis as it comes, seeing only immediate evils, and seeking inadequate solutions such as merely ending the war, or merely changing our domestic priorities. A longer-range view is necessary.

What is the nature of the present American crisis? Most of us see it as a collection of problems, not necessarily related to each other, and, although profoundly troubling, nevertheless within the reach of reason and reform. But if we list these problems, not according to topic, but as elements of larger issues concerning the structure of our society itself, we can see that the present crisis is an organic one, that it arises out of the basic premises by which we live and that no mere reform can touch it.

1. Disorder, corruption, hypocrisy, war. The front pages of newspapers tell of the disintegration of the social fabric, and the resulting atmosphere of anxiety and terror in which we all live. Lawlessness is most often associated with crime and riots, but there is lawlessness and corruption in all the major institutions of our society—matched by an indifference to responsibility and consequences, and a pervasive hypocrisy that refuses to acknowledge the facts that are everywhere visible. Both lawlessness and evasion found expression in the Vietnam war, with its unprincipled destruction of everything human, and its random, indifferent, technological cruelty.

2. Poverty, distorted priorities, and law-making by private power. America presents a picture of drastic poverty amid affluence, an extremity of contrast unknown in other industrial nations. Likewise there is a superabundance of some goods, services, and activities such as defense manufacture, while other needs, such as education and medical care, are at a starvation level for many. These closely related kinds of inequality are not the accidents of a free economy, they are intentionally and rigidly built into the laws of our society by those with powerful influence; an example is the tax structure which subsidizes private wealth and production of luxuries and weapons at the direct expense of impoverished people and impoverished services. The nation has a planned economy, and the planning is done by the exercise of private power without concern for the general good.

3. Uncontrolled technology and the destruction of environment. Technology and production can be great benefactors of man, but they are mindless instruments; if undirected they career along with a momentum of their own. In our country they pulverize everything in their path: the landscape, the natural environment, history and tradition, the amenities and civilities, the privacy and spaciousness of life, beauty, and the fragile, slow-growing social structures which bind us together. Organization and bureaucracy, which are applications of technology to social institutions, increasingly dictate how we shall live our lives, with the logic of organization taking precedence over any other values.

4. Decline of democracy and liberty; powerlessness. The Constitution and Bill of Rights have been weakened, imperceptibly but steadily. The nation has gradually become a rigid managerial hierarchy, with a small elite and a great mass of the disenfranchised. Democracy has rapidly lost ground as power is increasingly captured by giant managerial institutions and corporations, and decisions are made by experts, specialists, and professionals safely insulated from the feelings of the people. Most governmental power has shifted from Congress to administrative agencies, and corporate power is free to ignore both stockholders and consumers. As regulation and administration have grown, liberty has been eroded and bureaucratic discretion has taken the place of the rule of law. Today both dissent and efforts at change are dealt with by repression. The pervasiveness of police, security men, the military, and compulsory military service show the changed character of American liberty.

5. *The artificiality of work and culture.* Work and living have become more and more pointless and empty. There is no lack of meaningful projects that cry out to be done, but our working days are used up in work that lacks meaning: making useless or harmful products, or servicing the bureaucratic structures. For most Americans, work is mindless, exhausting, boring, servile, and hateful, something to be endured while "life" is confined to "time off." At the same time our culture has been reduced to the grossly commercial; all cultural values are for sale, and those that fail to make a profit are not preserved. Our life activities have become plastic, vicarious, and false to our genuine needs, activities fabricated by others and forced upon us.

6. *Absence of community.* America is one vast, terrifying anti-community. The great organizations to which most people give their working day, and the apartments and suburbs to which they return at night, are equally places of loneliness and alienation. Modern living has obliterated place, locality, and neighborhood, and given us the anonymous separateness of our existence. The family, the most basic social system, has been ruthlessly stripped to its functional essentials. Friendship has been coated over with a layer of impenetrable artificiality as men strive to live roles designed for them. Protocol, competition, hostility, and fear have replaced the warmth of the circle of affection which might sustain man against a hostile universe.

7. *Loss of self.* Of all the forms of impoverishment that can be seen or felt in America, loss of self, or death in life, is surely the most devastating. It is, even more than the draft and the Vietnam war, the source of discontent and rage in the new generation. Beginning with school, if not before, an individual is systematically stripped of his imagination, his creativity, his heritage, his dreams, and his personal uniqueness, in order to style him into a productive unit for a mass, technological society. Instinct, feeling, and spontaneity are repressed by overwhelming forces. As the individual is drawn into the meritocracy, his working life is split from his home life, and both suffer from a lack of wholeness. Eventually, people virtually become their professions, roles, or occupations, and are thenceforth strangers to themselves. Blacks long ago felt their deprivation of identity and potential for life. But white "soul" and blues are just beginning. Only a segment of youth is articulately aware that they too suffer an enforced loss of self—they too are losing the lives that could be theirs. . . .

As a mass phenomenon, consciousness is formed by the underlying economic and social conditions. There was a consciousness that went with peasant life in the Middle Ages, and a consciousness that went with small town, preindustrial life in America. Culture and government interact with consciousness; they are its products but they also help to form it. While consciousness is the creator of any social system, it can lag behind a system, once created, and even be manipulated by that system. Lag and manipulation are the factors that produce a consciousness characterized by unreality. If we believe in free enterprise, but the nation has become an interlocking corporate system, we are living in unreality as the victims of lag, and we are powerless to cope with the existing corporate system.

To show how this has worked out in America, and to show the true meaning of the new generation, we have attempted to classify three general types of consciousness. These three types predominate in America today. One was formed in the nineteenth century, the second in the first half of this century, the third is just emerging. Consciousness I is the traditional outlook of the American farmer, small businessman, and worker who is trying to get ahead. Consciousness II represents the values of an organizational society. Consciousness III is the new generation. . . .

Soon after Americans began their experiment in a new community, the assumptions upon which the nation was based were threatened by the rise of two powerful forces, worldwide in influence: the competitive market economy and scientific technique. The forces came as benefactors (as in large part they were), offering men in all countries the possibility of liberation from static toil. The market system transforms all men into competitors in order to get them to be more aggressively productive; it does this by defining man's labor, his environment, and his culture as commodities which can be valued in money and exchanged for money, and by permitting "successful" competitors to accumulate "profit" and "surplus" in return for the exploitation of labor and resources. Scientific technique is a philosophy concerned with the basic values of life; it asserts that all activities should be carried on in that manner which is scientifically or technically "best" and "most efficient." It is technique which dictates specialization of labor, the use of machinery, systems of organization, and mass production. These forces threatened the most fundamental aspects of the American dream: the physical-human environment that made possible the pursuit of happiness, and the form of government that rejected arbitrary power.

Prior to the coming of the industrial revolution, most people were born, lived, worked, and died in the same place, among people they knew and saw every day. There was no separation between work and living. Ties to the community were strong and seldom severed; each man lived within a circle which did not depend upon his own action, began before him, and lasted beyond him. Food and shelter were communal enterprises;

no one grew fat or starved alone. The scale of everything was smaller: tools, houses, land, villages. There were no large, impersonal institutions— apartment houses, factories, or hospitals. Scale and activity were influenced by nature (for example, time was measured by the daily sun and the seasons). Laws were administered by visible local people. Most important of all, man's economic activity was rooted in, and subordinate to, his social system. That is, there were no purely economic or scientific "laws." Customs or religion—communal traditions, in short—were the regulators of life. Play, art, ritual, ceremony, and the spiritual were not separated from the other aspects of life; they were an integral part of the whole. Activity of all kinds was rooted in folk and religious culture which developed "irrationally" and without conscious design, in response to human needs. This world, both in Europe and in frontier America, was destroyed in the making of our modern world. . . .

Beginning with a few individuals in the mid-1960s, and gathering numbers ever more rapidly thereafter, Consciousness III has sprouted up, astonishingly and miraculously, out of the stony soil of the American Corporate State. So spontaneous was its appearance that no one, not the most astute or the most radical, foresaw what was coming or recognized it when it began. It is not surprising that many people think it a conspiracy, for it was spread, here and abroad, by means invisible. Hardly anybody of the older generation, even the FBI or the sociologists, knows much about it, for its language and thought are so different from Consciousness II as to make it virtually an undecipherable secret code. Consciousness III is, as of this writing, the greatest secret in America, although its members have shouted as loudly as they could to be heard.

We must pause over the origins of Consciousness III, lest it seem too improbable and too transitory to be deemed as fundamental as Consciousness I and Consciousness II. One element in its origin has already been described: the impoverishment of life, the irrationality, violence, and claustrophobia of the American Corporate State. But how did this corporate machine, seemingly designed to keep its inhabitants perpetually on a treadmill, suddenly begin producing something altogether new and unintended? The new consciousness is the product of two interacting forces: the promise of life that is made to young Americans by all of our affluence, technology, liberation, and ideals, and the threat to that promise posed by everything from neon ugliness and boring jobs to the Vietnam war and the shadow of nuclear holocaust. Neither the promise nor the threat is the cause by itself; but the two together have done it.

The promise comes first. We have all heard the promise: affluence, security, technology make possible a new life, a new permissiveness, a new freedom, a new expansion of human possibility. We have all heard it, but to persons born after World War II it means something very different. Older people learned how to live in a different world; it is really beyond them to imagine themselves living according to the new promises. The most basic limitations of life—the job, the working day, the part one can play in life, the limits of sex, love and relationships, the limits of knowledge and experience—all vanish, leaving open a life that can be lived without the guideposts of the past. In the world that now exists, a life of surfing *is* possible, not as an escape from work, a recreation or a phase, but as a *life*—if one chooses. The fact that this choice is actually available is the truth that the younger generation knows and the older generation cannot know.

The promise is made real to members of the younger generation by a sense of acceptance about themselves. To older generations, particularly Consciousness II people, great issues were presented by striving to reach some external standard of personal attractiveness, popularity, ability at sports, acceptance by the group. Many lives, including some outstanding careers, were lived under the shadow of such personal issues; even late in life, prople are still profoundly influenced by them. Of course the new generation is not free of such concerns. But to an astonishing degree, whether it is due to new parental attitudes, a less tense, less inhibited childhood, or a different experience during school years, these are not the issues which plague the younger generation. If the hero of *Portnoy's Complaint* is the final and most complete example of the man dissatisfied with the self that he is, the new generation says, "Whatever I am, I am." He may have hang-ups of all sorts, insecurities, inadequacies, but he does not reject himself on that account. There may be as many difficulties about work, ability, relationships, and sex as in any other generation, but there is less guilt, less anxiety, less self-hatred. Consciousness III says, "I'm glad I'm me."

The new generation has also learned lessons from technology, by being born with it, that the older generation does not know even though it invented technology. It is one thing to know intellectually that there is a Xerox machine that can copy anything, a pill that can make sexual intercourse safe, or a light motorcycle that can take two people off camping with ten minutes' preparation, but it is quite another thing to live with these facts, make use of them, and thus learn to live *by* them.

These experiences and promises are shared to some extent by the youth of every industrial nation, and the new consciousness is, as we know, not limited to the United States. But Consciousness III, the specifically

American form, is not based on promise alone. A key word in understanding its origin is *betrayal.*

Older people are inclined to think of work, injustice and war, and of the bitter frustrations of life, as the human condition. Their capacity for outrage is consequently dulled. But to those who have glimpsed the real possibilities of life, who have tasted liberation and love, who have seen the promised land, the prospect of a dreary corporate job, a ranch-house life, or a miserable death in war is utterly intolerable. Moreover, the human condition, if that is what it is, has been getting steadily worse in the Corporate State; more and more life-denying just as life should be opening up. And hovering over everything is the threat of annihilation, more real and more terrifying to the young than to anyone else. To them, the discrepancy between what could be and what is, is overwhelming; perhaps it is the greatest single fact of their existence. The promise of America, land of beauty and abundance, land of the free, somehow has been betrayed.

They feel the betrayal in excruciatingly personal terms. Between them and the rich possibilities of life there intervenes a piercing insecurity—not the personal insecurity their parents knew, but a cosmic insecurity. Will the nation be torn apart by riots or war? Will their lives be cut short by death or injury in Vietnam? Will the impersonal machinery of the state—schools, careers, institutions—overwhelm them? Above all, will they escape an atomic holocaust (they were, as many people have pointed out, the generation of the bomb). Insecurity sharpens their consciousness and draws them together.

Parents have unintentionally contributed to their children's condemnation of existing society. Not by their words, but by their actions, attitudes, and manner of living, they have conveyed to their children the message "Don't live the way we have, don't settle for the emptiness of our lives, don't be lured by the things we valued, don't neglect life and love as we have." With the unerring perceptiveness of the child, their children have read these messages from the lifeless lives of their "successful" parents, have seen marriages break up because there was nothing to hold them, have felt cynicism, alienation, and despair in the best-kept homes of America. And will have none of it.

Kenneth Keniston, in *Young Radicals,* found that one of the most telling forces in producing the political ideals of the new generation is the contrast between their parents' ideals (which they accept) and their parents' failure to live these same ideals. Keniston found that young radicals show a *continuity* of ideals from childhood on; they simply stayed with them while their parents failed to.

We might add to this that our society, with its dogmatic insistence on one way of seeing everything, its dominating false consciousness, and its ever-widening gap between fact and rhetoric, invites a sudden moment when the credibility gap becomes too much, and invites cataclysmic consequences to the consciousness of a young person when that occurs. For so vehemently does the society insist that its "truth" be accepted wholly and undeviatingly down the line, and so drastic are the discrepancies once seen, that a single breach in the dike may bring a young person's entire conversion. All that is needed is to participate in one peace demonstration and find the *New York Times*' report of it inexcusably false, and the whole edifice of "truth" collapses. Such "conversions" are constantly seen on campuses today; a freshman arrives, his political views are hometown-Consciousness I, and suddenly he is radicalized. The fabric of manufactured "truth," spread taut and thin, breaches, and one breach leaves it irrevocably in tatters.

If a history of Consciousness III were to be written, it would show a fascinating progression. The earliest sources were among those exceptional individuals who are found at any time in any society: the artistic, the highly sensitive, the tormented. Thoreau, James Joyce, and Wallace Stevens all speak directly to Consciousness III. Salinger's Holden Caulfield was a fictional version of the first young precursors of Consciousness III. Perhaps there was always a bit of Consciousness III in every teen-ager, but normally it quickly vanished. Holden sees through the established world: they are "phonies" and he is merciless in his honesty. But what was someone like Holden to do? A subculture of "beats" grew up, and a beatnik world flourished briefly, but for most people it represented only another dead end. Other Holdens might reject the legal profession and try teaching literature or writing instead, letting their hair grow a bit longer as well. But they remained separated individuals, usually ones from affluent but unhappy, tortured family backgrounds, and their differences with society were paid for by isolation.

Unquestionably the blacks made a substantial contribution to the origins of the new consciousness. They were left out of the Corporate State, and thus they had to have a culture and life-style in opposition to the State. Their music, with its "guts," contrasted with the insipid white music. This way of life seemed more earthy, more sensual than that of whites. They were the first openly to scorn the Establishment and its values; as Eldridge Cleaver shows in *Soul on Ice*, and Malcolm X shows in his autobiography, they were radicalized by the realities of their situation. When their music began to be heard by white teen-agers through the medium of rock 'n' roll, and when their view of America became visible through the civil rights movement, it gave new impetus to the subterranean awareness of the beat generation and the Holden Caulfields.

The great change took place when Consciousness III began to appear among young people who had endured no special emotional conditions, but were simply bright, sensitive children of the affluent middle class. It is hard to be precise about the time when this happened. One chronology is based on the college class of 1969, which entered as freshmen in the fall of 1965. Another important date is the summer of 1967, when the full force of the cultural revolution was first visible. But even in the fall of 1967 the numbers involved were still very small. The new group drew heavily from those who had been exposed to the very best of liberal arts education—poetry, art, theatre, literature, philosophy, good conversation. Later, the group began to include "ordinary" middle-class students. In time there were college athletes as well as college intellectuals, and lovers of motorcycles and skiing as well as lovers of art and literature. But the core group was always white, well educated, and middle class.

Among today's youth, the phenomenon of "conversions" is increasingly common. It is surprising that so little has been written about these conversions, for they are a striking aspect of contemporary life. What happens is simply this: in a brief span of months, a student, seemingly conventional in every way, changes his haircut, his clothes, his habits, his interests, his political attitudes, his way of relating to other people, in short, his whole way of life. He has "converted" to a new consciousness. The contrast between well-groomed freshman pictures and the same individuals in person a year later tells the tale. The clean-cut, hard-working, model young man who despises radicals and hippies can become one himself with breathtaking suddenness. Over and over again, an individual for whom a conversion seemed impossible, star athlete, an honor student, the small-town high school boy with the American Legion scholarship, transforms himself into a drug-using, long-haired, peace-loving "freak." Only when he puts on a headband and plays unexpectedly skillful touch football or basketball, or when a visitor to his old room back home catches sight of his honor society certificate, is his earlier life revealed.

As the new consciousness made youth more distinct, the younger generation began discovering itself as a generation. Always before, young people felt themselves tied more to their families, to their schools, and to their immediate situations than to "a generation." But now an entire culture, including music, clothes, and drugs, began to distinguish youth. As it did, the message of consciousness went with it. And the more the older generation rejected the culture, the more a fraternity of the young grew up, so that they recognized each other as brothers and sisters from coast to coast. That is its history up to this writing; let us now try to describe the content of Consciousness III.

A few warnings are needed. First, in attempting to describe Consciousness III systematically and analytically, we are engaging in an intellectual process which Consciousness III rejects; they have a deep skepticism of both "linear" and analytic thought. Second, we shall be talking about an idealized consciousness, and not about something that is to be seen in all aspects in any one person. The members of the new generation have their doubts, hang-ups and failings too, and Consciousness III may coexist with earlier patterns and values. Third, Consciousness III itself is just in an early stage of development, and probably the elements of it would have to be described differently in one or two years.

The foundation of Consciousness III is liberation. It comes into being the moment the individual frees himself from automatic acceptance of the imperatives of society and the false consciousness which society imposes. For example, the individual no longer accepts unthinkingly the personal goals proposed by society; a change of personal goals is one of the first and most basic elements of Consciousness III. The meaning of liberation is that the individual is free to build his own philosophy and values, his own life-style, and his own culture from a new beginning.

Consciousness III starts with self. In contrast to Consciousness II, which accepts society, the public interest, and institutions as the primary reality, III declares that the individual self is the only true reality. Thus it returns to the earlier America: "Myself I sing." The first commandment is: thou shalt not do violence to thyself. It is a crime to allow oneself to become an instrumental being, a projectile designed to accomplish some extrinsic end, a part of an organization or a machine. It is a crime to be alienated from oneself, to be a divided or schizophrenic being, to defer meaning to the future. One must live completely at each moment, not with the frenzied "nowness" of advertising, but with the utter *wholeness* that Heidegger expresses. The commandment is: be true to oneself.

To start from self does not mean to be selfish. It means to start from premises based on human life and the rest of nature, rather than premises that are the artificial products of the Corporate State, such as power or status. It is not an "ego trip" but a radical subjectivity designed to find genuine values in a world whose official values are false and distorted. It is not egocentricity, but honesty, wholeness, genuineness in all things. It starts from self because human life is found as individual units, not as corporations and institutions; its intent is to start from life.

Consciousness III postulates the absolute worth of every human being—every self. Consciousness III does not believe in the antagonistic or competitive doctrine of life. Competition, within the limits of a sport like tennis or swimming, is accepted for its own pleasure, although even as athletes III's are far less competitive (and sometimes, but not always, poorer athletes as a result). But III's do not compete "in real life." They do not measure others, they do not see others as something to struggle against. People are brothers, the world is ample for all. In consequence, one never hears the disparagements, the snickers, the judgments that are so common among I's and II's. A boy who was odd in some way used to suffer derision all through his school days. Today there would be no persecution; one might even hear one boy speak, with affection, of "my freaky friend." Instead of insisting that everyone be measured by given standards, the new generation values what is unique and different in each self; there is no pressure that anyone be an athlete unless he wants to; a harpsichord player is accepted on equal terms. No one judges anyone else. This is a second commandment.

Consciousness III rejects the whole concept of excellence and comparative merit that is so central to Consciousness II. III refuses to evaluate people by general standards, it refuses to classify people, or analyze them. Each person has his own individuality, not to be compared to that of anyone else. Someone may be a brilliant thinker, but he is not "better" at thinking than anyone else, he simply possesses his own excellence. A person who thinks very poorly is still excellent in his own way. Therefore people are in no hurry to find out another person's background, schools, achievements, as a means of knowing him; they regard all of that as secondary, preferring to know him unadorned. Because there are no governing standards, no one is rejected. Everyone is entitled to pride in himself, and no one should act in a way that is servile, or feel inferior, or allow himself to be treated as if he were inferior.

It is upon these premises that the Consciousness III idea of community and of personal relationships rests. In place of the world seen as a jungle, with every man for himself (Consciousness I) or the world seen as a meritocracy leading to a great corporate hierarchy of rigidly drawn relations and maneuvers for position (Consciousness II), the world is a community. People all belong to the same family, whether they have met each other or not. It is as simple as that. There are no "tough guys" among the youth of Consciousness III. Hitchhikers smile at approaching cars, people smile at each other on the street, the human race rediscovers its need for each other. "I felt lonesome, so I came looking for some people," a III will say. Something in the makeup and pride of a I or II will keep him from "confessing" that "weakness" in quite such an open way. But III does not want to stand head and shoulders above the crowd. III values, more than a judgeship or executive title, the warmth of the "circle of affection" in which men join hands. In personal relations, the keynote is honesty, and the absence of socially imposed duty. To be dishonest in love, to "use" another person, is a major crime. A third commandment is: be wholly honest with others, use no other person as a means. It is equally wrong to alter oneself for someone else's sake; by being one's true self one offers others the most; one offers them something honest, genuine, and, more important, something for them to respond to, to be evoked by. A work of art is not valued because it changes itself for each person who views it, it retains its own integrity and thus means something unique and marvelous to those who see it. Being true to oneself is, so Consciousness III says, the best and only way to relate to others. Consciousness III rejects most of what happens between people in our world: manipulation of others, forcing anyone to do anything against his wish, using others for one's own purposes, irony and sarcasm, defensive stand-offishness. III also rejects relationships of authority and subservience. It will neither give commands nor follow them; coercive relations between people are wholly unacceptable. And III also rejects any relationships based wholly on role, relationships limited along strictly impersonal and functional lines. There is no situation in which one is entitled to act impersonally, in a stereotyped fashion, with another human being; the relationship of businessman to clerk, passenger to conductor, student to janitor must not be impersonal.

But to observe duties toward others, after the feelings are gone, is no virtue and may even be a crime. Loyalty is valued but not artificial duty. Thus the new generation looks with suspicion on "obligations" and contractual relations between people, but it believes that honesty can produce far more genuine relationships than the sterile ones it observes among the older generation. To most people, there is something frightening about the notion that no oath, no law, no promise, no indebtedness holds people together when the feeling is gone. But for the new generation that is merely recognition of the truth about human beings. Moreover, getting rid of what is artificial is essential to make way for what is real, and Consciousness III considers genuine relationships with others, friendship, companionship, love, the human community, to be among the highest values of life.

The premise of self and of values based on human life leads directly to a radical critique of society. Many people are puzzled by the radicalism of Consciousness III—have they been infiltrated by communists, are they influenced by "a few left-wing agitators," have they been reading Marx? It does indeed seem astonishing that naïve young people, without political experience, should come up with a critique of society that seems to have escaped the most scholarly as well as the most astute and experienced of their elders. But there is no mystery, no conspiracy, and very little reading of Marx. Older people begin by assuming that much of the structure of the

Corporate State is necessary and valid; starting there they never get very far. The young people start with entirely different premises, and all is revealed to them.

What Consciousness III sees, with an astounding clarity that no ideology could provide, is a society that is unjust to its poor and its minorities, is run for the benefit of a privileged few, is lacking in its proclaimed democracy and liberty, is ugly and artificial, that destroys environment and self, and is, like the wars it spawns, "unhealthy for children and other living things." It sees a society that is deeply untruthful and hypocritical; one of the gifts of the young is to see through phoniness and cant, and Consciousness III sees through the Establishment verities of our society with corrosive ease.

Consciousness III sees not merely a set of political and public wrongs, such as a liberal New Dealer might have seen, but also the deeper ills that Kafka or the German expressionists or Dickens would have seen: old people shunted into institutional homes, streets made hideous with neon and commercialism, servile conformity, the competitiveness and sterility of suburban living, the loneliness and anomie of cities, the ruin of nature by bulldozers and pollution, the stupid mindlessness of most high school education, the coarse materialism of most values, the lovelessness of many marriages, and, above all, the plastic, artificial quality of everything; plastic lives in plastic homes.

All of Consciousness III's criticisms of society were brought into sharpest focus by the Vietnam war. For the war seemed to sum up the evils of our society: destruction of people, destruction of environment, depersonalized use of technology, war by the rich and powerful against the poor and helpless, justification based on abstract rationality, hypocrisy and lies, and a demand that the individual, regardless of his conscience, values, or self, make himself into a part of the war machine, an impersonal projectile bringing death to other people. Those who said they could not go believed that compulsory service in a war they hated would be so total a destruction of their genuine values that even if they did return to the United States, they could never return to the ranks of the genuinely living.

The initial premise of self leads not only to a critique of society, it also leads, in many representatives of Consciousness III, to a deep personal commitment to the welfare of the community. This may sound contradictory to those who wrongly equate the premise of self with selfishness, and it may seem to contradict the premise that the individual, not society, is the reality. But there is no contradiction. It is quite true that the individual does not accept the goals or standards set by society. But of course he recognizes that society has a vast influence on the welfare of people everywhere, including his own desire to be an independent being. Mostly he sees this influence as bad, but he also sees how much better things could be. And therefore, for the sake of the welfare of individuals, he is committed to the improvement of society. It is the manner of commitment that differs from II.

There is one essential qualification to what we have said: dedication to the community is not to include means that do violence to the self. A Consciousness III person will not study law to help society, if law is not what he wants to do with his life, nor will he do harm to others in order to promote some good, nor will he deny himself the experiences of life for any cause. The political radical of Consciousness III is thus very different from the radical of the Old Left, the communist, socialist, or civil libertarian ready to dedicate himself and his life to the cause, puritanical, sour, righteous. To the new consciousness, to make himself an object to serve the cause would be to subvert the cause.

Subject to this qualification, the key to the Consciousness III commitment lies in the concept of full personal responsibility. In the case of Consciousness II, commitment to society means commitment to reform in the general direction already established by society (equality, better education), the notion of "reform" merely meaning that the "liberal" is somewhat ahead of where society is at. And the commitment has limits; the liberal enjoys his high status, his elegant house, his security, and comfort, and fights his battle from that position. Consciousness III feels that, if he is to be true to himself, he must respond *with* himself. He may take a job, such as teaching in a ghetto school, which offers neither prestige nor comfort, but offers the satisfaction of personal contact with ghetto children. He must live on a modest scale to retain the freedom that his commitment demands. He must take risks. And at the same time, he must be wholly himself in what he does. He knows that he is an agent of change, whether he plays music or works in a ghetto, so long as he affirms himself in his work, and so long as his work expresses the full responsibility of his feelings.

It is this notion of personal responsibility which makes the new generation, when it finds itself excluded from the decision-making process, demand a part in that process. For the liberal, it is sufficient to say, "I oppose air pollution, but in my job I have nothing to do with it, no responsibility in that direction, all I can do is try to influence those who do." That, to Consciousness III, is not being responsible; if one is not part of the decision-making process, responsibility requires that one gain such power.

It is this same personal responsibility that makes the young student feel himself to be an adult, not a person getting ready for life. By attempting to be fully alive *now*, young people grow more serious, more thoughtful, more concerned with what is happening in the world. Many adults of the older generation have smooth baby faces, the faces of men interested only in the Sunday ball game, the nearest skirt, or the bowling league, as if they were permanent juveniles, as if they never, not once in their lives, faced their world and took its concerns on themselves, or accepted the responsibilities of full consciousness. The faces of Consciousness III seem to have lived more, even in their short years. A look at a college classbook of today, compared with one of fifteen years ago, tells the difference. That is one reason why the people of Consciousness III have a sense of each other as a generation with something in common.

During the Columbia confrontation, a group of Columbia varsity athletes were invited to an alumni meeting to receive awards, then disinvited when they asked to make statements on the campus situation. The alumni didn't want to think of athletes having political views. The athletes, fencers who had won a national championship and basketball players who had won the Ivy League championship, then picketed the alumni meeting in a driving rain in their varsity C blazers, until the alumni finally let them in and let them speak (*New York Times*, 25 May 1968). It wasn't the athletes' "job" to picket in the rain; they could have signed a letter if they wanted to express themselves. But they were not the smooth-faced, ever-juvenile jocks of American expectations. They were serious adults. And they thought it essential, if they were to be *whole* as selves, to make a *personal* response, and thereby, as Sartre's Orestes did in *The Flies*, assume responsibility that "was not theirs," and thus achieve a full existence. It is interesting that journalists, in writing about the new generation, tend to use the term "a youth" with some of its older meaning—not merely a young man, but the hero of a story—a person who possesses the qualities of boldness, action, and moral purpose. It is as if young people have recaptured courage, and the ability to take action, and thus recovered a measure of power over their fate.

Because it accepts no imposed system, the basic stance of Consciousness III is one of openness to any and all experience. It is always in a state of becoming. It is just the opposite of Consciousness II, which tries to force all new experience into a pre-existing system, and to assimilate all new knowledge to principles already established. Although we can attempt to describe the specific content of Consciousness III at a given moment, its lasting essence is constant change, and constant growth of each individual. . . .

The essence of Consciousness III is not something that is inherently limited to youth. That essence is recovery of self. Youth are in the process of recovering self from the world of their parents, from the pressures of school and from the looming demands of role, career, and the draft. But there is an even greater need on the part of workers and older people to recover self. They are the prisoners of the technological state, exploited by its economy, tied to its goals, regimented by its factories and offices, deprived of all those sides of life which find no functional utility in the industrial machine.

Up to now, the forces within the Corporate State that have produced a new consciousness in a segment of youth have had no similar impact upon workers or older people. Apparently some factor that decisively influenced the new generation is missing, or some factor not applicable to youth is holding the minds of the middle class in check. If we can bring these differences to light, we can uncover the route to a change of consciousness that would extend beyond the ranks of youth.

The basis for a change in consciousness exists today in the middle class as a whole. Their dissatisfactions are at least as great as those of their children; the middle class feels a sense of betrayal of the American dream, and a sense of personal claustrophobia, that is very much like the feelings of young people. What they do not feel as strongly is the promise—the promise that gives the new generation its optimism and joy, and its liberation. But the promise is there, waiting to be seen by everyone. The road taken by the new generation is open to all others. . . .

How can our society be changed? No matter how many people join the ranks of Consciousness III, the Corporate State seems likely to go on as before. There is no convincing plan, no political strategy, for turning new consciousness into something effective in structural terms. Quite the contrary: there is every reason to fear that the State is growing ever more powerful, more autonomous, more indifferent to its own inhabitants. But the liberals and radicals who despair because there is no plan or strategy are simply looking for the wrong thing. They would not recognize the key to dismantling the Corporate State even if they saw it. The Corporate State cannot be fought by the legal, political, or power methods that are the only means ever used up to now by revolutionists or proponents of social change. We must no longer depend wholly upon political or legal activism, upon structural change, upon liberal or even radical assaults on existing power. Such methods, used exclusively, are certain to fail. The only plan that will succeed is one that will be greeted by most social activists with disbelief and disparagement, yet it is entirely realistic—the only means that is realistic, given the nature of the contemporary State: revolution by consciousness. . . .

Neither lawful procedures nor politics-and-power can succeed against the Corporate State. Neither can prevent the steady advance of authoritarian rule. If the new consciousness sticks to these tactics, it will throw itself away on an ideology that fails to take account of its real power. The power is not the power of manipulating procedures or the power of politics or street fighting, but the power of new values and a new way of life.

For the road to a new society is there nonetheless. Consciousness is capable of changing and of destroying the Corporate State, without violence, without seizure of political power, without overthrow of any existing group of people. The new generation, by experimenting with action at the level of consciousness, has shown the way to the one method of change that will work in today's post-industrial society: changing consciousness. It is only by change in individual lives that we can seize power from the State.

PART TWO

The Establishment School—
System and Sentiment

5

THE STATE SYSTEM, SCHOOLING, AND COGNITIVE AND MOTIVATIONAL PATTERNS*

Yehudi A. Cohen

Analysis of the development of specific social institutions depends on the premise that social forms can only emerge, flourish, and be sustained in sociocultural atmospheres that are conducive to them. Each of these social forms must be regarded as an aspect of a population's adaptation to its total environment. This milieu includes the sociopolitical institutions of the society, in addition to natural elements. I am going to treat the existence and imperatives of civilizational states as primary stimuli to the development of schools.

In terms of the strategy of research, it is often necessary to select certain variables that are taken as points of departure in order to break

* This is a revised and shortened version of my chapter, "Schools and Civilizational States," in *The Social Sciences and the Comparative Study of Educational Systems*, ed. Joseph Fischer (Scranton, Pa.: International Textbook Company, 1970). I want to express my deepest appreciation to Professor David G. Mandelbaum who stimulated many of the ideas in it. I also want to thank David A. Fredrickson, Vera-Mae Fredrickson, Margaret Mead, Lionel Tiger, and David Riesman for their helpful comments and suggestions. Needless to say, I alone am responsible for any of the paper's shortcomings. I also want to thank Lucille Walker for preparing this manuscript for publication.

into chicken-and-egg relationships. But the selection of such variables is not entirely arbitrary, especially if it can be shown historically that given features of social organization regularly and recurrently precede others. Thus, if it can be shown that the development of civilizational states are the repeated antecedents of schools, we can safely conclude that we have broken into the circle of the social systems of these societies. "At a more abstract level, the main course of cultural evolution increasingly has come to be viewed as a succession of adaptive patterns, each new cultural type tending to spread and differentiate at the expense of less efficient precursors." [1]

Another way of saying this is that the development and elaboration of a particular institution is an aspect of the natural history of a society, or of the stage of cultural development of which it is representative. This axiom has to be made explicit in order to stress that man has little (if any) deliberate and conscious control over the emergence or loss of specific institutions in society. All other things being equal—such as the limitations of the natural environment—he acts out the inexorable dictates of the stage of cultural development reached by his society. Man may affect the character of the institutions he creates, but their emergence in the first place, or their loss, are not matters of deliberate social policy. Naturally, men develop rational legitimating ideologies to justify the institutions they mold and in which they play their roles, but it is doubtful whether people in most societies know why their institutions have been developed. The regularity with which we observe the growth and ebb of specific social forms under similar conditions in widely dispersed areas of the world, sometimes at intervals of thousands of years, and in societies that could not have had contact with—or awareness of—each other requires an overview of society based on a concept of the natural history of social systems.

A comparison of societies at all stages of cultural development reveals a striking correlation: school systems are aspects of the formal organization of state societies, but not of all of them. A comparison of state societies that have independently created school systems with those that have not discloses that school systems are developed autochthonously in state societies that are parts of civilizations.

A civilization is a network of nations. One of the outstanding features of a civilizational network is the mutual dependence of the member nations on one another for their economic viability; intimately related to this is regional specialization within the network. Another prominent characteristic of such a network is the nations' political interdependence; this is often interlaced with common religious symbolization.[2] These areas of economic and political interdependence—which are generally insepara-ble—give rise to an interlocking set of institutions that govern the relationships among societies in the network. These are described below.

This is not to suggest that only civilizational societies are economically interdependent and that it is only at this stage of sociocultural development that intergroup relationships are interlaced with common religious symbolizations. The contrary is in fact the case. With the rarest of exceptions, almost all societies at all stages of development have been involved in such relationships. The exchange of economic goods—sometimes across great distances—has been a feature of human society long before the emergence of civilizations. In many noncivilizational societies, autonomous villages and other sociopolitical units have often symbolized their social relationships by means of religious organizations.

As an entity, a civilization gives rise to its own institutional configurations. These institutional complexes are adaptive mechanisms that are designed to meet the challenges created by the particular sociocultural environment of a civilization; these pressures are different from those engendered by the atmospheres of noncivilizational cultures. Hence there are institutional features to be found in civilizational societies that are not found in others. Schools are one of these.

Examples of noncivilizational states are the precontact Ashanti, Basuto, Dahomeans, Kazaks (of the Sultanate Period), Swazi, those of Polynesia, and the like. Examples of civilizational states are ancient Egypt, Rome, Greece, Babylonia, the Ethiopians, Aztecs, Inca, Japanese, Hebrews (of the Davidic Period), and the like. I am going to confine my analysis to the level of cultural development represented by the latter group; all these societies developed schools indigenously.

I will neglect here the relationships of schools to the social systems of colonized societies into which schools have been introduced by conquest civilizational states.

When school systems are introduced into tribal or other societies (including noncivilizational states) from without, the stimulus to their introduction is an instrument of a conquering or expanding civilizational state which has already developed an indigenous school system of its own: religious or medical missionaries, soldiers, trading companies, political bureaucrats, or secular teachers. These correlations not only require an exploration of the linkages between schools and state systems but also a distinction between civilizational and noncivilizational states. Schools have not always been the direct concern of the political sectors of the states in which they have arisen. Because schools are institutions generated by the atmospheres of state societies, however, they do ultimately come under the direct control of the political sector. For example, Marrou notes that education was not subject to direct political control in every Hellenistic city in ancient Greek civilization. "Since it was a matter of general interest the State could not be indifferent to it and therefore, almost everywhere, it was an object of the city's attention; but not always to the same degree, nor in the same way at the different degrees." [3] The first truly state-sponsored universities arose in Castile in 1208–9 and in Naples in 1224.

Among its other characteristics, a civilization is a sociopolitical system. It need not be an institutionalized system with deliberative and legislative bodies, coercive force, or a bureaucratic apparatus. Anthropologists have long known that political systems, such as those among the technologically least advanced societies, can function very well without formal apparatus and bureaucracy. But the political sphere of a civilization may be institutionalized, as in transnational religious guises or in the current civilizations' United Nations and transnational communist bureaucracy. Importantly, the United Nations has bureaucratic offices specializing in educational matters.

Before going to a discussion of schools as adaptive responses to the pressures engendered by participation in a civilizational network, it will serve to clarify some of the concepts in this paper to portray the institutional relationships among and within civilizational nation-states in diagrammatic fashion. This paradigm is presented in figure 1, in which I confine myself to only two hypothetical civilizational nations for heuristic purposes; in reality, every such network is composed of many nation-states.

An important qualification has to be kept in mind in connection with this paradigm. It suggests that the pressures of participation in the civilizational network impinge equally upon, and produce uniform consequences in, each of the nations; the contrary is, of course, the case. The rates and nature of adaptive responses to these pressures vary considerably from one society to another. This is due partly to the fact that not all are equidistant from the political center of gravity in the network, they have differential endowments with natural resources, unequal access to trade routes, and other natural features. Local customs and aspirations within the political structure of the network, and the like, also modify and maximize these pressures. This, then is an ideal-type formulation. More specifically, the paradigm is intended as a methodological outline rather than as a substantive description of the civilizational level of sociocultural integration.

Each of the circles in figure 1 represents a nation-state; together they constitute a civilizational network. However, their relationships to each other, and the institutional structures of each, are to be found on different planes. Participation in a civilizational network does not produce uniform consequences throughout a society's institutional configurations. Although, in reality, there is probably not a single institutional area which remains

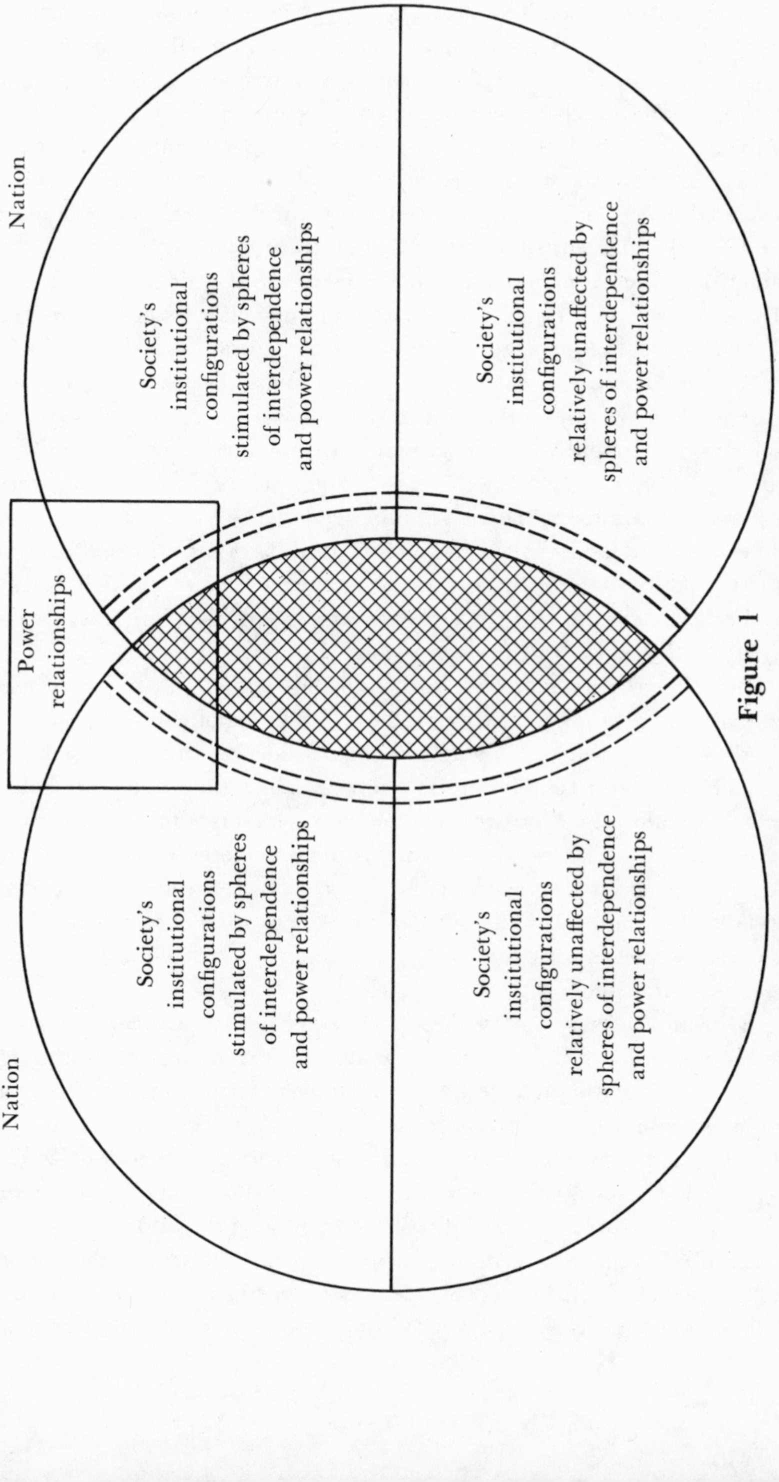

Figure 1

Paradigmatic illustration of relationships within a civilizational network

Nation

Nation

Power relationships

Society's institutional configurations stimulated by spheres of interdependence and power relationships

Society's institutional configurations relatively unaffected by spheres of interdependence and power relationships

Society's institutional configurations stimulated by spheres of interdependence and power relationships

Society's institutional configurations relatively unaffected by spheres of interdependence and power relationships unaffected by the society's participation in the network, it is nevertheless possible to establish a hierarchy of priorities.

The cross-hatched area of overlap between the two states represents their major spheres of interdependence. Some of these are mutual participation in energy systems, such as waterways and shipping or overland routes, electricity (as in the power grids joining Canada and the northeastern United States or adjoining European states), air routes, atomic power; regional specialization; formal knowledge, religion, and its associated myths and epics; international control of trade routes; intersocietal marketing, distributive, and monetary systems; and aesthetic standards. These spheres of interdependence constitute a relatively self-contained institutional area, although they affect and are in turn affected by local customs and institutional configurations.

During the early stages of a civilization's development, this is a relatively narrow and limited area. All things being equal until the civilization's decline and replacement by another, however, this area continues to expand; this expansion is represented in figure 1 by the broken lines paralleling the area of interdependence. As this area expands, it affects—if it does not take in—more institutions of each of the individual societies. A correlate of this expansion is that a commensurately greater number of the state's polity become directly involved in this area of interdependence. As will be seen below, this leads to an increase in the absolute size of a society's elite, although the ratio of elite to commoners generally remains fairly constant. The outer limits of this expansion are probably determined by the length of time of the civilization's existence as well as by the nature of relationships between elites and commoners within the individual states. More importantly, however, it is within this area that a civilization's existence as an entity is most vulnerable. When nations' interdependence is destroyed in the spheres of energy systems, regional specialization, and trade, the civilizational network will in all likelihood also disintegrate; and each society will devolve to a noncivilizational level of sociocultural integration.

Growing directly out of these spheres of interdependence, but also overlapping with an important segment of the society's institutional configurations, is the area of power relationships within the civilization. This is represented by the box in figure 1. Making up this area are the spheres of military relationships, diplomacy, political institutionalization (as in the Roman Catholic church, the United Nations), and legal systems. These spheres in civilizational power relationships serve to regulate and maintain economic and commercial interdependence among the sectors. As suggested above, the latter spheres of interdependence are the heart of a civilizational network. This is not to imply that economic and commercial relationships are the forces that set a civilizational network into motion. Instead, what is probably more to the point is that these relationships are initiated by the elites of states to serve their political controls and to maintain their standards of living.

Power relationships can be conceptualized as boundary institutions. The people who fill the roles of these institutions are boundary role players. The interdependence of societies within a civilizational network suggests a steady situation of what anthropologists call "contact" between cultures. Such contact invariably leads to an interchange of goods, ideas, customs, techniques, and the like. But it does not take place by itself like two masses of air. Instead, the relationships among the members of the network must be mediated by designated individuals whose roles are to preserve the integrity of the boundaries of their respective societies as well as to regulate the exchange of cultural elements. Murphy has suggested the very apt concept of the boundary role player, which is extremely useful in this connection:

> The role players in these boundary roles are, of course, holders of social statuses within their own societies. The role sets of the boundary roles and the sets pertinent to roles within the society may be kept well segregated—in fact, better segregated than most roles—and this tends to inhibit communication of information, or culture, through the role relationship. Boundary roles are at one and the same time the communication lines between related societies, insofar as the same actor may successfully segregate his duality of roles. In a situation of language differences in which the occupant of the boundary role must be bilingual, this can be quite easily done.
>
> However, much role segregation may exist, and however pertinent this may be to cultural transfer, the fact that the boundary role player has other roles within the society and the very fact that boundary roles exist, have profound effects upon the social system. . . . Just as there are boundary roles, there is also a boundary culture. We cannot accept the premise that a stable system of social interaction is predicated upon shared and internalized values, for it assumes a degree of similarity in socialization processes that would be most difficult to find in contact situations. Yet the people do get along with each other and share common expectations that are cognitively held to be part of the situation and are accordingly manipulated. The expectations are rules and norms rather than values, and they signify the acceptance of each society's status as well as providing a common language for social encounter. Today's boundary culture can, of course, become incorporated tomorrow.[4]

Schools are an integral element of the boundary culture of a civilizational state; the schooled elite of a civilizational state are among its most significant boundary role players. While schools ultimately become incorporated into the culture of the entire polity—both as an aspect of the transmission of privilege to the entire polity and as an aspect of national integration and unification through the transmission of common symbols to the masses—it is with their initial introduction to the social systems that I am concerned here.

Different types of sociopolitical systems require different types of boundary role players. In a state society, the first requisite for such a person is that his ideological, and thus psychological, commitment be to the state rather than to any local source of solidarity and allegiance, such as kin group, community, ethnic group, region, and the like. With few exceptions, schools do not initially teach or transmit cultural norms, customs, or legitimating ideologies. Schools become vehicles for the transmission of culture only long after they have been developed, when the state has begun to succeed in subverting local nexuses of authority and allegiance. When schools were first developed, they were almost invariably devoted to little more than rote and catechetical instruction. Moreover, they were generally reserved for the elite of the civilizational state. The notion that schools were developed as institutions designed to foster scholarship or the life of the mind has no basis in historical fact.

The aim of developing boundary role players through schooling was clear in early Greek civilization.

The problem that faced the Sophists, and which they succeeded in solving, was the fairly common one of how to produce capable statesmen. In their time this had become a matter of the utmost urgency. After the collapse of tyranny in the sixth century, most of the Greek cities, and democratic Athens in particular, developed an intensely active political life; and exercise of power, the management of affairs, became the essential concern, the noblest, the most highly-prized activity in the eyes of every Greek, the ultimate aim of his ambition. He was still anxious to excel, to be superior and effective; but it was no longer in sport and polite society that his "valor" . . . sought to assert itself: from now on it expressed itself in political action. The Sophists put their talent as teachers at the service of this new ideal of the political [sphere]: the training of statesmen, the formation of the city's future leaders—such was their programme.[5]

The aim of developing boundary role players through schooling was clear in England in the latter part of the nineteenth century.

Much has been written by nostalgic owners of the Old School Tie, praising the "Cheltenham and the Haileybury and Marlborough chaps [who] went out to Boerland and Zululand" and there "lived or died as gentlemen and officers." Certainly the imperialists of the nineties often mentioned England and their schooldays in the same breath; certainly many of them saw the public school as a generator of imperial enthusiasm.

Just as certainly their eulogies were exaggerated. . . . But it is not the contention here that the Victorian public schools helped create an empire. Once the empire was mainly built, however, public school education did partly contribute a faith and a rationale to the men who were going to administer and defend that empire.[6]

The curricula of the earliest schools generally consisted of little more than highly stylized texts devoted almost exclusively to the recitation of the exploits of kings, gods, and other national culture heroes. Whether confined to a social elite or to urban residents—and the two often coincided—the emphasis in this formal instruction was on the rote learning of national glories, not of regional or other local culture history. Furthermore, these topics were almost always suffused with religious themes. The emphasis in English public schools on Latin, Greek, and religious indoctrination bears a striking similarity to ancient elite education.

This interlacement served several purposes. First, and most apparent, it provided religious-ideological legitimation for national integration and centralized authority: the glories of palace and temple heroes were inseparable. Second, since one means used by a state in its subversion and erosion of local sources of authority and allegiance is the replacement of local religious symbols and cults by a national religious system together with the displacement of the pantheons of local heroes by national figures, the early schools of civilizational states were important adaptive mechanisms for shaping the minds of the elites who were most directly involved in interstate relations in addition to ruling the masses within the state.

How does schooling—whether rote, catechetical, or other—facilitate students' identifications with the state? Most children want to be like and attempt to emulate those people who meet their needs, including those people who teach them the things they want to learn.[7] Because learning is generally a rewarding experience for most children, despite their frequent protestations to the contrary, they tend to identify with those who teach them. Thus, at least as important as what is taught to children is who teaches them. An important source of identification with family and kinsmen in many primitive societies is the systematic instruction of children by these people.

But words alone never suffice for the inculcation of basic social identifications. The sense of anchorage that people are expected to develop must be driven deep and implanted with such permanence and fixity that it becomes almost a "physical" part of the individual. It is one aspect of the personal counterpart of the societal value system, and its stance must be firm and irrevocable. It must become so much a part of the personality that it is not questioned; it must be open neither to debate nor to justifying rationalization. As far as it concerns the person in whom this sense is instilled, and as far as the social system cares, it is synthesized like an integral part of the body. As far as the cultural value system is concerned, it is a law of nature, one of the man "most obvious things in the world." The sense of anchorage must be implanted in the mind from the earliest age, constantly, at every available opportunity. And the ways in which this is done must be tied to the institutional and value structures of the society.[8]

When a state becomes tied to a civilizational network and thus requires people who, among their other roles, are going to serve the state's interests in its relations with other states, it must be able to rely on them without question. Economic and political rewards are insufficient, the tenets of behavioristic psychologies notwithstanding, because someone else might offer greater rewards: we are all, or at least most of us, potential Calibans who follow the largest flask of liquor that is extended. The indispensable counterpart of a state's ability to rely implicitly on those who will serve its interests is that these people's sense of identification with the state will become so much a part of the personality that it is not questioned and is open neither to debate nor to temptation. Most states succeed in this quite well. (Treason is, after all, a very rare occurrence.) One of the most important ways by which this is accomplished is by removing the individual from parochially oriented education and placing him in a situation in which his training is focused on the state.

An illustration of the hypothesis that schools are not designed to foster scholarship or the life of the mind is provided by Wilkinson in his analysis of the sociopolitical functions served by the English "public school."

> There were . . . profound reasons . . . for the public school failure to encourage criticism and questioning. In the final analysis, the education system viewed the intellect itself as hostile to loyalty.

. . . The system instilled loyalty not by explicit dogma but by custom and etiquette, devices that played on a community mysticism and the aesthetic emotion of "good form" rather than on reason. To the extent that the dictates of "good form" were tacit dictates, influencing the individual unconsciously, their effects might even be called subliminal.

But it was not simply the method employed that made the public school treatment of loyalty anti-intellectual. Loyalty itself was considered a virtue which the exercise of reason could easily destroy. . . . Public school headmasters related Character to athletic vigor rather than to intellectual activity; [it is also important to note] The Times's [sic] defense of "school spirit" as a force which induced boys to distrust their individual intellects and do an unselfish job. Public school loyalties formed part of a faith rooted firmly in unquestioned assumptions about the gentleman's moral duty and his relation to the society about him. The same faith provided the public schoolboy with self-assurance and decisiveness. He took command easily because he did not often question either his right or his worthiness to take command. Self-assurance and rational inquiry were kept well apart.[9]

The essence of schooling is that it serves the adoption of universalistic values, criteria, and standards of performance; this is also the value system fostered by a state, as in the assertion that all citizens, regardless of community or region of origin, are subject to the same laws and regulations.

In his comparison of ancient Chinese and modern education with contemporary professionalism, Wilkinson observes that

all three phenomena—the Chinese examination system, American Ph.D. training, and examination in business—sprang in part from an equalitarian impulse, the wish to select candidates according to individual merit. Chinese experience, indeed, suggests that whenever there are a large number of candidates to be processed, increased reliance may be placed on impersonal examinations as a way of guaranteeing impartial selection. But Chinese experience also suggests that, however democratic its rationale, heavy reliance on examinations will generate its own form of elitism. A separate breed of men may spring up, talking the special language and thinking the special thought processes of their examinations.[10]

The thrust of schooling is that "who states a proposition is as such irrelevant to the question of its . . . value." [11] One of the most important factors in schooling is the student's awareness that he is learning precisely the same things as his peers—whether in terms of the society as a whole or of a particular class or caste—throughout the realm, and that he must give the same responses. When the content of this education is phrased in terms of gods (temple) and kings (palace), he also learns what the authority for this is and whence it derives. And not only do young people identify with those who teach them, but they also, as is well known, have a strong proclivity to identify with sources of authority.

In connection with the earliest Greek schools, for example, "we must not forget that we are speaking of what was originally an aristocracy. . . . In the earliest times schools did not exist, and when they did come into being they . . . existed merely to give technical instruction, not education." [12] Homer provided the basic text of the earliest Greek schools.

> It was not primarily as a literary masterpiece that the epic was studied, but because its content was ethical, a treatise on the ideal. . . . They attempted to extract from this fundamentally profane epic a veritable catechism. Nor was this catechism to teach only (as in fact it did) a theogony and the golden legend of gods and heroes, but also a whole theodicy, indeed a whole system of apologetics, a summarization of man's duties to the gods—more a handbook of practical morality, illustrating precept by example, beginning with good manners for children. [13]
>
> Like the [English] public schools, Chinese education supported a national elite style which stood out above regional differences. Against a profusion of dialects and a background of mass illiteracy, the ability to speak mandarin and to write fluently carried a cosmopolitan flavor. The advantage was also aesthetic, since education gave both bureaucrat and Emperor the ability to dignify State memorials with exquisite language and calligraphy. [14]

Although the man behind the plow or knee deep in the mud of a hillside terrace was profoundly affected by the economic, religious, legal stratification, and political institutions of the civilizational state, and although his state's relationships with others strongly influenced the structures of social relations in which he engaged daily, he was not necessarily conscious of them. "The way of life of the 'great society' directly affected only a small minority of the people who lived in the land and never penetrated deeply into the daily round of the basic agrarian communities." [15] Moreover, even if the common man did know that his state's rulers were deeply involved with others, he did not need—and, in fact, was not expected—to know the nature of these dealings. His obedience to the state was maintained by the redistributional authority of urban economic institutions, courts, taxation, religious institutions—subserved by legitimating ideologies—and the like, but not through the school system, which was generally reserved at first for the elite.

Wittfogel has described this process clearly in his classic study of what he called hydraulic society:

> Our survey reveals that even under the simplest conditions the ruling class in hydraulic society is divided into several subsections. Under more differentiated conditions it tends to be a fairly complex entity. How conscious of the peculiarity and superiority of their class position are the members of the various subsections? . . .
>
> To be sure, their class-consciousness did not always express itself in images which underlined their greatness as ranking officials. The serving men of Ottoman Turkey were proud to be the "slaves" of their sultan. The glory of the ruling class, as they saw it, rested upon its autocratic ruler. The political ideologists of Hindu India stressed the prominence of the king as the supreme protector of the dominant religion. The glory of the ruling class, as they saw it, rested upon its priestly advisors. The Confucian philosophers paid homage to their absolute sovereign, but they extolled the gentleman-scholar, who, because of his training, was likely to become a gentleman-bureaucrat. The glory of the ruling class, as they saw it, rested upon its properly educated officials.
>
> Confucianism presents the sociopolitical aspect of the matter with unusual clarity. By designating the gentleman-scholar as chün-tzu, Confucius emphasized the political quality of his ideal man. The chün-tzu was thoroughly versed in the cultural tradition of the hereditary ("noble") officialdom, but his qualifications had an essentially political intent. The word chün-tzu originally connoted "a ruler," "a man engaged in the business of ruling." After being properly trained, the chün-tzu was ready to be used as a government official. He was ready to rule the "little man," the mass of the population.[16]

Also in this connection, Wittfogel observes that while education in ancient China was confined to the elite,

> The competitive examination system was an excellent means for thoroughly indoctrinating ambitious commoners and for compelling the talented sons of officials and bureaucratic gentry families to submit to a most comprehensive ideological training.

The examinations were open to commoners during the first six hundred years with serious restrictions, and during the last six hundred years without such hindrances. But how many commoners did actually rise to official position in the government of imperial China through this method? . . . During the T'ang period (618–907) some 83 per cent of all socially definable officials had an upper-class background: about 70 per cent were from families of officials. Almost 7 per cent were "barbarians" (the T'ang ruling house, was at least in part, of Turkish origin). And less than 10 per cent were commoners.[17]

It is clear that the first schools served to implant national political symbols and to serve centralized political control. It is in terms of the provenience of schools that the curricula of primary and secondary schools in modern nations must be understood; the inclusion of colleges and universities within state bureaucracies as serving the aims of national institutions is a historically logical outcome of this process. Consider ancient Sumer:

Education was neither universal nor compulsory. Most of the students came from wealthy families; the poor could hardly afford the cost and time which a prolonged education demanded. . . . In the thousands of published economic and administrative documents from about 2000 B.C., some five hundred individuals listed themselves as scribes, and for further identification many of them added the name of their father and his occupation. . . . Fathers of the scribes—that is, of the school graduates—were governors, city fathers, ambassadors, temple administrators, military officers, sea captains, high tax officials, priests of various sorts, managers, supervisors, foremen, scribes, archivists, and accountants. In short, the fathers were the wealthier citizens of urban communities. Not a single woman is listed as a scribe in these documents, and it is therefore likely that the student body of the Sumerian school consisted of males only.[18]

It is in terms of the foregoing historical illustrations that we can understand another major purpose served by the establishment of schools for the elites of civilizational states. The members of these strata are responsible for maintaining very different institutions from those of the mass of ordinary men behind their plows. Classical education was essentially an initiation into the Greek way of life, moulding the child and the adolescent in accordance with the national customs and submitting him to a particular style of living—the style that distinguished man from the brutes, Greeks from barbarians.[19] The members of an elite by definition occupy positions of social, economic, political, and legal power over the commoners. This implies that the two participate in vastly different role and status systems, although they are dependent on each other. Hence they must be shaped by different experiences which will commit them to different legitimating symbol systems. At least during the early stages of civilizational states' development, the formative institutions of the commoner masses are intimately tied to local boundary systems— household, lineage, community, and the like—while those of the elite are tied to the state. Each gives rise to its own value orientations and symbol systems.

Although there have certainly always been differences in the modes of upbringing in household, kin, peer, community, and other relationships between elites and commoners—that is, different formative experiences in daily and spontaneous interaction—it would be a mistake to focus on these sources of personality difference to account for the cognitive gulf between the ruling and subordinate sectors of a civilizational state. In addition to the fact that elites are boundary role players, such homilies as "gentlemen [elite] are born to rule" are neither mere words nor handy targets for the editorial cartoonists of egalitarian philosophies. They are designed in large part to accentuate the difference between rulers and ruled, to drive them home with such force that neither sector in the society is likely to forget them. They are designed to underscore a sense of exclusiveness in each.

Nor is this sense of exclusiveness confined to the mechanical aspects of ruling and being ruled, of directing and being directed, of having privileges and being denied them. It goes to the very heart of self-definition. In the predilections of many behavioral scientists for such generalizing concepts as "national character," it is often overlooked that in societies in which women of the commoner classes are kept in quasi-feudal social shackles, women of the elite classes are often granted a measure of freedom that is not dissimilar to the men's. This is to be seen in Latin America, England and other parts of Europe, India, and the like. What this teaches us, among other things, is that elite status is not just a convenient classificatory device or concept, but that it has a profound effect on the individual, especially with respect to self-definition. It contributes greatly to a heightened awareness of a sense of difference from the masses, assuring their participation in distinct boundary subsystems within the society.

It is not coincidental that such differences go hand in hand either with school systems that are exclusively elite institutions or with very different curricula and schools for elites and commoners.[20] When schools are extended to the masses—as in compulsory universal education—states make certain in one way or another that differences between education in elite and commoner schools at all levels of the curriculum are maintained.

More importantly, children are not unaware of the types of schools that they attend or the nature of the curricula vis-à-vis others'. I am not suggesting that these social policies are conscious and deliberate; instead, they must be seen as aspects of the natural history of civilizational states.

Another way of putting this is that the authoritative structure of a state organization requires a pronounced degree of social distance between rulers and ruled. As a result, a state must adopt measures that will help to promote such distance. Different institutionalized formative experiences—of which, as I have suggested, we can be sure that both strata are conscious—are among the important means adopted by civilizational states to maintain this ideological separateness. Important to note in this connection is that civilizational states do not develop school systems in order to maintain social distance between elites and commoners. Schools are developed as adaptive mechanisms in response to the pressures engendered by the mutual intersocietal dependence of culture sectors within a civilizational network. Once established for these purposes, they become integrated into the stratification system. We must conclude that schools are adaptations to the pressures of civilization because not all states develop school systems; only civilizational states develop them autonomously.

Ideological convictions to the contrary notwithstanding, schools in contemporary societies continue to serve as the principal training grounds for elites who fill power and boundary roles. An American president who desperately seeks the compliance of the school-educated elite—whose numbers in the polity are out of proportion to the vigor of the wooing—in connection with his wars of dubious legality (and even more dubious morality) is not only seeking votes but is also implicitly expressing the apprehension that these personnel might refuse to fill the boundary roles for which they are being trained. In its outward appearances, formal education in contemporary nations appears to be very different from its ancient adumbrations, but the difference is more apparent than real. Although schools have begun to filter down from the elite to the commoner statuses, the gap between strata in respect to education continues.

In earlier civilizations education was largely confined to rote and catechetical instruction and was intended almost exclusively for the elite; the man behind the plow or the market stall was excluded. In contemporary civilization, the man behind the modern equivalents of the plow or market stall is schooled, but the gap between his education and that of the schools from which the elite boundary personnel are recruited continues to be as wide, quantitatively if not also qualitatively. It requires no elaborate demonstration that with every major advance in the education of the commoner statuses there has been at least an equally great advance in the curricula of the schools from which the state recruits its elite. Consider the financial support provided by, for example, the centralized American state to the universities and professional schools from which it recruits its elite as compared to the schools devoted to the education of the commoners behind the modern equivalents of the plow or market stall. The gap between the leading few universities from which the elite are recruited and the land-grant state colleges, junior colleges, and the like, is not only a matter of prestige or parental aspiration to be boasted about over cocktails and golf clubs. It is an integral feature of the formal organization of a civilizational state. Consider the fact that in ancient civilization the bulk of the elites were concentrated in and around the ceremonial and redistributional centers and that, in like manner, "the Washington [D.C.] area now ranks first in the nation for scientific personnel (per 1,000 population), although the major product is company promotion and politics rather than science." [21]

But training for elite status in a contemporary nation like the United States does not begin with the university. It begins with the earliest schooling. I know of no studies in this connection, but I am certain that a census of children who go to school between the ages of three and five years would, like the social origins of Sumerian students described in the quotation from Kramer above, reveal that they are the children of elite parents. The introduction of such curricular innovations as "the new mathematics" is ordinarily confined to schools in which the children of elite parents predominate. More than teaching intellectual skills, such innovations have all the earmarks of socially differentiated and stratified education; they are not uniformly introduced into all elementary and secondary schools. Such practices at the college or university level as "educational years abroad" are ordinarily confined to students in elite schools; they are designed to accentuate the gulf between elite and commoner education and to include firsthand experience with other nations in the civilizational network. One of the clearest and most institutionalized examples of the differences between elite and commoner curricula is to be found in the English school system.

Another example of class stratification in education, and thus of preparation for elite status, and paralleling the above instances, is to be seen in the area of language instruction. Since the days of Sumerian schooling, one of the most important ingredients in the education of people who are being prepared for boundary roles has been the teaching of foreign languages. It is self-evident that knowledge of the languages of other nations within a civilizational network is an integral part of performing boundary roles; also in this connection it is interesting to observe the high prestige enjoyed by linguistic studies in contemporary civilizational states. With the introduction of compulsory mass education and the teaching of foreign languages in secondary schools to the polity as a whole, it is understandable—in terms of the natural history of a civilizational state—that attempts will be made to find a way of reestablishing the gap between strata in this regard. Thus, we have observed in recent years the instruction of American elementary school students in foreign languages. But this has not been uniform throughout the realm; it has largely been confined to the schools attended by the children of elite parents. This innovation, too, is an attempt to foster a sense of exclusiveness among the latter, since they and their lower-status peers are fully aware that this has not become an aspect of mass elementary education.

The interlacement of stratified school systems, language instruction, and political organization is illustrated in the history of England.

Admittedly, the Victorian public schools did their bit to create unequal opportunity: by helping to crystallize an "Establishment" style and accent, they made it all the harder for a working-class person without that style and accent to be accepted in the top circles of power. Likewise, the emphasis on classics, however nobly viewed, provided the schools with a neat formula for offering free and reduced-fee scholarships and still excluding the lower-class boy. The formula worked because, at primary school level, Latin and Greek were a virtual monopoly of private education—the "prep" school and family tutor. By stressing Latin, public school entrance examinations deterred working-class families from even seeking entry to the schools.

Having said all this, the fact remains that in the social conditions of Victorian England it was practically impossible anyway for a working-class individual to attain high public office. For their part, the Victorian public schools did at least help set a pattern of extending the gentry's privileges to new classes. Had the public school of more recent times developed the pattern still further, had they admitted talented individuals from the working class, they would not have been perpetrating revolution. Viewed against the full march of public school history, the extension of privilege would have been a restoration, for many of the oldest and most famous public schools were founded with the express purpose of providing a good education for poor scholars. But, as we all know, the restoration was never made.[22]

What must be reiterated in this connection is that the English public schools were the principal avenues to political power and elite status.

As times change, so does the composition of a society's elite. At least in the United States, the elite are not to be found riding to hounds or on palatial yachts. Instead, they are to be found in bureaucratic offices, on commuter trains, and often mowing their lawns on Saturday mornings. The new American elite is less and less recruited from the propertied class and more and more from a select few universities to fill decision-making positions in governmental and business bureaucracies. (In fact, as many observers have been noting, the line between the two bureaucracies is becoming increasingly blurred.) Bazelon[23] has noted that the principal means to prestige and power in contemporary American society—what I am referring to as boundary and other elite roles—are higher academic degrees and educational qualifications; these have replaced ascribed statuses and personally (or parentally) amassed wealth. He observes that university education is now the crucial steppingstone to power in business, governmental, and general management roles in the society at large. Thus the growing relationship between elite-university education (and it is important to bear in mind that not all universities and colleges serve as such passports) and elite status is unmistakable. In the United States, the principal elite universities, from which boundary role players are recruited, are (more or less in terms of their relative rank) Harvard, Yale, Princeton, Columbia, the University of Pennsylvania, the University of Chicago, and Stanford.

This may also be seen in modern England. In the April 1966 elections for the House of Commons, 68 new members were of the Labour party. Of these, approximately one-fourth are teachers in universities and technical colleges; about 10 percent teach in secondary schools; lawyers, physicians, and scientists constitute more than 15 percent of the group. Also, the main features in the profile of these new members not only accentuate youth but also teachers of economics or political science at one of the redbrick universities.[24]

Thus, a historical perspective enables us to place the relationship of education to the rest of the social organization in balance. One of the cardinal features of a civilizational state, as well as other states, is a marked degree of social stratification, at the bedrock of which is a cleavage between elite and commoner statuses. In the 4,000 years or so of the history of civilizational states, there has been no fundamental change in this. Nor are there any current developments which suggest that this will change. My contention has been that the elites of civilizational states occupy a dual position: rulers and decision makers within the society and boundary role players in the society's relationship with others within the civilizational network. Schools have always been an important training ground for these elites.

Where are elite personnel to be found? In all contemporary

civilizational states they are to be found in the modern counterparts of earlier civilizational states' palaces, and (in some of these societies) in the temples. They are also to be found in the decision-making centers of national and intersocietal policies, corporate board rooms, principal banks, upper echelons of elite universities, and the like. These are the men who set the standards for the control and deployment of labor forces, determine the sites and often the rates of expansion of cities, control the strategically most important property, proclaim war, control trade among nations within the civilizational network, change money and set rates of interest, or control the principal sources of energy and lines of communication between and within societies.

These are the men who determine the rates of taxation, wage scale; for their own immediate servants in the elite stratum, and the standards of living of different strata beneath them. They are often the men who, if they do not actually codify the ideologies of the commoners, including egalitarian ideologies, at least control their fulfillment. They are the men who design programs for the redistribution of a fraction of the wealth ("welfare programs") in order to sterilize the seeds of discontent, but which go no further than the limits permitted by Calvinistically rationalized aggrandizement.

Universities, especially of elite status, are among the major sources from which these elites are recruited. It is in university-based laboratories, or laboratories staffed by university-trained personnel, that the bases are laid for elite-controlled technological advances; it is in university offices, or offices staffed by university-trained personnel, that ideas are formulated for the implementation of elite policies. Schools have thus always been important to the elites of civilizational states; if they have not always been steppingstones to elite status, they have been important in bringing commoners a little closer to the rulers, either illusorily or in their service. As far back as Hellenistic times, "the rich young men who went to the college wanted to be properly prepared for the life of the fashionable society to which they belonged, and the cultivation of the mind could no longer be left out. And so along with the sport there grew up lessons, lectures and audition." [25]

Similar patterns of recruitment of boundary role players and others of elite status from the more prestigious educational institutions are clearly discernible in other major sectors of the contemporary civilizational network, as in the Soviet Union, Japan, France, and South America. Almost all observers of the processes involved in the emergence of states out of colonial holdings have noted the intimate relationship between formal education and elite status. However, as Philip Foster has suggested, "by themselves the schools cannot create class differentiation on the basis of occupational criteria, but they can reinforce class boundaries, and increasing differentiation within an educational system may become an indirect index of the process of class formation." [26] In large measure, this occurs because, as suggested above, civilizational states—or states that are trying to gain participation in a civilizational network—develop schools in adaptive response to the pressures engendered by participation in a civilizational network. Once established for these purposes, schools become integrated into the stratification-power system.

It is generally accepted among observers of political development that formal education is inseparable from political socialization. The latter concept "refers to that process by which individuals acquire attitudes and feelings toward the political system and toward their role in it, including cognition . . . feeling . . . and one's sense of political competence (what one's role is or can be in the system)." As Almond has put it, "Political socialization is the process of induction into the political culture. The educational system is one of the agencies involved in this process, which begins at birth and, although its imprint is most pronounced during the impressionable formative years, continues well into adulthood." [27]

It is against this background that we can evaluate the steady and increasing diffusion of education at all levels within modern civilizational states. The schools of a given society cannot be viewed as a whole. Instead, it is necessary to distinguish carefully between elite and commoner schooling. Social scientists have done this with considerable ease in studies of other societies, but we have been remiss in this regard in studies of the American educational system.

Recent attempts in American society, and in other modern nations, to extend schooling, and improve its level, among the lower strata of the population are not to be seen as diffusions of elite training or the equalization of access to elite status. Nor can extensions of college and university training to greater numbers in the population be understood in such terms. The proliferation of such institutions in American society as "community colleges," "junior colleges," "state colleges," educational skill centers, and the like, serves entirely different purposes in the total social system. It is not accidental that they are designated by different terms than centers of elite schooling. They ordinarily recruit personnel from the lower social strata, not those who are expected to fill boundary and power roles. More specifically, these schools are designed to train individuals in the skills which make it possible to man the modern equivalents of the plow and the market stall.

Decisions to extend such schooling to the lower social strata are decisions of the society's elite; one inherent characteristic of elites is that they are conservative and reluctant to permit or encourage encroachments on their privileged positions from below. The history of education in England is hardly unusual in this respect. "Taken together, the attitudes and values inculcated by the Victorian public school very nearly comprise a definition of conservatism." [28] When elites do stimulate the diffusion of education to lower social strata, they are not inviting competition for statuses and roles. Instead, they are being quite self-serving by bringing the commoners' level of technical knowledge slightly closer to the elites' so that the former can carry out the economic and political activities required by those in decision-making capacities. The computer technologist, to take a somewhat overworked (but culturally relevant) example, has not been catapulted into elite status; but it is in the interests of the elite that he be trained in this technological procedure so that the elite can better make and carry out their decisions and maintain their privileged positions.

> School officials [in Amherst, Massachusetts] have refused to readmit a 12-year-old boy to junior high school until he takes off a black armband that he wears to protest the Vietnam war. The officials view his action as part of a larger "behavior problem" that interferes with the orderly environment of the Amherst Pelham Regional Junior High School. The boy . . . was expelled from school June 2 [1967]. He has refused to remove the armband since then.[29]

At the same time that a civilizational state adaptively develops a schooled elite who are going to occupy its boundary and power roles, it must also develop mechanisms that enable it to win and maintain the obedience and loyalty of all the polity. The diffusion of education from the elite to the commoner strata is one of the means by which this is achieved. This is not an automatic process, however. Education is almost never injected into the polity en masse. Instead, its deployment must be seen in historical perspective, especially as an aspect of the state's attempts to integrate its subordinate classes into a homogeneous entity who will subscribe to a uniform ideology and who will replace local allegiances with loyalty to the state.

One of the principal characteristics of a state, as discussed above, is that it must subvert local groups that might serve as competitors for the individual's loyalty and obedience. The reasons for this are readily apparent. In stateless societies, the checks, balances, and controls over behavior which are among the prerequisites of all social life are exercised through local institutions at the community level, without the intervention of supracommunity nexuses of authority. Local autonomy is the key factor in the maintenance of order and conformity, and is expressed in many ways, as in economic self-sufficiency, the right to feud and wage war, the administration of land tenure, and the application of juridical controls. Even in chiefdoms, which are redistributional societies with permanent central agencies of economic and other matrixes of coordination, there are multiple power centers; one of their central characteristics, as conceptualized by Service, is a notable resistance to centralization of authority.[30]

By contrast, the integrating principle in a state society is the vertical entrenchment of civil authority, and this is almost always accomplished at the expense of the lineage system and other local nexuses which strive for autonomy. Thus a state is a subversive organization; one of its most important means to the end of entrenching itself vertically is the erosion of local autonomies, allegiances, and authority.

This incompatibility is a conflict between boundary systems, in which one gains in firmness at the expense of the other. The strongest conflicts in a society's institutional structure are between boundary systems whose aims overlap, that is, those that serve the same functions. Part of the course of a state's vertical entrenchment is its arrogation of the right to wage war, enact and administer laws, control productivity and redistribute wealth, lay claim to rights of eminent domain and administer laws; these are the rights which are also claimed by corporate kin groups and communities. Since only one of the two boundary systems may exercise such authority and carry out such political activities autonomously, one of them must be subverted.

Mass education in a civilizational state has to be seen as a manifestation of two cross-cutting principles. The first of these is the civilizational state's need to train an elite who will fill the boundary roles in addition to ruling within the society; this is an adaptive outgrowth of the pressures engendered by the civilization as a network. The second is to establish ideological uniformity throughout the society by eliminating local boundary systems which can serve as the seedbeds of particularistic and antistate symbol systems; this is an adaptive outgrowth of the pressures engendered by the state per se. In other words, elite education is an adaptive response to the pressures generated by a society's participation in a civilizational network; mass education is principally a response to the forces stemming from civilizational and state pressures in juxtaposition.

By definition, the existence of a group—whether a family, secret society, age or work group, community, or society—connotes that its members respond in fairly uniform ways in respect to complex sets of expectations, rules, norms of behavior, modes of cognition, and symbols. Thus, given the truism that human life is inseparable from social life, conformity is an integral part of what is often referred to as the human condition.

But without going into the question of the degree in which conformity is necessary for the maintenance of viable group life, what is important to remember in this connection is that there are different ways of being human: different types of social systems require, among other things, different modes of conformity. Each type of social system (nomadic bands, different kinds of horticultural societies, pastoralists, agriculturists) is marked by relatively distinct symbol systems, criteria of allegiance and affiliation, and sources of authority to which the polity are expected to respond in relatively uniform manner. Furthermore, in each society there are techniques for inculcating, as well as eliciting, such uniform responses to the symbol systems of the culture. School systems play an important role in this regard in state societies that are sectors within a civilization.

One aspect of the overriding importance of a society's boundary systems is that they provide the social-emotional anchorages and sense of identity for the members of the society and thus constitute the point of convergence, if not inseparability, of ego and social structure. In the charge that a society makes to the individual to preserve the integrity of the total social system is the corollary promise that his integrity as a total person will also be maintained. This charge and promise are made to the individual by the total society conceived as a political system; they are always sustained, in part, by a highly particular system of legitimating symbols and ideologies. In state societies, it is expected that the individual will find his social-emotional anchorage in the state as a boundary-maintaining system.

Commensurately, the diffusion of formal education throughout the polity is one of the vehicles for the dissemination of legitimating symbol-systems and ideologies. In other words, an important aspect of a group's definition of itself as a total society, and of the individual's experience of this, is the symbolic representations of the total society. This is an expression of a process that is basic to social life generally, that all social relationships that are of primary significance to a social system are almost invariably given material or other symbolic expression. It is in these terms that a state's sponsorship of mass education is inseparable from its subversion of local boundary systems.

As is well known, as culture advances kinship plays a correspondingly weaker role in social relationships and in the maintenance of conformity. The direction of these developments has been largely inexorable, though different societies start from different points and move along different paths and at different rates toward this. Thus, as Goode notes in connection with contemporary patterns,

Being achievement-based, an industrial society is necessarily open-class, requiring both geographical and social mobility. Men must be permitted to rise or fall depending on their performance. Moreover, in the industrial system, jobs based on ownership and exploitation of land (and thus inheritance) become numerically less significant, again permitting considerable geographical mobility so that individuals are free to move about in the labor market. The neolocality of the conjugal system correspondingly frees the individual from ties to the specific geographical location where his parental family lives.[31]

In view of the importance of geographical and social mobility to the organization of industrial society and the requirement that people be able to act without reference to considerations of kinship in order to succeed in this social system, individuals must be trained at an early age to be mobile and to act without reference to considerations of kinship. This does not mean that all individuals in the society must, or will be, trained in this manner, because in a civilizational society, not everyone is expected to fill the jobs—viz., those of elite and high prestige-value that require the most mobility and the greatest freedom from particularistic criteria for behavior. Specifically, as in many contemporary Western societies, access to such occupations is generally limited to the offspring of parents who themselves hold such jobs. And it is these children who receive the most intensive or elite training in these modes of behavior.

One means to this is the seemingly obvious fact that the children of mobile parents are themselves mobile. Not only does this geographic mobility during their childhood provide them with the techniques they will need later in their lives for adapting to new and unfamiliar surroundings, but it also means that they more often than not grow up without the surrounding networks of kinsmen who are likely to be part of the social-emotional landscape of sedentary households. A child who grows up seeing grandparents and other kinsmen only a few days a year (if that often) and for whom such contacts are regarded as "special" occasions— who does not see his parents respond regularly to the pressures and expectations of a kinship network—has an entirely different orientation to the social world than a child who is brought up in a kinship-oriented environment. I contend that the insularity from extrahousehold kinship in the experiences of mobile children is not a coincidental by-product of mobility but is, instead, a socially designed mechanism of preparation for a particular kind of life style.

Another means by which this is accomplished, and closely related to the foregoing, involves the educational system directly—namely, the practice of sending children to colleges away from home. The correlates and consequences of this are not dissimilar to those observed in kinship-based societies in which children are sent to live elsewhere or to sleep outside the household at night—that is, to weaken ties to the household of orientation in the service of dominant social goals. The fact that the practice of sending children away from home for a college education tends to be found most often in higher-status families, at least in contemporary American society, is not due exclusively to financial considerations. The game of musical chairs that is played every September, in which every college and university center depletes itself of older adolescents and is replenished by in-migrants—and the desirability of being educated in cities away from the natal household that is explicitly expressed by the students themselves, as well as by their parents—suggests that a basic social value is being acted out. This value is the high premium that is placed on freedom from household and extrahousehold kinship as bases for the maintenance of conformity, as criteria for the formation of social relations, and as the source of educating personnel.

It is also in connection with the role of kinship in the individual's preparation for adult roles that it is possible to observe an important difference between elite and commoner education in contemporary society. As noted above, the strongest pressures for behaving according to nonkinship standards (or even antikinship principles, as in antinepotism laws and rules) are exerted on people who occupy elite roles. Correspondingly, the game of musical chairs referred to above is played most prevalently by those students who attend the elite schools, those who are being prepared for participation in the boundary and power roles of the society. Those who attend the less prestigious schools—the junior and community colleges, and the like—remain more closely tied to kinship groups, especially the family. Viewed in terms of their total development during their years of maturation, kinship and the particularistic values served by it play a much larger role than among those who attend elite schools. Needless to say, attendance at such institutions as "preparatory" and other "boarding" schools are important aspects of training the members of the elite classes in nonkinship patterns at a much earlier age.

Thus kinship is not only separated from the maintenance of conformity in the technologically most advanced societies but also from education, especially in the elite strata. Schools are relatively late developments in the evolution of social organization and it is significant that in any randomly drawn sample of societies that have schools including those to which educational institutions were introduced by colonial conquerors as part of the process of subjugation, in only a very few (approximately 8 percent) may teachers be kinsmen as well as nonkinsmen; they are nonkinsmen in all the others.

Unfortunately little is known about the rules governing the selection of teachers in most societies in respect to their kin statuses in relation to their students. However, it may be assumed that a society that has effectively separated kinship from the maintenance of conformity in general would also tend to avoid having children taught in schools by their kinsmen. There are indications that such quasi-formal rules exist in contemporary American society. For example, in northern New York there is a preference for hiring teachers who are nonresidents of the community or who are transient, partly in order to avoid the commingling of education and kinship.[32] Similar rules appear to have obtained in portions of the Midwest;[33] sometimes, if residents of the community are hired, they are required to be unmarried women, for whom the likelihood of having close kinsmen as students is small.[34]

Like kinship, religion plays an important role in the maintenance of conformity, and is strongly correlated with educational activities, in many preindustrial societies. Schools very often began under direct religious sponsorship or have a strong religious orientation; this, of course, includes schools established by the missionary arms of colonial governments. Religious influences over schools have persisted longer than kinship influences; correlatively, it appears that the religious sphere contributed to the maintenance of social conformity for longer periods in the history of human societies than the kinship sphere. Writing of post-Puritan New England, Tocqueville seemed to have taken it completely for granted that "every citizen receives the elementary notions of human knowledge; he is taught, moreover, the doctrines and evidences of his religion, the history of his country, and the leading features of its Constitution." [35] Most commentators on the history of American education, which is not unique in this regard, have noted the religious-denominational sponsorship and orientation of schools during the early periods of American history.[36] However, despite its long involvement in education, the differentiation of religion from educational and other spheres of activity in some industrial societies, such as contemporary United States, indicates that religion is dispensable to the field of conformity and is not a necessary correlate of educational activities.

Although there are not enough systematic data in the ethnographic literature to substantiate this conclusively, it is my impression that most societies whose organizations are based on kin-focused communities commingle religiously sanctioned social authority—what is often referred to as secular authority—with education. The impact of this interfusion as a basis for the maintenance of conformity in later life can hardly be overestimated. But what is even more important in this connection is that the loci and boundaries of political control in such societies are extremely close to the individual in social and territorial space. The ultimate sources of authority to which he is subject, and the boundary systems within which he finds his social-emotional anchorage, are characterized by immediacy and proximity. The people who exercise this authority are known to him personally, and the symbols legitimating their rightful power to act and command are part and parcel of his daily intimate social relations. Correlatively, the sources of his instruction in becoming a member of his society are directly tied to the small-scale boundary-maintaining group within which he carries out most of his significant daily social activities. It is the local group as a boundary system, and not any other beyond its social perimeters, which shapes his mind and to whose pressures and demands he is taught to respond. It is the symbols and imperatives of the local group (community, lineage, sodality) which he learns, and none other. Inseparable from this is that the religious dogma he learns and by which he lives is the dogma of the local group, and none other.

Schools in almost all major civilizations were long under the domination of religious personnel, and some still contain religious orientation and content. This commingling has persisted until very recently, and is still to be observed in some industrial nation-states, if not in pockets in almost all of them. Now it is not possible to explain the continuation of religious control of, or commingling with, education over many centuries and across several stages of social evolution only by the observation that religious personnel were generally the best educated in most of the societies with educational systems and that religions tended for many centuries to retain monopolistic control over formal knowledge and its transmission. The correlations are obviously true. But, more importantly, we need to ask why religious personnel were the best educated until recently, and why there was a monopoly by vertically entrenched religions over formal knowledge and its transmission.

I suggested above, when discussing the provenance of schools as an aspect of civilizational states, that the commingling of religion and education provided an ideological and legitimating basis for the identification of boundary role players with the state. But there is another aspect to the interlacement of education with religious ideology. Education is intimately tied to religious activity when the latter is one of the principal spheres serving the field of conformity. And religion plays a major role in maintaining conformity when the social organization is anchored to well-bounded communities in which kinship and other face-to-face relationships predominate in the structure of social relations. The organization of social relations is not only tied to small bounded communities and kin groups in stateless societies but also, importantly, during the early periods of nation-states; in the latter, the two matrixes crosscut in the integration of society and in the exercise of legitimate authority. While the pressures of the state promote universalistic standards of recruitment and evaluation, those of the small local nexuses support systems of particularistic values. When the universalistic value systems of the state—that is, when the standards of recruitment and evaluation are determined by individual ability as measured by decree of the state's bureaucratic and legal machinery—supplant the particularistic value systems that are appropriate to the personalized relationships of the bounded local community, religion begins to lose its position as a legitimating symbol-system in the maintenance of conformity.

Naturally, educational instruction also helps prepare people for necessary economic and technical skills, and this is especially important at the more advanced levels of technological adaptation. Such training becomes increasingly important as the economy expands its dependence on the harnessing and application of increasingly efficient extrapersonal sources of energy. The increasing reliance of contemporary industrial technology on electronic and other fuel sources of energy is a matter of common knowledge. Members of the commoner strata must be trained in the necessary skills in connection with these; this education is not only necessary to enable them to gain a livelihood but also for important political ends.

An important element in the sphere of economic activity that contributes significantly to the maintenance of conformity is the routine and schedule of productive activities, as well as those of consumption. Schools often serve in one way or another as models or prototypes for the routine of adult economic activities. The discipline—if not the attenuation—of spontaneity, originality, and personal expressiveness that results from learning by rote and catechetical procedures is not unrelated to the school schedule; both serve in part to prepare people for keeping to the routines that will be necessary in later life.

These routines are twofold adaptations. On the one hand, they are important sources of the stability and predictability in social life that underlie the smooth flow and integrity of the political system, broadly conceived. On the other hand, they are important adaptations to the round of productive activities. No social system—whether its basic economic activities rest on the care of domesticated animals, on the careful regulation of water flow, or on the idealization of a missile countdown—can tolerate a polity in which each man follows his own whims to think, enjoy a pretty butterfly, or make love in lieu of necessarily routinized productive activities. One consequence of sending children to school at, say, three years of age is not so much to have them learn a body of knowledge, it is to instill in them the routine and regularity of adult activities at a very early age. The imprint of such regularity in the consciousness of schoolchildren from the days of the earliest civilizational schools is a matter of record.[37]

As noted above, the political systems in which schools first arise are invariably characterized by formalized class, and sometimes caste, structures. In most of these societies the pressures for economic discipline and routine appear almost always to have been applied first to the elite classes. This was not only an inevitable accompaniment of elite-exclusiveness with regard to education, it was also an expression of value differences in regard to routine and personal discipline in different social strata; the two are inseparable. In Tokugawa Japan, for example, "it was on maintenance of the samurai's supremacy that the whole [social] system depended. In the economically simpler society of the early seventeenth century, when agriculture provided the bulk of the nation's total production, the samurai, whose fiscal system was well designed to tax agriculture, had no difficulty in maintaining that supremacy." [38]

Correlatively, there were two distinct segments in the educational system of Tokugawa Japan, each of which was crisscrossed by different types of schools. ("The education of samurai women was carried on in the home. It was a lower-class custom to send girls out to school with boys and no fiefs provided schools for women.")[39]

Regular attendance at school was so highly valued in samurai schools that "in some schools regular attendance was enough to get a prize. Thus, at Kochi, a complicated schedule of prizes was related to the number of days' attendance at the school or at military training establishments." [40] On the other hand, there were important attitudes toward commoner education. "If few writers on education actually held (publicly) that the common people were better illiterate, there does seem to have been in some districts a prejudice against farmers—or at least their wives—learning to read and write." [41] Even when commoner children did attend school with those of the samurai class, "they were clearly second-class citizens and on no occasion did they actually study with the other students." [42] Correlatively, in commoner schools,

> Hours of attendance were irregular—there were no clocks in any case—and the usual practice was for pupils to go to the teacher for their day's brief lesson as soon as they arrived and then settle at their desks to practice what they had learned. They did not necessarily go every day. One Gifu village teacher, for instance, whose records have been examined, held classes on seven or eight days of each month, and most of his pupils attended for only three or four.[43]

The plaint is often heard from teachers of children from the lowest social strata in contemporary American society that it is often almost impossible, or at least very difficult, to win acquiescence by these children in regard to routine and discipline, especially with respect to clock-measured time. It is also often observed that these children have few, if any, adult models of regularity and routine, and that this phenomenon is rooted in the society's socioeconomic structure. Such assertions are undoubtedly true, but what is important about them in terms of our present considerations is their inseparability. Patterns of child and adult behavior are not separate phenomena, counterpoised like opposing armies or separate islands across a gulf. They are of a piece. Patterns of child behavior are not only preparations for adult life, like the final preparations of experimental animals for dissertation runs; they are also inextricable parts of the adult world, and adults are integral elements in the world of their children. Thus, what must be kept in mind is that schools are adult institutions in which children participate; they are also childhood institutions in which adults play all-important roles. This is equally true of elite and commoner schools.

An important basis for the establishment of adult regularity and conformity is to be found in the use of examinations, which have been a central feature of educational systems since the first school systems. The manifest purpose of examinations is to determine the degree in which a student has engorged material and is able to return it; this is especially adaptive in connection with rote and catechetical learning. However, there is also a latent function in examinations that is significant at the primary and secondary school levels. This centers around the fact there is only one correct answer to an examination question. There is no room for dissent, speculation, disagreement, or imagination; and this is what a child learns, among other things, as a result of repeated examinations. These examinations become part of the individual's experience at a very early age, when he is most impressionable, and when he is first learning modes of relationship to the social system. That there is only one correct standard for the evaluation of the individual in the most impressionable years of schooling is underscored not only by the authority of teachers and others in the educational institution but also by the ubiquitous national flag, religious symbol, or portrait of a culture hero. These are the symbols of authority in society, and whether anyone is consciously aware of it or not, the child comes to associate everything he learns, including the notion that there is only one correct answer and standard of performance, with the state's symbols that face or envelop him while he is learning.

Today this is one of the most important bases for adaptation to life in a state society, namely, that there is only one standard of loyalty, allegiance, and conformity. A child being examined learns that he is giving precisely the same answers to precisely the same questions as all other children throughout the realm. The later realization that he must behave in many institutional areas in precisely the same way as all others throughout the realm, and often at precisely the same moment, is easy to achieve once the first has been successfully implanted. Although there are exceptions, every state system knows that a "good" student becomes an obedient subject. Repeated examinations in arithmetic and biology are integral aspects of what is called "political socialization."

In seeking to understand the ubiquitous commingling of the educational and political spheres of society, especially with regard to mass education, it is also necessary to draw attention to the continuity in civilization from its rural-based past to its contemporary forms, which are based on industrial urban centers. The majority of the populations of civilizational societies have not always lived in urban settlements; but there has been a steady growth in the proportion of the total populations of civilizational states who lived in urban centers. In either case civilizational states have almost always been dominated and governed by urban institutions.

It is thus also necessary to point to the similarity between rural peasants and modern urban dwellers in their relationships to their total societies, especially their political sectors. Speaking of rural peasants, Wolf has observed that they are "cultivators whose surpluses are transferred to a dominant group of rulers that uses the surplus both to underwrite its own standard of living and to distribute the remainder to groups in society that do not farm but must be fed for their specific goods and services in turn." [44] These groups of rulers are the occupants of power and boundary roles. Urban-industrial people, whether entrepreneurs or workers, do not cultivate, but they produce surpluses nevertheless; these industrially produced surpluses, to use Wolf's conceptualization, are "transferred to a dominant group of rulers that uses the surplus both to underwrite its own standard of living and to distribute the remainder to groups in society that do not [produce industrial products] but must be fed for their specific services in turn."

Members of the commoner strata must not only be educated in skills that will enable them to earn a livelihood but also to serve the interests and needs of the ruling elite. Skills involved in connection with medicine, the microscopic study of the workings of the law, the production of chemicals and fuel systems, the piloting of vehicles and reading navigational charts, the repair and operation of computer systems, or industrial farming underwrite the standard of living of the elite strata and provide economic surpluses which are then redistributed by these elites, among their other functions.

In the words of John Galbraith,

> Trained manpower is now the decisive factor of production. One very important thing to bear in mind is that the education explosion of recent years is not some new enlightenment. It is a response to the needs of modern industrial society. To a much greater extent than we realize, education is a reflection of industrial needs. In the last century and the early parts of this century, when the new industry, the new capitalism, required hundreds of thousands of unlettered proletarians, that is what the educational system provided. Now that it requires specialists—octane engineers and public relations experts —this increasingly is what the educational system is providing.[45]

Hence, among other goals served, radical alterations in the stratification aspects of educational systems—the wedge in the door through scholarships in England, the American school desegregation decision of 1954 by the Supreme Court (a central institution in the American elite structure), to name just two—must be seen partly as policies of elites who need to broaden the surplus-providing base in society. The expansion of this base not only provides greater surpluses for the elite and an increase in their standards of living, but it also provides them with greater surpluses which can then be redistributed in the forms of livelihood to those who do not produce goods.

One of the most important aspects of the curriculum of a state's school system is the instruction of students in the "history" of their society; this, as we have seen, together with examinations, has been a central element in school curricula since man's first educational systems. That this is always ideologically rewritten—if not often distorted—history needs no demonstration. Every society demands that its growing members learn that their society's road to the present is paved with righteousness. American students are not taught about their country's barbarity toward the Indians, who are instead often depicted as the predatory aggressors against a peace-loving people. American teachers and texts do not mention the policies of concentration camps (antiseptically known as "reservations" and "internment camps") for Japanese-Americans during World War II or for American Indians. American expansionist policies and support of totalitarian regimes are redefined as support for democratic ideals. Spanish students do not learn about the Inquisition. Russian and Chinese students are not taught of the brutalities in their domestic and intersocietal histories. Such instruction—the thrust of which is that one's state is always virtuous—has been eminently successful in meeting the goals of the society as a political system.

But it is not enough for a state to encourage the elimination of enduring outspoken dissent. It must also subvert and erode differentiated boundary-maintaining systems within the society. Intimately related to this is that what is learned in schools is uniform throughout the society and is not rooted in localized kin groups, communities, ethnic enclaves, and the like. Schools that are staffed by nonkinsmen outside the household and other kin relationships—and in which students are made aware that they are learning the same standardized or stereotyped information as their peers throughout the realm—are important steps in establishing uniformity of thought; one result of this is to facilitate alienation from local groups and sources of loyalty. This is one reason why schooling in so many societies of different levels of complexity involves the residence of students in places that are distant from their natal households, at least for the duration of their educational careers. Such practices simultaneously underlie the person's alienation or estrangement from local sources of anchorage in the service of the state organization's entrenchment and his conformity to national patterns of thought and behavior.

The removal of children from local settings for educational pruposes in agricultural and many industrial civilizational societies is consonant with another aspect of the evolution of social organization, namely, the increasing distance between the individual and the loci of authority. There are several aspects of this. The first is the tendency for the centers of power and control to become increasingly remote from the individual in social as well as physical space at successive levels of cultural development. Second, these loci of power and control embrace increasingly larger numbers of people and wider territorial areas at successive levels of cultural growth. Third, the individual, at each succeeding stage of social evolution becomes tied to—and comes to feel that his fate depends on—more inclusive sociopolitical systems. Thus, "the sequence which communities seem to follow as they develop their component institutions . . . is always unidimensional, cumulative, and appears to lead in the direction of greater participation in the national social structure, regardless of the political ideology that may be present." [46] The development of educational institutions in states is clearly part of this process.

This must be done because one of the tasks confronting a state is the establishment of an ideology, if not a reality, of uniformity among its polity in as many respects as possible. One way in which this is done is by the inculcation of a uniform and standardized system of symbols to which all can be trained to respond uniformly. Such symbol-systems must be implanted early if they are to be effective, and they must be uniform throughout the society. Whether an American child begins his school day by an oath of allegiance to a flag and faces it all day, or whether a Soviet or Chinese child does the same toward his flag and a portrait of Lenin or Mao, the fundamental goals are no different. Similar sociopolitical goals are realized in the monastery schools of the Sherpas and the Burmese; the Brahman seminaries of the Bengali; the Moslem education of the Siwah, Atjehnese, and Hause; as well as in the rote learning of Tokugawa Japan, the Catholic catechism, the Jewish cheder, and the like. It is also in these terms, as many observers have noted, that we can understand the lengths to which Western colonial powers have gone to "educate" their subjects in Africa, Asia, the Americas, and elsewhere.

There is merit in the notion that "the book tends to be a solvent of authority," [47] but—like alcohol which is often a solvent of the superego—a book's effects vary considerably with its setting. Just as schools have considerably different repercussions, depending on whether they are commingled with religion and kinship in the maintenance of conformity, or whether they are intended as elite or commoner education, so will "the book" have quite different effects on man's relationship to sociopolitical authority depending on whether its force is emotionally (and demonologically) charged by religious authority or not, or on the individual's status in the social system.

In either case, I suggest that the idea that "the book tends to be a solvent of authority" is an ideology of the elite; it does not constitute the legitimation of mass education. One characteristic of elite status is that people in this stratum always enjoy privileges that are withheld from those of lower strata. Elites enjoy a measure of freedom from authority—and there is no gainsaying that "the book" plays a role in this, especially in contemporary society—partly because it is the elites who wield the authority. If "the book" were really a diluent of authority, elites would be less eager to provide education for the masses. High school administrators whose talents seem to reside exclusively in measuring their students' haircuts, or the dean of a junior college who posts a sign on the door to a study lounge proclaiming that no one will be admitted unless properly attired, do not seem particularly intent on liberating the mind or providing solvents of authority.

I have tried to show in this paper that schools were first developed as aspects of states' adaptations to pressures engendered by participation in civilizational networks. One of the most outstanding of these pressures was to create boundary roles; elites, who were always the first to be schooled, were the people who filled these roles. I have also tried to show that the existence of civilizational networks continues to generate these pressures and that civilizational states adaptively continue to train personnel to fill these boundary roles. Correspondingly, as education diffuses to the commoner strata, partly in the service of maintaining conformity and strengthening the state's control, gaps are created between elite and commoner education to maintain the gulfs that are integral elements of a system of stratification.

The study of the evolution of social organization from the most primitive levels of sociocultural integration to the level represented by modern civilizational states inevitably raises questions about the future. If this evolution does, indeed, constitute a grand movement or sweep in a given direction, and if we assume (as we must) that we are part of this movement, it is necessary to conclude that the processes involved will continue. An inescapable conclusion is that because every sociopolitical system adaptively creates its own mechanisms of education, and because a civilization represents a sociopolitical entity as such, it will develop its own relevant educational institutions. This is not an entirely new development; it has been characteristic of civilizational networks since Hellenistic time.[48] It was also characteristic of the Roman Catholic church when it represented the political institutionalization of Western European civilization. There is thus every good reason to anticipate that the civilization of the present, as well as of the future, will develop its educational system; but this will have to await an increase in the effectiveness in the civilizational network's institutionalization, currently represented in the United Nations. All such developments, as noted above, are slow and fumbling, if not sometimes painfully frustrating.

However, as suggested, a civilizational network—like any other sociopolitical entity—must also create its own legitimating ideology. Because this is part and parcel of the network's institutionalization, it is no more rapid. One reason for the slow pace in this is that the legitimating ideology of a civilization is in conflict with the ideologies of sovereignty in each of the nations of the network, just as the ideology of a state emerges out of the competitive struggle with the ideologies of local corporate groups.

Boundary roles are integral parts of the social organization of a civilization. Hence, it is among the players of these roles that the legitimating ideology of a civilizational network must first take root. The commoners oppose this, as do many boundary role players themselves, albeit for different reasons. Furthermore, since elite schools are among the principal training grounds for these boundary personnel, these educational institutions are among the major seedbeds of this legitimating civilizational ideology. And since this ideology is regarded as subversive from the point of view of the state's ideology, it is understandable that such schools are often regarded with some suspicion in the polity.

It is in these schools that we now observe some of the most vociferous expressions of this ideology, especially in regard to expansionist wars which are seen as conflicting with the emergence of a civilization encompassing the entire world. These ideological expressions—held by a minority, to be sure—must be regarded in anthropological terms as anticipations of a civilizational sociopolitical entity.

NOTES

1. Robert McC. Adams, *The Evolution of Urban Society: Early Mesopotamia and Prehispanic Mexico* (Chicago: Aldine, 1966), p. 8.

2. For concise descriptions of this interlacement, see Eric R. Wolf, "The Social Organization of Mecca and the Origins of Islam," *Southwestern Journal of Anthropology* 7 (Winter 1951): 329–56; W. F. Leemans, *The Old Babylonian Merchant: His Business and Social Position* (Leiden: Brill, 1950); W. F. Leemans, *Foreign Trade in the Old Babylonian Period* (Leiden: Brill, 1960); Karl Polanyi, Conrad M. Arensberg, and Harry W. Pearson, eds., *Trade and Market in the Early Empires* (New York: Free Press, 1957).

3. H. I. Marrou, *A History of Education in Antiquity* (New York: Mentor Books, 1964), p. 150.

4. Robert F. Murphy, "Social Change and Acculturation," *Transactions of the New York Academy of Sciences*, Series II, 26 (1964): 849–50.

5. Marrou, *History of Education in Antiquity*, pp. 77–78.

6. Rupert Wilkinson, *Gentlemanly Power: British Leadership and the Public School Tradition, A Comparative Study in Making of Rulers* (London: Oxford University Press, 1964), p. 100.

7. Yehudi A. Cohen, *The Transition from Childhood to Adolescence* (Chicago: Aldine, 1964), p. 39.

8. There is a very good discussion of the British "public school" in these terms (without using the concepts explicitly) in "The British Commune," *Encounter*, 6 (February 1961): 24–28.

9. Wilkinson, *Gentlemanly Power*, p. 83.

10. Ibid., p. 127.

11. Talcott Parsons, *Essays in Sociological Theory* (New York: Free Press, 1954), p. 42.

12. Marrou, *History of Education in Antiquity*, pp. 56–57.

13. Ibid., p. 30.

14. Wilkinson, *Gentlemanly Power*, p. 157.

15. W. H. McNeil, *The Rise of the West: A History of the Human Community* (New York: Mentor Books, 1956), p. 77.

16. Karl Wittfogel, *Oriental Despotism* (New Haven: Yale University Press, 1956), p. 320. For a description of third-millennium Hindu education, see A. L. Basham, *The Wonder that was India* (New York: Dover, 1959), pp. 162–65.

17. Wittfogel, *Oriental Despotism*, p. 351.

18. Samuel Noah Kramer, *History Begins at Sumer* (Garden City, N.Y.: Anchor Books, 1959), pp. 2–3.

19. Marrou, *History of Education in Antiquity*, p. 143.

20. For an excellent description of this, see R. P. Dore, *Education in Tokugawa Japan* (Berkeley: University of California Press, 1965).

21. H. L. Nieburg, *In the Name of Science* (Chicago: Quadrangle, 1966), p. 187.

22. Wilkinson, *Gentlemanly Power*, pp. 95–96.

23. David T. Bazelon, "The New Class," *Commentary* (August 1966): 48–53.

24. *New York Times*, 3 April 1966.

25. Marrou, *History of Education in Antiquity*, p. 256.

26. Philip Foster, *Education and Social Change in Ghana* (Chicago: University of Chicago Press, 1965), p. 196.

27. James S. Coleman, ed., *Education and Political Development* (Princeton: Princeton University Press, 1965), p. 18.

28. Wilkinson, *Gentlemanly Power*, p. 110.

29. *New York Times*, 9 June 1967, p. 9.

30. Elman R. Service, *Primitive Social Organization: An Evolutionary Perspective* (New York: Random House, 1962), pp. 143–77.

31. William J. Goode, *After Divorce* (New York: Free Press, 1962), pp. 11–12.

32. Arthur J. Vidich and Joseph Bensman, *Small Town in Mass Society: Class, Power, and Religion in a Rural Community* (Garden City, N.Y.: Anchor Books, 1960), p. 85; Edgar Friedenberg, personal communication.

33. Robert S. Lynd and Helen Lynd, *Middletown: A Study in American Culture* (New York: Harcourt, Brace, 1929), pp. 206–10.

34. August B. Hollingshead, *Elmtown's Youth: The Impact of Social Classes on Adolescents* (New York: John Wiley, 1949), pp. 128–32.

35. Alexis de Tocqueville, *Democracy in America* (New York: Vintage, 1954), I:327.

36. See, for example, Bernard Bailyn, *Education in the Forming of American Society: Needs and Opportunities for Study* (New York: Vintage Books, 1960).

37. See, for example, Kramer, *History Begins at Sumer*, pp. 8–11; Marrou, *History of Education in Antiquity*, pp. 362–63.

38. Dore, *Education in Tokugawa Japan*, p. 11.

39. Ibid., p. 67.

40. Ibid., p. 69.

41. Ibid., p. 215.

42. Ibid., p. 221.

43. Ibid., p. 271.

44. Eric R. Wolf, *Peasants* (Englewood Cliffs, N.J.: Prentice-Hall, 1966), pp. 3–4.

45. John Kenneth Galbraith, "The World through Galbraith's Eyes," *New York Times Magazine*, 18 December 1966, p. 88.

46. Frank W. Young and Ruth C. Young, "Toward a Theory of Community Development," *Science, Technology, and Development* 7 (n.d.): 23.

47. David Riesman, *Abundance for What? and Other Essays* (Garden City, N.Y.: Anchor Books, 1965), p. 403.

48. See Marrou, *History of Education in Antiquity*.

6

THE SOCIAL SYSTEM
OF THE SCHOOL

Adam Scrupski

Contemporary society has been characterized conceptually as involving structural differentiation, extension of inclusiveness, and promoting adaptive and normative upgrading.[1] The accelerating interdependency among the three phenomena, the tendency for structural differentiation to develop increasing specialization of function in hitherto unspecialized spheres, of such specialization to enhance the adaptive capacity of the society, thus providing impetus for further differentiation as new knowledge is created and discretely identified, is likely to produce certain discontinuities between men's private and public identities.[2] Thus, Philippe Aries reports that in seventeenth-century France there was no disjuncture between the two identities, indeed *two* identities did not exist; functionaries of various sorts mingled in all kinds of what are now called "private" affairs, mixing "business" with friendship in the kitchen or in the street, with no temporal or spatial separation between the two spheres.[3] In contemporary structurally differentiated society, however, the attainment of a discrete public identity seems a necessary and problematical affair; the fact of differentiation alone implies a certain objectification of self or selves. As differentiation proceeds identities are multiplied and self becomes a more thoroughly conducted and harmonized entity. The necessity for coordination among differentiated and upgraded functions requires an unprecedented measure of role taking which enhances the objectification of self. The requirement for upgraded specialization seems to ensure at the same time a long period of increasingly complex cognitive experiences. Enter the public school.

The school then becomes the agency that constructs the individual's initial public identity and ensures a more complex objectification of self, as it participates in the adaptive upgrading of the society. This process is a major focus of the exposition that follows.

As John Kenneth Galbraith has observed, it is education or the potential to be mobilized as a technical adjunct to the industrial system, a function of adaptive upgrading, that has replaced capital as "the difference that divides," for it is education that qualifies personnel for positions in various strata of the technological society.[4]

Yehudi Cohen has emphasized the division of inhabitants of a civilizational state, decision makers and boundary role players on the one hand and commoners on the other; but he notes the existence of several substrata within each of the two major divisions and observes that in the United States today

. . . the elite are not to be found riding to hounds or on palatial yachts. Instead they are now to be found in bureaucratic offices, on commuter trains, and often mowing their lawns on Saturday mornings.[5]

Cohen suggests that university education is now the route to an elite status of some kind or degree. The proliferation of the new elite positions seems to have made the pre-university education of those so destined more thoroughly a public school affair; while the older, exclusive private boarding schools still maintained their socially elevated positions and enrollments, they seemed not to be able to accommodate the increasing number of elite participants. These students are instead accommodated by the public school, where the interests of exclusiveness and segregation tend to be reconstructed in the form of ability grouping and tracking.

H. Schelsky has observed

. . . mobility among individual families, which has weakened class solidarity and given rise to a kind of family or small-group egotism typical of present-day society. . . . Since this highly mobile society is characterized by widespread anxieties and a craving for security, it tends to degenerate into an eternal wanting-to-have-more and wanting-to-be-more.[6]

Thus, given the significance of education for occupational qualification (occupation being the primary if not only mode of advance), the school will essentially be dealing with the "social claims of the family." [7] The value of Schelsky's essay is that it translates a manpower allocation "function" from the societal realm to the everyday world of pupils, teachers, and parents. For Schelsky it is individual nuclear families, supercharged intra-sentimental units that are concerned for their social status and pursue its enhancement and security in the schools. Such families, of course, are the product of the same evolving social forces of technology and industrialism that have reconstituted the labor force, the economy, and the supporting governmental functions. The point is made historically by Philippe Aries in his *Centuries of Childhood*. Aries suggests that the modern phenomenon of social class is strongly related to the shrinking of the family to its nuclear base, that in some way the modern family has given up a former concern for neighborly relationships for a contemporary severely private concern, investing its energy in the "interests of a deliberately restricted posterity." [8]

In any case, the school seems to have become the family's agent for maintaining or processing its social-status claims. This fact accounts in large part for much of the phenomena explicated below: for the tension between teachers and their clients; for the role prescriptions teachers construct for administrators; for the development of the guidance counseling position, whose major concern now is with educational, not occupational, placement beyond high school.

That learning of a cognitive sort, even learning that "sticks" somewhat, takes place in school is, of course, not to be denied. There seems little doubt that over the long haul schooling produces learning that is not produced elsewhere. That schoolwork is taken more seriously, by children and adolescents as well as their families, than has been the case in the past seems evident. The curricular reforms of the 1950s and '60s with their emphasis on a "structure of knowledge" to be made available to students at any level of development and the replacement of "arithmetic" with "modern mathematics" represent a kind of academic upgrading consistent with the adaptive upgrading characteristic of society at large. However, the emphasis in this essay is not on the cognitive in a narrowly academic sense; it takes academic upgrading as a kind of "given" and focuses on the socialization of attitudes and orientations, primarily those related to achievement, competence, responsibility, and independence that seem to make differentially available to students the more complex organization of subject matter as it is elaborated in an increasingly longer academic career.

The basic exposition is two-pronged, comprising first an examination of the manner in which the corporate-technological society is reflected in and reconstructed by the social system of the school. The school as a social system is conceptualized as involving four interrelated social processes: (1) classroom social processes which are seen as stratifying achievement and socializing clients through a formal public sanctioning pattern enhanced in valence by occasional demonstrations of affectivity; (2) bipolar group processes in the school as they tend to ensure a measure of autonomy for their members and as they combine with formal school structure to further the stratification of clientele on an affective axis; (3) counseling activities considered as an integrative process, matching clients and curricula and cooling out client aspirations deemed unrealistic. (The fourth substructure of social relationships in the school, involving administration as a focus, is examined in a later chapter.)

Then (the second "prong") attention is given to the manner in which ascribed social status of students interacts with school structure to ensure the reproduction of the pattern of unequal participation in the activities and rewards available in contemporary society.

The Classroom and What Is Learned There

At the center of the formal educational enterprise resides the school class. The term "class" retains here either or both of its common meanings in the everyday parlance of the school. On the one hand, it refers to the group of children, usually 25 in number (a figure that seems to represent a curious unchanging norm and, as shall be explicated, may have its source in more than mere economic expedience), assigned to a single teacher usually in a designated room. On the other hand, "class" may refer to an entire age cohort of children in the school, all of whom have progressed to a particular stage (e.g., the freshman class). The tendency here is to focus on the first connotation, though by mere extension the second may in many cases be equally well served.

Thus, a school may be defined in a sense as a collection of classes, graded with respect to age, gathered under a single roof (though the single roof is not necessary; in an era of expanding school populations many administrative units were composed of several classes in temporary quarters such as church basements and volunteer firehouses). The common criticism of school structure implied in the terms "egg-crate architecture" and "cells and bells" reflects this definition of a school. A collection of one to 25–30 set interaction patterns, to borrow Chapple's and Arensberg's term,[9] is what the modern school tends to be, whether "self-contained" (each teacher working all day with the same group of students) or departmentalized. Thus, in Talcott Parsons' sole excursion into the sociology of education he chose for his title "The School Class as a Social System";[10] for Parsons it is essentially the school class, as the school's basic unit, which performs the basic function of formal education in contemporary society.

CLASSROOM STRUCTURE AND THE STRATIFICATION OF ACHIEVEMENT— Parsons suggests that the school class performs two basic functions: socialization and selection. For Parsons, socialization is "to the basic values of society" and while he speaks briefly of the development of orientations to achievement and universalism, he tends to emphasize the selection function of schooling, in particular elementary schooling. By the end of eighth grade, the point of decision with respect to high school program of studies, the cohort of students who had entered kindergarten nine years prior has been differentiated on the "axis of achievement." [11] Students are then separated basically into two groups, those who are allowed to enroll in college preparatory courses and those who are not,[12] thus, college-goers and noncollege-goers (or in the recent period of community and state college proliferation, goers to Ivy League colleges, goers to state universities, goers to state colleges, etc.).

To this point Parsons presents no remarkable insights; indeed, Willard Waller presented a similar case in his chapter on vertical mobility and the school more than forty years ago.[13] It is when Parsons points to "the four primary features of the elementary school situation" that ensure the school's differentiation function that he ingenuously and intuitively makes his essay's most significant contribution; for not only do these features comprise a structure which ensures the school's selection function, the same structure, it shall be argued below, ensures the school's basic socialization function.

These four primary features of the elementary school classroom situation are

1. . . . the initial equalization of the "contestants' " status by age and by family background, the neighborhood being typically much more homogeneous than is the whole society.

2. . . . the imposition of a common set of tasks which is, compared to most other task areas strikingly undifferentiated.

3. . . . the sharp polarization between the pupils in their initial

equality, and the single teacher who is an adult and represents the adult world.

4. . . . a relatively systematic process of evaluation of the pupils' performances . . . particularly (though not exclusively) in the form of report card marks . . . [constituting, from the pupil's point of view] reward and punishment for past performance.[14]

A basic "contest" pattern seems to be established by these features. Its consistency with Ralph Turner's contest mode of mobility seems obvious.[15] The contest is ensured by the following:

1. A set of contestants no one of whom seems to enjoy an unfair advantage over the others. (Equality for children tends to the temporal, an equality of age or seniority. When George Homans cites "investments" as a factor in social behavior, wherein equal investments are expected to bring equal rewards, he cites age as a significant illustration.)[16]

2. A set of undifferentiated tasks to be completed, that is, the same course to be run by all.

3. A systematic procedure for identifying winners, losers, and runners-up (the grading system).

4. A single judge or referee; inconsistencies in judgment, an opportunity to play one judge off against another, the chance of getting help—which by definition in a contest is "unfair"—are all thus obviated.

In the contest context all these features seem logically as well as empirically related to one another. A radical change in any one would seem to require a change in the others, or a movement to bring the deviant feature "back into line." Each of the features seems to have long been the target of educational reformers who have decried the contest pattern as unnecessarily competitive and constitutive of extrinsic motivation for learning. Thus, reformers have sought to replace cryptic "grade"-oriented report cards with narrative or simple pass-fail approaches. They have asked that differentiated, individualized tasks replace the common curriculum. They have advocated a more "natural" grouping arrangement, of a multi-age sort, as a replacement for the narrowly age-homogeneous arrangements. They have asked that the teaching function be extended beyond the person of the single teacher, to include community personnel, older students, or even other teachers (team teaching). Yet, perhaps because most of the attempts at reform focused on one or another of these features relatively independent of the others, in a short time it seems that the reform faded and the preexistent characteristic reasserted itself.[17] Such reformist attempts seemed also to ignore the network of basic societal interdependencies in which these features were involved. To that we now turn.

CLASSROOM STRUCTURE AND STUDENT SOCIALIZATION: THE SUPERORDI-NATE SUBSYSTEM–The same primary features of the elementary school classroom situation that seem to ensure the selection function seem also to ensure the schools' basic socialization function. Robert Dreeben contrasts the social relations in today's intimate nuclear family with those of impersonal corporate society and suggests that the process of schooling functions to internalize for its subjects norms that act ultimately as standards for governing adult conduct in contemporary industrial society.[18] Noting a certain discontinuity between standards governing life in the nuclear family and those governing public life in society at large, Dreeben suggests that schooling constitutes an institutionalized way of ensuring that the child will develop orientations of universalism rather than particularism, specificity rather than diffuseness, achievement rather than ascription, and independence rather than dependence.[19]

Social relations in the family are characterized by particularism; that is, family members tend to see and interpret behavior directed toward one another in terms of the peculiar, particular heritage of experiences *they* have undergone together. Orientations in the family are diffuse rather than specific; that is, one's significance for another is defined in terms of his entire personality and a broad range of shared activities and interests. Also, family members tend to be more concerned with what others in the family are rather than with what they can do (ascription vs. achievement). Last, the family as an intimate solidary interacting unit tends to emphasize dependence upon one another, a certain going-for-help when an obstacle is met, rather than a basic independence orientation to tasks.

Of course, fathers and mothers are also concerned about whether their children "measure up" to others of similar age (universalism), about whether or not a child of theirs is a good reader or a good shortstop (achievement), or if he can perform certain caretaking activities by himself (independence). But it should be noted that mutual exclusivity is not being asserted; what is suggested is that the balance of family orientation compared to societal (or as we shall see, school) orientation is on the side of particularism rather than universalism, ascription rather than achievement, dependence rather than independence.

The development for children of the norms of universalism, specificity, achievement, and independence seems assured by the four primary features of the classroom situation. The polarization of status, a single teacher, and at least twenty-five students of the same age means that there will be too many students for the director of learning to be particularistic about; clear categorization is present; both tend to produce universalistic orientations. The homogeneity of the student groups allows each student to see himself in the same boat as others, making the universalistic approach legitimate; the concern on the part of schoolchildren for "fairness," given their age-equal position, seems to force universalistic approaches on the teacher. The set of undifferentiated tasks also reinforces universalism, since each student may be assessed in terms of the same criteria; a systematic scheme for reporting ensures that children will be asked to "measure up."

The same features tend to encourage orientations of specificity rather than diffuseness between teacher and student; too many children for a single teacher to know as "whole" persons, identical tasks for all children to accomplish—leaving little opportunity for idiosyncratic performances, a necessity to rank order children vis-à-vis a performance—leading to the establishment of criteria for undimensional measurement.

Achievement rather than ascription as a norm governing children's behavior seems ensured by the homogeneity of the pupil group—all of whom seemingly should be relatively equally capable of accomplishing the same task, a compulsion laid on the teacher to "rate" or rank students in terms of performances, and the set of undifferentiated tasks—existing as a set of "challenges" to all students at a given grade level.

Independence seems to be ensured also by the four primary features of the classroom situation. In school, a child is expected to do for himself, to persevere somewhat or at least to try again before going for help. The collection of age-equals allows the participants to reinforce independence demands in that the chances of some children being in a position where they can legitimately give help to others is obviated; the obvious equality of status makes it fair to expect a child to try to accomplish a given task without assistance ("If others your age can do it, why can't you?"); of course the necessity to rank or grade means that the teacher, to be "fair," must be able to assure himself and others that each child's grades are a reflection of his own independent efforts; the polarization of position, a single teacher, and at least twenty-five children makes the giving of very much help by the teacher problematical (there are too many students to help).

Thus, the same features of the classroom which ensure a contest situation and the stratification of an age-cohort of children with respect to scholastic achievement also function to develop for these children habitual orientations of universalism, specificity, achievement, and independence, learning unavailable in the particularistically oriented nuclear family and apparently necessary to life in structurally differentiated corporate society.

THE PROBLEM OF TEACHER SANCTIONS–Dreeben observes that as a socializing agent directing the day-to-day learning and order-keeping experiences of the classroom, the teacher faces the problem of finding for sanctioning purposes some substitute for the general affective involvement that characterizes the parent-child relationship in the nuclear family. Such a relationship is unavailable to the teacher in view of the relatively great number of children in his charge. The solution, it seems, lies in the fact of publicity of student response and behavior in general. Public response on the pupil's part is enhanced in value because of the age homogeneity of the group; all find themselves in the same boat and thus the kinds of exceptions that are typically made in the age-heterogeneous family for failure ("He's so much younger, what do you expect?") or great success ("Of course he can hit better, look at how old he is!") are not available in the classroom. Each pupil is expected to perform equally in terms of the tasks presented. Thus, the teacher may play on the pupil's sense of self-respect. "Each pupil is exposed and vulnerable to the judgment of adults in authority and of his equals." [20] Indeed, as Jules Henry has observed, the pupil group may be enlisted by the teacher, in whom social power resides, in this enterprise, though, of course, it is the teacher's public approval that lies at the base of the sanctioning pattern and is utilized to manipulate the peer group. (Henry refers to "carping criticism" directed at individual pupils by classmates and elicited by the teacher.)[21]

In essence what the teacher does in the primary grades is to establish teacher approval (later to take the form of grades) as the primary sanction for the school. In a sense this phenomenon has been identified by Philip Jackson in his *Life in Classrooms* in terms of "crowds, praise, and power." [22] That is, given the *crowd* of children confronting the teacher and necessitating a distribution of pupil responses such that each child figuratively "waits in line" to contribute or respond and obviating the possibility of something approaching a genuine Socratic dialogue, given the social *power* of the teacher in the primary grades where the age and size disparity between children and adults is greatest it is likely that public *praise* and its negative counterpart, public censure, will be used as the primary general sanctioning mechanism. Over time, teacher praise is translated into such things as gold stars and ultimately into grades or marks. Of course, Jackson's tri-pronged description involves three of

Parsons' four primary features of the classroom situation, age homogeneity (crowds), polarization of teacher and taught (power disparity), and the systematic scheme for reporting (teacher praise).

Of course, the schools do not independently elaborate their structure in the directions noted. Strong expectations are levied upon the school by its sponsoring parent clientele. Margaret Mead has suggested that parents in modern nuclear families, shorn of their relationships to grandparents and other extended family elders who might assure them of their child's worth, lacking any basic internalized standard against which to assess their children, tend to resort to comparing their children with others. Such parents, says Mead, are interested in public validation of their children's worth. "The child is valued in comparative terms, not because he is of the blood and name of his parents, but because of his place on some objective rating scale of looks and potential abilities." [23] It seems that such a disposition is at the root of parents' demands for grades (marks), for some indication from the school of how their children "measure up" vis-à-vis others. The interdependency between such grades, age homogeneity of pupils, and curriculum has been demonstrated.

CLASSROOM PRACTICES–Matthew Miles has remarked

> . . . the presence of a body of subject matter, an adult and some children tends to create role pressure toward "explaining," asking for recitation, etc., relatively independently of the personality of the particular incumbent at hand.[24]

While Miles "cops out" on an explanation of this phenomenon, it is suggested here that the structure he elaborates interacts with the four primary features of the classroom situation noted above. Explaining, asking for recitation, etc., constitutes what we might call a central group pattern, in that the teacher tends to "orchestrate" the contributions and responses of the students around his or her own periods of lecture; the teacher is the "star" performer and students come in on cue as the teacher directs.[25] It may be noted that a decentralized pattern would probably enhance the *teaching* function of the teacher; such a pattern would make increments of teacher personal assistance available to children on a wholesale basis, destroying the contest situation and mitigating strongly the universalistic disposition of the teacher. For if some children, any children, are given help by the teacher on a particular piece of schoolwork in terms of the childrens' peculiar difficulties, is it "fair" for this help to improve their grades vis-à-vis the grades of those not given help at the same time? Thus, then, the strength and resilience of the central group pattern.

In exploring the central group pattern one may cite evidence recently collected by Raymond Adams and Bruce Biddle.[26] Confirming similar findings of long standing, Adams and Biddle seem to have discovered the Chapple-Arensberg one-to-twenty-five set interaction pattern, apparently a consequence of the polarized social arrangement and the initial equality of the students. After carefully examining hours of videotaped classrooms in action in grades 1, 6, and 11, the investigators concluded that for 75 percent of the time only a central communication group was in existence. For another 10 percent of the time, there existed a central group with one or two peripheral groups (presumably spontaneously generated student-to-student interaction of a sotto voce sort). Thus, the classroom is identified as a "public" arena.

> For most of the time whatever is being done demands the attention of all pupils. Small enclaves of private interaction emerge from time to time, but typically they are transitory.[27]

(Thus, the significance of Dreeben's comment noted earlier; the publicity of pupils' responses gives teachers the opportunity to play on student self-respect as a sanctioning device.)

The teacher in the Adams and Biddle study was a principal actor 84 percent of the time and an audience (for, say, student-student colloquy or argumentation) only 7 percent of the time. Most of the students are watching the teacher's performance and awaiting an opportunity to participate. Information dissemination, primarily on the part of the teacher, accounted for 65 percent of classroom time with only 20 percent spent on intellectualization (reasoning, opining, deducing, etc.),[28] testifying, it seems, to the significance of the evaluation process, wherein the requisite quantification and stratification of performance may more easily be based on information retention and regurgitation than on the process of reasoning, inference, deduction, etc.

In attempting to explain the continued existence of the basic central group as the essential organizational scheme for the classroom, Adams and Biddle suggest that "the specter of loss of control continues to haunt teachers," making them unwilling to create informal pupil activity situations, which would be hard to supervise closely. Here, of course, what is being noted is the basic structural isolation of the teacher, a function of the polarization feature, which because of the fears it generates tends to perpetuate itself.

Adams and Biddle make an interesting discovery, which may consist of a built-in engine of stratification in the central classroom group situation. They find that in the central-communication-group situation (in existence 85 percent of the time) teachers tend to concentrate their attention on only a few students located in what is called the "action zone," an area encompassing the front-center of the conventional pupil-seating arrangement. Apparently a function of proximity and attention-set, this tendency results in some 60 percent of pupil classroom contributions coming from three front-center single locations; if the area is expanded to include locations on either side of the front-center file, almost 100 percent of pupil contributions are accounted for. A similar pattern is exhibited with respect to teacher communication directed to individual students.[29]

What this pattern suggests is that built into the conventional classroom physical structure are unequal opportunities for pupils to participate and that either by chance, teacher design, or pupil self-selection, only certain pupils are afforded these opportunities. Thus, perhaps at the very outset of students' school careers, a stratification of participation and presumably reinforcement and achievement is ensured. At the same time the investigators exhibit the structure by which the publicity of pupil response makes it possible for the manipulation of pupil self-respect to become the teacher's major sanctioning device. The central-group arrangement, in existence 85 percent of the time, with only one person "holding the floor" at a time, provides opportunities for students to contribute, one at a time, in view of all other students, and in which evaluations and assessments of performance by the adult in charge are immediately communicated to the entire group. Such an operation enhances the teacher's significance and power, thus making it likely that he will persist in this mode of classroom operation, particularly if he is haunted by the "specter of loss of control."

STUDENT SOCIALIZATION AND THE SUBORDINATE SUBSYSTEM–What has been outlined above, of course, is a socialization process; a process, however, which cannot be readily accomplished without attention on the part of socialization agents to the initial predisposition of socializers, what Parsons has called the "subordinate subsystem." As Parsons observes,

Those who play a strategic part as agents of control must play at least a dual role. They must to some important degree, participate with the "deviant" in at least a limited way "on his own terms." But at the same time they must play an authentic role in the wider system, relative to which the subsystem is defined as deviant. The socialization agent uses his interaction in the subordinate subsystem to motivate the child by forming an attachment to him. He then uses his other role as in some sense defining a "model" for the child to emulate and as a basis of "leverage." [30]

In the case of classroom socialization, of course, the "wider system," as noted above, is constituted by the norms of universalism, specificity, independence, and achievement and the structural characteristics which ensure them. The "subordinate subsystem" involves the immediate social world of the child as child (contrasted to the child as pupil) as a member of what Waller has referred to as "the closest of all the primary groups," the nuclear family,[31] in which, as Dreeben has pointed out, relationships are characterized more by particularism, diffuseness, dependence, and ascription than by universalism, specificity, independence, and achievement, certainly as compared to the school situation and the "wider system."

The teacher superordinate role seems to imply what Waller calls "institutionalized leadership." In his examination, Waller seems to have uncovered a variant of Barnard's "zone of indifference." [32] Citing Simmel, Waller outlines the nature of superordination and subordination.

. . . subordination is possible because the relationship is meaningful to the dominant person, and relatively, not meaningful to the subordinate one. . . . The subordinate . . . strives to achieve psychic reorganization which will reduce the meaning of the relationship to nothing.[33]

What Waller seems to be saying is that as long as the teacher-student relationship is one in which the teacher's plans are substituted for the students,[34] there will be a strong tendency for students to empty teacher plans of meaning.

In an age of short-term preparation for work, in which the structure of the work force required cohorts of production workers and unskilled underlings who knew how to take orders and survive, such a socialization to obedience and meaningless work may be seen as a functional necessity. However, in the development of a work force requiring greater specialization and expertise and a longer-term preparation, in which children's motivation, it seems, must be more thoroughly captured in the interest of formal education, some variation of the subordinate subsystem role seems essential. Parsons' characteristic dual role, noted above, seems to be what Waller was attempting to describe when he noted that the "rhythm of the teacher's movements" daily is characterized by an alternation of his authority role with one in which he says in effect, "But I am a human being, and I try to be a good fellow. And you are all fine people and we have some good times together, don't we?" [35]

The nature of teaching seems inevitably to involve some variation of the subordinate subsystem role, a degree of *Gemeinschaft* relationship with pupils. Bryan Wilson emphasizes strongly this aspect of teacher role, noting

> . . . the living process in which the establishment of rapport, the impact of personality, are necessary to the stirring of the imagination and the awakening of enthusiasm involved in the learning process.[36]

Dreeben refers to this subordinate subsystem role as involving the creation of a sense of goodwill, a sense of diffuse attachment, suggesting that the teacher who relies solely on the dispensation in a quid pro quo fashion of rewards and punishments will find such sanctions exhibiting a progressive marginal efficiency unless they are complemented with the sense of diffuse attachment.[37]

Gertrude McPherson, in her observations of elementary school classroom life, points to the uncomfortable constraints of the teacher's formal role when she quotes a teacher as saying, "It is hard work, never to smile, never to let down, never to have fun with them." [38] That there may be some independent cultural-personal impetus to the teacher's establishment of diffuse contact with students is further supported by McPherson's observation that "the Adams teacher wanted the pupils to like her, not just to be afraid of her." [39] Indeed, McPherson reports at length the process of identification with their pupils that teachers manifest as the year goes on, suggesting that it weakens somewhat the impact of the teacher-group's solidary universalistic-specific orientation to children. Of course, McPherson is speaking of the elementary school, where the "self-contained" organizational structure more easily permits such an identification.

Nevertheless, the characteristics of the classroom situation identified earlier, the homogeneity of clients, the polarization of status, the undifferentiated curriculum, the systematic reporting scheme, set limits to the particularistic-diffuse relationships between teachers and pupils. Indeed, as children progress through school, it might be expected that the socialization will be effective and that they will value less and less the diffuse attachment coming from the classroom teacher. Evidence to this effect is provided by Musgrove and Taylor, who summarize several studies reporting that home rather than school is still the main source of "expressive, emotional satisfactions" for high schoolers, who seem primarily concerned with the teacher's instrumental rather than expressive role.[40] They cite Wright's finding that "pupils value their teachers mainly for their intellectual abilities; they are little concerned with their more general, human qualities." [41] At the same time, Musgrove and Taylor found in their own study, "Whereas the children emphasized 'teaching,' the teachers emphasized 'personality,' " [42] a peculiar set of reciprocal expectations whose balance must apparently be worked out in practice.

That the balance will be on the side of impersonality and *Gesellschaft* relationships rather than personal and *Gemeinschaft* orientations seems further ensured by the practice within graded education of changing teachers every year. This practice, which assigns a teacher to a single age group of children for a year at a time (thus, a fifth-grade teacher will see no one but eleven-year-olds for a year at a time—year after year) tends to freeze childhood in a particular stage for a teacher. The teacher is unable to experience the long pull of childhood; he is unable to see or feel growth in the child. Thus, in a temporal sense the teacher is kept from seeing children whole; not only are they "pupils" rather than "children," but they are pupils frozen in time, cut off from past and future; hardly human, hardly children, they are fifth graders or in high school, "CPs" or "generals."

With respect to the balance of teacher instrumentalism or task orientation vs. expressiveness or "personality" orientation, recent research tends to suggest that only a moderate exhibition of expressivism or teacher personality combined with considerable task orientation seems most functional for student development.[43]

In a sense, then, what schools teach children is how to play a role in contemporary society. To play a role is to concern oneself with behavior looked upon specifically, the division of labor being what it is in both society at large and in school, and universalistically, since the objective is to be a "good" doctor, or mechanic, or father, or fifth grader, or math student. A role in addition tends to involve discrete acts, which can be attributed to a single person and a single person only; it must be played independently. Lastly, a role is concerned with performance; while one can conceive, as Neal Gross has, of "role attribute," even such attributes may be identified and attested to largely through action; presumably, if they exist, they will be manifested in overt performance. Doing is still being.

In school a child learns that he is a pupil, similar to many other pupils, all of whom are treated relatively similarly by a single teacher, who, it will be perceived by the pupil as he meets a succession of teachers, is also playing a role. If socioeconomic systems can only be energized through persons playing roles, then learning to play roles, to see one's own behavior universalistically and specifically, conceived with independent achievement of expectations held for one by others reciprocally bound to one, seems essential for life in contemporary society. Such life the school ensures by teaching children to play roles.

Peer Groups in the School: Conflict, Autonomy, and Differentiation

Absent from the functionalist descriptions of schools constructed by Parsons and Dreeben is the element of conflict. Yet conflict is so endemic to the school that the most insightful of all sociologies of education, Willard Waller's *Sociology of Teaching*, has been called a conflict model of schooling.

> The teacher, as a member of the institutional faculty, desires the scholastic welfare of children even at the expense of other aspects of their development; parents usually take their stand for a more harmonious development.
>
> Thus . . . conflict . . . is accentuated by the fact that parents and teachers are involved in different alignments of group life affecting the child. For the parent the child is a fellow member of the closest of all the primary groups and a warmly personal attitude toward him is the result. But the teacher . . . still sees him mainly as a member of a secondary group over which the teacher must exert control by the mechanisms of secondary group life.[44]

What Waller has so incisively noted, of course, is the contrast between the particularistic-diffuse orientation of the family toward the child and the universalistic-specific orientation of school personnel. For Waller, however, the conflict is not one to be permanently resolved; indeed, it may constitute a benefit for the child in his development, if the balance between the two is maintained.[45] The mitigation of the conflict is seen by some as the function of parent-teacher work, as in the Gresham Sykes essay "The PTA and Parent-Teacher Conflict." [46]

There seems to be another source of conflict in the school arising somewhat later in the chronology of pupilhood, probably as children enter the latency stage and ultimately replacing the contrast between teacher and parent as the primary source of conflict. This later conflictual source lies in the contrasting (with respect to adult society at large) orientations of the adolescent peer group. Waller again puts the situation

> . . . pupils are much more interested in life in their own world than in the desiccated bits of adult life which teachers have to offer. . . .

Teacher and pupil confront each other with attitudes from which the underlying hostility can never be altogether removed.[47]

In this regard, Waller notes a tendency for pupils to withdraw from a personal relationship with teachers, the pupil group perhaps sensing the cooptive danger. Such a tendency, of course, reinforces the segmental, universalistic orientation characterizing the formal teacher-pupil relationship. Teachers who enter the school desirous of behaving as whole persons, exhibiting a common humanity, seem to be rather quickly and painfully socialized by students to the "real" teacher role. The social distance so guarded by teachers as a protection for their authority role is further strengthened from the other direction by the proscriptions placed by the peer group of students upon intimacy with teachers.[48]

The pupil-peer group's function is somewhat broader than the maintenance of social distance from the teacher (which makes superordination tolerable). Waller speaks of "the well-known school-boy code, the rule that students must never give information to teachers which may lead to the punishment of another student." [49] Perceptively Waller notes also the myths among students that cut the teachers down to size in their minds, one that of a student once attendant at the school who defied the authorities, laughed at disciplinary action, and ran away from home not to be seen again; and another of a nearsighted teacher whose students played leap-frog in the rear of the room.[50] Such myths seem to serve a tension-management function.

Noted also by Waller is the tendency of students to make nice discriminations between activities appropriate to particular age and grade levels, suggesting an intrinsic child and adolescent-sponsored support for the age gradedness of the school and other youth-serving institutions in contemporary society.

Both S. N. Eisenstadt and Talcott Parsons have contributed explanations of the age-grading phenomenon in society, explanations which, while they focus on the functional contribution age grading for youth makes to personality and occupational role taking and playing, nevertheless imply the potential for conflict noted above. Eisenstadt suggests that fullblown youth groups and youth cultures flourish in societies in which familial and *Gemeinschaft* socialization process is not sufficient for the development of adult public and private identities. Eisenstadt's point is that the school cannot itself account totally for the development of these identities. The emphasis in school on "preparation," the polarization of status which emphasizes the discontinuity between the social world of children and that of adults, the concentration of power and authority in the hands of adults, the downplaying in school of sexual maturation all tend to comprise a system which does not satisfy the needs of the child's and adolescent's personality at this "period of transition from the family to total society." [51] For this reason, says Eisenstadt,

> . . . the child and adolescent always develops the predisposition to join in age groups in which the dignity of his current dispositions and values will be affirmed, within which a greater spontaneity of activities will be permitted, and in which in some cases will also have a more direct relation to the symbols of identification of a total society. [52]

Parsons has contrasted the increasingly dependent position of the child in today's shrunken, isolated nuclear family (a dependence which appears to foster the inter-identification necessary for achievement motivation) with the independence necessary to perform adult roles in contemporary society, an independence required in mate selection, occupational and career contingencies, and the necessity for independent interpretation of rules and norms that no longer cover problematical situations as specifically as they once did (the latter an explanation of what Parsons calls "normative upgrading"). [53] Parsons suggests that relationships with teachers learned in school, though they may be universalistic and specific are also hierarchical, involving the child or adolescent in the taking of a clearly subordinate role. However, the child is destined ultimately to behave during much of his adult years in relationships with others that are basically egalitarian rather than hierarchical. As Waller says, "Subordination to the teacher does not prepare the child for anything, because there will be no teachers where he is going." [54] For Parsons, the society of age peers provides the child and adolescent with the opportunity to relate significantly to social equals. The adolescent peer group exists as a field for the exercise of independent action free from adult control, with unresolved dependency needs displaced onto the peer society itself, appearing in the extreme as a kind of slavish conformity to peer-group dictates.

Parsons notes further that in contemporary society family and school as institutions are "far down the line in the propagation of the effects of change." [55] This leads adolescents to sense that these agencies are "out of tune" with the tenor of the times and that it is somewhat unfair to be rigidly controlled by them. It should not be surprising then, that as the significance of formal education increases (children and youth tend to accept the importance of schoolwork)[56] and the period of basic dependency is therefore increased, that there should be exhibited a greater sense of rebellion, of disparagement of contemporary society and its establishment. David Matza identifies youth as a kind of minority group, suggests that in an age of affluence its dependency is ameliorated and that the amelioration, throwing strongly into question the basic subordination of the earlier position, will elicit demands for greater amelioration in the name of "justice." [57] (Jerry Farber's essay "The Student as Nigger" comes to mind.)[58]

There is a sense in which the informal peer group of students may be seen as the agency for the maintenance of what Alvin Gouldner calls "functional autonomy" for its members. Gouldner criticizes Parsons for his concentration on interdependence and his ignoring of the problematical nature of interdependence, suggesting that interdependence may not be a metaphysical given, but must be an empirically demonstrated fact; system parts (role players or collectivities) must be conceived as concerned with their functional autonomy; much of their behavior can only be interpreted as designed to maintain that functional autonomy and to limit the extent to which they are dependent upon other system parts. It seems to be in this sense that peer groups maintain a pattern of values that maximizes members' autonomy and reduces constraints issuing from their dependence upon others. The extent to which these groups share values common to the system as a whole may be seen, as Gouldner alludes to, as something to be negotiated albeit from perhaps a commonly acculturated base.[59] The system's values are not nearly as situationally specific as their subsystem translations—something which enables a culture to outlast transitory social systems. Thus, the peer group of students enforces social distance from teachers (no "entangling alliances" or social "debts"), places a fierce proscription on "informing" (thus protecting the sphere of autonomous activity), prescribes how much "work" is due a teacher for a given teacher output of reciprocal service (as described by Becker and Geer in their treatment of medical students),[60] and fills in the unelaborated terms of the student-teacher contract in a way that is most beneficial to its members in terms of expenditure of effort and the rewards it gains.

What the solidary or identificatory peer group provides is "resonance" for complaints and demands peculiar to the structural position of its members. It lends a basic moral justification to these demands. It constitutes and maintains them as values and provides consensual validation for them. Thus armed, its members may sally forth individually and collectively and negotiate their exchanges as role partners of dissimilarly positioned others, holding out, in the interests of justice, for as favorable a bargain as possible, and diminishing the possibility that their reciprocal acts will undergo what Gouldner refers to as an inflationary spiral (each conforming act, because it is so readily delivered, earning less in reciprocity from the "other").[61] As such, the entire process seems to constitute a protection for the group's autonomy, for indeed, if it can define the social situation as one in which performances on the part of "complementary others" are already owed or are a part of other's basic commitments, such performances are due no return service and a constraint is lifted from the group's members. The drive for "professionalization" of formerly lower-level occupations (even, paradoxical as it may seem, the professionalization of some amateur statuses with its accompanying associations) may be seen as a drive for autonomy in an increasingly complex but increasingly pluralist society in which individuals exhibit multiple discrete identifications.

THE TEACHER GROUP AND TEACHER AUTONOMY–That spheres of autonomy, particularly teacher autonomy, must be considered in an examination of the school as a social system has been demonstrated by Fred Katz. He, like Gouldner, insists that it is the degree of interdependence that is problematical in a system and that the school as a social system must ensure that its specialists are allowed to function autonomously, in the case of teachers, free from illegitimate intrusions of coordinators and presumably clients and their sponsors.[62]

Protection for autonomy on the part of teachers is exhibited by the teacher informal group. Waller notes:

> The primary group of teachers gives a sub-group sanction to the attitude of the teacher toward students and community; they support him in his struggle for mastery, comfort him in defeat, and advise him as to ways and means of further struggle.[63]

Waller perceptively cites the advice of William Bagley to teachers with respect to what is called the "craft spirit" in the teacher group. There, the teacher, says Bagley, will find "the comfort that really cheers, the advice that really helps, the idealism that really inspires." [64] And one must add, quoting Bagley's advice with respect to control of students, the conviction that "you have on your side right, justice, and the accumulated experience of generations of teachers." [65] Teachers so informed, so oriented, are likely to be hard bargainers in the field, unlikely to give up something for nothing, more likely, through their actions, demands, assertions, and refusals to define the situation in terms that enhance their freedom from constraint and reduce their dependency on others.

Gertrude McPherson illustrates the "justice-is-on-our-side" negotiation function of the informal group of teachers when she notes of the school she studied,

> The barriers between upstairs and downstairs, old guard and new, regular and special, primary and intermediate teachers were all

important, but all of those became somewhat less important to the teacher than her unity with her colleagues when she was face to face with the important member of her role-set—the pupil, the parent, or the administration. . . .[66]

The teacher expected more than that the group should merely passively defend her. She expected colleagues . . . to help justify her feelings and her actions. . . .[67]

The congruence of one teacher's attitudes and behaviors with the other teachers was increased by her contact with them. As she listened to the comments about pupils and the experiences of others, she found justification as well as standards.[68]

Iannacone has observed that the informal group of teachers may be a better agent of teacher participation in the running of the school than the popular formal devices for "democratic administration," noting that administrators in confronting a particular teacher are well aware that at the same time they are confronting the demands of the entire teacher group, to whom decisions or dispositions are likely to be immediately referred and resonantly judged.[69]

As an extreme illustration of the phenomenon under examination, we may cite Chapple and Sayles who note that "wildcat" strikes (autonomy run amok) seem to be endemic to work situations where workers perform identical functions and are in frequent contact with one another, ensuring solidarity, resonance, and the magnification of complaints and a sense of injustice.[70]

That the informal group performs a tension-management function seems obvious. Note McPherson's observation:

No teacher believed that she could allow herself to take out on the pupil the anger and hostility that his recalcitrance produced in her. If she did take them out on him she must then assuage her guilt through some group support. As Miss Tuttle said, after a group discussion in which each teacher humorously told how cruel she had sometimes been to her pupils, "I feel much better about how I behaved. Just sitting around talking and eating makes it all seem much less awful." [71]

What seems to have been identified is the existence in the form of the informal group of Parsons' pattern-maintenance and tension-management function performed not by a single solidary group, but by two contrasting, frequently conflicting groups, corresponding to that bipolar age distribution which for Waller most distinctly characterizes the social life of the school. That basic socialization functions of a pattern-maintenance sort are performed by these groups seems implicit in the examination conducted above. The sanction in the hands of the socializing agent or agents, of course, seems to be the willingness or unwillingness to manage the tension of the socializee. In that such socialization involves a supported thrust toward autonomy for the role player (teacher or pupil); that is, the development of the capacity to make demands or refuse to "come across" with behavior demanded, it perhaps leads to that sense of self-regard that Gouldner sees as a necessary element in the fully functioning personality and as resulting from a sense of autonomy.

> Self regard comes from conflictual validation, which the self may experience when it manifestly becomes something to be reckoned with, even if not approved by others, and when it thus validates its autonomy.[72]

THE PUPIL PEER GROUP AND THE STRATIFICATION OF PUPIL AUTONOMY—In that socialization in the informal group must be to the status or identification of teacher generally or peer-group member generally, rather than to that of teacher vis-à-vis parent or teacher vis-à-vis administrator or adolescent vis-à-vis teacher or adolescent vis-à-vis counselor, a structurally differentiated parallel is suggested with the general socialization in the basic pattern-maintenance and tension-management societal unit, the family. It is in the family of orientation, says Gouldner, that socialization ensures "a measure of functional autonomy for the individual by preparing him to participate in various groups." [73] Gouldner suggests that the more general diffusely oriented socialization which takes place in the nuclear family tends to produce an autonomous self which rejects total encapsulation in any one or even a series of roles; that such autonomy when exhibited in a refusal to behave in terms of normative role produces a sense of self-regard which is contrasted with the sense of self-esteem produced by normative role playing and its consequent social approval on the part of complementary others.

In parallel fashion, one might suggest that the general socialization structure of the informal group also makes possible, as noted above, a degree of autonomy and presumably a sense of self-regard in terms of the identity in question. Of course, this explication departs from Gouldner's in that the autonomy nurtured by the informal group of teachers or students is presumably that of teacher per se or adolescent peer-group member, involving still a basically universalistic orientation. While the exercise free of adult control made possible through adolescent peer-group membership may be functional for the development of a certain independence, it is still independence supported by the norms of a contrasting group. Though

Parsons hints that projection of dependency needs upon the peer group is a temporary affair for adolescents, he is not explicit with reference to the transition to general personal autonomy. Indeed, the rigorous uniformity enforced by such groups suggests that for the majority of members they may even be impediments to the development of the autonomous self projected by Gouldner. (Presumably they become Riesman's "other-directed" men.) It may be suggested that the school's participation in the construction of child and adolescent society has the effect of stratifying its client cohorts in such a way that only a minority (ultimately perhaps Cohen's boundary role players and decision makers) attain something approximating a sense of genuine personal autonomy.

AUTONOMY, SOCIOMETRIC STANDING, AND ACADEMIC ACHIEVEMENT–What is being further asserted here, and which will be discussed in greater detail in our later examination of the way in which ascribed (social-class) factors interact with the school's organizational and cultural structure, is that there is an interdependent relationship between a sense of independence or autonomy and cognitive competence, that the two "interact" with and reinforce each other, and that opportunities and experiences made differentially available to individuals in one realm will result in a parallel differentiation in the other. Such an asserted relationship is implicit in the following exposition which focuses on the relationship between sociometric standing on the one hand, which is assumed to be both cause and effect of a sense of personal autonomy or independence, and academic achievement on the other.

One of C. Wayne Gordon's adolescent respondents tells of the way in which the publicity of response in the formal classroom situation working on a pupil's self-respect articulates with peer-group development to affect position in the group,

> My first years in school I think were my happiest school years. . . . I made friends very easily and was quite a "big wheel." . . . In the third grade it started getting hard for me. When the teacher would call on me and I wouldn't know the answer, without taking a while to figure it out, the kids would tease me. It got so I dreaded to hear the teacher call my name. . . . I became more quiet and had very little to say in class. . . . The next few years were very much the same except my popularity standing started to slip. I gradually slid from the top popularity group into the middle popularity group.[74]

And Denise Kandel and Gerald Lesser note in their study of American and Danish adolescents:

Members of the leading crowd do in fact attain high levels of academic achievement. Furthermore, data on school performance show that ability and school performance of boys nominated three or more times for ["leading crowd"] are higher than those of their classmates.

Furthermore, at the same high levels of ability, leaders achieve at a higher level than nonleaders.[75]

There seem to be interactive effects between academic achievement and informal group position, as indicated by Glidewell and his associates, who report relationships between position in the informal classroom social structure on the one hand and mental health, utilization of intelligence, and measured academic achievement, on the other hand. There is a suggestion that teacher imputation of academic achievement, even when involving randomly chosen children, affects the students' own attributions of competence within the student group. Finally, these authors report that all the research of the last several years suggests a general tendency toward a hierarchical organization of status within the informal group of students.[76]

Other studies demonstrate a relationship between sociometric standing and academic performance. Gronlund's survey of elementary school studies found an association between school achievement and sociometric status.[77] Ryan and Davie found a similar association among high school students.[78] Schmuck found a relationship between cognized peer-association status and academic achievement of elementary school students.[79] Though Sarane Boocock, in summarizing such studies, suggests that the associations discovered may depend upon a value climate wherein academic work is valued, Parsons' suggestion that increasingly children and youth in all social classes are coming to value scholastic performance must be kept in mind. Whether or not the notion that education is the route to the good life is merely a myth (as Christopher Jencks and his colleagues have recently suggested),[80] it seems that it is an increasingly widely held belief and arguments put forward by such as Schelsky, Galbraith, and now Daniel Bell, who suggests that theoretical knowledge has replaced property as the axial stratification principle,[81] tend to justify its validity.

Kandel and Lesser present an interesting paradox associated with their research. While the adolescent school leaders they identified do better in school than nonleaders, these leaders value schoolwork less, placing other pursuits ahead of schoolwork. It is suggested that such a finding may be explained in terms of the adolescent's predisposition to identify good schoolwork in public school with obedience and conformity to adult dictates. Thus, while these leaders, as others, comprehend the importance of schoolwork and share this comprehension with their teachers and parents, nevertheless as leaders are constrained to convey overt depreciation of such activity as demeaning to their increasingly emancipated status.

EXTRACURRICULAR ACTIVITIES: AN AGENT OF DIFFERENTIATION– Important as academic performance may be, there may be an at least equally significant (and related) way in which schools affect the development and differentiation of adolescent society; that is, through the institution of what are called club programs and extracurricular activities, seemingly a universal phenomenon in American high schools.

That adolescent peer groups would exist without the institution of extracurricular activities is certain. However, it seems almost equally certain that these activities give added visibility to those who participate, indeed, allow a distinction to be made between those who do and do not participate, and in that the activities tend to be ranked with respect to prestige, affect the sociometric standing of participants and nonparticipants.

In a sense, then, extracurricular activities constitute a supplement to the school class as an ensurer of differentiation or stratification among students. Thus Kandel and Lesser found in their comparison of Danish and American adolescents that nearly one-half of the Danish high schoolers were unable to respond to a question concerning the existence of a "leading crowd" while in the corresponding American case less than 30 percent could not respond.[82] The authors then observe that among the American adolescents leading crowd members were much more likely to be members of school clubs than were nonleading crowd members. In the Danish high school, however, clubs and extracurricular activities were reported to be weak, almost nonexistent. Thus, Kandel and Lesser conclude that clubs and club membership facilitate the visibility of leading crowds and act as agents of differentiation.[83] It might be noted that James Coleman uncovered a similar phenomenon, finding in only one of the ten high schools he studied a relatively "democratic" adolescent social structure, where girls "were bound together in large, unbroken chains, more than in any other community." [84] This school exhibited a relative absence of clubs and extracurricular activities. As Coleman notes, "it was the only school in which a question about school clubs prompted queries about what was meant." [85]

The manner in which participation in school activities interacts with academic performance and informal social life to produce prestige-stratified structure has been explicated by Gordon in his study of a small midwestern high school. Gordon refers to "one general function which all [school] organizations served: to provide the members a means for defining their social status within the informal system of the school." [86] Gordon was able to adduce the prestige rank of fifty student organizations from basketball, football, national honor society, and cheerleading at the top to roller skating and knitting clubs at the bottom. Gordon notes that organizations whose memberships and positions were achieved through competition ranked high while purely voluntary organizations did not.[87] Gordon found also that the sheer quantity of organization membership was significant for student standing in the social structure. One of his respondents observed:

> A person's popularity is based somewhat on how many clubs, sports or committees you participate in. . . . On the whole, you become acquainted with many more people and teachers when you belong to a wide spread of clubs and activities.[88]

This comment refers to the significance of the acquaintance with teachers as a consequence of organization membership. Gordon notes that teachers behave toward students they get to know through sponsorship of clubs and activities differently from the way in which they behave toward nonparticipating students.

> Differential association [between teachers and students] resulted in diffuse, affectively toned relationships with some students, compared to specific affectively neutral relationships with non-participants. The result was for the teacher to particularize with those he knew well in the distribution of rewards and apply universalistic standards with greater affective neutrality in the distribution of rewards and punishments to least active, least known students.[89]

The implication is clear. Not only are participating (in activities) students afforded the opportunity of more particularistic, affective relationships with teachers (implying greater equality; noting Homans' observations on social distance and equality),[90] but these particularistic, affective relationships seem to result in attribution of better academic performance to these students, thus strengthening and validating the academic component of student prestige ranking. One may even hypothesize that those students who interact more frequently and informally with those status occupants (teachers) who are granted the most authority and autonomy in the basic school situation are likely themselves to feel a greater sense of autonomy. The entire formal structure of the school, then, both curricular and extracurricular, seems to operate to produce not only a stratification of competence, but also a stratification of personal autonomy.

Of course, peer-group leaders may have the opportunity to depart from the group's norms to a greater extent than do others. Homans has observed that while leaders are expected to exemplify the group's norms better than anyone else, they also, paradoxically, have the power to depart from these norms at much less cost to themselves. One of Gordon's female respondents said:

> One who is a leader can wear something out of the ordinary and "get by" with it because they are accepted and anything rather odd that they do has a chance of becoming the style.[91]

Perhaps leaders of adolescent groups stand the greatest chance of freeing themselves from slavish conformity to group norms and developing a genuine autonomous self.

It may be noted that it takes some degree of personal autonomy to enlist and persist in these student organizations. That is, unlike formal, academic organization where a student is compulsorily assigned to one class or another, extracurricular activities require a student's active voluntary enlistment; only the most autonomous may join one without some kind of "company," or social support from friends (and of course, those lowest in the social structure are likely to have the fewest friends—thus narrowing their disposition to join any specific activity—presuming one must find some commonality of interest in order to get a friend to join also). The more competitive activities seem to require even greater personal autonomy and perhaps social support, in order to persist in the face of competition.

Waller has correctly noted the competition involved in these informal activities.[92] It is suggested here that even the more recent youth-culture-related activities such as pottery making, weaving, and film making involve considerable competition, though the judges in this case may not always be formally appointed faculty sponsors, but the ubiquitous "jury of their peers" that David Riesman identified several years ago.[93] Informal observations in high schools suggest that such groups may be the most exclusive, most elitist of all, despite ideological protestations to the contrary.

The immediate attractions of extracurricular activities for students require little explication. The visibility, prominence, and status validation they give to members of the adolescent society have been noted. The belief that colleges weight rather heavily participation in such activities seems to be widely held among college-aspiring students. And no doubt some students are attracted to an activity because of a coincidence with their interests or "hobbies." But why do teachers sponsor and guide such activities? Of course, the belief, as noted by Waller, that such activities actually prepare one for life, that they help students develop habits of constructive use of leisure time, that they "give every student a chance to succeed at something," all the formal educational justifications that school administrators haul out for questioning board members may be cited by teachers also. But might there not be something more personal involved?

One suspects that American teachers are not oblivious to the common demeaning stereotype of their occupation held by most Americans and so incisively outlined by Waller as that of an "optical illusion," overconcerned with artificially inflated dignity, authority, rules, and petty rewards and punishments. Given this stereotype and a contrasting egalitarian ethic, which, as noted above, seems in many respects to characterize American culture, it is not surprising that Waller can also observe teacher attempts to escape from their stereotyped occupational role:

> . . . to break through the stereotype which shuts him off from others and to impress himself upon his fellows as a human being of note.[94]

Extracurricular activities, the opportunity to sponsor a dramatic society, a golf team, a film-making group, a folk-singing ensemble—in which students participate voluntarily, may indeed even be selected by the teacher (and excluded, if they misbehave)—may allow the teacher to categorize for his most significant audience, students (and, therefore, for himself), as something more than a teacher, as a genuine human being.

It may also be suggested that extracurricular-activity sponsorship by teachers constitutes an institutionalization on secondary school level of what has earlier been referred to as subordinate-subsystem interaction; an amelioration of, or a kind of role distance from, the normative authority or superordinate subsystem role. The more thorough segmentation of teacher personality that the more severely departmentalized high school exhibits (relative to the "self-contained" single-teacher classroom arrangement in elementary school) requires a more formally institutionalized arrangement in which students and teachers can meet and identify one another in a particularistic-diffuse-affective manner. Though, as noted above, such subordinate-subsystem interaction may involve primarily the more autonomous, leading-crowd types of students, it may be just these students whose opinions are most valued by the student body at large and whose general approval is most significant for legitimation of teacher authority. As such, it may be as close as teachers can come to approximating a kind of "charismatic," as contrasted with "traditional" or "bureaucratic" authority.[95]

With respect to the current drift of school organization, until recently Daniel Bell's "logic of size" seems to be involved.[96] Most definitive explication of this logic for the educational sphere seems to have been provided by James Conant in his *American High School Today*.[97] Conant recommended that high schools be made large enough to make economically available to students advanced placement courses in various academic areas, thoroughly equipped science laboratories, well-stocked libraries, and relatively esoteric subjects like calculus and Chinese language, opting strongly for consolidation of small high school districts. Indeed, this seems to be precisely what has been happening.

Of course, the consolidation of high schools in the interests of specialization and acceleration is consistent with, indeed is one facet of, the development of the technological society. However, it must be pointed out that with increased size of school goes a diminished distribution of student participation in extracurricular activities. Barker and Gump have reported that the number and variety of activities do not increase commensurate with an increase in school size (numbers of teachers and students). Nearly all small high school students in their study participated in ten or more extraclass settings and only a small proportion participated in an excessively large or small number of these settings. In the large high school, on the other hand, a relatively large proportion of students participated in ten or fewer extraclassroom settings and a small proportion participated in a great many settings. Small-school students performed more actively in the activities in which they participated than large-school students. Forty-two percent of large-school students took active roles (as contrasted with audience or passive roles) in extracurricular settings; while 80 percent of small-school students took active parts.[98] Barker and Gump report further,

> According to the reports of the students, "everyone" in the small school felt that he had a chance at the rewards provided by the settings and that the settings, and the other persons in them, needed his contribution.[99]

In contrast the large school had a sizable number of outsiders. In addition small-school students gave more response indicative of acceptance of responsibility than did large-school students.[100] Thus, it seems that the interests of hierarchy in the adolescent society are served by the combination of extracurricular activities, designed naively to involve *all* students in school activities, and increasing secondary school size.

Thus, while the conflict of contending informal groups of teachers and students in the school serves the immediate interests of maintenance of autonomy for their members as they maintain contrasting patterns of values in the interests of such autonomy as they manage their members' tension, the organization of activities as an integral socialization substructure, interacting with formal curricular structure and teacher attempts at the preservation of a "sacred" or whole personality, works to differentiate the age cohort of students with respect to social status and differentially socialize students to a sense of genuine personal autonomy and competence.

GUIDANCE COUNSELING: EDUCATIONAL DECISION MAKING–Guidance counseling as a discrete activity or "profession" has been described as an illustration of structural differentiation in contemporary society.[101] At one time, decisions concerning occupational and educational pursuits were intrafamily affairs. Today, however, the individual reaching the end of or even planning his secondary school career faces a multiplicity of occupational and educational choices. Certainly no family agent outside or within the school, no teacher or administrator, is in a position to comprehend the qualifications, requirements, and strategies involved in effecting satisfactory placements. The bill seems to have been filled by the guidance counselor, by now an almost universal phenomenon in the secondary schools and a growing one in the elementary schools. Data presented by Armor indicates that the number of full-time counselors quintupled between 1951 and 1965, grew by 150 percent between 1958 and 1965, when there were 30,000 full-time counselors in the United States.[102]

Despite official doctrine which would have counselors develop genuine agency behavior in students (each student the agent of his own education) largely through a Rogerian quasi-therapeutic approach, it seems that counselors remain essentially what Aaron Cicourel and John Kitsuse called them in their study of counseling, *The Educational Decision-Makers.*[103] What counselors do, it seems, is to act as agents of societal manpower allocation within the school system, institutionalizing and ensuring the selection function, which in elementary school was attributed by Parsons to the structure of the school class. As Cicourel and Kutsuse observe, counseling personnel are primarily responsible for the assignment of incoming high school freshmen to the categories of college-preparatory, general, and usually, commercial "tracks," each constituting a set of course offerings. This assignment, of course, represents the high school's "seal of approval" that Parsons suggests is placed upon the child's identity as a college-goer or noncollege-goer after it is achieved over the elementary school years.

The essential allocating function of counseling is revealed by David Armor, who presents data concerning counselor use of tests to determine not only the categorization of students as "underachievers" and "overachievers" but to deny students assignment to college-preparatory courses. Armor points out that while counselors are heard officially to deprecate educators' reliance on ability tests, privately these counselors rely very heavily upon these tests in making their allocations. Armor found in his Boston area study that counselors heavily preferred IQ or aptitude tests to other measures (grade average, achievement test scores, teacher recommendations) as representations of student intellectual ability.[104] Armor reports further that almost three-quarters of the counselors "believed" in a cut off point in IQ scores (about 110) below which a student would not be successful in college ability. Testing, it seems, is widely accepted by counselors as an educationally diagnostic tool, a way of categorizing and identifying clients.

Thus, the problem for the counselor in his educational counseling, which over the entire sample takes up at least one-half of counselor time, is one of getting students to make "realistic" decisions. Realistic decisions, it seems, are acceptances of counselor categorizations based on IQ test scores. This "realistic" decision making seems to be at the heart of "educational counseling." And the ability test tends to be used "not . . . as a means of raising a student's aspirations but rather as a means of lowering them if the aspirations seem too high compared to test scores and grades." [105] "Realistic" decision making on the part of counselees seems to have a "cooling-out" connotation for the counselors. As such, the counselor is indeed embracing an integrative role and performing an integrative function. The function seems to be performed immediately for the institution, in matching children of given ability and disposition to study with teachers assigned to specific courses. Educational "counseling" has to do with getting students to be "realistic" about their aspirations and abilities; it is functional both for the school, where presumably disgruntled students, believing they have been prevented unjustly from implementing their aspirations, may cause "trouble," and for society in that such students' scaling down of aspiration presumably is a more or less permanent affair—in a self-fulfilling kind of way.

STUDENT PROBLEMS AND THE COUNSELOR AS THERAPIST–Armor finds support[106] for the Cicourel and Kitsuse suggestion that the recently discovered phenomena of underachievement and overachievement are artifacts of routine counselor operations—comparing ability test scores to school grades. It is pointed out that when an ability test score is high relative to grades, there are several possible explanations among which may be a suggestion that the ability test is not valid or that the instructional program is not well adapted to the development of the ability in question. However, counselors tend to conclude that both test and curriculum are valid and that the child is an "underachiever," a problem student whose problems are likely to be seen as a deep-seated sort and amenable only to quasi-psychiatric approaches. Thus the routinization of counseling operations—the routine comparison of students' test scores and grades—produces a technology based on measured ability and measured performance which systematically identifies students who must be "cooled-out" of high aspirations and make "realistic" plans instead, and identifies personality problems upon which counselors may work and use to maximize their self-images as therapists—having selected psychiatry as that reference profession most conducive to the enhancement of professional status.[107]

THE STUDENTS' RESPONSE TO COUNSELING–The routinization of educational counseling and its major concern with a "realistic" match between student IQ and aspiration and the consequences for student categorization are perhaps perceived and resisted by students—to the point of neutralizing somewhat the potential effect of counseling in the very area counselors seem to hold most dear—personal counseling. Armor points out that when students were asked whom they considered the most important sources of advice on future plans (an area lying squarely in the middle of the counselor's bailiwick), very few selected counselors. Among middle class students none selected counselors as either a first or second choice, preferring family, teachers, friends, or "other." Urban working classes selected counselors (11 percent named counselors as a first choice) behind family (68 percent named family as first choice) and teachers (14 percent) as the most important source of advice on future plans.[108]

Such evidence seems further to confirm the counselor's basic function as that of allocation and integration (of "adjustment" rather than construction of motivation) and not that of "therapy." Essentially, counselors seem to be specialists in integration, matching students to curricular tracks in terms of tested ability and for the student himself, aspirations to the same tested ability. It is in this regard that counselor operations are consistent with the technological society. Jacques Ellul has pointed out that the essence of technique and the technological phenomenon is its quest for the most efficient method, the "one best means," the technical means.[109] A man as a role player, as an instrument of the socioeconomic system, may then be conceived of as destined for one best slot or occupational role in the technological society. Such a mission for guidance counseling was outlined in 1925 by Arthur Payne.

> . . . within limits there is one best person for every job. Each person is better adapted for work in some one vocational field than in some other. It is the function of guidance to discover and bring together the right person to the right life activities.[110]

The Social System of the School and the Ascribed Status of Its Clients

The social system of the school has been described in terms of three of its basic substructures: (1) the classroom, where the basic formal functions of the school, the socialization of cognitive and social competence, are met; (2) the informal peer group where personalities and values are supported through solidarity, tension-management, and resonance; and (3) the counseling program, where students are allocated to various strata of academic activity.[111] The element of stratification has been present in each case. It has been noted with respect to classroom activity that the four basic features of the class, in addition to ensuring an emphasis on universalism, specificity, independence, and achievement, also ensure the differentiation of the age cohort of students in terms of formal achievement. It has been observed that student peer groups, functioning to reflect and produce a sense of autonomy for students, seem to effect a stratification of informal rank related to the stratification of achievement, whose source tends to be classroom activity. And counseling programs, in an attempt to allow students to realize their potential through accurate placement in terms of curricula of varying rigor, act as informal agents of manpower allocation, sorting students into "tracks" whose varying termini constitute the reconstruction of contemporary social class structure. The question arises, however, as to what extent the school merely re-creates a stratification complex for each generation of students or to what extent it assists in perpetuating the social-class position of families within the class structure, assigning a family's children ultimately to the same social class.

ASCRIBED STATUS AND ACADEMIC ACHIEVEMENT–Basically the position taken here is supportive of the Coleman Report conclusion that the most important determinant of children's success in school is what the children bring with them from home; what comes out of schools is basically, in terms of differentials among students, related to what goes in.[112] "What goes in," of course, is strongly related to social class.

Cognitively, the association between intelligence or IQ and academic achievement is well known.[113] Almost as well known is the relation between conventionally measured intelligence (IQ) and social class. As Boocock observes, "The relationship between I.Q. and socioeconomic status is a worldwide phenomenon documented by an extensive crosscultural literature." [114] To what extent these social-class differences are genetically determined is an issue not yet resolved. Certainly, if the skills inventoried by Martin Deutsch are related to the development of cognitive ability as measured by IQ tests, a case can be made for environmental determination, for surely the development of these skills, which are related to stimulus enrichment or deprivation, is related to socioeconomic deprivation and social class.[115] In this case, however, we prefer to focus on affective or attitudinal variables as they are differentially exhibited in the school's socialization process. What might be considered here is the relationship between these "affective" variables on the one hand and the cognitive variables presumably involved in school success on the other. Lawrence Kohlberg sums up the position.

> "Affective" development and functioning, and "cognitive" development and functioning are not distinct realms. "Affective" and "cognitive" development are parallel.[116]

To take one affective variable that we have focused on strongly, self-direction, we may note the suggestion of M. Brewster Smith that the development of self-direction is related to the variety of relatively ordered personal and non-personal stimuli in the infant's environment. The absence of variety and change, suggests Smith, constitutes the absence of intrinsic motivation "which in the short run means apathy and in the long run should lead to retardation." [117] Smith suggests that the instigation of the infant's actions is based upon a discrepancy from an accustomed set of perceptions and experiences. "He acts to reestablish sights and happenings to which he has become emotionally attached during the process of increasing familiarization." [118] Smith then relates this initial impetus to intrinsic motivation or self-direction to a sense of discrete self and to generalized orientations of competence and achievement. Thus, stimulus enrichment, a variety of familiar stimuli which for Deutsch is related directly to intelligence is for Smith indirectly related to competence and achievement through its effect on a sense of intrinsic motivation and a sense of self. Stimulus enrichment and deprivation, of course, seem closely related to social class.[119]

Parsons has said "the most important single predispositional factor with which the child enters the school is his level of independence. By this is meant his level of self-sufficiency relative to guidance by adults, his capacity to take responsibility and to make his own decisions in coping with new and varying situations." [120] Independence in approaching school tasks is one of the norms that Dreeben suggests the structure of the school class is set up to teach. Those who have been socialized to independence in the home then presumably have a kind of "head start" over those who have not; a head start whose manifestation in school presumably affects success in academic activity as well as student social life.

In several studies, Melvin Kohn has found a relationship between child rearing for self-direction (rather than obedience) and social class. Kohn attributes this relationship to the occupational activities of the parents—primarily the father—suggesting that people who are expected to perform autonomously on the job come to value autonomy as a human trait and rear their children accordingly.[121] Self-direction, it is suggested here, is a more necessary requisite for scholastic success than obedience. Docility and obedience, it seems, have been overemphasized as personality traits necessary for school success; certainly there is a strain toward docility and obedience as a reciprocal function of the teacher's autocratic role and the school's peculiar value structure, as Waller has so aptly pointed out; however, the sustenance of effort, even in rather rigorously assigned schoolwork, requires a measure of self-direction; particularly since as the child goes through school, an increasing amount of such work must be done at home, without benefit of teacher supervision. As the child continues up the grades assignments seem to become increasingly open ended, taking on the "report" or "project" character and further requiring autonomy and self-directed effort. The capstone, or course, is the doctoral dissertation, which judging by the number of doctoral candidates who founder at this stage, requires more than ordinary self-directed effort.

The fact that there is a relationship between scholastic success and social class,[122] just as there is between social class and child rearing for self-direction, suggests a relationship between scholastic success and self-direction. Indeed, there may be a reciprocal effect between the latter two phenomena. A record of academic success may render the student less susceptible to teacher influence and constraint and thus more autonomous and self-directive. Wallace reports high-academic-ranking freshman college students considerably less subject to teacher influence than low-ranking students.[123] In addition, we have the finding by Kandel and Lesser that both Danish and American adolescent leaders report high academic achievement and at the same time a reduced valuation of the student role.[124] A similar pattern was found by Coleman. The conventional student role, of course, involves more of obedience than autonomy. Paradoxically, for a student to be thoroughly socialized to the norms of universalism, specificity, independence, and achievement is to be released at some point from the student role, to be emancipated not only from familial adult direction but from schoolteacher direction as well. The relationship to student peers, however, must be kept in mind, for as noted above, it seems strongly related to, reflecting and affecting, the sense of autonomy which is also facilitated by (and facilitates) academic success.

Boocock reports several studies relating children's independence positively to school achievement;[125] she reports also Elder's study which found a negative relationship between parental dominance (presumably the antithesis of child rearing for self-direction) and educational attainment.[126] Boocock's demurrer, that independence may be related to achievement only in some societies and under certain conditions, tends in terms of the evidence presented to suggest that contemporary American society may constitute such a case. Perhaps it is through its participation in the development of achievement motivation that independence training makes its contribution to achievement;[127] but it seems reasonable nevertheless to suggest that it operates independently to affect disposition to join in aspects of school social life, approach school personnel, and the like.

Samuel Bowles enunciated a point similar to that made here when he noted that the contribution of schooling to ultimate social-class position can be explained not by the effect of schooling on cognitive skills per se, but by the personality characteristics of those who go further in school. The point of departure between the two positions, however, is represented in Bowles' citation of Herbert Gintis' work in support.[128] Gintis argues that schooling develops in its subjects (its most successful subjects) a sense of subordinacy, discipline (punctuality and quiescence), and "cathection of external reward," all, says Gintis, traits necessary for success in occupational enterprise in American society today.[129] The position taken here, however, is that while punctuality, quiescence, and subordinacy are requisites for occupational success in some areas of American enterprise, they are by no means requisites for success in all areas.

Indeed, it seems that the number of positions requiring independent judgment, autonomy, and flexibility are increasing. These are the positions referred to in census data as professional and technical, and managers and officials, which have increased from 1900 to 1968 from 10 percent of the labor force to 24 percent and which are expected to continue to increase over the next several years, at the expense largely of unskilled and semiskilled labor.[130] These are the same positions whose occupants, says Melvin Kohn, tend to value self-direction rather than obedience, tolerance rather than intolerance of conformity, trustfulness rather than suspicion, change rather than the status quo.[131]

C. Wright Mills has observed that there are "two Harvards," the

Harvard of the exclusive East Coast boarding school graduate and the Harvard of the public high school graduate, and that it matters mightily in terms of personal future which of the two Harvards one goes to.[132] The reason that researchers such as Christopher Jencks have found diminished relationship between occupational position and educational attainment may lie in the neglect of the "two Harvards" phenomenon;[133] for there are not only two Harvards, there are two (or more) Podunk High Schools and it matters just as mightily which Podunk High School one goes to. Which Podunk High School one goes to will depend on which Podunk High School one perceives and experiences, with which associates and in what position vis-à-vis those associates one approaches and experiences the school, how well one does in school, and so on. It is suggested here that social-class position of family of orientation strongly affects the student's "approach" to school, his initial and continuing definition of the high school situation and related experiences, and whatever self-fulfilling prophecy is consequently constructed for him by teachers and classmates.

ASCRIBED STATUS AND SOCIOMETRIC POSITION–The effect of social-class position on informal peer-group status seems evident, whether it is perceived to work directly, indirectly (through variations in academic achievement which, as noted above, seem to be related to peer group status), or as hypothesized here, to be a function of reciprocal relationship between formal and informal status in the school. From Hollingshead's careful demonstration that social class strongly affected participation in dating, clique membership, and extracurricular activities[134] to the finding of Kandel and Lesser that "leaders come from the more privileged social-class groups," [135] most research studies report a relationship between social class and informal social position of students.[136]

As noted earlier, Gordon's data suggest that students' informal social position even influences teacher grading habits, perhaps an illustration of what Merton calls the "Matthew effect": "To him who hath shall be given, from him who hath not shall be taken, even that which he hath" [137] (particularly in view of the well-known tendency of teachers to "curve" grades). Such a benevolent cycle (for those initially identified as leaders, who tend to be also the socially advantaged) must lead to the further hierarchization of the student social structure, in view of the tendency of academic performance in turn to react favorably upon informal status. It should not then be surprising (as it seems to have been to Hollingshead, the discoverer) that lower-class students, while complaining of the elite's monopolization of student government offices, nevertheless themselves vote for upper-class students in student government elections.[138]

ASCRIBED STATUS AND COUNSELING–Cicourel and Kitsuse have investigated the relationship between the social-class position of students and students' involvement in counseling operations. They correctly focus on the allocative responsibilities of counselors, for, as Armor seems to have demonstrated, students apparently do not perceive counselors as sources of effective personal guidance—even in the area of educational plans. Cicourel and Kitsuse note first the tendency for counselor effectiveness to be measured in terms of the number and quality of college placements among fourth-year high school students. They suggest that such a criterion elicits a strain on the part of counselors toward concentration on the more socioeconomically advantaged students, who besides being more likely to have a college education financed (thus being a better "bet" for counselor efforts) also exhibit a family orientation more pressing for college; such a press is frequently imposed on counselors directly, but also acts indirectly through its effect on students' college aspirations.[139]

Beyond such global and unfortunately empirically unsupported assertions, Cicourel and Kitsuse assess the effect of students' social class on counselor assignment of college-preparatory courses. While they find a certain association between social class and such assignment, they also find an association between "social type" (a translation of social class as it operates in the adolescent status structure) and informal counselor achievement-type designations of students (the designations presumably affecting strongly the counselor's allocative decision making). This suggests a tendency for counselors to be influenced by students' position in the student social structure.[140] Also noted was the influence of social class directly on counselor achievement-type classification; all but one student classified as "excellent" by the counselor had also been named as being in the highest social class.[141]

It should be noted that counselors reliance on ability and aptitude tests in educational counseling and placements, in view of the strong demonstrated association of social class and IQ, seems by implication to constitute a social-class bias in counseling operations. The consequent detrimental effect of tracking and streaming on student motivation and achievement of those placed in noncollege tracks, a "labeling" effect that amounts to a kind of self-fulfilling prophecy, demonstrates the significance of ability tests as a placement criterion for the perpetuation of social-class position.[142] A recent study has demonstrated that noncollege-track students tend to improve their scholastic averages (over their high school career) much less than college-track students, that noncollege students drop out of school at a much greater rate (36 percent for noncollege, 4 percent for college), that track position is related strongly to participation in extracurricular activities (only 21 percent of college-track students were nonparticipants compared to 58 percent of noncollege-track students) and that track position was strongly related to delinquency, both in and out of school. The same study found a strong relationship between social class and track placement, but the detrimental effects of track placement were still strong, even when IQ, social class, and previous performance were controlled.[143]

A sense of self-direction or autonomy which seems to be related to social class, as noted above, may in turn be related to the disposition to make use of the counselor. For a student to interrupt his daily schedule (considering the bureaucratic entanglements such interruption implies; in most schools the schedule is a "sacred" item) to approach and make an appointment with a counselor and then to press his case upon the counselor seems to require a degree of personal self-direction which constitutes one aspect of dealing with a bureaucracy, an inclination which working and lower classes have not been famous for. Thus to discuss educational plans; to request a change in classes to a different track or a more appealing or "better" teacher (students seem not to be bad judges of teaching ability; they are the only firsthand observers we have that are in continuous contact with teaching performances); to inquire about a trip, club, or activity; to inquire about or protest a teacher grade—all common guidance-counselor-referral items—requires some sense of initiative, of self-direction.

It is suggested here that the "benevolent cycle" noted earlier makes such a disposition available only to some and that these some tend to be initially advantaged by superior social position. Thus, Boocock reports studies demonstrating that students from middle- and upper-class families, students in college-prep tracks, and students highly engaged in extracurricular activities are more likely to discuss future educational plans with counselors; very few lower-class students are reported as seeing counselors for these purposes.[144]

Summary

The social system of the school operates to socialize children to norms of universalism, specificity, achievement, and independence. These are functional necessities, it seems, in an increasingly structurally differentiated, technologically upgraded society. The school system interacts with children's ascriptive identities, through curricular and extracurricular activities, to maintain a class order and patterns of inequality of life chances. As such, this chapter has treated school largely as a reflection and an agent of convergent forces, whose consequences are structural differentiation and adaptive upgrading. In chapter 8, dealing with school administration, the fourth structural unit of the school's social system will be filled in and the manner in which convergent forces manifest themselves in administrative operations will be identified.

NOTES

1. Talcott Parsons, "Youth in the Context of American Society," *Daedalus* 91, no. 1 (Winter 1962): 103–5.

2. Ruth Benedict, "Continuities and Discontinuities in Cultural Conditioning," in *Personality in Nature, Society, and Culture*, ed. C. Kluckholn, H. A. Murray, and D. M. Schneider (New York: Alfred A. Knopf, 1953), pp. 522–31.

3. Philippe Aries, *Centuries of Childhood* (New York: Vintage Books, 1965), pp. 392–93.

4. John Kenneth Galbraith, *The New Industrial State* (New York: Signet Books, 1965), p. 254.

5. Yehudi A. Cohen, "Schools and Civilizational States," in *The Social Sciences and The Comparative Study of Educational Systems*, ed. Joseph Fischer (Scranton, Pa.: International Textbook Company, 1970), pp. 94–95.

6. H. Schelsky, "Family and School in Modern Society," in *Education, Economy, and Society*, ed. A. H. Halsey, J. Floud, and C. A. Anderson (New York: Free Press of Glencoe, 1961), p. 416.

7. Ibid., p. 417.

8. Aries, *Centuries of Childhood*, p. 406.

9. Eliot D. Chapple, with the collaboration of Conrad M. Arensberg, "Measuring Human Relations," *Genetic Psychology Monographs* 22, no. 1 (1940).

10. Talcott Parsons, "The School Class as a Social System: Some of its Functions in American Society," in Halsey, Floud, and Anderson, *Education, Economy and Society*, pp. 434–55.

11. Ibid., p. 436.

12. Of course, for some students concerning whose "track" placement uncertainty exists, the decision will be considered tentative and subject to review and revision in the light of subsequent student performance, but these students seem few in number; one either takes college preparatory math or he doesn't and the tentative placement, one suspects, tends to become a self-fulfilling prophecy much like the initial reading-group placement in first grade.

13. Willard Waller, *The Sociology of Teaching* (New York: John Wiley, 1965), pp. 15–32.

14. Parsons, "The School Class as a Social System," pp. 437–38.

15. Ralph H. Turner, "Modes of Social Ascent Through Education: Sponsored and Contest Mobility," in Halsey, Floud, and Anderson, *Education, Economy, and Society*, pp. 121–39.

16. George C. Homans, *Social Behavior: Its Elementary Forms* (New York: Harcourt, Brace, 1961), p. 75.

17. John R. Seeley, R. Alexander Sim, and Elizabeth W. Loosley, *Crestwood*

Heights: A Study of the Culture of Suburban Life (New York: Basic Books, 1956), pp. 279–80.

18. Robert Dreeben, *On What is Learned in School* (Reading, Mass.: Addison-Wesley, 1968).

19. Ibid., pp. 63–90.

20. Ibid., p. 38.

21. Jules Henry, *Culture Against Man* (New York: Vintage Books, 1965), pp. 302–5.

22. Philip Jackson, *Life in Classrooms* (New York: Holt, Rinehart, & Winston, 1968), chap. 1.

23. Margaret Mead, *And Keep Your Powder Dry* (New York: William Morrow, 1965), pp. 86–88.

24. Matthew Miles, "Some Properties of Schools as Social Systems," in *Social and Cultural Foundations of Guidance*, ed. E. M. Lloyd-Jones and N. Rosenau (New York: Holt, Rinehart, & Winston, 1968), p. 132.

25. The orchestral analogy is given visual form in Frederick Wiseman's film, *High School*, in which the camera moves first to a shot of two student percussionists awaiting the orchestra director's cue to hit their drums and then to classroom after classroom, in which are seen students similarly awaiting a teacher's cue to participate.

26. Raymond S. Adams and Bruce J. Biddle, *Realities of Teaching: Explorations with Videotape* (New York: Holt, Rinehart, & Winston, 1970).

27. Ibid., p. 37.

28. Ibid., pp. 39–40.

29. Ibid., pp. 49–51.

30. Talcott Parsons and Robert Bales, *Family, Socialization, and Interaction Process* (New York: Free Press, 1955), pp. 58–59.

31. Waller, *The Sociology of Teaching*, p. 69.

32. Chester Barnard, *The Functions of the Executive* (Cambridge, Mass.: Harvard University Press, 1938), p. 167.

33. Waller, *The Sociology of Teaching*, pp. 193–94.

34. Jackson, *Life in Classrooms*, p. 30.

35. Waller, *The Sociology of Teaching*, pp. 385–86.

36. Bryan R. Wilson, "The Teacher's Role: A Sociological Analysis," *British Journal of Sociology* 13, no. 1 (March 1962): 25.

37. Robert Dreeben, *The Nature of Teaching: Schools and the Work of Teachers* (Glenview, Ill.: Scott, Foresman, 1970), pp. 98–99.

38. Gertrude McPherson, *Small Town Teacher* (Cambridge, Mass.: Harvard University Press, 1972), p. 172.

39. Ibid., p. 34.

40. F. Musgrove and P. H. Taylor, "Pupils' Expectations of Teachers," in *Social Psychology of Teaching*, ed. A. Morrison and D. McIntyre (Harmondsworth, Middlesex, England: Penguin Books, 1972), p. 172.

41. D. S. Wright, "A Comparative Study of the Adolescent's Concepts of His Parents and Teachers," *Education Review* 14 (1962), as quoted in Musgrove and Taylor, "Pupils' Expectations of Teachers," p. 174.

42. Musgrove and Taylor, "Pupils' Expectations of Teachers," p. 178.

43. Mary E. Bredemeier, "Teacher-Student Transactions and Student

Growth" (Ph.D. dissertation, New Brunswick: Graduate School of Education, Rutgers University, 1973), pp. 200–201.

44. Waller, *The Sociology of Teaching*, pp. 68–69.

45. Ibid., p. 69.

46. Gresham Sykes, "The P.T.A. and Parent-Teacher Conflict," *Harvard Educational Review* 23, no. 2 (Spring 1953): 86–92.

47. Waller, *The Sociology of Teaching*, p. 196.

48. Ibid., p. 110.

49. Ibid.

50. Ibid., p. 111. The writer, a former principal, was amazed to learn from a former student, years after leaving the principalship, of the implicitly believed stories (among students) of the times when students had locked him in the school vault!

51. S. N. Eisenstadt, *From Generation to Generation* (New York: Free Press, 1956), p. 165.

52. Ibid., p. 166.

53. Parsons, "Youth in the Context of American Society," pp. 106–12.

54. Waller, *The Sociology of Teaching*, p. 314. A strain toward egalitarian relationships in American society has recently been noted by Robin Williams, *American Society: A Sociological Interpretation* (New York: Alfred A. Knopf, 1970), pp. 472–79.; Herbert Gans, "The Equality Revolution," in *The Impact of Social Class*, ed. Paul Blumberg (New York: Thomas Y. Crowell, 1972), pp. 100–110, and Talcott Parsons, "Equality and Inequality in Modern Society, or Social Stratification Revisited," in *Social Stratification: Research and Theory for the 1970's*, ed. Edward O. Laumann (Indianapolis: Bobbs-Merrill, 1970), pp. 13–72.

55. Parsons, "Youth in the Context of American Society," p. 112.

56. Ibid., p. 115.

57. David Matza, "Position and Behavior Patterns of Youth," in *Handbook of Modern Sociology*, ed. Robert E. L. Faris (Chicago: Rand McNally, 1964), pp. 193–96.

58. Jerry Farber, *The Student as Nigger* (North Hollywood, Calif.: Contact Books, 1969).

59. Alvin W. Gouldner, *The Coming Crisis of Western Sociology* (New York: Basic Books, 1970), pp. 215–18.

60. Howard Becker and Blanche Geer, "Student Culture in Medical School," *Harvard Educational Review* 28, no. 1 (Winter 1958): 70–80.

61. Gouldner, *The Coming Crisis of Western Sociology*, pp. 232–33.

62. Fred E. Katz, "The School as a Complex Social Organization," *Harvard Educational Review* 34, no. 3 (Summer 1964): 428–55.

63. Waller, *The Sociology of Teaching*, p. 57.

64. W. C. Bagley, *Classroom Management* (New York: Macmillan, 1908), quoted in Waller, *The Sociology of Teaching*, p. 432.

65. Ibid., p. 307.

66. McPherson, *Small Town Teacher*, p. 81.

67. Ibid., p. 72.

68. Ibid., p. 73.

69. Laurence Iannacone, "An Approach to the Informal Organization of the School," in *Behavioral Science and Educational Administration*, ed. Daniel E. Griffiths (Chicago: National Society for the Study of Education, 1964), pp. 226–31.

70. Eliot D. Chapple and Leonard R. Sayles, *The Measure of Management* (New York: Macmillan, 1961), pp. 83–85.

71. McPherson, *Small Town Teacher*, pp. 73–4.

72. Gouldner, *The Coming Crisis of Western Sociology*, p. 221.

73. Ibid., p. 219.

74. C. Wayne Gordon, *The Social System of the High School* (New York: Free Press, 1957), p. 114.

75. Denise B. Kandel and Gerald S. Lesser, *Youth in Two Worlds* (San Francisco: Jossey-Bass, 1972), pp. 33–34.

76. John C. Glidewell, Mildred B. Kantor, Louis M. Smith, and Lorene A. Stringer, "Socialization and Social Structure in the Classroom," in *Review of Child Development Research*, ed. Martin L. Hoffman (New York: Russell Sage Foundation, 1964), pp. 227–46.

77. Norman E. Gronlund, *Sociometry in the Classroom* (New York: Harper & Brothers, 1959).

78. F. J. Ryan and James S. Davie, "Social Acceptance, Academic Achievement and Aptitude among High School Students," *Journal of Educational Research* 52 (November 1958): 101–6.

79. Richard A. Schmuck, "Some Relationships of Peer Liking Patterns in The Classroom to Pupil Attitudes and Achievement," in *Learning in Social Settings*, ed. M. B. Miles and W. W. Charters, Jr. (Boston: Allyn & Bacon, 1970), pp. 151–68.

80. Christopher Jencks, Marshall Smith, Henry Acland, Mary Jo Bane, David Cohen, Herbert Gintis, Barbara Heyns, and Stephan Michelson, *Inequality: A Reassessment of The Effect of Family and Schooling in America* (New York: Basic Books, 1972).

81. Daniel Bell, *The Coming of Post-Industrial Society* (New York: Basic Books, 1973), pp. 18–20.

82. Kandel and Lesser, *Youth in Two Worlds*, pp. 22–24.

83. Ibid., p. 38.

84. James S. Coleman, *The Adolescent Society: The Social Life of the Teenager and its Impact on Education* (New York: Free Press, 1961), p. 216.

85. Ibid., pp. 211–12.

86. Gordon, *The Social System of the High School*, p. 54.

87. Ibid., pp. 59–61.

88. Ibid., p. 64.

89. Ibid., pp. 47–48.

90. Homans, *Social Behavior*, pp. 323–27.

91. Gordon, *The Social System of the High School*, p. 115.

92. Waller, *The Sociology of Teaching*, p. 112.

93. David Riesman, with Reuel Denney and Nathan Glazer, *The Lonely Crowd* (New Haven, Conn.: Yale University Press, 1950).

94. Waller, *The Sociology of Teaching*, p. 421.

95. Here we are citing Weber's typology of authority, *Max Weber: The Theory of Social and Economic Organization*, ed. Talcott Parsons (New York: Free Press, 1947), pp. 324–62. In this regard Amitai Etzioni has suggested that normative organizations like the school commonly require some variant of charismatic authority, but that the teacher's position is such that typical charisma is denied him. Amitai

Etzioni, *A Comparative Analysis of Complex Organizations* (New York: Free Press, 1961), pp. 211–13, 220.

96. Daniel Bell, *The End of Ideology* (New York: Collier Books, 1961), pp. 230–31.

97. James B. Conant, *The American High School Today* (New York: McGraw-Hill, 1959).

98. Roger G. Barker, Paul V. Gump, Wallace V. Friesen, Edwin P. Willems, "The Ecological Environment: Student Participation in Non-Class Settings," in Miles and Charters, *Learning in Social Settings*, pp. 25–30.

99. Ibid., pp. 35–36.

100. Ibid., p. 36.

101. David J. Armor, *The American School Counselor* (New York: Russell Sage Foundation, 1969), p. 44.

102. Ibid., pp. 33–37.

103. Aaron V. Cicourel and John I. Kitsuse, *The Educational Decision-Makers* (Indianapolis: Bobbs-Merrill, 1963).

104. Armor, *The American School Counselor*, pp. 76–80.

105. Ibid., p. 67.

106. Ibid., p. 90.

107. Cicourel and Kitsuse, *The Educational Decision-Makers*, pp. 81–82.

108. Armor, *The American School Counselor*, p. 122.

109. Jacques Ellul, *The Technological Society* (New York: Alfred A. Knopf, 1967).

110. Arthur F. Payne, *Organization of Vocational Guidance* (New York: McGraw-Hill, 1925), quoted in Armor, *The American School Counselor*, p. 38.

111. These three substructures plus a fourth, the administrative, which shall be examined in the following chapter, seem to correspond roughly to Parsons' four primary subsystems of a social system, the adaptive (classroom), the pattern-maintenance and tension-management (informal peer groups), the integrative (counseling), and the goal-attainment (administrative). Though no attempt at it is made in this case, it seems that exchanges of the sort Parsons has outlined may be traced between the substructures in the school situation. See Parsons, "Equality and Inequality in Modern Society," pp. 56–59, for a recent illustration.

112. James S. Coleman, Ernest Q. Campbell, et al., *Equality of Educational Opportunity* (Washington, D.C.: U.S. Government Printing Office, 1966).

113. Sarane Spence Boocock, *An Introduction to the Sociology of Learning* (Boston: Houghton Mifflin, 1972), p. 98.

114. Ibid., p. 100.

115. Deutsch lists the skill handicaps of the lower class child including "poor auditory discrimination, insufficient experience with correction of enunciation, pronunciation, and grammar, less developed memory function." Martin Deutsch, "The Disadvantaged Child and the Learning Process," in *Education in Depressed Areas*, ed. A. Harry Passow (New York: Bureau of Publications, Teachers College, Columbia University, 1963), pp. 163–79.

116. Lawrence Kohlberg, "Stage and Sequence: The Cognitive-Developmental Approach to Socialization," in *Handbook of Socialization Theory and Research*, ed. David A. Goslin (Chicago: Rand McNally, 1969), p. 349.

117. M. Brewster Smith, "Competence and Socialization," in *Socialization and Society*, ed. John A. Clausen (Boston: Little, Brown, 1968), p. 295.

118. Ibid.

119. Deutsch, "The Disadvantaged Child and The Learning Process."

120. Parsons, "The School Class as a Social System," p. 437.

121. Melvin L. Kohn and Carmi Schooler, "Class, Occupation, and Orientation," *American Sociological Review* 34, no. 5 (October 1969): 659–78; Melvin L. Kohn, *Class and Conformity: A Study in Values* (Homewood, Ill.: Dorsey Press, 1969).

122. Bernard Goldstein, *Low-Income Youth in Urban Areas* (New York: Holt, Rinehart & Winston, 1967), pp. 31–34.

123. Walter L. Wallace, *Student Culture* (Chicago: Aldine, 1966), p. 80.

124. Kandel and Lesser, *Youth in Two Worlds*, pp. 38–39.

125. Boocock, *An Introduction to the Sociology of Learning*, p. 73.

126. Glen H. Elder, "Family Structure and Educational Attainment," *American Sociological Review* 30 (1965): 81–96, cited in Boocock, *An Introduction to the Sociology of Learning*, p. 296.

127. Bernard C. Rosen, "Family Structure and Achievement Motivation," in *Social Stratification in the United States*, ed. Jack L. Roach, Llewelyn Gross, and Orville R. Gursslin (Englewood Cliffs, N.J.: Prentice-Hall, 1969), pp. 537–52.

128. Samuel Bowles, "Unequal Education and the Reproduction of the Social Divison of Labor," in *Schooling in a Corporate Society*, ed. Martin Carnoy (New York: David McKay, 1972), p. 59.

129. Herbert Gintis, "Education, Technology, and the Characteristics of Worker Productivity," *American Economic Association Proceedings* 61, no. 2 (May 1971): 266–79.

130. Bell, *The Coming of Post-Industrial Society*, pp. 134–35.

131. Kohn and Schooler, "Class, Occupation, and Orientation," pp. 666–67.

132. C. Wright Mills, *The Power Elite* (New York: Oxford University Press, 1956), pp. 57–70.

133. Jencks, *Inequality*, pp. 180–90, 220–24.

134. August B. Hollingshead, *Elmtown's Youth* (New York: John Wiley, 1949).

135. Kandel and Lesser, *Youth in Two Worlds*, p. 39.

136. Goldstein reports several studies supporting the proposition that social status of students affects sociometric position. Goldstein, *Low Income Youth in Urban Areas*, p. 46.

137. Robert Merton, "The Matthew Effect in Science," *Science* 159, no. 3810 (January 1968): 56–63.

138. Hollingshead, *Elmtown's Youth*, p. 201.

139. Cicourel and Kitsuse, *The Educational Decision-Makers*, pp. 144–45.

140. Ibid., pp. 70–73.

141. Ibid., p. 70. Unfortunately, the authors did not attempt to relate social class or social type directly to college or noncollege placement, thus not allowing any test of the hypothesis that student social position affects formal counselor decision making.

142. Informal observations in schools lead the author to suggest that teachers like ability grouping because they feel less constraint with higher-ability groups. Teachers report that with these groups they can "let their hair down" somewhat, that is, step out of conventional teacher role, and that these students will not "take advantage" the way the other groups do. Such a relationship between teacher and

students, less hierarchical, warmer and more personal, it is suggested, is productive of a sense of autonomy for students. (Kandel and Lesser observe that adolescents who exhibit the greatest autonomy are also those who have the warmest, most intimate relationships with parents.)

143. W. E. Schafer, C. Olexa, and K. Polk, "Programmed for Social Class: Tracking in High School," in *Sociology Full Circle: Contemporary Readings on Society* (New York: Praeger, 1972), pp. 145–50. See also D. Hargreaves, *Social Relations in a Secondary School* (London: Routledge & Kegan Paul, 1967).

144. Boocock, *An Introduction to the Sociology of Learning*, p. 184.

7

ADOLESCENT CULTURE:
REFLECTIONS OF DIVERGENCE*

Elise Boulding

An examination of literature about a phenomenon variously labeled youth culture, the counterculture, or the adolescent society highlights three interesting facts: (1) there is no agreement that such a thing exists; (2) if it exists, there is no agreement on what the phenomenon is; and (3) only adults write about it. No representatives of the adolescent society (if it exists) participate in this all-adult debate.

Is there a youth culture? If there is, it would have to be grouped conceptually with subcultures in general. A recent study of the sociology of subcultures quotes this definition of a subculture: "a set of conduct norms which cluster together in such a way that they can be differentiated from the broader culture of which they are a part." [1]

Those who argue that there is no youth culture may claim that adolescence is "a kind of cultural disease . . . an interruption of

* Thanks are due to Shirley Jessor, for helpful discussions on her research as it relates to the topic of this chapter; to Susan Boulding, for sharing perspectives on adolescence gained while acting as coordinator of volunteers for the Boulder Attention Homes; to William Boulding, for sharing perspectives from "inside" the teen culture; and to Dorothy Carson for invaluable assistance with bibliographies, tables, and final preparation of the manuscript.

developmental continuity," [2] or, conversely, find no evidence of a distinctive adolescent value system.[3] Offer concludes from his study of Chicago suburban teen-agers that they "were by and large an integral part of the culture within which they lived. They were proud of their schools, their communities, and the achievements of their parents." [4] Bettelheim agrees that an adolescent culture exists in modern society, but only as an abnormal phenomenon resulting from the fact that "fully pubertal human beings [are] being kept in dependency—and someone else foots the bill." [5]

Since many students of adolescents focus entirely on phenomenon of deviance and delinquency (see, for example the studies cited in Arnold), it is not surprising that youth culture is so often seen as pathological and destructive. At the other extreme are the social philosophers who feel that the youth counterculture will save us all. Some middle-aged apostles of the youth culture mix together in one huge mystical stew the Aquarians and the followers of a variety of recent imports of pieces of great religious traditions of the East, the sturdy communitarians in the great utopian till-the-land tradition, and the equally sturdy politically oriented urban communitarians who seek to build alternatives in the ruins of megalopolis. While careful discriminating analyses of various elements in the stew can be found,[6] the distinctions keep getting blurred in a romanticization of youth culture as an escape hatch from adult failures.

Few of the current debaters about youth culture seem to have read Eisenstadt's *From Generation to Generation*.[7] This comprehensive study of the phenomenon of youth groupings in societies at all levels of complexity— from pre-industrial to post-civilized—puts the issue in a much-needed historical perspective. He points out that in agrarian societies the main integrative principles regulating family and kinship behavior are also those regulating behavior in the larger social structure; the individual therefore experiences a smooth transition from familial to civic solidarity. In industrial societies, however, there are sharp differences between family-appropriate behavior and the behavior in the public sphere; so the individual has to change her behavior at a certain point in her life career to achieve full status in society.[8] The youth society therefore becomes a transition society, where the young person is protected from adult pressures by familistic peer-group support, while she nevertheless tries out the new behaviors which will shortly give her adult status.

Taking into account the divergences of approach to the phenomenon, we can I think say, yes, Virginia, there *is* a youth culture. And while we will build on Eisenstadt's structural argument of a transition space in which to create new social roles, it should also be pointed out that the extent of the felt presence of this subculture, and the intensity of its impact, is a reflection of something beyond social discontinuities. It has to do with unprecedented segregation in the 1950s and '60s of the population bulge of teen-agers in school settings away from the rest of society. In 1900, 10 percent of young people went to high school. Now 80 percent do. This means that formerly youth were spread all through society in all kinds of age-heterogeneous groupings at work and play during their adolescent years. Today they are, almost literally, under lock and key in large centralized schools. Sanity dictated the development of somewhat privatized teen cultures if these youth were not to submit to becoming automatons.

Rapporteurs about the Youth Culture

EDUCATORS–It is not surprising that educators, who are the custodians of this exploding and explosive group, are our chief rapporteurs about the youth culture. James Coleman was one of the first to describe the teen-age culture,

A set of small teen-age societies, which focus teen-age interests and attitudes on things far removed from adult responsibilities, and which may develop standards that lead away from those goals established by the larger society.[9]

His purpose was "to learn how to control the adolescent community as a community, and to use it to further the ends of education."[10] While Coleman described adolescent cultures in schools representative of various social statuses, on the whole he (and his successors in research) saw these cultures, whatever the class status, as struggling with the same problem. All adolescents, according to this view,

are caught between two fundamentally opposed cultures; the culture of the school based on deferred gratification, cognitive skill, individual achievement and deference to authority, and the out-of-school "youth culture" based on immediate gratification, physical skill, group solidarity and the equality of group members. Hence, they are forced to choose one or the other.[11]

In this view of the teen culture, either you are a good teen-ager, work hard and obey adults, and get your goodies when they say you can have them; or you are a bad teen-ager, goof off, don't obey adults, and take your goodies now—anyway you can get them.

A recent study of the youth culture and schools in England led the researchers (Murdock and Phelps) to conclude that the earlier studies were wrong because they assumed too monolithic a view of youth culture. In fact there are two youth cultures, say these British authors, the street culture and the pop media culture.

> Street cultures are rooted in inner urban neighborhoods and are based on the characteristic leisure activities of working-class male peer groups. . . . The central values of "street cultures," solidarity with the group, physical prowess, and the ability to "look after yourself," are derived from, and supported by, the wider value system of the working-class neighborhood. . . . Working-class girls tend to share the same basic values. . . . "Pop media culture" is based on activities, values and roles which are sponsored by those sectors of the mass media which are produced primarily for adolescent consumption. The central values are immediate gratification and the expression of emotional and physical capacities. . . . However, the fact that these media disseminate styles and values which are potentially available to all adolescents, does not mean that all adolescents are equally involved in them, and it is the failure to recognize this which accounts for many of the inadequacies of past conceptualizations.[12]

While the referents are British, the comments apply to American working-class and middle-class culture as well. Murdock and Phelps further subdivide the middle-class into (1) a group that accepts *both* the deferred-gratification patterns of the school *and* the immediacy of the pop media culture, and (2) a group that rejects the deferred-gratification patterns of the school and accepts only the immediate-gratification patterns of the pop media culture. This study represents a crack in the armature of the youth-culture-as-immediate-gratification theory, in its recognition of a teen culture variant which *also* accepts school values of deferred gratification. However, it still resorts to a very limited definition of youth culture, and continues the view of the school as the main carrier of desired social values. By and large, the view still prevails that the schools and youth are simply at war.

OTHER INFORMANTS–Besides educators, who are our other informants about youth culture? One category comprises professional youth workers working for federal, state, or local agencies, church youth workers, and the personnel of large national youth-serving bureaucracies such as the scouts and YMCA and the YWCA. All share many of the characteristics and orientations of the educator.

The remaining sets of informants are to be found in the business world and in the family—i.e., parents and adolescents themselves. The world of business long ago discovered the adolescent as consumer, and the Samuel K. Grafton *Youth Reports*[13] keeps up with the entire range of youth subcultures. Parents are usually complainers but not articulate informants, and that leaves us with one last information resource—the teen-agers themselves.

Since the American teen-ager already has more schooling than most of her age mates around the world are ever going to get,[14] she is obviously equipped to write some fairly sophisticated commentaries on her own scene. Yet the teen-ager as author is rare. Even *The Soft Revolution*,[15] which is written as a how-to-manual on initiating radical social change in the high schools, is written entirely by adults. *High School*,[16] another adult enterprise, at least has a lively and informative section written by youth.

Occasionally there is a remarkable eruption into print of a poignant adolescent experience with significant social dimensions such as *The Diary of Ann Frank*[17] or Jessica Reynolds' *Jessica's Diary*,[18] the account of her family's protest voyage into the Pacific during the nuclear test explosions of the 1950s.

Since the teen-liberation movement has not yet reached the stage of articulateness in print that other movements have reached, we must make the best of what we have in this chapter.

The picture we will be developing here of adolescent culture-worlds is a complex blend of continuities and discontinuities with the cultures of the larger society. To some extent the youth subcultures reflect the range of adult subcultures, rooted as they are in ethnic, racial, socioeconomic, religious, and other special cultural orientations. They are not reflections of, but adaptive reactions to, these adult cultures—and yet more than reactions, since they also have an element of independent culture creation. As a prelude to constructing a model of the development of youth culture, and a typology of existing youth subcultures, let us examine the issues of continuity and discontinuity on the one hand, and the issues of system maintenance and system change on the other, as they relate to the conceptualization of youth culture.

Continuities

Seen in historical perspective, the tradition of a youth counterculture representing a critique of industrial society, a new view of the potentials of humankind, and alternative life styles emphasizing the organic unity of humans with one another and with nature is a very old one. Eisenstadt suggests that it was born in the Romantic movement, particularly in Germany.[19] An early forerunner was Johann Gottfried von Herder

(1744–1803), who saw "the whole earth as a school," [20] and who opposed to crude rationalism a theory of psychic forces affecting humankind which, for any particular period of human history, went to make up the *Zeitgeist* (spirit of the age). The contemporary counterculture movement might be seen as the latest manifestation in a series of rebellions against the progressive technologization of society. Table 1 presents a five-generation picture of these counterculture movements, beginning with hypothetical great-great grandparents at the close of the nineteenth century in Europe and America. Saint-Simon and Fourier in France, Robert Owen and Ruskin in England, each represented the (adult) counterculture of their time. The countercultures of the nineteenth century in the United States are vividly described in Charles Nordhoff's *Communistic Societies.*[21]

Studies of the college-student protest movements confirm this continuity theme by emphasizing the fact that these students are the children of parents who in their own youth were also protesters, and who today continue to be strongly liberal in their views, though not so radical as their offspring.[22] Today's youth protest movements are more multidimensional than our movements in the 1940s and '50s, as I hope to show.

An interesting bit of evidence on this increasing sophistication in the analysis of social problems among youth as compared with their parents is found in the questionnaire data collected by Harold Guetzkow from conscientious objectors during World War II on the development of their own attitudes of conscientious objection to war.[23] A substantial number of conscientious objectors indicated that their parents held similar, but much simpler views of war. They perceived that they had used parental teachings as a point of departure for further and more sophisticated analysis of world problems.

To do the theme of continuity justice, it must be pointed out that not only dissenting views of the world and counterculture perspectives are passed on from generation to generation, but establishment views of the world are also handed on in the same manner. There are obviously no simple relationships between parental and adolescent world views, or the sense of the generation gap would not be so acute.

Models of Adolescent Culture Choice

It is useful for us to have a model in mind of the process by which youth acquires its cultural values, which will account for the great variety of youth cultures we are to examine. The elements of this model should include individual personality characteristics and relevant social environments. A series of longitudinal studies by Shirley and Richard Jessor and associates at the University of Colorado, of socially defined problem

Table 1. The Counterculture as a Five-Generation-Plus Enterprise

	GENERATION			
1800–1899 GREAT-GREAT GRANDPARENTS AND THEIR FOREBEARERS	1900–1919 GREAT GRANDPARENTS	1920–1939 GRANDPARENTS	1940–1960 PARENTS	1960–1975 YOUTH COUNTERCULTURE
"Romanticism" in full swing in Europe, as reaction to failures of rationalism; early problems of urbanization and industrialization.	Social Darwinism increasing sophistication of technological and social adaptations to urbanization and industrialization. War fought to end war.	Flaming '20s, "Back to the Land '30s." Worldwide depression; fascism in Europe.	Social quietism, breakdown of some earlier adaptations to technology; mounting problems of environmental pollution, population explosion, poverty.	Consciousness III. Reaction to failures of technological society; contemporary problems of urbanization.
Vision of new organically whole human being to create new society.	Automobile age begins; era of optimism, all things possible through science and technology.	Cultural-lag theory popular; pessimism about capacity to make social adaptations to technology.	New kind of war without start or finish (Vietnam).	Human potential movement; vision of new, organically whole human being to create new society.
Birth of German youth culture, *Wandervogel.*	Entire society perceived as involved in creation of new life styles.	Experiments with communes, alternative life styles.	Experiments of returned veterans and conscientious objectors with communes, alternative life styles.	Experiments with communes, alternative life styles.

behavior (e.g., drug use, problem drinking, premarital sex, activism) with junior high, senior high, and college populations are of great help in developing such a model. The Jessors are amassing data that will eventually enable us to say a good deal about the interrelationships between (1) individual personality; (2) the social environments represented by the family, peer groups, other community environments including the media culture; and (3) cultural value choices and behaviors. One general finding of interest to date is that the personality characteristics associated with engaging in a particular kind of problem behavior are similar for a whole range of problem behaviors. They also found that behavior choices (such as drug use) can be predicted from measured personality and social characteristics a year prior to the change in behavior status.[24] This means that adolescents are not erratic and unpredictable in their behaviors, even in their nonconforming behaviors, but act out of a stable context of perceptions and response tendencies. This stability of response patterns will be important as we consider our youth culture types.

ELEMENTS OF THE MODEL: PERSONALITY CHARACTERISTICS–What personality characteristics are particularly relevant in determining the youth subculture an adolescent will identify with? Extent of *alienation* is one trait that all writers on adolescence agree on. *Aspiration level* (or achievement orientation) is another, and the *gap between aspiration level and performance capacity* a third. The Jessors make use of all three in their work, and also *independence* (particularly from adults). Two more traits that do not appear in this form in the Jessor studies, but which are important for our purposes are *autonomy*—extent to which choices are made independently both of peers and adults—[25] and *levels of tolerance for frustration and personal discomfort*. This concept of frustration and discomfort tolerance goes beyond the simple notion of ability to defer gratification for the sake of future rewards, and deals rather with the capacity to endure possible hardship for the sake of long-term goals. Three of the above personality characteristics—alienation, aspiration level, and frustration tolerance—will be taken account of in our typology of adolescent cultures.

ELEMENTS OF THE MODEL: SOCIAL ENVIRONMENTS–*1. The Parental Culture as Social Environment.* In addition to response consistency for adolescents, Shirley Jessor has found a significant relationship between mother's ideology and adolescent behavior.

> . . . the less conventional the mother's ideology, the more nonconforming behavior the adolescent reported engaging in. The results

were stronger and more consistent for the girls, but were supportive for boys as well.[26]

These findings . . . indicate a degree of continuity between parental socialization and adolescent behavior even with respect to behaviors often represented as institutionalized in and primarily influenced by the peer culture.[27]

The fact that maternal influence can be identified even after the peer-culture influence has fully been taken into account gives strong support to the view taken here that there are powerful continuities in youth cultures with the cultures of the parent society.

2. *Other Social Environments.* Since class status and racial and ethnic identity contribute to determining subculture affiliation for adults, it seems reasonable to assume that these determinants also operate in the arena of adolescent society. The general theory of subcultures as discussed in Cressey[28] apply.

Since each local community offers its own distinct range of choices to children growing up in its environs, depending on its size, economic base, racial and ethnic diversity, civic pride, etc., the community itself is an important determinant of adolescent culture choice.[29] The mass media provide a different dimension of environment, but certainly create a highly significant set of social spaces in which adolescents spend substantial amounts of time. The Jessor studies suggest that high involvement with television produces teen-age conformers. While there is no basis in their studies for imputing a causal relationship, they suggest interactive relationship:

Television contributes to socialization by reinforcing prevailing social standards for its viewers, and viewers who become involved with the medium are those already responsive to the values and standards it projects.[30]

ELEMENTS OF THE MODEL: INSTITUTIONALIZED STRUCTURES FOR YOUTH– While institutionalized structures for youth properly belong under social environments, they are such a specialized set of structures that they can be conceptually distinguished from other social environments. Certainly they are one of the most significant contributors to the youth culture, in that they all contribute to the segregation of adolescents from the larger society. The *school* contributes by keeping children and teens physically isolated. *Youth agencies* contribute by treating their needs as youth needs, not human needs. *Adult-organized youth organizations* contribute by creating separate opportunity structures for their every interest or recreational activity.

Movement organizations contribute by channeling youthful ideas into the side alleys of the movement, thus avoiding having to confront new ways of thinking, new solutions to old problems.

The adolescent, pushed and pulled in every direction in the name of socialization, and preparation for life in the larger society, somehow emerges with a youth culture identity. Table 2 is a schematic representation of the various determinants we have been discussing in this section.

Socialization, System-Maintenance and System-Change

Adolescents are usually viewed as a troublesome lot of raw materials, who if properly handled at school and at home, will grow up into successful "maintenance men (women)" for the society that has been preserved for them. They are not considered as a resource for social change.

Ignoring the adolescent culture as a source of social change in a society that is daily confronting social change of agonizing dimensions can be serious. Let us review the crises of social change that youth and age alike face, and then examine how youth cultures deal with these problems.

As we near the end of the twentieth century, four major areas of social challenge, each representing a pressing set of social problems, might be categorized:

1. Development of nonhierarchial patterns of organization and decentralist working and living patterns that can function for globe-spanning organizational structures as well as for national and local units.
   a. These patterns to ensure maximum participation of all members of society at each system level.
   b. These patterns to evolve systems of access to valued physical and social resources for all members of society.

2. Development of more stable world system with deemphasis on nation-state units, increasing emphasis on transnational association and UN-type agencies.

3. Development of nonviolent techniques of dealing with conflict situations, at all levels from local to global.

4. Development of new perceptions of the ecological balance of the planet, new values and habits about human consumption and human reproduction, and new resource-economizing physical technologies.

Table 2. Determinates of Choice of Youth-Culture Patterns by the Adolescent

FAMILY CULTURE *Parental Values*	PERSONALITY CHARACTERISTICS OF THE INDIVIDUAL ADOLESCENT	SOCIAL ENVIRONMENTS	INSTITUTIONALIZED STRUCTURES FOR YOUTH	YOUTH-CULTURE PATTERN
	Achievement Orientation	*Racial, ethnic community*	*School*	
	Aspiration-Performance Gap	*Class status*	*Public youth Agencies*	
	Alienation	*Geographic Community*	*Adult-organized youth organizations*	
	Autonomy	*Mass media*	*Political, civic, and movement organizations with youth sections*	
	Levels of tolerance for frustration and personal discomfort			

We know very little about how to start on any of these challenges, and yet substantial progress must be made on all four of them in the next fifty years if we are to survive as a human society. Most of you who read this will have reached retirement age before those fifty years are up. That makes it very important to understand where the younger-adolescent age sector of our society is "at" in relation to these problems. If the stereotyped images of the adolescent culture are correct, they are nowhere in relation to these problems, and are instead doing their own thing in a cozy niche labeled "alternative life styles."

If we abandon the simplistic view that all adolescents either play the game provided them by the Establishment society and take their goodies later, or don't play the game and grab their goodies now, we can start instead looking at what kinds of "goodies" adolescents want, and how they go about seeking them. We will find that their social values and goals, their attitudes to the Establishment and their role concepts, are all more diverse and complex than is usually considered.

One obstacle to an accurate social perception of adolescents as possible change agents is lack of historical understanding of change-agent roles adolescents have played in the past. Just as enslavement of blacks made it impossible for the average American to visualize blacks as autonomous participators in society, so the enslavement of children—a process that could be variously dated but might be located for our purposes with the onset of industrialization—[31] makes it impossible for the average Westerner to visualize children and adolescents as autonomous participants in society.

The few records that have come down to us from history of adolescents as change agents (children, like women, have been written out of history and must now be put back by painstaking scholarship) come from periods of great social upheaval. If the stories end in tragedy, so, often, do stories of adult efforts at social change. The Children's Crusades are an extraordinary record of children taking it into their hands to do what they saw the adults around them were not able to do—rescue the Holy Land from the infidels. All the children's naiveté and adult exploitation that attended those crusades does not take away from the basic facts of (1) an amazing social vision on the part of a few adolescents twelve to fifteen years of age, and (2) some solid organizing ability at the start that got the actual troops of children moving. (See *Children's Crusades* for an account of this.)[32]

Quakerism, born at the onset of the industrial revolution, was at first to a considerable degree a children's movement.

. . . there were fiery children of the light walking the length and breadth of England to tell their astonished countrymen that Jesus had come to teach his people himself. They were fifteen-year-olds—who would today probably be studying a carefully-graded edition of the Quarterly, in a sunny Sunday school room well-designed and so placed that there would be no danger of an excited youngster's voice disturbing adults at their worship.[33]

In this century there are two examples of adolescents and pre-adolescents forming their own societies in times of great social upheaval and suffering. In the early 1920s Russian civil-war orphans, the *Besprisornji*, numbering in the hundred thousands,

were forced to fight for physical survival after their parents and relations had been killed by the Whites or the Reds. Although this was not a voluntary or spontaneous opting out of society, but was enforced by practically unthinkable hardship and the will to survive, these children and adolescents did organize themselves into well-functioning gangs.[34]

A similar phenomenon took place during the civil war in Colombia in the early 1950s.[35] Similar events could certainly be documented in Vietnam today. And while the social suffering is of a very different order, the rise of the children's liberation movement in the major cities of the United States in the past decade is part of this same historical tradition.

Change agents in the youth culture, as in adult society, have always been in the minority. That makes them more, not less, important to study. Those who are not change-oriented can be divided into the system maintainers—those for whom socialization into the mainstream of society takes perfectly—and the system-neutral youth. The latter do not actively take up the roles the adult society provides for them, nor identify with mainstream values, but neither do they protest them. They drift, and some of them become dropouts both from school and society. We will take account of all three categories in developing our typology.

Table 3. Class and Ethnic-Related Orientations of Youth to System Maintenance and System Change: The General Model

Social Class and Ethnicity	→	Extent of Alienation	→	Achievement Goals	→	Frustration Tolerance	→	Commitment to Social Change

The attitudes toward change and the Establishment are by no means class-determined, though class and ethnic identification significantly affect the perspectives of teen-agers. Table 3 suggests a general sequence in development of orientation to the social system which is then broken down for subgroups in table 4. Within each broad category of social class there are ethnic and racial groups who experience that class culture differently. Some groups of young people in each of these class/ethnic groups identify positively with the society, some feel alienated. Beyond general attitude sets of adaptation or alienation, youth subcultures variously adopt or reject the achievement ethic (not necessarily the achievement goals) of the larger society. We label youth as achievers or drifters. This includes both teen-agers who drift within the system and those who drop out. They are treated as one group here in order not to make the typology too complex. Groups can be further characterized in relation to their tolerance of frustration and personal discomfort. This distinction is isomorphic with the achiever-drifter distinction, since one characteristic of achievers is that they do have tolerance for frustration; drifters do not. The drifter is one for whom there has been too great a discrepancy between aspirations the larger society would like him to hold, and his performance capacity (not his genetic, but his socially shaped performance capacity). Having low frustration tolerance he has lowered his aspirations and settled for drifting. An inspection of table 4 shows that there are all three orientations to the social system in both the working class and the middle class—each class spawns system maintainers, system changers and youth who are system neutral. The upper class produces two main types—the Ivy Leaguers who are system maintainers and the Jet Set who are drifters. There is a fine line between system maintenance and system change for the most idealistic of the Ivy Leaguers (Jay Rockefeller, IV, for example, as an adolescent was already active in international tension-reducing projects), but there is no recognizable group of Ivy League adolescents committed to system change.

The Typology

Utilizing the variables of social class, ethnicity, education-related performance, and commitment to the social system, we are now prepared to develop a typology that will cover in a rather broad way the diversity of adolescent subcultures. In table 5 we use class as an "organizer" in the presentation of the typology. It will quickly be seen that we cannot do justice with this approach to the actual diversity of teen culture. Instead of treating black, Chicano, and Amerindian and teen women's cultures separately, we are lumping them together under "ethnic." Teen-age

Table 4. Class and Ethnic-Related Orientations of Youth to System Maintenance and System Change

	Ethnicity	Attitude	Result	Frustration Tolerance	Social-Role Orientation
BLUE COLLAR	Anglo →	Adapted →	Achiever →	High →	System Maintainer
	Anglo →	Alienated →	Drifter →	Low →	System Neutral
	Ethnic →	Adapted →	Achiever →	High →	System Changer
	Ethnic →	Alienated →	Drifter →	Low →	System Neutral
MIDDLE CLASS	Anglo Mainstream →	Adapted →	Achiever →	High →	System Maintainer
	Anglo Mainstream →	Alienated →	Drifter →	Low →	System Neutral
	Ethnic Mainstream →	Adapted →	Achiever →	High →	System Maintainer
	Anglo Protest →	Alienated →	Achiever →	High →	System Changer
	Anglo Protest →	Alienated →	Achiever Dropout →	High →	System Changer
	Ethnic Protest →	Alienated →	Achiever →	High →	System Changer
UPPER CLASS	Anglo Ivy League →	Adapted →	Achiever →	High →	System Maintainer
	Anglo Jet Set →	Alienated →	Drifter →	Low →	System Neutral

Table 5. Adolescent Subculture Typology
for American High School Age Youth

Working Class

    Blue-collar achiever
    Blue-collar drifter
    Ethnic blue-collar achiever[a]
    Ethnic blue-collar drifter

Middle Class

    Mainstream achiever[b]
    Mainstream drifter
    Ethnic mainstream achiever
    Protest achiever
    Protest dropout
    Ethnic protest achiever

Upper Class

    Ivy League achiever
    Jet Set drifter

[a] The term ethnic refers to Chicano, blacks, and Amerindians; other ethnic or sex-based (women's liberation) teen-age movements are too small to mention separately, but would share the characteristics to a considerable extent of one or another of the three "ethnics" mentioned.

[b] There are so few ethnic mainstream culture drifters that this category is omitted.

women's liberationists are usually found in the protest movements, and would therefore share to a considerable extent the characteristics of the "ethnic protesters." There are religiously oriented adolescent subcultures in both the working class and the middle class which are not given separate attention. They are important in their own way, and cannot easily be subsumed under any of the other types, but had to be eliminated to keep the analysis from becoming too complex.[36] Since the meanings of social class are important for the typology, we will examine this before moving to descriptions of individual culture types.

MEANING OF SOCIAL CLASS FOR ADOLESCENT CULTURE–Earlier descriptions of the American working-class or blue-collar society tended to lump together stable and unstable, secure and insecure, economically self-sufficient and poverty-stricken groups; and the general picture of the blue-collar family was of one in which parents were fearful of the world outside, inarticulate in their relationships both within the family and with outsiders, and intent on socializing their children to give no trouble. In sum, these people were considered generally incompetent to deal with life's problems. A landmark in the development of a more analytically sophisticated—and realistic—picture of the working class was reached with Shostak and Gomberg's *Blue Collar World*.[37] By now a host of writers[38] have established the distinctions between stable and coping, and marginal, noncoping families,[39] between tradition-minded and modern families,[40] between upwardly mobile and contented families,[41] and so on. Perhaps the most important single concept to emerge from these reconceptualizations of the "lower classes" is that of working-class skills of adaptation. Blue-collar workers in working-class neighborhoods, or poverty-level welfare recipients in slum ghettos of whatever race or ethnic group, are all seen as making ingenious and socially sophisticated adaptations to the realities of their situation. A lowering of aspiration levels, avoidance of planning activities, and operating with foreshortened time horizons are all realistic adaptations to a life situation where efforts frequently do not produce results and plans are destroyed by financial or other catastrophes. Since the disciplines associated with deferred gratification and the capacity to endure present discomfort for future goals rarely pay off for the poor, these traits are often not developed. When disciplines are relevant, such as the disciplines of the gang, they develop them.

A capacity for realistic analysis of one's life situation is the unifying trait for these classes. This is particularly pronounced when examining adolescent lower-class culture. Realism, adaptability, toughness, and humor characterize many youth groups. Drifting too may be a realistic adaptation when attempts to drop anchor have never succeeded. Working-class adolescent achievers are therefore a special group who have made the most of very limited opportunity structures.

Middle-class achievers have everything going for them—they have been brought up to expect reward for effort. However, since a climate of continual expectation of achievement can be as damaging as one in which no effort is rewarded, we also have the middle-class drifters, who have chosen their own escape from pressure. The protesters on the other hand are achievers, different from their mainstream brothers and sisters mainly in having opted for other social goals. They share with more conventional members of their peer group the experience and expectation that effort will be rewarded, but they can hold out through prolonged periods of discomfort when necessary.

The "love-culture" was born among middle-class teen-agers, responding to excessive pressures and dehumanization in the adult world by developing an expressive, affectionate style of interpersonal interaction. The new gentleness is oddly paired with the loudness of rock music, but together they create a style of coping with dehumanization.

Upper-class achievers often have to seek the climate of heightened expectation which their middle-class brothers and sisters know so well. Those that never discover expectations join the Jet Set.

Each social-class status, and each ethnic subculture within that class, provides its own set of opportunity structures and frustrations. As pointed out earlier, however, youth do not respond to these opportunity structures either by simply developing mirror images of their parent cultures, or by simply negating them. Youth cultures are more or less creative responses to the life experience of the young, products of individual personalities dealing with family and community environments. Perhaps a review of table 2, Determinants of Choice of Youth-Culture Patterns, would be useful for the reader before going on to the discussion of specific subculture types.

Characterizations of Adolescent Subculture Types

A further spelling out of the meaning of the labels given the subculture types in table 5 is found in table 6. Here the variables from the mode in table 3 of sequences in the development of subcultures are arranged to fit our types. An indication of the primacy of public vs. private goals has been added for each type. It is generally assumed that adolescents have mainly private goals and lead privatized lives, but as we shall see, this is not always the case. All drifters have only private goals, but some achievers have important public goals, other achievers do not. For those groups having public goals, they have been spelled out along the lines developed in the discussion on system-change goals earlier. A careful inspection of table 6 will show the great diversity of orientations and social values among different youth subcultures both within and between social classes. Table 7 emphasizes the same point, this time showing subcultures by commitment to system maintenance or system change. Social policy aimed at a more effective incorporation of adolescents into our society, whether in the school system or in civic life, that does not take this diversity into account will fail to achieve any meaningful change. Our discussion of adolescent culture types will follow the pattern of organization in table 7.

One caveat in regard to the types. These are "ideal types" in the Weberian sense, abstractions from reality, and do not correspond to concrete manifestations of adolescent society. Certain traits have been

Table 6. Social-System Orientations of Adolescent Subcultures, Grouped by Social Class

	ATTITUDE TO SCHOOL-SOCIETY, "ESTABLISHMENT"	FRUSTRATION TOLERANCE	SOCIAL-ROLE ORIENTATION TO SYSTEM	PRIMACY OF PUBLIC VS. PRIVATE GOALS	SPECIAL PUBLIC INTERESTS
WORKING CLASS					
Blue-collar achiever	Adapted	High	Maintainer	Private	—
Blue-collar drifter	Alienated	Low	Neutral	Private	—
Ethnic blue-collar achiever	Adapted	High	Changer	Public	Equal opportunity
Ethnic blue-collar drifter	Alienated	Low	Neutral	Private	—
MIDDLE CLASS					
Mainstream achiever	Adapted	High	Maintainer	Public	Econ. development / Int'l system
Mainstream drifter	Alienated	Low	Neutral	Private	—
Ethnic mainstream achiever	Adapted	High	Maintainer	Public	Equal opportunity
Protest achiever	Alienated	High	Changer	Public	Denationalization
Protest dropout	Alienated	High	Changer	Public	Debureaucratization
Ethnic protest achiever	Alienated	High	Changer	Public	Equal opportunity / Ecological balance
UPPER CLASS					
Ivy League achiever	Adapted	High	Maintainer	Public	Econ. development / Int'l system
Jet Set drifter	Alienated	Low	Neutral	Private	—

Table 7. Social Characteristics of System-Maintaining, System-Changing, and System-Neutral Adolescent Subcultures

	Attitude to School-Society, "Establishment"	Frustration Tolerance	Class Status	Primacy of Public vs. Private Goals	Special Public Interests
System Maintainers					
Blue-collar achiever	Adapted	High	Working	Private	—
Mainstream achiever	Adapted	High	Middle	Public	Econ. development Int'l. system
Ethnic mainstream achiever	Adapted	High	Middle	Public	Equal opportunity
Ivy League achiever	Adapted	High	Upper	Public	Econ. development Int'l. system
System Changers					
Ethnic blue-collar achiever	Adapted	High	Working	Public	Equal opportunity
Protest achiever	Alienated	High	Middle	Public	Denationalization
Protest dropout	Alienated	High	Middle	Public	Debureaucratization
Ethnic protest achiever	Alienated	High	Middle	Public	Equal opportunity Ecological balance
System Neutral					
Blue-collar drifter	Alienated	Low	Working	Private	—
Ethnic blue-collar drifter	Alienated	Low	Working	Private	—
Mainstream drifter	Alienated	Low	Middle	Private	—
Jet Set drifter	Alienated	Low	Upper	Private	—

chosen for emphasis but in real life these traits would not appear in the exaggerated form they appear in here. Social involvements and orientations are never as clear-cut as they have been made to look, and many young people would claim they belong in none of the boxes we have constructed for them. As long as these features of abstraction and exaggeration are borne in mind, however, these types should help us to understand the variety of kinds of mini-societies that adolescents live in.

SYSTEM MAINTAINERS–The system maintainers all have certain things in common. The blue-collar achievers, the mainstream achievers, the ethnic mainstream achiever, and the Ivy League achiever all have a certain level of knowledge about how the larger social system works, a desire to develop the skills that make for success in that system, and career ambitions that are a mix of private and public goals—making it oneself, and also helping society make it. The female system maintainers tend to live in a more private world than the males, and accept traditional female roles in both public and private settings.

The blue-collar achievers. These teen-agers come largely from that successful, small-homeowning sector of the "modern" working class, the "blue-collar joiners" [42] who work very hard to achieve middle-class values. Their fathers moonlight and their mothers have jobs outside the home, and family life is oriented around saving enough to send the children to college. Girls, however, are less likely to be sent to college than boys. They have grown up in a nonpolitical environment, with a powerful work ethic which they have internalized. They are disciplined, obedient to authority, work hard at home and in school, and participate in relatively sedate church and neighborhood recreation. They see themselves as becoming somewhat more successful replicas of their parents, and do not develop ideas or recreational patterns that separate them very much from their elders. This is a "youth culture of preparation" for an already familiar future.

Mainstream achievers. These teen-agers come from suburbia—their families have nice homes and solid incomes, mother is active in the community. This is the American dream family pictured by the ad man. The teen-agers studied by Offer[43] fall in this group—happy with their way of life, proud of their parents, eager to succeed in their parents' world. They are neither rebellious nor cause-oriented.

> The vast majority are not visible in the social field; they do not demonstrate, take drugs, or engage in delinquent activities. Though they might object to the war in Vietnam all will go if drafted.[44]

They are happy consumers of the "pop media culture" and keep businessmen very happy indeed. The girls all go to college and accept the line of reasoning which says that higher education will make them better wives and mothers. Offer estimated that about 30 to 40 percent of the teen-agers of suburbia fall into this category. This, like the blue-collar achiever culture, is a "culture of preparation" for an already familiar future.

Ethnic mainstream achievers. Middle-class black and Chicano teen-agers have many characteristics in common with the mainstream achievers described above, except that they do not often live in the same neighborhoods. With housing desegregation an increasingly prevalent phenomenon for middle-class minority families, there will be less and less distinction between Anglo mainstream achievers and others. They are somewhat more disciplined than their Anglo counterparts, work harder, are more likely to have ulcers, and have more heartaches over social slights—all reflections of the fact that they are still not fully accepted by Anglo mainstream teen-agers. The "black is beautiful" movement and its counterparts for other minorities have made it easier for them to take pride in themselves and ignore these slights, but they do not participate in minority liberation activities. Lewis Jones gives an illustration of this type from the black world, which he calls "accommodaters":

> My aims, ambitions, and goals in life are to become an educated and well-informed citizen of my community. I desire to obtain my Masters in education. . . . Marriage and a family is an idea that often concerns me. Social equality is too a concern of mine; thus, I may say that my goals include those things that will enable me to have a fairly well-rounded life, which for me includes education, religion, marriage and social activities.[45]

Andrew Billingsley has described very well the sources of the achievement culture in black families in his *Black Families in America*. He traces the descendants of five hundred extended black families in existence in 1860 and shows how most black professionals today come from these families, which systematically encouraged achievement and gave strong family support for that achievement.[46] The continuity theme is impressive here, and the informant quoted above is precisely in that achievement tradition. Black middle-class girls expect just as much of themselves, if not more, than boys do, and aspire to more than family roles. These teen-agers too participate in a culture of preparation.

Ivy League achievers. The Ivy League achievers are the descendants of the white counterparts of the black "500 families," young people steeped in a tradition of public service. They have fathers and grandfathers and uncles and great-uncles who have held public office, and the women in their families have been prominent in civic and welfare activities (organizers of charity balls in an earlier day). The Kennedys and the Rockefellers are good examples. The distractions of affluence, and all the choices that affluence opens up, sometimes capture them, but there is an identifiable group of upper-class adolescents who begin taking active leadership roles in prep school. It is a prep school culture, another culture of preparation, but develops international links early, as in the case of Jay Rockefeller cited earlier. These people might be labeled nonprotest peace activists, in their own upper-class style. Since girls' prep schools are more sheltered from larger social realities than boys' prep schools are, teen girls emerge less visibly as having social concerns.

These four types of achievers, all actively involved in youth cultures of preparation for mainstream adult society, are the ideal targets for most of the work that youth professionals are prepared to do. Professionals know how to communicate with them, and motivation is no problem. The reason that our school system and related youth-system structures work as well as they do is because there are enough of these achieving adolescents around, in all statuses of society from working class to upper class, to make them work.

SYSTEM CHANGERS–The system changers, like the system maintainers, come from the working class as well as the middle class, though there are no upper-class representatives. They are equally disciplined, have equal capacity for hard work, and give even more primacy to public goals as compared to private ones. Except for the ethnic blue-collar achiever they are alienated from society, unlike their brothers and sisters in the previous groups described, and their public interests have to do with system change. While some of them reject the love culture, many of them share in it, and bring gentle ways to their protest activities.

Ethnic blue-collar achiever. The ethnic blue-collar achiever is a system changer by default rather than by intention. The prototypes are the courageous black children and adolescents who in Clinton and Little Rock and Charlotte walked through hostile crowds simply to exercise their right to go to school with whites. This was something no adult could do for them. In spite of all the background work done beforehand, when it came to entering hitherto forbidden schools, they had to do it for themselves. They were not seeking system change, they were seeking the proper operation of a system which in theory guaranteed rights that were in fact denied. Jones calls these the "transcenders"—those who accept new opportunities in education and occupation no matter how difficult the conditions, and strive to meet qualifications no matter how demanding. They are "study-hard, self-development youth" who change opportunity structures by making them function the way they are supposed to function.[47]

From time to time slum-child adolescents manage to pattern themselves on a middle-class self-development model, often with the help of a religiously oriented family and strong church ties. Rainwater describes the boy who makes this difficult choice:

> He stands aside from the excitement of the street and ignores the possibilities of interesting adult activities like drinking, heterosexual relations, and stealing. Instead, he devotes himself to school accomplishments, to becoming a leader of organized activities in school and church; he may have a part-time job, and he spends his remaining time at home.[48]

Even gang members in slum settings can make these choices. Suttles, in *The Social Order of the Slum*, describes Chickie, a member of the Erls gang, as a quiet boy who was often absent from gang activities because he had "to study." This was accepted matter of fact, and he gradually dropped out of gang life and moved toward the middle-class world.[49]

The mothers and fathers of these ethnic achievers are in themselves an interesting group. The teen-agers are not achieving in a vacuum. The poverty mothers who have swarmed into the Head Start Supplementary Training New Careers Program, many of them high school dropouts of twenty years earlier, are struggling over their books side by side with their teen-agers at the kitchen table.[50] Chicano-initiated programs like Migrants in Action are doing the same thing with an even stronger whole-family orientation to schooling and achievement. Active poverty mothers become significant role models to teen girls, for whom the ghetto provides even more obstacles than boys to achievement because of the ever-present facts of early pregnancies. Some ghetto youth from these success-story families are even leaving Harlem to work in Wall Street, in a new banker-initiated program for the training and employment of ghetto youth.[51]

Many of these young people are isolates, participating in the achieving adolescent culture in an essentially mainstream style, through sometimes almost superhuman overcoming of immediate obstacles presented by the nonachieving adolescent cultures within which they are immersed. They have a "culture of preparation," but it is invisible to the average observer. The fact that opportunity structures have actually changed over the past decade owes more to the willingness of these teen-agers to sacrifice their own comfort and pleasure than the adult world generally recognizes. Not all significant social battles are won either in the courts or on the streets. Some of them are won by persisting daily treading of new but apparently insignificant footpaths in the social mazeways.

The protest achiever. We are distinguishing between the protest achiever, the protest dropout, and the ethnic protest achiever because they are all working in distinctly different social milieus and have recognizably different cultures.

The Anglo middle-class protest achiever is the familiar and yet not so familiar teen-age radical. From "good" liberal homes, politically aware as part of their parental heritage,[52] they are alienated from society in the positive sense of being dissatisfied with things as they are but dedicated to making them better. The girls are the first generation to mature during the Women's Liberation movement and are careful to educate their brother activists about sexism. They insist on and take active leadership roles in movement activities.[53]

These young people are the leaders of the children's liberation movement in the big cities. They fought for the right, during the flowering of the SDS movement on college campuses, to have high school SDS groups. Discovering that they did not have freedom of association as their requests to form such groups, and in general to participate in antiwar activities, were rejected again and again, they began to turn to civil liberties organizations for help in establishing the rights of the adolescent in court.[54]

Working from a firm base in both family and school, they nevertheless participate in the creation of alternative community structures such as free schools, people's clinics, People's Yellow Pages (directory of alternative services based on barter instead of exchange of money), and the publishing of underground newspapers. They share with mainstream achievers a capacity for hard work and in addition can endure considerable personal discomfort on behalf of social goals. Able to succeed in the "Establishment" if they want to, usually doing well in school, they choose to work sometimes with, often around, the system, always with a commitment to changing it. Some of these were at the 1971 White House Conference on Youth, regularly preparing minority reports to offset oversimplified statements on social problems.[55]

Usually nonviolent in protest (but not always), their involvement with drugs, sex, and alcohol is minimal compared to the hippie culture, though the complaint has been made in recent years that it is getting harder to tell the hippies and the radicals apart.[56] An overlay of somewhat similar surface life style is deceptive, since following a protest achiever around for twenty-four hours would give one a very different picture of the radical as a hard worker than her appearance may seem to indicate. The cream of this crop are a secure, altruistic group whose earlier socialization experiences prepared them for dealing with hostility and violence without getting uptight. They have had enough success in their own lives so they can help others at some risk to themselves, and have an image, albeit vague, of a possible different society—more peaceful, more just, less bureaucratic, less technological.[57]

The protest dropout. The protesting dropout shares many characteristics with the protesting achiever who stays in the system, including the capacity for hard work and achievement. Their choice, however, is to enter the counterculture and begin now to develop the alternative system that will be needed when society crumbles. They are more radical, less patient, but have similar commitments. They will be found in politically oriented communes with slightly older young people, and communes of people of all ages such as the Life Centers in Philadelphia and elsewhere, or Catholic Worker Houses, or community residential centers set up for this growing category of youth by friendly community people. They could easily get high school accreditation but choose not to bother. Problem-oriented, they work around the clock at times of peak protest actions.

Like working-class dropouts, they spend a lot of time on the streets, but their activities are very different. They are usually "organizing." Sometimes they move to rural communes, but the commitment to social change is such that they are continually on the move between rural pads and urban centers. Some of them are part of a group known as Movement for a New Society, associated with a growing cluster of communes in major cities across the country. (The first book to come out of this movement, by an older member, is *Strategy for a Living Revolution* by George Lakey.) [58]

In addition to protest against militarism they single out sensitive points in local community institutions as well as national ones that reflect serious injustice. They also work on developing the alternative networks that their brothers and sisters still in school also work on—the free schools, people's clinics, People's Yellow Pages. Since their skill levels are not always high, though their commitment is strong, much of their work appears on the surface to be ineffective. These alternative life-style networks are from time to time alluded to in the press.[59] They are often short-lived because of the proportion of people working in them who do not have sufficient organizational skill. How many of these protest dropouts will later return to school when they have a better sense of things they need to learn, one cannot be sure. Some of them have already returned, however, and more probably will.

The protest dropout path is a hard way of life, and few teen-agers can take it for long. Furthermore, they don't remain teen-agers; they age and move into some variant of adult protest culture. The status of the girl dropout is more ambiguous than that of the boy. She has to work harder to maintain her activist stance, and only strong-minded girls try.

While I may have exaggerated the work ethic of these political communes, since they also have spiritual concerns and believe strongly in a greater emphasis on warm human relationships, my own limited observation leads me to believe that more spiritually oriented concerns often suffer because of action demands.

Some potentially creative protest dropouts do not find their way into a protest counterculture and become drifters instead, often in the drug culture. They do not have the characteristics of the drifters as described further on, and are an identifiable enough population to have spurred the establishment of a special experimental school, Lindisfarne, which will take these protesters-become-drifters and bring them back to a realization of their unusual potentials. Lindisfarne[60] is unique in that it draws on spiritual as well as intellectual traditions in its educational enterprise.

The ethnic protest culture. For lack of space we will mention here only the black protest group, though there are active Chicano and (very recently) Amerindian teen-age cultures also. Jones[61] has pointed out how diverse activist black youth orientations are, and we cannot begin to reflect that diversity here. Most of them are committed to a radically different society, relatively few to violence and then chiefly, as in the case of the Black Panthers, because a hostile white world pushes them into it. Black separatists are sometimes violence-prone, and urban schools often foster violence when whites and blacks feel keenly in competition. We are here describing socially oriented protest groups, however, and their "purposive" violence should not be confused with the aimless violence of the ghetto.

An example of the black social activist, while it comes from the earlier days of the movement, is still probably typical of many black teen-agers:

> Well, you see, I'm very confused about my role in life. I have an inferiority complex about being negro [sic] and about being me. I have tried to gain respect by participation in the movement (civil rights, SNCC). Last year working in SNCC, putting my heart into demonstrations gave me purpose. As a result of my actions (plus others) many places were opened to negroes [sic]. My reaction to this has been, "so what! So what if a few places do serve my people now; that really doesn't help the problem." [62]

Just a couple of years later black high school youth, with solid experience under their belts, were coming on clearer. Detroit and Newark studies[63] show teen-agers as having increasing feelings of racial pride and even racial superiority. The Detroit studies of a sample of twelve- to eighteen-year-old black students showed that the black teen-agers who were supportive of riot activities did well in school and had higher internal control scores than nonsupportive teen-agers, and also a greater awareness of the external constraints which keep black people in a disadvantaged position. These black protesters are very much like the Anglo protesters described above, only working in a deprived milieu that has radicalized and educated them in a very short period of time.

The joyous "soul culture" weaves in and out of the black protest culture to give it a flavor Anglo protest groups lack. Girls have an increasing place in the culture, which they fought hard for. Working-class culture is largely sex-segregated, and teen-age women are fighting their way out of that one.

SYSTEM-NEUTRAL CULTURES–Much of the adult attention that is focused on adolescent society is in fact focused on that segment which is system neutral. We mean by this that the values and behaviors of these groups do not contribute either to the maintenance or the change of the existing social structures—they simply do not affect society at all, but simply drift through it. Some of these cultures can be thought of as a series of "niche cultures." The young people we are talking about in this section are either drifters in the mainstream or dropouts in niches.

They receive such a lot of attention because they are what society considers its failures—young people who are not headed for any identifiable social roles in the adult world. While from the adult point of view they appear to be failures, the youth will be seen to have made a kind of—for them—workable adaptation to an unfriendly world. I would have preferred another word beside drifters, which would give more recognition to the kind of social adaptations that have been made by these adolescents. With the system-maintenance, system-change framework of our analysis, however, I cannot come up with a better descriptor for our "neutrals." While all drifters hit rough spots in the social system that system-related people never feel, girl drifters have an even harder time than boy drifters. Annie Hilliard's poignant description of The Street Chick [64] based on her own experience of street life for a few months, shows the chick as receiving a social and physical buffeting which it is hard for a person to endure and remain psychologically intact.

Blue-collar drifters, Anglo and ethnic. While the dynamics of discrimination which leads to their situation of severe cultural disadvantage is somewhat different for Anglos and ethnics, the resulting deprivations and lack of perceived opportunity structures for achievement are the same for all poverty groups. We will therefore treat them together.

The great convergence of research on slums and ghettos that has produced a new image of the cultures of poverty as adaptive has already been discussed here.

The problem for poor youth is not that they lack future orientations, but, indeed, that they lack a future. They are made aware of this early because there is so little meaning in their present. A limited gratification exists in striving for the impossible, and as a consequence, poor youth create styles, coping mechanisms, and groups in relation to the systems which they can and cannot negotiate. Group values and identifications emerge in relation to the forces opposing them. Poor youth develop a basic pessimism because they have a fair fix on reality. They rely on fate because no rational transition system is open to them. They react against schools because schools are characteristically hostile to them.

Despite the seeming hopelessness of their chances in life, poor youth do develop coping skills and strengths. It is a mistake, for instance, to characterize them as inarticulate, or non-verbal. Although their academic command of language may be lamentable, urban low-income youth possess a colorful and complex verbal style. In the face of a forbidding system in which they seem to have no stake, they struggle to establish codes, groups, values, and goals which will provide a basis for identity, a standard for behavior, a status, a competence.[65]

Vivid descriptions of gangs and various kinds of youth activity groupings are to be found in Suttles' *The Social Order of the Slum*[66] and Rainwater's *Behind Ghetto Walls*,[67] in the Morland study of a mill town,[68] and in the Purcell study of the hopes of Negro workers for their children.[69] A common theme runs through these accounts—early aspirations that fit mainstream aspiration patterns, which in time become more and more discrepant with the surrounding reality, and finally a rueful, but often good-humored revision of aspirations. So the Milltown child who wanted to go to college and become a doctor enters the mills instead.[70] Alice Walker, who wanted to finish high school and become a secretary gets pregnant in her junior year and resigns herself to early marriage and family responsibilities. In the light of the literature on the necessity of getting lower-class youth to have aspirations, the poignancy of the well-nigh universal ghetto phenomenon of environmentally constrained revision of aspirations is almost unbearable.[71]

Maybe they finish high school, maybe they drop out early. Either way, they have a life of economic insecurity ahead, probably babies to provide for. If they fall through all the nets they wind up in skid row, but most just drift through the side streets of America's ghettos. Since these streets are literally their "living rooms," they make them as comfortable as they can, staking out private areas whose boundaries are generally respected by adults and other teens. The territoriality of gangs has often been remarked on, but Suttles introduces a somewhat different note in his description of the homeyness of ghetto streets.[72] The humor of the young who live on these streets, their realism and their skills of social manipulation, are their only tools in dealing with an unfriendly reality.

The mainstream drifter and the Jet Set. The flower children are the mainstream drifters. High schools across the land, trying to find ways to respond to the young who simply refuse to accept school as they have known it, are developing their own alternatives in experiments like Project Hold. For teen-agers, Project Hold with its arts and crafts and human-encounter emphasis becomes a way to drop out of the system while staying in. For high school administrators, it becomes a reassurance that, after all, "the system" is working. While differently perceived by teen-agers and administrators, it does seem to provide a mutually acceptable counter-culture niche for alienated middle-class youth who don't fit anywhere else. Its expressive style seems to suit males and females alike.

"Drifter" may seem an inappropriate categorization, after all that has been written about Consciousness III and the counterculture. The commitment of these youth to the present, to process, to relationship, to feelings and visionary perceptions, in environments heavy with incense and delights in the discovery of the human potential (which they often equate with sex and drug trips), makes them difficult to place in relation to social structures. While they *live* alternative life styles (either at home or in hippie pads), it would be hard to say that they actually create alternatives. Their very commitment to openness, and their absorption in easy crafts (simple jewelry and candles) runs counter to the basic conditions for social creativity, which includes a talent for critical analysis, capacity for self-discipline and endurance of discomfort, as well as a capacity for joy.

Yet who, in the days of the great love-ins, could receive a dandelion from a gently smiling flower child—as I did during the Belle Isle Detroit love-in back in 1967—and not hear an inner music too long muted by the roar of machines? Of course they are rebelling against a ridiculous society, locked in by machines and robots, where nobody smiles anymore. In their own way, like the ghetto dropouts, they are making an adaptation. And if they go around loving us, is not that a teaching for us?

While our flower children teach us, their Jet Set brothers and sisters among the rich seem to have little to teach, except the dangers of too much wealth and too little love.

In this examination of the variety of cultures of adolescence, we have observed both convergence with adult society and divergence from it—and we have observed some degree of adolescent autonomy with respect to the adult society. Can we now pick one of the subcultures and say, this one has the most promise—let's put all our resources into strengthening it and discrediting the others? I think not. It has been my intention to show the strengths as well as the weaknesses of each of these adolescent subsocieties. They are all a part of us. They all have their contribution to make. Mostly, we have ignored these societies as resources, have ignored our teen-age brothers and sisters as collaborators in the ongoing business of living. This analysis is not intended to give policy makers new clues for manipulation of the young, even on behalf of the best of social goals. It is intended to introduce a new set of partners into the social process: our teen-agers.

NOTES

1. Donald R. Cressey, "Differential Association and Delinquent Subcultures" (Paper presented in Helsinki, June 1965), p. 5.
2. Carl Frankenstein, *The Roots of the Ego* (Baltimore: Williams & Wilkins, 1966).
3. Daniel Offer, *The Psychological World of the Teen-ager: A Study of Normal Adolescent Boys* (New York: Basic Books, 1969).
4. Ibid.
5. Bruno Bettelheim, as quoted in William Braden, *The Age of Aquarius* (New York: Quadrangle Books, 1970), p. 63.
6. Theodore Roszak, *The Making of a Counter Culture* (New York: Doubleday, 1968); Braden, *The Age of Aquarius*; and Jacob Needleman, *The New Religions* (Garden City, N.Y.: Doubleday, 1970).
7. S. N. Eisenstadt, *From Generation to Generation* (New York: Free Press, 1956).
8. Ibid.; Ruth Benedict makes the same point in the quoted "Continuities and Discontinuities in Cultural Conditioning," *Psychiatry* 5, no. 1 (1938): 161–67.
9. James S. Coleman, *The Adolescent Society* (New York: Free Press, 1961), p. 9.
10. Ibid., p. 12.
11. Graham Murdock and Guy Phelps, "Youth Culture and the School Revisited," *The British Journal of Sociology* 23, no. 4 (December 1972): 478.
12. Ibid., p. 479.
13. Samuel K. Grafton, *Youth Reports.*

14. I.e., Scouts, Ys, and other community children's organizations.

15. Neil Postman and Charles Weingartner, *The Soft Revolution: A Student Handbook for Turning Schools Around* (New York: Delta, 1971).

16. Eliot Wigginton, ed., *The Foxfire Book* (Garden City, N.Y.: Doubleday, 1972); and Eliot Wigginton, ed., *The Foxfire Book II* (Garden City, N.Y.: Doubleday, 1973).

17. *Anne Frank: The Diary of a Young Girl*, trans. B. M. Mooyart (rev. ed.; Garden City, N.Y.: Doubleday, 1967).

18. Jessica Reynolds, *Jessica's Journal* (New York: Holt, Rinehart & Winston, 1958).

19. H. Brunswick, *La Crise de l'Etat Prussien du XVIIIe Siècle et la Genèse de la Mentalité Romantique* (Paris: 1949).

20. Howard Becker and Harry Elmer Barnes, *Social Thought from Love to Science*, vol. 2 (3rd ed.; New York: Dover, 1961).

21. Charles Nordhoff, *Communistic Societies of the United States* (New York: Schocken Books, 1965; first published in 1875).

22. Richard Flacks, "The Liberated Generation," *Journal of Social Issues* 23 (July 1967): 52–75.

23. Unpublished data made available to the author by Harold Guetzkow, now at Northwestern University.

24. Richard Jessor, Shirley L. Jessor, and John Finney, "A Social Psychology of Marijuana Use," *Journal of Personality and Social Psychology* 26, no. 1 (1973): 1–18; Richard Jessor, Mary I. Collins, and Shirley L. Jessor, "On Becoming a Drinker: Social-Psychological Aspects of an Adolescent Transition," *Annals of the New York Academy of Science* 117C (25 May 1972): 199–213; Russell H. Weigel and Richard Jessor, "Television and Adolescent Conventionality: An Exploratory Study," *Public Opinion Quarterly* 37 (1973): 76–90.

25. The Jessors' variable, independence, while it theoretically refers to the trait of making decisions for oneself and not having them made by others, in fact appears to be interpreted by respondents as being independent of parents, and does not necessarily reflect considered independence of peers.

26. Fathers' behaviors were not related to behaviors of either sons or daughters. Men's liberation, please take note!

27. Shirley L. Jessor and Richard Jessor, "Maternal Ideology and Adolescent Nonconformity," *Development Psychology* 10 (May 1973): 246–54.

28. Cressey, "Differential Association and Delinquent Subcultures."

29. Coleman illustrates this particularly well in *Adolescent Society*, through his choice of ten different types of community school settings for his study of youth culture (p. 5).

30. Weigel and R. Jessor, "Television and Adolescent Conventionality," p. 88.

31. Ollendorf suggests that it began when patriarchies succeeded matriarchy in human civilizations; Robert Ollendorf, "The Rights of Adolescents," in *Children's Rights: The Liberation of the Child*, ed. Paul Adams et al. (New York: Praeger, 1971), p. 92.

32. George Z. Gray, *Children's Crusade: A History* (New York: William Morrow, 1972; reprint of 1870 edition).

33. Elise Boulding, "The Place of the Child in the Society of Friends," *American Friend* (July 1969): 205.

34. Ollendorf, *Children's Rights*, pp. 96–97.

35. Ibid.

36. The working-class and middle-class youth who participate in the Crusade for Christ movement, for example, are a special marginal group who have some of the characteristics of the achiever, but not in a mainstream way, yet they are not oriented to system-change either.

37. Arthur B. Shostak and William Gomberg, eds., *Blue Collar World* (Englewood Cliffs, N.J.: Prentice-Hall, 1964).

38. Gerald Handel, "Persistence and Change in Working-Class Life Style," in Shostak and Gomberg, *Blue Collar World*, pp. 36–41; Louis Kriesberg, *Mothers in Poverty* (Chicago: Aldine, 1970); S. M. Miller, "The New Working Class," in Shostak and Gomberg, *Blue Collar World*, pp. 2–9; Lee Rainwater, Richard Coleman, and Gerald Handel, *Working Man's Wife* (New York: McFadden Books, 1959); David Riesman, *The Lonely Crowd* (New Haven: Yale University Press, 1950); Frank Riessman, *The Culturally Deprived Child* (New York: Harper & Row, 1962); Hyman Rodman, "The Lower Class Value Stretch," *Social Forces* 42, no. 2 (December 1963): 205; Alvin Schorr, *Slums and Social Insecurity* (Washington, D.C.: U.S. Government Printing Office, 1963); Alvin Schorr, *Poor Kids* (New York: Basic Books, 1966).

39. Miller, "The New Working Class," p. 9.

40. Ibid., p. 2.

41. Murray Hausknecht, "The Blue-Collar Joiner," in Shostak and Gomberg, *Blue Collar World*, pp. 207–14.

42. Ibid.

43. Offer, *The Psychological World of the Teen-ager*.

44. Braden, *The Age of Aquarius*.

45. Lewis W. Jones, "The New World View of Negro Youth," in *Problems of Youth*, ed. Muzafer Sherif and Carolyn W. Sherif (Chicago: Aldine, 1965), p. 80.

46. Andrew Billingsley, *Black Families in White America* (Englewood Cliffs, N.J.: Prentice-Hall, 1968), pp. 97–121.

47. Jones, "The New World View of Negro Youth."

48. Rainwater et al., *Working Man's Wife*, pp. 289–90.

49. Gerald D. Suttles, *The Social Order of the Slum* (Chicago: University of Chicago Press, 1968).

50. John C. Flynn, "A Coordinated Approach to Exploiting Federal and Foundation Funds to Serve the Educationally Disadvantaged" (Report prepared for the Conference Preparation of Paraprofessionals, University of Tennessee, May 1969). Mimeographed.

51. Grafton, *Youth Reports*.

52. Flacks, "The Liberated Generation."

53. See "On De-Segregating Stuyvesant High," by high school student Alice de Rivera, in Robin Morgan, ed., *Sisterhood Is Powerful* (New York: Vintage Books, 1970), pp. 366–71.

54. Ibid.; also see Jean Strause, "To Be Minor and Female: The Legal Rights of Women Under 21," *Ms.* 1, no. 2 (August 1972): 70–75, 116.

55. See Recommendations and Resolutions, 1971 WHCY, which published all minority reports as well as regular commission reports. While this in a way justified the faith of the change-committed youth who attended, the entire

conference and monumental-but-never-to-be-read report is an example of token approaches to youth which do not involve taking seriously the careful thinking both mainstream and protest youth did at the conference. It will not be found on best-seller lists, nor referred to in widely read literature on the young.

56. Braden, *The Age of Aquarius*, p. 209.

57. See Elise Boulding, "The Child and Nonviolent Change," in *Design for Nonviolent Change*, ed. Israel Charny (forthcoming), for a discussion of socialization experiences which prepare children for creative change roles.

58. George Lakey, *Strategy for a Living Revolution* (San Francisco: Freeman, 1973).

59. For example, Patrick Conover, "The Potential for an Alternate Society," *Futurist* 7, no. 3 (June 1973): 111–16.

60. "The Mechanists and the Mystics," an interview with William Irwin Thompson, *Time*, 21 August 1972, pp. 36–38; and "The Individual as Institution," an essay in *Harpers*, September 1972.

61. Jones, "The New World View of Negro Youth," pp. 80–82.

62. Ibid., p. 81.

63. N. S. Caplan and J. M. Paige, in *Report of the National Advisory Commission on Civil Disorders*, ed. O. Kerner et al. (New York: Bantam Books, 1968), pp. 127–37; and N. S. Caplan and J. M. Paige, "A Study of Ghetto Rioters," *Scientific American* 219, no. 2 (August 1968): 15–21.

64. Ann Hilliard, "On the Street," *Colorado Daily* (Boulder, Colo.), 5 March 1971.

65. Arthur Pearl, "Youth in Lower Class Settings," in Sherif and Sherif, *Problems of Youth*, p. 93.

66. Suttles, *The Social Order of the Slum*.

67. Lee Rainwater, *Behind Ghetto Walls*, (Chicago: Aldine, 1970).

68. J. Kenneth Morland, "Kent Revisited: Blue Collar Aspirations and Achievements," in Shostak and Gomberg, *Blue Collar World*, pp. 134–43.

69. Theodore V. Purcell, "The Hopes of Negro Workers for Their Children," in Shostak and Gomberg, *Blue Collar World*, pp. 144–54.

70. Morland, "Kent Revisited."

71. For facts on these environmental constraints, see Alvin Schorr, *Poor Kids*; Patricia Cayo Sexton, *Education and Income* (New York: Viking Press, 1961); and Daniel Schreiber, ed., *Profile of the School Dropout* (New York: Vintage Books, 1968).

72. Suttles, *The Social Order of the Slum*.

PART THREE

Innovation of the Establishment

8

EDUCATIONAL MANAGEMENT: PROMISE AND FAILURE

Adam Scrupski

The Plight of the School Administrator

An examination of school administration might begin with a comparison of successful and unsuccessful innovations in education. There is available, collected in the same volume,[1] Richard Carlson's description of the diffusion of modern mathematics as a curricular innovation in Allegheny County, Pennsylvania,[2] and a description of the failure of a "major organizational innovation" provided by Neal Gross, Joseph B. Giaquinta, and Marilyn Bernstein.[3]

Carlson reports the rather facile adoption of "the new math" in Allegheny County as a correlate of the sociometric structure of local school superintendents, that is, school superintendents who acted as agents of influence upon one another to diffuse the curricular innovation throughout the county. The adoption of such curricular change is usually a board of education's responsibility, usually responding to an administrative recommendation. Such changes involve the substitution of a given set of materials and "methods" for another set, changes to which teachers over the years seem to have become accustomed to adjusting. As such, these changes are hardly central to the basic pattern of teacher-pupil activity; they tend to amount to no more than a substitution of one set of texts for another. In the case of modern mathematics many school districts conducted "workshops" where teachers were expected to "brush up" their mathematics and learn something of the substance of modern mathematics, but such workshops were seldom more than cursory; ignorance of the mathematical law in this case was no excuse for not having "new math."

On the other hand, the study conducted by Gross, Giaquinta, and Bernstein reported the fate of a proposed innovation in the activity and interaction of teachers and pupils in the classroom, wherein it was expected that children would learn according "to *their* interests rather than in terms of a prescribed curriculum," wherein pupils were to have "maximum freedom in choosing their own activities" and to have "primary responsibility for directing their own learning." [4] In this case a principal was the originator and agent of the innovation; he "was well known as an educational innovator and as a person who had strong beliefs about the necessity of educational change." [5] The principal had come from a position of some note outside the school district (he was, thus, not a "prophet without honor") and was given "considerable" autonomy and freedom to select his own faculty. Teachers were initially receptive to the innovation. The investigators reported, however, that six months from the time the innovation was introduced "no effort was being made to implement the innovation . . . and all teachers were still behaving in accord with the traditional role model." [6]

It may, of course, be the case that the current structure of teacher-pupil relationships, related as it is to such primary features as the isolated classroom and current class-size norms and in turn to general societal social structure, is impervious to the kind of change Gross and his colleagues have described. "Leadership" in school administration, then, may have to be content with the innovation of new "programs" or curricula, such as modern mathematics and marginal changes in educational structure (e.g., "modular scheduling and team teaching").

Yet genuine leadership in education, leadership which aims at more than the substitution of one textbook series for another, seems to comprise a large portion of the administrator's ego ideal. The principals in Seymour Sarason's study viewed their roles in such a way. [7] Certainly graduate courses in educational administration dwell at length on the problems of leadership and the position of the school administrator as educational leader, and while a few realists like Ronald Corwin lament the belief that a principal is ultimately responsible for everything that goes on in his school, [8] the belief that the principal is basically at fault if the school exhibits an "outmoded" (or unfashionable) educational program seems to be held by both the public at large and, in a buck-passing manner, by many teachers as well.[9] And when the quality of life in classrooms, a function of teacher-pupil relationships, comes in for the kind of strong criticism that has been delivered recently by such as Herbert Kohl, John Holt, Charles Silberman, and Christopher Jencks (whose readership surely constitutes a significant public for the administrator), the principal's leadership identity seems correspondingly expanded. Sarason describes the typical principal in his study as

> constantly wrestling with the problems of leadership, with the feeling, which increases in strength over time, that he is losing the battle, that he is not the leader he expected to be, or would like to be, or others expect him to be.[10]

Such a plight seems to demand an explanation. One will be assayed here.

School Administration Circumscribed: The Cult of Efficiency

At the conclusion of his classic treatment of school administration as a "cult of efficiency," Raymond Callahan laments the fact that in a study led by Neal Gross administrators were judged by themselves and board members to do their best work in the areas of finance, personnel, and school plant management and their poorest work in the area of direction of instruction, a demonstration of the heritage of the cult of efficiency.[11] Callahan's work is a history of school administration through the years when it was said "the business of America is business." [12] The development of school administration as a professional field paralleled the development of administration generally. That the classic bureaucratic model should have served education as it did business and industry should not be surprising. As Callahan suggests, this was a period of burgeoning school populations, accelerated by immigration, the decline of apprenticeship, and a lengthened period of formal education. Economy seemed to dictate increased size as well as centralization of control. Thus, considerations of hierarchical ordering, line and staff organization, and "span of control" came to characterize educational administration as they had business administration.

What is especially interesting about Callahan's descriptions of the cult of efficiency in education is that in attempting to relate some measure of cost to a measure of productivity, administrators tended always to assume the character of the teacher-pupil activity and interaction pattern as an ultimate given, selecting some consequence of this given pattern as the measure of productivity. Thus, early studies attempted to relate school expenditures to measures of educational retardation, using as a measure of school effectiveness the percentage of "repeaters" found in a given school, and ignoring completely variables related to particular school situations which might lead teachers to promote or retain students independent of instructional effectiveness as well as variables related to the nature of the instructional process taking place in the classrooms in question. Later studies used the developing testing approach in a measure of educational productivity. (In this way the cult of efficiency seems to have given strong impetus to the testing movement.)

Callahan notes early studies of class size comparing classes of 18–25 with those of 33–42 which found little difference in achievement between the two. Again, teaching methods and their outcomes were accepted as given. What was considered amenable to reconstruction were *not* the nature and quality of teacher-pupil relationship, that which presumably allowed a class of 20 to achieve similar to a class of 40, such achievement measured by a procedure which itself was constructed for large group administration; [13] what *was* considered amenable to reconstruction were class size (between the size of 20 and 40; even Coleman recently found little difference in achievement among classes varying between these limits),[14] scheduling, textbooks, and areas such as finance and personnel.

Callahan draws the parallel clearly. That which was accomplished by teachers in classrooms, it seems, was directly comparable to what was accomplished by assembly-line workers. Teaching and learning were to be as standardized and quantifiable as parts to a Ford motor car. Given the hierarchy adopted from industry, that which identifies the school board as a "board of directors," the superintendent as a "general manager," principals as "foremen," and teachers on the lowest rung as "hands," why should the integral activity of the hands get any more attention than that analogous to Frederick Taylor's stopwatch?

The school administrator's analog of the stopwatch seems to be the checklist or "evaluation instrument," wherein points are given for such things as teacher appearance and voice, classroom housekeeping, and "skill in making assignments"; points are then added to arrive at a total score which is presumed to be a measure of the teacher's worth.

Of course, the scientific managers were not immediately awed or discouraged by what Matthew Miles has called the "goal diversity" in education; [15] if goals were diverse, the problem would be resolved in terms of a kind of "consumer" demand; and the most powerful and important consumers at the time were business interests. The manner in which schools served those interests through such things as thrift and savings programs, courses in salesmanship, and sponsorship of Junior Achievement programs represents what Callahan calls the "service station" conception of schools, an orientation which implies an abdication by schoolmen of their basic professional responsibility in favor of a willingness to serve the interests of their commercial public. This public was to provide the specifications for the educational "products" to be turned out by the schools. The diffusion of educational practices may resemble the diffusion of commercial consumer fads: in American education it is important to be able to say that one's school system is abreast of the latest development. But the core of the educational process, the nature and quality of student experience, went unexamined; and its conventional definition was accepted as a given.

School Administration as a Response to Societal Forces

Art Gallaher presents an alternative explanation of the school administrator's leadership plight. Gallaher denies the role of genuine and effective change agent to the school administrator, suggesting that schools, as service organizations responsible to an autonomous local client group, constitute a cultural situs particularly inhospitable to notions of professional authority. For Gallaher, as for George Spindler, the school administrator is the "man in the middle," mediating between contrasting and sometimes contending professional and client interests.[16]

> His job is in large part that of maintaining a working equilibrium of at best antagonistically cooperative forces. This is one of the reasons why school administrators are rarely outspoken protagonists of a consistent and vigorously profiled point of view.[17]

It is suggested here that the leadership function of such a position-holder will tend to be limited by strong social constraints to the implementation of changes designed and advocated in other societal sectors. In this vein Callahan has suggested that the vulnerability of school administrators to public criticism and to the pressure built into the local control pattern accounts for their ready acceptance of the Conant recommendations,[18] as well as post-sputnik curricular changes. What this vulnerability suggests, however, is a susceptibility to demands consequent or correlative to larger societal changes. For example, the Conant proposals, particularly that calling for consolidation of small high school districts, seemed to coincide with a significant demographic phenomenon, the suburbanization of formerly rural areas by middle-class urbanites, the resultant overloading of small rural high schools (or the exclusion of "sending district" pupils from the overcrowded neighboring established high schools), the consequence of which was the construction and regionalization of larger high school districts. These schools tended to be larger schools perhaps because the kind of advanced placement and other semi-esoteric curricula that only a larger school could economically provide had been available to these middle-class groups in their former urban setting and thus expected in the new setting.

With respect to curricular programs the introduction of modern mathematics seems to be a case in point. Impetus for its inclusion in the curriculum as a replacement for the algorithm-laden and unmathematical "social arithmetic" (as earlier math programs were often caricatured) seemed to arise as part of the general post-sputnik concern for rigor in the curriculum, exemplified by the antiprogressive criticisms of such as Hyman G. Rickover[19] and Arthur Bestor,[20] supported by the same government-sponsored scholars and workshops that gave us BSCS, PSSC, and other alphabet-soup curricula, and demanded by a middle-class public anxious for its children's competitive position vis-à-vis the proliferating national defense-sponsored mobility opportunities in technical and scientific fields.[21] After what Corwin has called "faddist" districts adopted modern mathematics,[22] a process of media and socially supported diffusion seemed to set in (as noted by Carlson, cited above). In an age of geographical mobility (middle-class parents seem to know what is going on in other school districts) as well as social mobility (the same middle-class parents want their children in a "competitive" position vis-à-vis college opportunities and their low-class equivalents—not always parents—following John Dewey, want the best for "their" children, too),[23] schools may be more competitive than Carlson's characterization of them as cared-for "domesticated" organizations implies.[24]

The school administrator's role, then, seems to be basically a conservative one, ensuring the balance of forces not only in system-environment (or professional-client) terms, but also in terms of forces internal to the school system, preserving and nurturing the measure of hierarchically derived formal authority necessary to make binding the modest decisions made in the interests of the system as a whole. Changes at the heart of the educational process, concerning the character of teacher-pupil relationships, seem to be resistant to the administrator's bureaucratic mode of operation and to require an altogether different approach, one which by its very nature may be self-defeating, as we shall see, a quid pro quo that ensures the maintenance of the status quo.

Classroom Structure and the Circumscription of Educational Leadership

To return to the case cited by Gross, Giaquinta, and Bernstein, where an innovation designed to change drastically the "heart of the educational process" proved a dismal failure, the investigators' proposed solution might be examined. The case is defined as one of ineffective "management," basically one of a failure to resocialize teachers to a new definition of their role. The tasks which presumably effect such resocialization consist of

1. Making clear new role requirements (the old watchword, "communications")

2. Making adjustments in organizational structure (basically the changing of lunchroom and physical education schedules)

3. The provision of instructional hardware and software

4. The provision of resocialization experiences for teachers

5. The provision of necessary supports and rewards to reinforce teacher efforts[25]

Now the last two recommendations seem to be only a restatement of the basic problem. Any resocialization experiences (in-service workshops, for example) are hardly likely to be effective unless they involve the actual behavior and its consequences; both are available only in working with pupils in the prescribed setting; the only rewards which presumably will reinforce changed behavior are the successes of the new endeavor, which is itself the objective of the resocialization recommendation. The first three tasks—communicating clearly about role requirements, making marginal schedule changes, and providing materials—constitute administration's old "caretaking" function, and, given the context of the situation, seem to deal with aspects of the problem in a way differing only in slight degree with steps already taken. In short, the recommendations seem largely redundant, trivial, and ineffective, testimony to the difficulty of effecting change in classroom operations and a resort to what Sarason has identified as a tendency for a principal when encountering resistance either to "assert his authority" or "withdraw from the fray." [26]

Why should the classroom behavior of teachers in interaction with their charges be so relatively impervious to formal bureaucratic methods? Dan Lortie has noted that the organizational structure of public schools meets only minimal criteria of bureaucracy; there is a hierarchy of offices filled through merit, but the hierarchy is relatively flat; there are divisions of labor, but the divisions are comparatively few; there are careers available, but because the organization is a flat one there are few chances for promotion, and many spend only a few years in such employment.[27] And, while there are rules of operation, they pertain more to problems of organizational management than to the actions and behavior of teachers' work in the classroom, which constitute the core of the educational enterprise. As Robert Dreeben suggests:

> Although teachers may have to follow syllabi handed down from the superintendent's office and follow directives issued by the principal and his administrative subordinates, many, if not most, of their day-to-day activities are governed by the exigencies and pressures of the classroom.[28]

"How," asks Lortie, "does one subdivide a warm and empathic relationship between teacher and pupil?"[29] Lortie further observes:

> Teachers face the problem of deciding when they have achieved the desired level of student response; in a sense, each teacher defines the outcomes she will consider gratifying and those she will consider unsatisfactory . . . teaching has a particularly interminable quality. One can easily define teaching outcomes in such a way that it is never finished.[30]

Both Dreeben and Bryan Wilson[31] call attention to the teacher's need to win the voluntary participation of pupils in the school's program; rules and routine procedures are not applicable to such behavior. Such voluntary participation on the part of students would seem to be a consequence of what has earlier been termed the subordinate subsystem role. Indeed, it might be suggested that it is just when the teacher's subordinate subsystem role becomes more crucial, that is, when the discontinuity between family and extraschool child role, on the one hand, and formal pupil role, on the other, becomes greater (as related to the development of child nurturance in the shrunken nuclear family; note Philippe Aries' *Centuries of Childhood*),[32] that bureaucratic chain-of-command operations break down as they reach the classroom. In this sense, in considering the teacher's developing subordinate subsystem role, we are speaking of a kind of "normative upgrading" demand laid upon the teacher, requiring greater on-the-spot spontaneity and autonomy in adapting to students in a supportive manner, paralleling the normative upgrading characteristic of society at large.

Lortie suggests that all this presses the teacher further into teaching and away from other aspects of his role.[33] He points out that teachers in his study of Dade County (Florida) schools, when asked what they would do with an additional ten hours of professional time per week, "chose core teaching tasks over organizational matters in a ratio of nine to one." [34] The significant sanctions for teachers, it seems, are in the hands of pupils, not administrators.

What, however, of the well-known observation-conference technique of teacher-supervision practices by school administrators? Such a practice consists of a visit to a teacher's classroom by an administrator (for purposes of "observation") followed by a conference between the two, supposedly a "cooperative" effort to improve instruction. Among administrators this technique has long been considered the "heart" of the supervisory process. If, however, our suggestions regarding classroom imperviousness to bureaucratic control have validity, we would expect the observation-conference technique to be honored more in the breach than in practice. That such is indeed the case seems to be indicated by recently gathered data, both hard and soft.

Lortie suggests that principals accommodate to what he perceives as the teacher's wishes for loose supervision. He reports studies by McDowell, reporting that Chicago principals expressed reservations concerning close supervision of tenure teachers; and by Trask, reporting great caution exercised by principals in initiating activity for any but beginning teachers.[35] Dreeben reports an NEA study in which 55 percent of the principals said they did not have enough time for accurate evaluation of teachers. More than a quarter of the teachers in the study reported no classroom visitations by any supervisor during the first half of the year. Only 44 percent of tenure teachers were visited, and the median number of visits was only three for both these and the nontenure teachers. The same study reports only half the teachers believing they were helped by a visit, while only 11.1 percent of probationary teachers and 14.8 percent of tenure teachers expressed confidence in the system.[36] With respect to the question of "help" coming from the principal, Lortie reports Dade County teachers citing other teachers as sources of the most help 41.5 percent of the time and the principal only 14.3 percent.

Estelle Fuchs sums up reported experiences of new urban teachers by referring to principal classroom visitation as merely a "rite de passage," representing a stage or hurdle in a teacher's career, suggesting that the most effective source of help for the new teacher are other teachers and specialists.[37] (Fuchs suggests that the principal, when he does "observe," is meeting administrative requirements of his own superiors; submitting reports that lend themselves to the perfunctory meeting of bureaucratic requirements rather than improving the quality of teaching.)

Seymour Sarason has given considerable attention to the problems faced by principals as elicited in interviews and observations at the Yale Psycho-Educational Clinic. Sarason asserts that principals view entering a classroom for purposes of evaluation as hostile to the teacher and rarely productive of instructional improvement.

> From the standpoint of the principal there is little that he feels he can do about what goes on in a classroom, particularly if the teacher has tenure or has been a teacher for a number of years. As a result, the principal tolerates situations that by his values or standards are "wrong." Because this toleration is frequently accompanied by feelings of guilt and inadequacy, it frequently has an additional consequence: the tendency to deny that these situations exist in the school.[38]

The significance of this last observation is obvious. If problematical situations are denied, they are hardly likely to be dealt with effectively.

There is some question concerning the teacher's definition of the visitation act, for Dreeben enters a demurrer to Lortie's assertion that teachers dislike close supervision by principals. Dreeben notes the Gross and Herriott study which reported that teachers *want* close supervision. Some of the questions to which teachers in this study responded might be interpreted as involving a kind of support rather than scrutiny, e.g., "require teachers to keep the principal informed of problem children," and "ask teachers to report all major conferences with parents to the principal." Nevertheless, other questions, such as "visit classes on a regular schedule to determine how well teachers are carrying out their jobs" elicit only a 20 percent negative response from teachers, suggesting that teachers may consider such close supervision much less of a threat than is widely assumed.[39] Is the loneliness of teaching and its many anxiety-generating difficulties such that principal attendance to the classroom may be viewed as a kind of support or at least a making available to the principal an acknowledgement of just how "tough" the teaching job is?

From Scientific Management to Human Relations

What Callahan has done for scientific management in education remains to be done for the human relations approach in educational administration, for just as educational administrators were strongly influenced by classical management approaches, so they seemed susceptible to the developing human relations approach in the 1940s and early 1950s. However, the acceptance of the human relations approach in education might be explained in terms other than subcultural diffusion. The attenuation of the classical bureaucratic model in educational administration seemed to coincide with the growth in popular acceptance of progressive education as an educational movement. Progressive education seemed to focus squarely upon the educational experience of the child and the transformed role of the teacher as the midwife of this experience. As educators turned their attention to what was going on between teacher and pupil in the classroom and made these relations problematical, the classical model had to be seen as ineffective for the transformation of the school that progressives called for; it was thus at least supplemented if not replaced during the 1940s with the "human relations" approach, one characterized by "democratic administration," concern for "motivation" of practitioners, group processes, and attention to workers' "morale." While progressive education's historians tend not to attend to administrative affairs,[40] it is nevertheless interesting to note that the human relations approach tended to coincide with the apex of progressive education as a movement; *Management and the Worker*,[41] the study which seemed to give birth to the human relations approach, was published in 1939, one year after the Progressive Education Association reached its maximum in enrollment.[42]

Writing in the 1930s, immediately prior to the advent of the human relations movement, John Dewey observed,

> Relations of teachers and pupils have been harmonized to a large extent. Older methods of "discipline" have been abolished or fallen into disuse. Much greater provision for activity within the school has been made in compensation for the curtailments enforced outside the school. Indoctrination in the school subjects has become more skillful and sugar coated. Above all, new subjects and new courses of study have been introduced with almost startling rapidity. . . . School expansion in subjects, in courses open to students and in numbers of students has kept pace with the industrial expansion.
>
> Nevertheless there has been no fundamental change in spirit and motivation. . . . Problems are brought up but only that they may be solved and put to bed. . . . The real alternative to settling questions is not mental confusion but the development of a spirit of curiosity that will keep the student in an attitude of inquiry and of search for a new light.[43]

In a field where the core operations seemed thoroughly insulated from formal controls, the human relations approach must have seemed peculiarly adaptive. Robert G. Owens suggests that the human relations movement had much greater impact on supervision as a separate field in education and elementary school administration than it did on school administration per se.[44] (Of course, the relatively smaller size of elementary schools compared to high schools usually precluded a separate supervisor; elementary principals were both administrators and supervisors. Also, the progressive movement seemed predominantly concerned with elementary education.) The point must be made that it was at this time that distinctions were being made between administration and supervision as professional fields. It seems that the construction of the field or concept of supervision separate from that of administration provided a hospitable reception for (and was perhaps a reaction to) the human relations approach.

However, to a conscientious administrator or supervisor the successful implementation of the human relations approach must have seemed to require some variety of magic power. What theory existed at the base of the human relations school was translated into prescriptions for action on the part of supervisors (or "leaders" as they tended to be called); in that sense human relations was as much a guide to action as classical bureaucratic theory. The sticking point for the practitioner had to be the difficulty of gaining the objectives of effective educational reconstruction without a clear direction for his own influence. To successfully "work" the human relations, the practitioner had to steer a tight course between complete laissez faire on the one hand and only thinly disguised manipulation on the other.

All this seemed to be reflected in one of the more quintessential guides of the day, *Supervision for Better Schools* by Kimball Wiles, published in 1950. Wiles suggests that the principal problem for the supervisor is the discovery of ways of working cooperatively *within* a staff rather than *on* a staff. The supervisor's "word" is not to carry any more weight than that of other members of his staff. "His vision is not expected to be superior to that of the combined intelligence of the working group." [45] The special function of the supervisor is to work for the conditions (principally high morale and effective group process) "under which people can think and work together about purpose and about ways of implementing them." [46] Wiles betrays the naiveté of the human relations approach when he observes "Low morale cuts down production. High morale increases it." [47] (Actually it has been demonstrated that there is no such linear relationship between morale, whatever it is, and productivity.)[48] Wiles' even more naive suggestion that supervisors treat all staff members equally ignores evidence gathered by Howard Becker that what is significant in this respect is equity, not equality; Becker found new principals experiencing difficulties because of their ignorance of the informal status hierarchy of a school staff.[49] In this respect Wiles advises supervisors to take pains to meet the staff on a "social" basis and to work his influence primarily by being a kind of role model. Where is there a more naive statement in the literature of supervision than the following?

> If he [the supervisor] is prompt, hard-working, and thorough, the staff will be the same. If he sets an example of coming to work easily and not leaving before the day is over, the staff will assume the same responsibility.[50]

The element of manipulation among all these prescriptions for democracy in educational policy making is betrayed by a casual statement early in the book, where Wiles asserts that the effective teacher "encourages the collection of sufficient information about each child to make it possible for the teacher to guide the child through an individualized curriculum." [51] The message seems to be clear, democratic group processes must be utilized in the interests of progressive method. To say that such a task approaches the superhuman seems an understatement. That administrators and supervisors were destined to be confused and frustrated in employing these approaches seems inevitable. That disenchantment would shortly set in seems equally to be expected.

In any case, the demise of human relations in educational administration seemed to be furthered by the antiprogressive, post-sputnik campaign for a more rigorous curriculum, which again seemed to accept the traditional classroom structure as a given, to be contended with primarily by the production of "teacher-proof" curriculum materials.

The Return of Imposition

Michael Katz, in exploring school reform in mid-nineteenth-century America, asserts that it was accomplished largely by imposition. Exploring the development of high school education in Massachusetts, Katz demonstrates that it was imposed upon the community by the most wealthy, prestigious, and powerful laymen, joined often by those at middle levels, in the interests of the perpetuation and enhancement of the social position of their own families, testified to by high school enrollments at the time, which exhibited very few lower-class children.[52]

In treating the development of a "soft" (progressive-humanistic) pedagogy Katz makes the same point, that such a pedagogy was imposed upon the schools by an increasingly centralized state apparatus (in this case sponsored by Horace Mann), again apparently in the interests of the mobility-conscious middle and upper classes.

Actually, the soft-liners' emphasis on the individual stressed the very qualities most necessary for social mobility and economic success. Their ideal product would be superbly equipped to enter the competitive arenas of Massachusetts life.[53]

There is a sense in which the curricular reform movement of the late 1950s and 1960s represents a similar social phenomenon, a similar process of imposition. Now allied with university scholars and wealthy foundations, purportedly in the national interest, powerful non-educators, inveighing against the educational establishment, imposed a set of curricula upon American schools in the interests of the acceleration of the social position of those who already "had"; that this movement should have been accompanied by an acceleration of tracking, ostensibly to "individualize" instruction, but effectively to set up segregated schools-within-schools for those whose *real* "head start" made these curricula available (at the outset, at least, and even to this day in many places, most of these curricula are considered to be "only for the gifted") seems a further illustration of Merton's "Matthew Effect." [54]

Concern with the core of the educational process did not die, of course, in the late 1950s and '60s. A growing preoccupation with the quality of school life by middle classes and with problems of academic stimulation and motivation by lower classes and their sponsors assured that attention would continue to be given to the nature of teacher-pupil activity and interaction and the teaching-learning process. Administrators were beginning to find themselves back where they started from, prior to the human relations experience. (Many adopted what seemed to be a contemporary elaboration of the human relations idea in the form of T-group or sensitivity training, but the same criticism might be made of this latest variation that was made of its progenitor.)

Human Relations' Successor

Amitai Etzioni refers in a general sense to a "structural" approach as the successor to the human relations school.[55] In an education-specific sense, Owens speaks of "behavioral theory" as the successor to the earlier approaches, citing concepts such as role and reference group in contrast to line and staff, span of control, and unity of command as representative of classical bureaucratic theory and morale, group dynamics, and participative supervision as representative of human relations.[56]

A more recent thrust in educational administration has been what is called a "systems" approach which has in some cases given rise to an emphasis on "behavioral objectives" and "accountability." As such it seems to constitute an alternative to the structural, behavioral theory-related leadership approach. However, since it is the subject of Professor Oliver's chapter, further treatment of it here will be omitted, except to suggest that it seems to be the natural descendant of classical bureaucratic theory and scientific management. Though lower-level personnel (teachers) are enlisted in the specification of objectives or goals, the approach seems only pseudo-democratic since the entire notion of "goals" seems in many respects foreign to the educational process and in a sense seems to constitute another return to imposition. (To witness literature or social studies teachers attempting to state "goals" concerning a given examination of a piece of literature or social study is a harrowing experience.)

The human relations approach neglected the significance of formal organization and formally assigned position, assuming that conflict based on formal position could be eliminated and that workers of various designations could all live together on (and off) the job in one happy family. The behavioral theory to which Owens refers and the structuralist approach described by Etzioni both seem to correct this imbalance. Both seem to constitute an empirically based, rather academic approach to life in organizations, one which, through an accumulation of empirical evidence, using the tools and approaches of the behavioral sciences, attempts to build up a "science" of administration.

There seems, however, to be a difference in kind between the classical approach along with its exaggerated scientific management form and the human relations approach, on the one hand, and the behavioral or structural approach, on the other. The earlier two each constituted a clear guide to action for the administrator. Difficult as action may have been in the case of the human relations approach, there were available to the practitioner relatively clearly defined approaches, derived from basic theory and some research. The behavioral and structural approach, on the other hand, seems to be largely an academic-scientific endeavor. An administrator must be a student of behavioral science in order to gain any line on possible directions to take. In this sense, the new approach seems to constitute an adaptive upgrading of the administrative function.

A new focus on leadership seems to be emerging from the behavioral theory approach to administration, one which makes distinctions between administration and leadership just as earlier distinctions were drawn between administration and supervision. There are significant and well-known studies of leader behavior,[57] "executive professional leadership," [58] expressive and instrumental leadership,[59] and "leadership effectiveness." [60] Several pose an analytical dichotomy between the needs of the personality (idiographic) which were heavily weighted in the human relations approach and the needs of the organization (nomothetic) which were emphasized in the classical bureaucratic orientation,[61] implying that there exists an essential reciprocity between the two if the organization is to be energized in an adaptive direction, that is, if it is to be successfully led.

From Supersubordination to Exchange

An illustration of the behavioral approach in educational administration seems represented in recent work by Dan Lortie who seems to have correctly identified the basic nature of the teacher-administrator relationship but whose identification requires some revision. Lortie's basic hypothesis is that since teachers' rewards are in the hands of pupils and not administrators, the teacher is released from bureaucratic control by the administrator, enabling the relationship to move to one of reciprocity or exchange rather than super and subordination.

> Caring less about school-wide than classroom affairs, the teacher is not reluctant to grant the principal clear hegemony over those matters which do not bear directly upon her teaching activities . . . the principal's primary sphere is the school at large, the teacher's is the classroom.[62]

Thus, Lortie suggests that the principal exchanges loose supervision of teachers ("as one approaches instruction the number and tone of administrative initiations change and the 'suggestion' becomes more characteristic than the 'order' ")[63] for a willingness on the part of teachers to submit textbook inventories, participate in curriculum revision, and comply with other routine nonclassroom-related policies. The principal gives the teacher the classroom and in return the teacher gives the principal the school. While this exchange may help to account for the propensity, when it comes to innovation, for administrators to initiate changes much more easily in the area of curriculum and organization rather than classroom teaching method, it seems to be less of a genuinely reciprocal affair, wherein each dispensation would vary with the other, than a relatively invariant aspect of the culture of the school. As Atwood has noted, teachers come to value what they do, working independently of all others within the four walls of their classrooms.[64]

The suggestion here is that contrary to Lortie's hypothesis, principals don't have to be bargained with for loose supervision. They tend to supervise loosely for the reasons noted above, time pressure, a declining expertise as teachers enhance their specialization and principals continue to ply administrative routines, and the difficulty of meeting the burden of proof of educational criticism. Teachers tend to do such things as fill out textbook inventories as such tasks are related to their basic "zone of indifference"; indeed a better illustration of this zone of Barnard's could not be found.[65] This is not to suggest that teachers do not require a basic freedom from administrative interference in order to function effectively. Fred Katz has incisively demonstrated such autonomy needs on the part of the teachers.[66]

We have earlier pointed to the normative upgrading phenomenon, which applied to the case of working with today's children (particularly with respect to what has been called subordinate subsystem interation) requires increasing spontaneity and autonomy on the part of the teacher. However, there is another sense in which the teacher must fashion a protection for his autonomous classroom direction, a service which lies within the principal's sphere. Such a service is the support given the teachers in cases of unruly pupils and "interfering" parents. As noted above, socialization in schools means socialization to orientations and relationships characterized by universalism, specificity, performance, and independence rather than particularism, diffuseness, quality, and dependence, all characteristics of family relationships.[67] It means, as Parsons has suggested, emancipation from these family orientations and relationships. Any institution that proposes to resocialize individuals who are at the same time living and existing in the "deviant" pattern of relationships is bound to find itself in conflict—both with official representatives of that "deviant" pattern (parents who tend to represent the pattern to the school) and with socializees who tend to resist resocialization (discipline problems).

Add to this the competing socialization agency of the peer group, which exists as an opportunity for the young increasingly to exercise independence from adult control and which therefore exhibits a tendency to behave in ways that are positively disapproved by adult representatives of society. There must also be added the schools' crucial role as an agent of selection (manpower allocation) as it stratifies pupils in terms of achievement, a function which jeopardizes the status position of the family on the one hand (leading to parental tendency to intrude) and tends to alienate the students who are continually unsuccessful while compelling them to attend (leading to discipline problems). Thus, it should not be surprising to find support in cases of pupil behavior and parental complaint that administrative activity which is most highly valued and demanded by teachers.[68]

This support is more than "consideration," friendliness, or Wiles' "social activity." It is an active coming across with protection and defense of teacher autonomy as it relates to teacher classroom activity. As we have seen, the teacher group tends to build the expectation for such support into a norm for administrative behavior. Lortie himself seems to recognize this when he says,

> A relationship of exchange implies that the teachers can assert as well as respond to claims. In the case of elementary teachers, her claims are buttressed by their legitimacy; "requests for assistance" can readily be justified in terms of her primary function as a teacher. Teachers press their principals for help in difficult discipline cases and with "problem" parents . . . the assertion of such claims is congruent with both teachers core tasks and the enhancement of work rewards.[69]

With respect to leadership in such a situation, Peter Blau in a variant of exchange theory says that it is the furnishing of needed contributions to a group that makes a man a leader, that makes followers of the group and disposes them to meet the leader's expectations. Thus, if there is to be an expansion of teacher disposition to comply beyond the basic zone of indifference noted above, it will depend upon the administrator's delivery of the requisite support.

On the other hand, Alvin Gouldner has observed,

> . . . if Alter feels that a given conforming act has been imposed upon ego—let us say as part of the minimal requirements of the position— we would expect Alter to value and reciprocate it less than if he defined Ego's conformity as "voluntary."
>
> Conversely, the more Ego's conforming action is defined by Alter as voluntary, the greater is Alter's tendency to appreciate and reward it. . . . In other words, reciprocity is a function of the degree to which the act is perceived as voluntary.[70]

In the school situation, it is suggested that to the extent that support from the principal is considered by teachers to be involuntary, obligatory just to meet the minimum demands of the role of principal, to that extent it will elicit little additional willingness to respond positively to administrative leadership. Thus, the significance of the informal teacher group in defining the parameters of rights and obligations in the problematical situation. For it is expected that this group will maximize teacher autonomy by providing resonance and a sense of justice concerning its demands for support. As Gouldner later notes,

> . . . a moral rule is given more support by a part [of the social system] when it furthers than when it restricts its autonomy. The tensions between the parts is reflected in the interpretations each seeks to impose on any rule.[71]

Thus, in the case of discipline problems, it is expected that the teacher group will opt for the rule that says a "good principal should support his teachers" rather than the one which says "a good teacher handles his own problems." [72]

If as Gouldner's observation implies, the teacher group is able to define administrative support as involved in the basic performance of the administrative job, as something "owed" to the teacher merely by virtue of the position he holds, to that extent administrative support will be perceived as involuntary, it will do little to advance the administrator's leadership potential, and a possible constraint upon teacher autonomy will be obviated.

Gouldner describes the process by which a given act performed for another may through repeated performances come to be taken for granted and thus earn no reciprocity.

> . . . the longer the sequence of Ego's conforming actions, the more likely is Alter to take Ego's conformity for granted. The more Alter takes Ego's conformity for granted, the less appreciative Alter will feel and the less propensity he will have to reward and reciprocate Ego's conforming actions . . . repeated identical acts of conformity modify —i.e., increase or reinforce—the expectation of conformity. Conformity is thus taken for granted and thereby the propensity to reciprocate is weakened.[73]

There may be a strain toward such a situation in the school administrative situation. Note the following observation by Sarason, made of a principal (whom teachers considered "strong" with children) who asked,

> "How do I get some of my teachers to be able to change what and how they are teaching them?" This principal, who spent most of his

time handling pupils sent "to the office," literally had no time to spend in classrooms or with those teachers he regarded to be as much of a problem as he did the children.[74]

While this explanation of the principal's failure to get his teachers to change seems valid, one suspects that his obvious "automatic" delivery of support reduced the propensity on the part of teachers to respond positively to his leadership.

Edwin Bridges has provided significant research in this area, which unfortunately has not been followed up in similar studies. Bridges reports that with increased experience, principals' attitudes toward their role approach the expectations held by teachers (and the more likely teachers are to fault him with respect to his behavior);[75] the absence of a "vice versa" here or in any other research suggests that the weight of resonance and the interpretation of the moral rule may lie on the side of the teacher group rather than on the side of the principal.

The author's own research in a small elementary school district composed of four schools has also uncovered a strain toward compliance on the part of the principal with teacher expectations; this compliance in the case of all but one of the four schools seemed to have undergone Gouldner's inflationary spiral. In the one school where principal support maintained its value and was reciprocated by teachers with a disposition to follow principal leadership, the staff had a peculiar history of relative independence, of both assistance from the principal and support from one another, thus reducing their demand for principal support.[76]

Effective leadership, then, under the conditions just examined seems hardly to have been advanced. If anything, the autonomy of professional staff personnel seems to be strengthened, both specifically, in furthering its insulation from particularistic intrusion, and generally, in rendering it further resistant to administrative influence. In this sense what may have been uncovered is a thrust that will ultimately issue in something approximating colleague control.[77]

The suggestion here is that the professional group's drive for autonomy through a demand for unconditional support or conformity may constitute a divergent force, a result of structural differentiation and adaptive upgrading. As Winston White has observed,

It has been the policy of the American labor movement that the rights of labor to some degree of autonomy in work processes . . . were best attained by eschewing participation in overall managerial responsibility.[78]

Correlatively, there is no assurance that sharing in administrative operations through "democratic administration" is the route to professional autonomy for teachers. As Iannacone has pointed out, the interests of teacher influence on policy making may be better served by strong informal organization, as noted in chapter 6.[79]

The notion of reciprocity involves basically horizontal rather than hierarchical relationships. As Lortie hints when he speaks of the teacher-administrator relationship turning "from subordination to exchange," [80] reciprocity denotes a certain equality of condition, furthered by increasing structural differentiation, which provides personnel with a more likely unique occupational identification and, in terms of occupational upgrading, makes close supervision of diverse specialist-experts by generalist administrators increasingly difficult. Changes in labor-force composition continue to see a reduction in the proportion of "production" workers and unskilled workers in favor of jobs concerned with people and data in some degree of complexity and requiring autonomous judgment, all a consequence of upgrading and structural differentiation. One would expect that such a process would produce an administrative ideology which retained in somewhat diminished intensity the morale-oriented concerns of the human relations school but which emphasized through its concern with "leadership" the specialized adaptive functions of administrators in gaining autonomously directed intelligent effort on the part of an increasing percentage of workers.

Conclusion

With scientific management having been rejected because of its mechanical and teacher-demeaning approach and its primary concern with the fringe areas of education, with the human relations combination of laissez faireism and manipulation unmasked, with the more recent leadership-influence approaches washing out in a stream of inflationary expectations, it seems that the informal group of teachers drawn together to maintain its autonomy opts for ever greater autonomy and freedom from constraint by increasingly restricting its domain to the academic through demands for equality of treatment and administrative support in cases of pupil misbehavior and particularistic interference. This option seems to constitute a further development of structural differentiation, leading perhaps ultimately to teachers' assumption of the role projected for them several years ago by David Riesman:

. . . I want to encourage some of them to give up trying to be psychiatrists, mothers, and moralists, to give up making citizens, democrats, and tolerant children. Could they not be persuaded to concentrate more than many now feel justified in doing on their roles as teachers of specific subjects? This is, after all, a job no one else is assigned to do.[81]

Further structural differentiation in education seems to be reflected in the increasing specialization in the form of child study teams, counseling, and special classes for socially and emotionally disturbed, neurologically impaired and perceptually impaired; such structural development tends to differentiate the affective from the cognitive function in education, removing many "problem" children from the regular classroom and in fact constituting a kind of tentative solution to the problem, pressing teachers further toward the core teaching function.

It might be noted that at Rutgers Graduate School of Education a faculty committee has recently recommended to the state teacher certification agency that even elementary teachers be expected to "specialize" in one subject or another. Such specialization would insulate teachers even further from the effective supervision of generalist administrators and further enhance teacher autonomy. Its implementation presumably would assist in the further upgrading of education and ultimately of society at large.

Jesse Newlon, speaking as early as 1925, suggested that school administrators should be students of the social sciences, of history, sociology, economics, psychology, and political science in terms of their educational implications.[82] Such an orientation is, of course, similar to but broader than the behavioral theory approach to administration explicated above. Newlon's administrator might then exemplify the scholarship prescribed by Dewey in his "Sources of a Science of Education," [83] scholarship in the field of humanistic studies as well as behavioral sciences, so that such studies might direct the identification of educational problems and then assist in solving them. Newlon's point is strongly made, that education is a social process, that it participates extensively and intensively in the social life of the community and that one who presumes to some leadership in the field must be thoroughly knowledgeable in the social studies. Such an administrator might, as Dewey suggested, identify forces with which educators, having made an assessment of the direction in which society is headed and the contending forces involved, might choose to align themselves. As such, implicit direction available to educators may be guided less by a romantic yearning for a return to a more pristine gemeinschaft existence and more by a program for action in a new and emerging social context.

In reading T. W. Bamford's book on the rise of the British public school, one is struck by two characteristics of the great headmasters. The first is that they viewed themselves as teachers, to the point of being obsessed with the need for inspiring the sixth form, which they thought the most important part of their work.[84] The second striking characteristic of these headmasters was their tendency to participate in the politics of controversy. Bamford observes,

> One might well ask how a man whose name appears regularly in the papers and who deliberately sets out to shock society can possibly fail to influence his pupils. This is not an idle question but one vital to the whole public school story, since the greatest headmasters have by common repute been violent radicals . . . while conversely, many with dim reputations were reactionaries . . . those headmasters who lacked this controversial dynamic quality are not considered in the top rank.[85]

While one would not advise today's administrators to engage in controversy for the sake of controversy (for one thing, they lack the prestigious ascriptive "connections" of the great headmasters), one might observe that scholarship in the social studies would make intelligent participation in community and societal political affairs available to school administrators (as well as giving administrators a discipline to teach in). Waller has suggested that teachers will continue to be imprisoned within the schoolteacher stereotype until they begin to participate as first-class citizens in the affairs of the community. In this sense school administrators might lead the way. Certainly their public political participation added a charisma to the authority of the great headmasters, and Etzioni has commented that normative organizations like the school can hardly do without a large measure of charismatic authority.[86] The hope then is still that announced by Newlon, that the educational administrator may be the leader of "a company of scholars engaged in the education of youth." [87]

NOTES

1. Matthew B. Miles and W. W. Charters, Jr., *Learning in Social Settings: New Readings in the Social Psychology of Education* (Boston: Allyn & Bacon, 1970).

2. Richard Carlson, "The Adoption of Educational Innovations," in Miles and Charters, *Learning in Social Settings*, pp. 672–90.

3. Neal Gross, Joseph B. Giaquinta, and Marilyn Bernstein, "Failure to

Implement a Major Organizational Reform," in Miles and Charters, *Learning in Social Settings*, pp. 691–706.

4. Ibid., p. 694.

5. Ibid., p. 695.

6. Ibid., p. 696.

7. Seymour Sarason, *The Culture of the School and the Problem of Change* (Boston: Allyn & Bacon, 1971).

8. Ronald G. Corwin, *A Sociology of Education* (New York: Appleton-Century-Crofts, 1965).

9. George Spindler, "The Role of the School Administrator," in *Education and Culture*, ed. George Spindler (New York: Holt, Rinehart & Winston, 1963).

10. Sarason, *The Culture of the School and the Problem of Change*, p. 130.

11. Raymond E. Callahan, *Education and the Cult of Efficiency* (Chicago: The University of Chicago Press, 1962), p. 254.

12. Calvin Coolidge, Speech before Society of American Newspaper Editors, 17 January 1925.

13. Callahan, *Education and the Cult of Efficiency*, p. 220.

14. James Coleman, Ernest Q. Campbell, et al., *Equality of Educational Opportunity* (Washington, D.C.: U.S. Government Printing Office, 1966).

15. Matthew Miles, "Some Properties of Schools as Social Systems," in *Social and Cultural Foundations of Guidance*, ed. Esther M. Lloyd-Jones and Norah Rosenau (New York: Holt, Rinehart & Winston, 1968), pp. 128–29.

16. Art Gallaher, Jr., "Directed Change in Formal Organizations: The School System," in *Change Processes in the Public Schools* (Eugene, Oregon: The Center for the Advanced Study of Educational Administration, University of Oregon, 1965), pp. 49–51.

17. George Spindler, "The Role of the School Administrator," p. 142.

18. James S. Conant, *The American High School Today* (New York: McGraw-Hill, 1959).

19. See Hyman G. Rickover, *Education and Freedom* (New York: Dutton, 1959); and *Swiss Schools and Ours and Why Theirs Are Better* (Boston: Little, Brown, 1962).

20. Arthur Bestor, *The Restoration of Learning: A Program for Redeeming the Unfulfilled Promise of American Education* (New York: Alfred A. Knopf, 1955).

21. Referring in 1959 to the scientific revolution and its consequent need for qualified scientists and technologists, the "Crowther Report" spoke of the "swing" on the part of young people to science and mathematics as subjects for specialization. "The Pressure of Economic Change," in *Education, Economy, and Society*, ed. A. H. Halsey, Jean Floud, and C. Arnold Anderson (New York: Free Press of Glencoe, 1961), p. 22.

22. Corwin, *A Sociology of Education*, pp. 388–89.

23. "What the best and wisest parent wants for his own child, that must the community want for all of its children," John Dewey, *The School and Society*. (Chicago: University of Chicago Press, 1900), p. 19.

24. Richard Carlson, "Environmental Constraints and Organizational Consequences: The Public School and its Clients," in *Behavioral Science and Educational Administration*, ed. Daniel E. Griffiths (National Society for the Study of Education, 1964), pp. 262–76.

25. Gross, Giaquinta, and Bernstein, "Failure to Implement a Major Organizational Reform," p. 701.

26. Sarason, *The Culture of the School and the Problem of Change*, p. 29.

27. Dan Lortie, "The Balance of Control and Autonomy in Elementary School Teaching," *The Semi-Professions and Their Organization*, ed. Amitai Etzioni (New York: Free Press, 1969), p. 9.

28. Robert Dreeben, *The Nature of Teaching: Schools and the Work of Teachers* (Glenview, Ill.: Scott, Foresman, 1970), p. 47.

29. Lortie, "The Balance of Control and Autonomy in Elementary School Teaching," p. 9.

30. Ibid., pp. 34–35.

31. Bryan Wilson, "The Teacher's Role—A Sociological Analysis," *British Journal of Sociology* 13, no. 1 (March 1962): 15–32.

32. Philippe Aries, *Centuries of Childhood: A Social History of Family Life* (New York: Vintage Books, 1965).

33. See also Howard S. Becker, "Social-class Variations in the Teacher-Pupil Relationship," in *The Sociology of Education: A Sourcebook*, ed. Robert R. Bell and Holger R. Stub (Homewood, Ill.: Dorsey Press, 1968), pp. 156–57.

34. Lortie, "The Balance of Control and Autonomy in Elementary School Teaching," pp. 34–35.

35. Ibid., p. 37.

36. Dreeben, *The Nature of Teaching*, pp. 62–63.

37. Estelle Fuchs, *Teachers Talk: Views from Inside City Schools* (Garden City, N.Y.: Anchor Books, 1969), p. 160.

38. Sarason, *The Culture of the School and the Problem of Change*, p. 120.

39. Dreeben, *The Nature of Teaching*, pp. 68–72.

40. See Lawrence Cremin, *The Transformation of the School* (New York: Alfred A. Knopf, 1961).

41. Fritz Jules Roethlisberger and William John Dickson, *Management and the Worker* (Cambridge, Mass.: Harvard University Press, 1939).

42. Cremin, *The Transformation of the School*, p. 324.

43. John Dewey, "The Schools in the Social Order," in *Intelligence in the Modern World: John Dewey's Philosophy*, ed. Joseph Ratner (New York: Modern Library, 1939), pp. 687–89.

44. Robert G. Owens, *Organizational Behavior in Schools* (Englewood Cliffs, N.J.: Prentice-Hall, 1970), p. 27.

45. Kimball Wiles, *Supervision for Better Schools* (New York: Prentice-Hall, 1950), p. 9.

46. Ibid.

47. Ibid., p. 39.

48. See Bernard Berelson and Gary A. Steiner, *Human Behavior: An Inventory of Scientific Findings* (New York: Harcourt, Brace, & World, 1964), p. 411; and George C. Homans, *Social Behavior: Its Elementary Forms* (New York: Harcourt, Brace, & World, 1961), pp. 276–81.

49. Howard S. Becker, "The Career of the Chicago Public Schoolteacher," in *Contemporary Society*, ed. Jackson Toby (New York: John Wiley, 1964), p. 34.

50. Wiles, *Supervision for Better Schools*, p. 36.

51. Ibid., p. 14.

52. Michael B. Katz, *The Irony of Early School Reform: Educational Innovation in Mid-Nineteenth Century Massachusetts* (Cambridge, Mass.: Harvard University Press, 1968), pp. 35–50.

53. Ibid., p. 146.

54. "To him who hath shall be given, from him who hath not shall be taken away, even that which he hath." Cited by Robert Merton, "The Matthew Effect in Science," *Science* 159, no. 3810 (January 1968): 56–63.

55. Amitai Etzioni, *Modern Organizations* (Englewood Cliffs, N.J.: Prentice-Hall, 1964), pp. 41–49.

56. Owens, *Organizational Behavior in Schools*, pp. 11–14.

57. Andrew W. Halpin, *Theory and Research in Administration* (New York: Macmillan, 1966).

58. Neal Gross and Robert E. Herriott, *Staff Leadership in Public Schools: A Sociological Inquiry* (New York: John Wiley, 1965).

59. Robert F. Bales, "The Equilibrium in Small Groups," in *Social Processes and Social Structures*, ed. W. Richard Scott (New York: Holt, Rinehart & Winston, 1970), pp. 290–301.

60. Fred E. Fiedler, *A Theory of Leadership Effectiveness* (New York: McGraw-Hill, 1967).

61. Jacob W. Getzels, "Administration as a Social Process," in *Administrative Theory in Education*, ed. Andrew W. Halpin (Chicago: Midwest Administration Center, University of Chicago, 1958).

62. Lortie, "The Balance of Control and Autonomy in Elementary School Teaching," pp. 35–36.

63. Ibid., p. 13.

64. Mark Atwood, "An Anthropological Approach to Administrative Change," (Ph.D. dissertation, Columbia University, 1960).

65. Chester Barnard, *The Functions of the Executive* (Cambridge, Mass.: Harvard University Press, 1938).

66. Fred E. Katz, "The School as a Complex Social Organization," *Harvard Educational Review* 34, no. 3 (Summer 1964): 428–55.

67. Robert Dreeben, *On What is Learned in School* (Reading, Mass.: Addison-Wesley, 1968).

68. See, for example, the following: Howard S. Becker, "The Teacher in the Authority System of the Public School," *Journal of Educational Sociology* 57 (September 1951): 136–44; Estelle Fuchs, *Teachers Talk*, p. 58; Gertrude McPherson, *Small Town Teacher* (Cambridge, Mass.; Harvard University Press, 1972), pp. 163–64; C. Wayne Gordon, *The Social System of the High School* (New York: Free Press of Glencoe, 1957), pp. 44–45; Norman J. Boyan, "A Study of the Formal and Informal Organization of a School Faculty" (Ph.D. dissertation, Harvard University, 1951), pp. 285–86.

69. Lortie, *The Balance of Control and Autonomy in Elementary School Teaching*, p. 76.

70. Alvin W. Gouldner, "Organizational Analysis," in *Sociology Today*, ed. Robert K. Merton, Leonard Broom, and Leonard J. Cottrell, Jr. (New York: Harper Torchbooks, 1965), pp. 425–26.

71. Alvin W. Gouldner, *The Coming Crisis of Western Scoiology* (New York: Basic Books, 1970).

72. Of course the latter dictum functions to cut down discipline referrals and thus maintains the effectiveness of principal support, so that one might expect teachers also to subscribe to such a norm to a considerable extent.

73. Gouldner, "Organizational Analysis," p. 425.

74. Sarason, *The Culture of the School and the Problem of Change*, p. 130.

75. Edwin M. Bridges, "Bureaucratic Role and Socialization: The Influence of Experience on the Elementary Principal," *Educational Administration Quarterly* 2 (Spring 1965): 19–28.

76. Adam F. Scrupski, "Administrative Support for Teachers and Teacher Legitimation of Administrative Authority: A Test of an Exchange Theory of the Social System of the School" (Ph.D. dissertation, Graduate School of Education, Rutgers University, 1970).

77. Note Warren Bennis, "Beyond Bureaucracy," in *The Study of Society: An Integrated Anthology*, ed. Peter I. Rose (New York: Random House, 1973), pp. 289–95; and Talcott Parsons' recent attention to "associationalism" rather than super-subordination as characteristic of contemporizing organizational structure, in *The System of Modern Societies* (Englewood Cliffs, N.J.: Prentice-Hall, 1971), pp. 104–6.

78. Winston White, *Beyond Conformity* (New York: Free Press of Glencoe, 1961), pp. 93–94.

79. Laurence Iannacone, "An approach to the Informal Organization of the School," in Griffiths, *Behavioral Science and Educational Administration*.

80. Lortie, "The Balance of Control and Autonomy in Elementary School Teaching," p. 34.

81. David Riesman, "Thoughts on Teachers and Schools," *The Anchor Review*, no. 1 (Garden City, N.Y.: Anchor Books, 1955), p. 55.

82. Jesse H. Newlon, *N.E.A. Proceedings* (1925), pp. 657–60, as quoted by Callahan in *Education and the Cult of Efficiency*, p. 203.

83. John Dewey, "Sources of a Science of Education," in Ratner, *Intelligence in the Modern World*, pp. 640–54.

84. T. W. Bamford, *Rise of the Public Schools: A Study of Boys' Public Boarding Schools in England and Wales from 1837 to the Present Day* (London: Thomas Nelson & Sons, 1967).

85. Ibid., p. 160.

86. Amitai Etzioni, *A Comparative Analysis of Complex Organizations* (New York: Free Press, 1961), pp. 219–22.

87. Jesse H. Newlon, *N.E.A. Proceedings*, as quoted by Callahan in *Education and the Cult of Efficiency*.

9

UTILITARIAN PERFECTIONISM AND EDUCATION: A CRITIQUE OF UNDERLYING FORCES OF INNOVATIVE EDUCATION

Donald Oliver

This essay explores an ideology that underlies the contemporary social and cultural conditions in which "innovative" education is currently operating, and in turn suggests an alternative to it. What will be termed "utilitarianism" in this essay serves as a dominant philosophical foundation for both conventional or "Establishment" education as well as innovative education. The application of utilitarianism is demonstrated most clearly in a series of projects, experiments, and programs which run the gamut from curriculum to the upgrading of teaching to "total" school reform. Humanistic or radical alternatives to educational reform have commonly failed, however, not only because they run counter to the dominant utilitarian thrust of the society, but also because they pay too little respect to natural conditions of human growth and community. Genuine educational reform must be grounded in a fuller and more realistic understanding of the paradoxical nature of human nature and the social context within which that nature can find reasonable expression.

A Second Lens from Which to View Efficiency and Accountability in Education

A central quality of "modern society" is a view of reality in which we come to see as quite natural the increasing differentiation and specialization of its various parts resulting in a larger, more efficient, and complex whole. We then take for granted that human activities including those of an essentially "helping" nature such as teaching the young or healing the ill or caring for the aged are to be carried on within specialized segregated institutions. We assume that these institutions will be run by professionals, and that defects or problems within such institutions can be adequately construed or managed *within the framework of the single activity itself.*

Improvement or "reform" in the teaching of the young is seen as quite a separate issue from the problems we have in caring for infants or the aged, the way we treat the mentally ill, the boredom and tediousness of factory work, poverty and violence in the inner city ghettos, or boredom of adolescents and housewives in the affluent suburbs. Progress in teaching the young is translated into improving the efficiency, the order, and morale of those who inhabit schools. This can be done by such devices as creating new curriculum; constructing and using behavioral objectives; developing more sophisticated methods of testing and evaluation; finding less stressful and more regularized methods of disciplining and controlling children and youth; and making more efficient the process of managing and using teachers, buildings, books, courses, school buses, and the whole apparatus we now call "schooling." Callahan, for example, documents the explicit use of the business metaphor applied to American schools in the early part of this century.

> The men who were leaders in educational administration in the period from 1910 to 1918 . . . represented a new type of school administrator. . . . To a man they were able, energetic, and practical, and, to an amazing degree they represented in their interests and actions the dominant tendencies in American life in the first decades of the twentieth century. They not only manifested a great interest in and admiration for businessmen and industrialists, but they resembled these men in their behavior. They were active in introducing and using business and industrial procedures and terminology in education, and they centered their attention almost exclusively upon financial, organizational, and mechanical problems.[1]

The contemporary controversy over the issue of "accountability"—whether or not individual teachers should be rewarded or penalized on the basis of test performances of their students—suggests that the "cult of efficiency" is still very much alive.

Within the past few years, however, a central premise of modern society itself—the premise that most of us should spend most of our time in highly specialized managed institutions separated from the common life of a human community—has come under reexamination. From the radical perspective, efforts to reform or improve the teaching of the young consist of minor variations on a common theme: How can some humans be more efficiently trained to carry out tasks that are structured and assigned by other humans? In more general societal terms the theme includes such elements as creating a national or corporate consciousness which increasingly tears apart any remaining fabric of common community life (e.g., neighborhoods, ethnic clubs, local church parishes, small family businesses) on the one hand while on the other isolating and individuating persons or nuclear families so they can function efficiently as competitive mobile interchangeable parts striving to succeed within the national economic arena. The goal of the overall system is a balance between corporate *efficiency* and *stability* based on meritocratic stratification and segregation. In sociological terms, an underlying central goal of schooling is to preselect and stratify children to make success and failure within the system seem reasonable, justified, and personally earned.

One of these radical critics, Michael Katz, is a student of the historical process in the nineteenth century during which schools became corporate institutions. He suggests that there were, in the early years of the Republic, a variety of competing models of schooling. These he conceptualizes and labels as paternalistic voluntarism (the charitable rich voluntarily civilizing the indigent poor); democratic localism (decentralized neighborhood schools); corporate voluntarism (e.g., private academies and schools); and the public bureaucracy. From casual observation it is clear that Katz's democratic localism was the model of schooling linked to neighborhoods and small towns—something akin to groups of people sharing a common life. It is also clear which model became dominant in the twentieth century. Katz summarizes his conclusions:

> There are no effective alternatives in American life . . . There is only one way to grow up in America if one wants to eat regularly, to be warm, and not to be harassed by the police. For the vast majority there is only one place to go to school, and that place is the same nearly everywhere.[2]

Nor is the school unlike its surrounding institutions. As Katz adds, "There is one city, one mode of production, one road to power. And there is little freedom." [3]

Regardless of rationales or apologies given by professional educators for the monolithic quality of their contemporary institutions, most practices of modern schooling make a good deal of sense within the framework of this kind of radical criticism. For example:

—Mass psychological testing and evaluation procedures are simply analogies to industrial quality control. Humans, like products, are valued for common uniform qualities. Testing is also a quick and efficient way to teach people their "place."

—Requiring teachers to draw up teaching units, lesson plans, or make explicit behavioral objectives are methods for training teachers and students that they are accountable to the larger society in concrete utilitarian terms.

—The stress on learning disabilities and remedial reading for "slow" children are ways of teaching them early that they are defective and can be corrected only by specialized professionals who have a body of esoteric knowledge and special skills.

—The coalition between educational specialists in the universities and commercial publishing companies leads teachers to believe that there are uniform materials and methods to carry out a professional public responsibility. The notion that the unique relationship between a teacher and a child or a teacher and a community has value (other than as a means toward uniform goals) then seems at best trivial, at worst wasteful.

—Educational hierarchies come to mirror corporate hierarchies with managers at the top (in consort with technical or scientific specialists). Teachers are seen as the "workers" who are organized for purposes of efficient production. Team teaching or the "house system" simply creates another layer in the hierarchy.

The radical twist in the above statements describing examples of modern practice or reforms in schooling is not simply a set of barbs aimed at bureaucratic excesses in corporate institutions. The critical attitude toward modern schooling is based on a fundamental disillusionment with the level of planning, control, management, and stratification that seem required to make what we euphemistically call "modern civilization" function. And beyond this is a growing suspicion that modern man, with all his planning and managing and intervening and evaluation and feedbacks, is not on some linear road to progress and perfection, but rather is increasingly anxious and alienated from a variety of circumstances "primitive men" and "peasants" took for granted: unconditional acceptance by small communities of humans who share a common life, a sense of relatedness if not harmony with one's natural surroundings, and a sense that the human career is punctuated by meaningful rituals and celebrations even for the aged and the dead.

The suspicions and skepticisms directed toward the rational planners and managers is based first on the rediscovery by some of us of what is perhaps the most obvious characteristic of the species, one that is constantly emphasized in literature, mythology, and religion: the paradoxical and contradictory qualities in man's nature; the sense of a species suspended and uncompleted. One need only observe, for example:

—Man has an incredible capacity to plan, to organize, to create a social and technical world of his own choosing, yet social relationships and technology seem constantly to flow of their own force in their own direction, mostly out of human control.

—Man has an awareness that he is separate from his social and natural environment—a narcissistic sense of his own separate being. Yet as he moves toward a greater sense of individuality he is haunted by the fear of loneliness and alienation.

—As far as we can tell, individual humans have exhibited differences in talent and temperament, differences in styles of loving and working: some exploitative and aggressive; some passive and receptive; some generous and supportive; some reflective and innovative; some stingy and retentive. Yet we resist in the most agonizing way to accept diversity and variety as "normal." We must search constantly for the perfect specimen as well as for educational techniques for creating it.

—Humans often yearn for freedom, freedom from the bonds of ascribed statuses of occupation, social class, religion, kinship groups, national groups; yet at the same time we yearn for "home"—neighborhood or village, the family, the religion, the tradition that will support and protect us from freedom.

—Man commonly believes that his senses and the rational processes by which sense information is made comprehensible will allow him to fully know the world. Yet he is plagued by an uneasiness that there are forces and realities which can be understood only dimly; and he seeks to build uncertain bridges of faith to cross over into these other realities.

One underlying basis of such human contradiction and paradox is man's multilayered nature. On one level he shares with his mammalian relatives very similar physiological metabolic limits and requirements. He has little control over an autonomic nervous system, which regulates his need for air, water, nutrition, exercise, warmth, and rest. At a second level, he has a set of biosocial characteristics some of which he shares in modified and attenuated ways with other primate relatives, e.g., male-female bonding, mother-child bonding, male dominance, the tendency to associate in small bands, the tendency toward social hierarchy. While the environment that allows man to meet his biosocial requirements seems less rigidly defined than conditions for metabolic regulation, there seems little doubt that the needs are real, that conditions required for social caring and trust, for example, are as essential to human life as water or food. The disintegration of a single organism occurs relatively quickly when metabolic requirements are not met; the disintegration of human societies and consequently of individual humans may take several generations when biosocial needs are not adequately met.

On a third level are strata of thought and emotion which are not only *adaptive* in that they allow man to construe and respond to the world in some systematic way; they also establish needs, requirements, and limits in their own right. In a rough way we might identify three such strata: unconscious dreaming or imaging; conscious concrete respresentation of reality; and finally, hypothetical formal reasoning. On the level of the unconscious, man relates to his needs in the phenomenal world through images and metaphors which are revealed only through inference from myths, totems, pictures, dreams, music, drama, and dance. For example, mother = earth; fire = life or sex; dry wood = tradition and continuity. (We assume that one takes seriously the work of Freud, Jung, and Lévi-Strauss.) At the level of concrete representation, man has the capacity to construe the world with diagrams and language reflecting the simple logic of time, space, and movement. At the hypothetical level, he has the capacity to create science and philosophy; to analyze and describe his environment in very abstract ways, and to analyze and describe the complex logic of such descriptions. The problem for *Homo sapiens* is that elements of a human life style or whole life styles themselves which would integrate and nourish the various levels of human personality simultaneously are only weakly connected or patterned by instinct.

Man thus runs the risk of creating life styles that may be consistent with one aspect of human nature and yet stifle another, e.g., thinking in conceptual, analytic, instrumental terms may enhance his ability to create technology—to cope with the requirements of metabolic comfort and survival; yet the emphasis he places on "scientific thinking," technology and work may inhibit his ability to maintain, "realize," or express his primitive connectedness with his natural environment, i.e., his ability to be "superstitious" and experience the presence of other living and nonliving forms who have shared his environment throughout his evolutionary development.

Our argument in simplest form is that *Homo sapiens* evolved over a period of millions of years, and that within each of us is a complex of social needs and requirements along a continuum from primitive to modern which make demands, often conflicting demands, on individuals and societies alike. We would speculate, for example, that one of the more stable and pressing of these primitive demands for most humans is that they live within "bands" or small communities.[4] The concomitants of band life are many. For example:

—Commitment to the full range of humans who are born in and live within the band is taken for granted; the aged, the halt, and the lame are cared for. (It is difficult for humans to allow members of their own band with whom they have direct personal contact to starve or otherwise to suffer.)

—It is difficult for centralized elites to control the band, at least from within, since the essential humanity—its weakness and strength—of all is obvious and visible. Powerful elites require social distance to legitimize their demands.

—The various functions that human societies must perform for survival tend to be integrated around a common culture or meaning system. Human attachment and caring, work, celebration, relaxation, decision making and conflict resolution tend to be woven together with symbol, ritual, and religion.

—The small nuclear family is less significant and less critical as a necessary base from which the quality of all other human relationships must flow. Extended kinship relationships allow for a great range of social affiliations very early in life.

—Although the individual may choose to venture forth and leave the band, there is always the sense that one will be sheltered and accepted somewhere.

—A great variety of human differences must be accepted and used within the culture, or at least tolerated, since it is intolerable to segregate or banish individuals except under the most unusual circumstances.

It is obvious that a large number of these characteristics is negated or reversed for modern man, who spends the majority of his life either in impersonal corporate groups or in the highly charged intimate nuclear family. For example:

—Commitment to other humans outside of the small nuclear family is difficult except on a quid pro quo contractual basis. The aged, the lame, and the halt are cared for in corporate institutions under contract with the government or relatives.

—Invisible, often inaccessible elites make the important decisions for the society.

—Pluralities of cultures, religions, and meaning systems are encouraged, since this allows none to be seen as genuinely true or sacred.

—Human differences are generally seen as negative and not accepted; all aspire to have those characteristics perceived to be common to the elite: youthful maturity, physical attractiveness, the capacity to cope competently and aggressively, intellectual brightness, the flexibility to move about socially and geographically.

Our assumption is that this dramatic reversal or negation of man's more primitive life style without any fundamental biologically based adaptive change in the species is not possible without substantial stress. This stress, described psychologically as alienation and societally by a host of "ills" or problems, e.g., crime, poverty, racism, absenteeism from work, communication gaps, brutalization in custodial institutions, must be meaningful within some ideological framework. The ideology of modern man we could call utilitarian perfectionism—the belief that the purpose for which the planet was created is the comfort, convenience, and perfection of the human species and that man's maximal comfort and convenience can be attained through large, highly differentiated social organizations (e.g., nations, corporations, factories) arranged to fit the requirements of complex technology.

It is our contention that this ideology is inadequate if not dangerous because it underestimates or discounts the more primitive needs of the human species; that continued educational development based on its premises will inevitably exacerbate rather than ameliorate the human condition on the planet; that the first order of business for philosophers, educators, and social scientists is to work toward a more adequate ideology, which better accounts for our current knowledge about the full range of human needs. And the first step in this venture is to understand better how deeply we are embedded in the myth of utilitarian perfectionism by comparing it with a more accurate and beneficial myth—what we shall call "evolutionism" or "communitarianism."

The Ideological Choice

The ideological content of utilitarian perfectionism is succinctly summarized by Stuart Hampshire:

> Utilitarianism has always been a comparatively clear moral theory, with a simple core and central notion, easily grasped and easily translated into practical terms. Its essential instruction goes like this: when assessing the value of institutions, habits, conventions, manners, rules, and laws, and also when considering the merits of individual actions or policies, turn your attention to the actual or probable states of mind of the persons who are, or will be affected by them. That is all you need to consider in your assessments. In the final analysis, nothing counts but the states of mind, and perhaps, more narrowly, the states of feeling, of persons; or, more generously, of sentient creatures. . . . From this moral standpoint, the whole machinery of the natural order, other than states of mind, is just machinery, useful or harmful in proportion as it promotes or prevents desired states of feeling.
>
> For a utilitarian, the moral standpoint, which is to govern all actions, places men at the very center of the universe, with their states of feeling as the source of all value in the world. If the species perished, to the last man, or if the last men became impassible and devoid of feelings, things would become cold and indifferent and neutral, from the moral point of view; whether this or that other unfeeling species survived or perished, plants, stars and galaxies, would then be of no consequence.[5]

The utilitarians, having placed the maximization of man's pleasure and the minimization of his suffering as central considerations about quality of life, are then more or less compelled to posit something qualitatively "special" about man as a species.

> . . . even if the transcendental claims of Christianity have been denied, any serious thought about morality must acknowledge the

absolute exceptionalness of men, the unique dignity and worth of this species among otherwise speechless, inattentive things, and their uniquely open future.[6]

The second view—call it "evolutionism"[7] or more narrowly communitarianism—takes off from a very different set of premises. The initial unit of moral consideration is not man set in the Garden with dominion over the plants and animals; it is the universal space and immense time in which energy, matter, and life exist and have existed on this planet. It generally views as moot whether or not any particular direction of evolution is positive, negative, or neutral. It assumes that life evolved from nonlife; man and insects evolved from simpler life forms, but would hold that neither is in any state of near-perfection blessed with a purposeful creator-protector. Over thousands and millions of years nonlife forms evolve—mountains, rivers, continents, and oceans; likewise, life forms come and change and go. Turtles and cockroaches and moss have been on the planet a long time and are likely to be here a long time; man has been on the planet a relatively short time and is likely to be here but a short time. Although he is clever in adapting through technology to a variety of climatic and ecological conditions, he is genetically unstable and extremely vulnerable to small changes in atmospheric radiation.

So the first major point of difference in viewpoint is in the way utilitarian perfectionists and evolutionists see human life and the relative importance of man's place on earth. Utilitarians place man at the center of things; evolutionists place man within a broad framework of time and space and see him as sharing the planet with or simply "living among" other forms of life and nonlife.

The evolutionist operates from a dual perspective: (1) that of the human species who has a conscious or unconscious bias toward creating the conditions which meet his own particular metabolic, biosocial, and intellectual-emotional requirements; and (2), the "friends of earth" perspective: the point of view which values the historical-geological continuity of living and nonliving forms on the planet. Each perspective has its own particular moral basis, although they are clearly related.

From the bias of *Homo sapiens* the evolutionary moral imperative is that man fulfill as best he can the underlying potential of his nature. This is, in fact, little different from a simple utilitarian position, since human fulfillment presumably leads to maximal pleasure and minimal suffering. Only when utilitarianism embraces a singleminded liberal perspective positing man as a totally flexible and hence perfectable species deserving unique and special moral consideration do we see it as a wrongheaded and dangerous ideology. There is no essential contradiction between an evolutionary and utilitarian position as long as the latter will grant the multileveled and paradoxical characteristics of man which complicate considerably how one construes "pleasure" and "suffering." Only when utilitarianism denies or diminishes in importance man's fundamental biological, biosocial, and unconscious needs and limitations—e.g., his mortality, the fragility and suffering of the physical body, the sense of loneliness and social loss when loved ones depart or die, the agonizing responsibility the strong feel for the infirm—do the two ideologies clash sharply.

The evolutionist assumes, moreover, that it is only when man gives due weight to the limits of his own nature—when he sees his own nature as continuous with and embedded within the evolution of a broader planet and universe—that he will embrace the more universal principle of historical-geological continuity.[8] That is, if one projects the condition of the planet from past to future, the evolutionist assumes that deliberate human efforts to create radical or massive shifts in the geological or biological continuity of the planet are likely to be harmful. For man lives within such a complex and interdependent web of relationships with living and nonliving forms which have evolved over billions of years that any substantial interference with these relationships is likely to be destructive. One can, of course, argue that man's obsessive development and use of technology and social organization to transform the planet for his purposes is also the product of "natural evolutionary forces." We would have to assert that if one places value on forces which enhance geological or biological continuity, man seems to be an evolutionary mistake. In his exceptional case we would assert that modern man is a threat to the continuity of other living and nonliving forms on the planet, just as a small number of cancer cells are potentially a threat to the living out of a normal existence of the whole organism from which the cancer cells evolved.

The doctrine of evolutionary continuity set forth here suggests that we take a major leap of faith by committing ourselves to a view of human life circumscribed by two conditions: (1) the *pace of time* over which the planet has evolved (4 to 5 billion years), including a deep reverence for the living and nonliving forms which have evolved during that period; and (2) the view of the planet *as an interrelated whole,* including a sense of the complexity among all the forms of matter and energy which exist on and surround the planet. From these premises we would argue, for example, that the extinction of a species because of gradual climatic changes on a continent (e.g., the Pleistocene extinction of the woolly mammoth in North America) is morally neutral, whereas the slaughter of the American bison during the nineteenth century by Europeans was a massive crime against nature, against the planet, as well as against other people, i.e., the American Indian.

CHANGE AND PROGRESS–A second major consideration in comparing the utilitarian-perfectionist and evolutionist orientations toward social amelioration is man's attitude toward change and progress. For the utilitarian, in Hampshire's words:

> both emotional sensitiveness and intelligence in the calculation of consequences can be expected to multiply and increase, as moral enlightenment spreads and as standards of education improve, into an indefinite and open future. In this future there will be less avoidable waste of human happiness, less considered destruction of positive and valued feelings, as the human sciences develop and superstitions become weaker and softer. The story of the past—this is the assumption—is essentially the story of moral waste, of a lack of clear planning and contrivance, of always repeated losses of happiness because no one methodically added the emotional gains and losses with a clear head and undistracted by moral prejudices. The modern utilitarian policy makers will be careful social economists, and their planning mistakes will be progressively corrigible ones; so there is no reason why there should not be a steadily rising balance of positive over negative feelings in all societies that have a rational computational morality. A new era of development is possible, the equivalent in morality of high technology in production.[9]

The evolutionist sees change initially in terms of geological and biological evolution, both of which seem largely out of man's control. The earth's orbit around the sun, the rise of mountains, the separation of continents, the covering of continents by sheets of ice, the creation and extinction of forms of life describe neither progress nor loss; only change. The notion that more complex and highly differentiated forms of life are somehow morally or functionally superior to "lower" forms seems simplistic and naive. They certainly seem less durable. So when the evolutionist arrives on the scene of ongoing human societies, he sees remarkable similarities and commonness in the behavior of humans. He sees the myth of progress in centralized complex societies as seductive and illusory. He sees the most obvious differences across modern and primitive human societies as technological, not as a gradation of underlying qualities of human feeling, motivation, or happiness, or moral superiority.

The utilitarian sees progress as civilization; he sees civilization as the development of man's "higher" capacities: literacy; contractural or legal modes of social relating; complex technology based on principles of science; centralized highly organized modes of social work and aesthetic achievement, e.g., symphony orchestras or cinema.

Conversely, the evolutionist who emphasizes the necessity for balance between the "higher" human capacities common to civilization and the more primitive needs of his biosocial and unconscious personality is more alarmed than impressed by the one-sided gains of human social and technological engineering. The evolutionist assumes that the various layers of human personality must be nourished by concrete elements of life style; that when man's life no longer allows him to express or work through his various needs and strivings, he tends to become alienated or disconnected from parts of self. In summary the evolutionist would speculate that civilization runs the constant threat of alienating or separating man (or any species) [10] from the basic conditions within which he evolved or adapted to cope for his own survival. If one asks, to what is man supposedly "connected," a variety of conditions can be cited:

1. The geological circumstances characteristic of the planet—sun, light, water, soil, wood, seasons, cold, fire, etc.—and man's relatedness to these conditions (the need for water; the use of energy represented by fire) that have borne a direct relationship to his evolution and survival

2. Flora and fauna on which human life depends and the biological relatedness of man with other forms of life

3. The process of growth and aging and death for man and for other living organisms

4. The process of coping for food, water, warmth, shelter, safety; the sense of competency in solving problems of coping

5. The sociality involved in kinship relationships—family, bands, clans as well as feelings of antipathy toward outsiders and out-groups

6. The sense of territory—the security that comes with familiarity not only with social group but with geographic surroundings

7. The sense of history—the security that comes with knowing the past out of which one's own life (and the lives of ancestors) evolved

8. Orderliness in social existence which comes with the sense of shared obligations and responsibility; the relationship between places in the social hierarchy and age, competence, and experience

9. The sense of fatefulness and unpredictability as it relates to suffering, joy, and the range of human experience

10. The obvious diversity within the species in age, sex, temperament, competence, physical strength, beauty, etc.

For the evolutionist there is always the precarious balance: man must remain connected to his geological and biological past, yet he has unusual flexibility. He constantly dreams of some trick of training, invention, or insight that will allow him to transcend either his biological or his primitive biosocial heritage. So quality of life for the evolutionist must be construed not simply as preventing alienation, but rather as establishing a tolerable balance between evolutionary connectedness and the sense of hope, freedom, or destiny which characterize his flexibility.

The utilitarian is little prone to ask about the extent to which the human species needs to remain connected with any evolutionary past. Man is thought to be unique among life forms in that he is free to invent his own cultural rules rather than remain enslaved to instinct. His faith in his own *freedom* is seemingly validated by the technology, organizational ability, and political power acquired by groups of men who have come to believe in it. Modern utilitarian man is bound and determined that he can rid himself of his evolutionary limits—that he can place himself in a linear track to progress now and, in the end, attain his own perfection.

HUMAN INSTITUTIONS–"Primitive," "village," or pre-industrial urban societies which have traditionally lived by evolutionist principles have been extinguished or are being rapidly transformed by utilitarian man. Fewer and fewer people are permitted to live in a neighborhood or village culture in *dignity*—even, as Paul Goodman said, to be decently poor. Neighborhood-village life is in a constant state of siege. While industrial-urban-village-agricultural complexes did in fact coexist for substantial periods of time to provide a link with man's social and natural evolutionary past, this no longer seems possible. A new ideological and structural force has emerged which subsumes agricultural life, village-neighborhood life, and the city, transforming all in its own service. The force and form has various names: the industrial state, technopolis, the purposive-rational society. It has a multiplicity of facets: the consolidation of smaller political units into large units called nation-states; massive use of inanimate machines which free man from dependence on human or animal energy; transportation of natural resources across great land masses to meet the needs of the new technology; the broad-scale use of rationally ordered human relationships (bureaucracy) to manage the new technology and the larger political units; the fragmentation of towns and pre-industrial cities into specialized functions with utilitarian efficiency the major criterion for the "success" of a function; the fragmentation of human behavior into specialized human roles centered mainly around work in highly specialized settings; family life in small transitory nuclear units, the location and quality of which is determined largely by the nature of one's work; the exploitation of both living and nonliving elements in nature as objects to serve man's pleasure; and finally, the exploitation of man himself to serve the requirements of the corporate and technological structures he himself has created.

The evolutionist views such a transformed world with alarm, predicting that post-industrial societies will decline and decay because they alienate man from primordial social and environmental conditions that are critical to nourish the full range of human personality. He sees the kind of primary group support represented by the extended family, by semipermanent sodalities or work parties, by small community neighborhood or village life, for example, as essential for the emotional well-being of most humans. He sees the integrative basis of social life in the corporate organization—the open contract where the individual freely negotiates conditions of work, love, consumption, recreation, and celebration—as a luxury purchased at the price of personal insecurity and the brutalization of others. A good many humans simply cannot cope or are prevented from coping with such a choice-oriented society: housewives isolated with small children; alcoholics; people living in inner-city ghettos; those institutionalized in rest homes, prisons, schools, and mental hospitals. Moreover, he sees the tension between cosmopolitan culture based on the life style of the open contract and the village culture based on the life style of the traditional neighborhood as a permanent source of conflict for the species.[11] In recent history, the dominant cosmopolitan culture has responded to this tension by continuing to destroy neighborhood life, and assuming that "villagers" could be reeducated away from their sense of alienation. Alienation, like any other psychic condition, is presumed by utilitarian man to be amenable to rational human control.

TWO MEANINGS OF HUMAN RATIONALITY–The shift that takes place when we move from a village-city complex to a technopolitan society is radical to the core. It universalizes and merges sacred and secular standards of "life success" into a single monolithic goal: useful economic activity. As Gouldner points out, historically the economic utilitarian standard of "human worth" as a legitimizing criterion for station and privilege is associated with the rise of the so-called middle class and the decline of aristocratic-feudal arrangements (at least in the West). Utilitarianism as a quasi-religious belief system carries with it a great deal of complex baggage we are only now coming to understand. The most radical shift is the way we see man himself.

In large reaches of our society and particularly in the industrial sector, it is not man that is wanted. It is, rather, the function he can perform and the skill with which he can perform it for which he is paid. If a man's skill is not needed, the man is not needed. If a man's function can be performed more economically by a machine, the man is replaced. . . . The useless qualities of persons are either unrewarded or actively punished should they intrude upon the employment of a useful skill . . . just as there is the unemployed man, there is also the unemployed *self.* Because of the exclusions and devaluations of self fostered by an industrial system oriented toward utility, many men develop a dim sense of loss, for the excluded self, although muffled, is not voiceless and makes its protest heard. They feel an intimation that something is being wasted, and this something may be nothing less than their lives.[12]

The *utilitarian-perfectionist view of man* along with its faith in the value and *necessity of rapid technological growth* have now merged into a single world view. Instead of beginning with man and his needs, we begin with the requirements of a self-generating technology and corporate-organizational form, and then seek to shape man to fit that environment. *Rational control of the means for doing* becomes the end itself.

In Habermas's terms:

The institutionalized growth of the forces of production following from scientific and technical progress surpasses all historical proportions. From it the institutional framework draws its opportunity for legitimation. The thought that relations of production can be measured against the potential of developed productive forces is prevented because the existing relations or production present themselves as the technically necessary organizational form of a rationalized society.

Here "rationality," in Weber's sense, shows its Janus face. It is no longer only a critical standard for the developmental level of the forces of production in relation to which the objectively superfluous, repressive character of historically obsolete relations of production can be exposed. It is also an apologetic standard through which these same relations of production can be justified as a functional institutional framework. Indeed, in relation to its apologetic serviceability, "rationality" is weakened as a critical standard and degraded to a corrective within the system: what can still be said is at best that society is "poorly programmed." At the stage of their scientific-technical development, then, the forces of production appear to enter a new constellation with the relations of production. Now they no longer function as the basis of a critique of prevailing legitimations in the interest of political enlightenment, but become instead the basis of legitimation. *This* is what Marcuse conceives of as world-historically new.[13]

Habermas then quotes Marcuse:

> In this universe, technology also provides the great rationalization of the unfreedom of man and demonstrates the "technical" impossibility of being autonomous, of determining one's own life. For this unfreedom appears neither as irrational nor as political, but rather as submission to the technical apparatus which enlarges the comforts of life and increases the productivity of labor. Technological rationality thus protects rather than conceals the legitimacy of domination and the instrumentalist horizon of reason opens on a rationally totalitarian society.[14]

Understanding the role of technology in modern society requires clarification of various ambiguities in the term "rational." In the Weberian sense, rationalism fuses three concepts: (1) instrumental-purposive work-oriented man, (2) the universal scientific characteristics of technology, and (3) organized social labor directed toward the use of technology. When man is behaving in a purposeful way, channeling his energy toward visible or publicly describable goals, he is rational. When he creates or invents tools to facilitate the attainment of visible public goals, he is rational. When he organizes and manages other men in instrumentally efficient ways, he is rational. Only when these senses of rationality are fused into a world view and become the primary purpose and exclusive meaning of rational behavior do we have what Marcuse calls a "totalitarian society." Modern man is so committed to the view that rational men must live in a highly structured society organized around and consuming in socially productive corporate organizations set up to operate efficient technical apparatus that alternative world views seem as unrealistic or romantic utopias.

As Habermas suggests, the critical deficiency in this view of rationality is that it excludes a complex set of elements that we believe are fundamental to any healthy or decent human society. Those elements we have associated with alienation and connectedness. They have to do with functions such as spontaneous human bonding (love, friendship, caring) as well as the creation of informal consensual norms within group life, norms or standards which evolve out of the basic fact of sharing a common life. In short, the function of man most susceptible to the more limited sense of "rational" implied in rational-purposive behavior is work; other functions such as various kinds of bonding, play, human ritual and celebration require a broader meaning of the term or much of what humans find meaningful comes to be construed as irrational, nonrational, or even irrelevant.

THE HELPING PROFESSIONAL: RESPONSIBLE ACTION TOWARD HUMAN DISTRESS IN MODERN SOCIETY–The evolutionist sees the stresses in the life style of utilitarian man as caused by alienation from the more primitive elements in the human community and personality. Man becomes alienated from *meaningful work*, for example, when its connection with communal needs or visible survival press is obscured by technology, specialization, and excessive leisure. Man becomes alienated from his normal *social impulses* when "purposeless" or nonwork activities such as play, gossip, ritual, and active celebration are discouraged because they conflict with the efficiency and structure of organized work. Man becomes alienated from his normal tendencies toward *cooperation and generosity* when the dependent and less competent among him are segregated and isolated so that he may not expend economically useful energy becoming emotionally or personally involved with them.

The utilitarian assumes that these various social stresses can be resolved by the same approach that caused them: the application of systematic rational thought to social action, i.e., by the further use of science and technology—practical intelligence. Alienation from meaningful work may be cured, for example, by requiring very little human work—work is automated. "Nonwork" can take the form of formal recreation, sensitivity classes, etc., and becomes "work" for those who direct and manage such activities. The generous human impulse is institutionalized in the form of "helping professions." Specialized professionals (doctors, psychologists, group leaders, pastoral counselors, teachers, social workers, lawyers, nurses, etc.) are trained to care for and hopefully "cure" or ameliorate the suffering of the exceptional people, i.e., those who cannot cope with alienation from meaningful work, reduced support from primary communal groups, or the guilt caused by an overly exploitative and affluent life style. Quite logically, the utilitarian criterion by which the helping professional is judged is not the quality of his concern or compassion or generosity. It is the same as for any specialized professional: the extent to which he can make the noncoper—his clients, students, or patients—effective, useful functionaries as either producers or consumers.

To attain legitimacy, the helping professional has developed elaborate theories and research methodologies to give the appearance of participating in the same scientific enterprise that characterizes other sectors in the economy. Medicine is the prototype. It has a sophisticated division of labor: chemicals and professional techniques are developed in research laboratories; medicines and hardware developed in the laboratory are then manufactured in factories, sold by salesmen, prescribed and administered by physicians, and sold in commercial drug and supply stores. Other helping professionals seek to legitimize their work in similar ways. Psychiatrists administer therapy created and tested in research settings in universities and mental hospitals. Educational research and development centers develop, test, and prescribe school organizational plans (open classrooms, team teaching), personnel training procedures, and curricula. This research and development is often based on elaborate theories which suggest how individuals and organizations can be made to function more efficiently.

In the past twenty years, for example, education has stumbled through one utilitarian-perfectionist school of thought after another: Skinnerian behaviorism; Bruner and the teaching of the disciplines; Rogers, Maslow, and the so-called third force of psychology; and more recently the developmental psychologists inspired by Piaget and Kohlberg. Each grasps one element of human potential and explodes it into a comprehensive theory of schooling.

How does the helping professional who sensitively attends to an inner calling toward social amelioration, who feels some special responsibility to help others, deal with the utilitarian trap within which he now finds himself? We would argue that one can come to terms with the futility and destructiveness of the helping professions as they are now commonly practiced only by a basic reassessment of the utilitarian-perfectionist doctrine, a doctrine which now looks at only *one part of the human condition:* man's capacity to conceptualize purposefully and manipulate his social and physical environment to satisfy his short-run appetites. This reassessment, we would argue, should move us in the direction of an evolutionary viewpoint which stresses (1) the limits placed on man by his need to remain connected to those primordial conditions within which a substantial part of his moral, intellectual, and physical nature evolved; and (2) the often paradoxical or contradictory relationship between man's more "primitive" self and his self-conscious, reflective, directed self. The paradox can only be taken seriously, moreover, when we recognize that his primitive needs are not to be stigmatized as "lower" or morally inferior. The need of most humans, for example, for social attachments to quasi-permanent primary community life must not be seen as the negative end of ideologically loaded dimensions such as tradition-freedom, rigidity-flexibility. Man can no more tolerate extreme freedom than suffocating tradition.

Utilitarianism, Community, and School Reform

We see models and justifications of various proposals for school reform as inextricably linked to which of the two visions of society one carries in one's head, or, for those who apprehend both models, the relative weight given the two visions. For the devout utilitarian the road to progress is straightforward and consists of making schooling more efficient and effective. For example:

1. Pushing teachers toward the use of explicitly stated behavioral objectives

2. Development of formulas to justify relative cost benefits for various school programs

3. Development of curriculum models along with teacher training experts (or consultants) who will install such models whenever and wherever wanted

4. Vocational education reform construed as training and channeling students with various talents into the most appropriate job slots in the economy

5. Ever-increasing specialization of job functions: creating new curriculum departments for affective education or value clarification; creating new coordinators to integrate increasing numbers of specialists

6. Devotion to highly specialized educational research which will answer critical questions relating to efficient instruction and administration, e.g., group size, methods of presenting material, various systems for teaching reading, math, etc.

7. Development of complex systems models to describe the educational process, usually involving complex loops, feedbacks, evaluation procedures, etc.

For the utilitarian with humanist tendencies educational reform is more complicated. Like the straight utilitarian, he sees the process of modern schooling as essentially necessary and correct. But he has a vague and uneasy sense that things aren't quite what they should be. He reads such dissenting "anarchist" literature as Paul Goodman or Michael Katz and catches a glimpse of alternative visions. He comes to see the corporate school as too specialized, too formal or impersonal, too large, too regimented, too task-oriented, too meritocratic, too bureaucratic, too separated from the "community" and searches for palliatives for each of these shortcomings.

If the school is too specialized, teams of specialists can work together. Subject-matter specialists can create core curriculum, student services personnel can work as teams to deal with troubled children and adolescents (psychologists, guidance counselors, teachers, administrators). Walls between the specialties can be lowered as long as one doesn't give up one's sense of being a specialist.

If schools are too formal and impersonal, they can be made informal and more impersonal. Call teachers by their first names. Give students flexible assignments and have them discuss work options with the teacher. Have subject matter teachers play softball with the students at the lunch break. Go on weekend retreats and sit around campfires rapping together.

If the schools are too large, break them into smaller units: institute the house system, increase the importance of home room and call them "family groups." Have teams of four or five teachers work with a hundred students and really get to know them.

If the schools are too regimented, eliminate the bells (or substitute chimes for bells), institute flexible scheduling or "arena scheduling" (where students get the chance to choose the time of day or the teacher who will administer Algebra I).

If the schools are too merit-conscious, substitute written evaluations for letter grades; or institute special curricula for the mediocre losers so they feel that they are being given special attention to remedy their lack of intellectual brightness.

If schools are too task-oriented, institute the open campus so kids can wander about casually during "study periods," or play cards, or simply sit around and talk.

If schools are too bureaucratic, give greater support to the student council or create special teacher task forces so everyone can have some say in running the school.

If schools seem too separated from the "community," or from the parents, institute a voluntary teacher-aid plan, put parent monitors on the school buses, have more PTA meetings; or send students into the community to participate in work-study programs.

Public school systems as well as private schools have implemented various comprehensive versions of these reforms, commonly called "alternative schools." It is our experience that more radical alternative schools, those which have begun with the premise that an "evolutionist" or communitarian culture will *evolve* from the needs and requirements of individuals sharing a common environment, common work, and common problems, have had very rough going. The following scenario is not unusual. One of the first "crises" in such schools is the dual problem of class attendance on the one hand and groups of kids hanging around doing nothing on the other. If one observes carefully the "hanging around" phenomenon, it tends to become increasingly regularized: friendship groups are formed; a limited set of activities come to characterize the different groups (e.g., playing cards, gossiping, eating, horseplay, record playing, etc.); territories are selected by different groups for different activities (corridors, empty work space, toilets). As this happens the class attendance or "cutting" problem becomes more serious. There is, then, a direct confrontation between the new and somewhat unstable beginnings of a communitarian culture (one might characterize it as a street culture) and the managed classroom culture. Teachers, administrators, and the more task-oriented responsible students tend to see the nascent street culture as "wasting time," at best; and as adolescents on the brink of orgiastic sex and violence, at worst. The crisis is resolved in a variety of ways, but the common result is to abolish the free time or unused space which supports the newly developing "street life," or, more accurately, "corridor life."

The high mortality rate of communitarian alternative schools is perhaps superficially caused by ambivalent adults (parents and teachers) and youngsters who are initially committed to the freedom of each to choose his own education, or to the pluralistic goal of allowing a variety of subcultures to emerge which suit the needs and temperaments and talents of different kinds of students. These hopes and visions, however, are soon challenged either by students' and parents' realistic fear of failure, or by outside pressures to meet standardized goals of conventional utilitarian institutions. The school is pressed to show that students are reading at grade level, that students can get into good colleges, or that the school will not become immersed in legal troubles because it harbors truants, drug users, or allows smoking on school grounds. These pressures are commonly handled by inefficient group-decision-making processes, which outstrip the ability of the school to cope, until finally everyone gives in to a more managed system in the hope of getting back to work. So ends an agonizing drama.

From our perspective, the most serious problem for communitarian alternative schools, however, is *not* the pressure to be accountable according to utilitarian standards, e.g., reading scores, college admissions, truancy. (Obviously, a great many conventional schools are failing miserably by these standards, but they persist.) The most serious problem is that settings that characterize communitarian cultures or institutions require conditions that are *generally unavailable for any kind of modern schooling*, e.g., the sharing of honest work, a broad mix of people of all ages and temperaments, or the sharing of a common religion or cultural tradition. The following illustrations should amplify and clarify this point.

AGE AND SEX DIVERSITY–Natural communities normally contain the full range of ages and both sexes. Out of this diversity commonly evolves various coalitions; for example, women of childbearing age, girls, and babies; young adolescent boys; older adolescent boys and mature men; old people and young children. We would speculate that these coalitions might be considered "natural" in the sense that they are self-selected and produce consensual (noncoerced or explicitly managed) order as a basis for work, recreation, celebration, and shared experience. Such coalitions evolve, presumably, out of mutual benefits for individuals, members of groups, and for the community as a whole. Girls gain status and a sense of adulthood by caring for young children, which frees adult women to talk or work nearby. The high activity and risk-taking physical acting-out of younger adolescent boys is drained away safely by their self-segregation. (Women, younger children, and old people are protected from the latent sadism of the boys by the older adolescents who have settled into more symbolic and less overt demonstrations of sex and aggression.)

Old people have a number of unique resources. Their presence tends to enhance peace and order, both because of their slow pace and because they are the focus of a large number of kinship bonds which can demand a good deal of paternal or maternal respect. Because of their long memories, they are the repository of the history of the group and have the leisure to care for, tell stories to, and indulge young children. Such coalitions tend to produce substantial order as well as a set of productive human relationships without a great deal of hassle over the need for formal rules or explicit sanctions for their enforcement. Modern schools consisting largely of children *or* adolescents and young or middle-aged adults provide little basis for such coalitions.

TEMPERAMENTAL DIVERSITY, COOPERATIVE ACTIVITY, AND DIVISION OF LABOR–Human communities carry on a variety of social functions which normally demand a diversity and range of talent and leadership. The great majority of activity requires a combination and integration of planning and symbolic manipulation as well as physical activity and routine, e.g., carpentry, cooking, farming, sports, dance. Human activity tends to be cooperative and division of labor tends to evolve on the basis of natural diversity in temperament and talent.

But most modern schooling, especially for older children and young adults, has neither the time, the imagination, nor the flexibility to have work parties engage in meaningful activities which combine symbolic planning, trial-and-error experimentation, physical effort, and routine, and which can draw upon diverse temperamental potential of a variety of humans. Schooling is largely sedentary manipulation of symbols (with activity breaks), in which human diversity in talent and motivation is looked upon as a problem—for all students are pursuing uniform goals. Those who can do the assigned tasks well are rewarded; those who do them poorly are encouraged to emulate those who do them well. Those who find the tasks too complex, meaningless, or repetitive are given remedial training.

BUILDING A COMMON CULTURE TO DESCRIBE A COMMON LIFE–Culture is a set of beliefs, rules, and images at least partly shared by groups of humans who also share a common life. The beliefs, rules, and images must be meaningfully interpreted at various levels of abstraction. In a highly segregated and fragmented society, where much of the work is invisible or infrequently seen or experienced by those who do not actually do it, there is, in fact, little common life; there can therefore be little common positive culture. (There are a number of shared prohibitions and sanctions, made highly visible by mass media, e.g., crime, police, detectives, and lawyers disseminated by novels, movies, comic books.)

Since there is little common shared life, the only culture modern man can construct must be highly complex and abstract. One can describe society in such abstract terms as industrial production, assembly line, advertising, marketing, distribution, consuming, recreation, housing, marriage, family, and the like; but the categories mean very different things for the gas station attendant, the corporation lawyer, or the welfare mother. Schooling exists, presumably, to transmit (or to operate within the framework of) a common culture. But if that culture, in order to be "common," must be stated in highly abstract and complex terms, it is available only to those who can think in complex and abstract ways. For other kinds of humans who tend to "think" visually, kinesthetically, or who are just plain simple and more concrete, there can be no common culture except as a set of transitory fragments (TV ads, popular songs, images of political leaders, etc.). And education without a sense of a common life and a common culture to reflect that life and give it meaning is either motivated out of instrumental self-interest or obedience to authority. A voluntary noncoerced community requires that there be meaningful senses of work, celebration, decision making, suffering, and the like which can be shared by all. In a society in which many of these relationships are either invisible or trivial, meaningful culture and hence meaningful schooling cannot exist without coercion or extrinsic rewards.

We see alternative schools failing for two reasons. First, their inventors are ambivalent and draw back when the risks of downward social and educational mobility become apparent from the unsettling anarchy that erupts as the constraints of a managed system are removed. But more importantly, alternative schools are unable to meet the complex conditions of community (e.g., availability of natural coalitions, visible division of labor, the sharing of a common life along with a set of religious myths to give that common life meaning) from which a new basis for order might evolve. The schools are still locked into a level of specialization (i.e., education is seen as a function to be segregated from the rest of the society) that makes a sense of the common life impossible.

The point is that one does not create "community" with superficial or transitory devices such as confrontation groups or weekend camping trips. One does not create community by calling one another by their first names or giving students and parents more control over curriculum or the selection of teachers. One simply tinkers with the structure of a managed system.

The Viability of "Community" as an Approach to Educational Reform

The most radical approach to communitarian educational reform is the creation of intentional communities. Such communities have a somewhat dreary record. Those with a strong and demanding religious base (e.g., the Amish, the Hutterites, or the Bruderhof) have the best record of longevity. Those based only on humanistic communitarian concerns seem to fall quickly by the wayside (e.g., Brook Farm of the last century and the countless communes of the last ten years).[15]

The more communitarian private schools (e.g., Summerhill and its followers) have very limited applicability as models for at least two reasons: they are not economically viable and depend wholly on the good graces of the well-to-do whom they usually serve; and more importantly, they eject those who do not get along—a fundamental violation of one premise of community.

What might be called "educational service communities" which relate to ongoing neighborhoods, towns, or cities would seem to be more hopeful examples of radical communitarian reform.

A good example of this approach is Myles Horton's Highlander Folk School, which has served for the past forty years as an adult residential center in Appalachia for the development of community leaders among school, church, civic, labor, and farm groups, as well as for liberal education. Horton's initial conception of the school is described as follows:

If I understood our purpose correctly, we will all be working at the same job but will be using different approaches. Our task is to make class-conscious workers who envision their roles in society, and to furnish motivation as well as technicians for the achievement of this goal.

In other words, we must try to give the students an understanding of the world in which we live (a class-divided society) and an idea of the kind of world we would like to have. We have found that a very effective way to help students to understand the present social order is to throw them into conflict situations where the real nature of our society is projected in all its ugliness. To be effective, such exposure must be preceded, accompanied by, and followed by efforts to help the observer appreciate and digest what he has seen. This keeps education from getting unrealistic. While this process is going on, students need to be given an inkling of the new society. Perhaps this can be done best by having a type of life that approaches as nearly as possible the desired state. This is where our communal living at the school comes into the picture as an important educational factor. The tie-in with the conflict situations and participation in community life keeps our school from being a detached colony or utopian venture. But our efforts to live out our ideals makes possible the development of a bit of proletarian culture as an essential part of our program of workers' education.[16]

Frank Adams summarized Highlander in 1972 as follows:

Through Highlander's programs, many people have been encouraged to find beauty and pride in their own ways to speak their own language without humiliation, and to learn of their own power to accomplish self-defined goals through social movements built from the bottom up.

People learn of unity by acting in unity. They learn of democracy by acting democratically. And each time they do these things as a result of experiences at Highlander they both renew their capacity to act in these ways again and demonstrate the process of education in action. Talk about this distorts, and is one step removed from the essential element—the people themselves doing. Writing words about the process is two steps removed. Education at Highlander is a synthesis of person, group, time, place, purpose, and problem.[17]

A second example of an educational service community is Synanon[18] and its related offspring (e.g., Daytop in New York; Marathon House in New England). In its early years Synanon was a residential drug rehabilitation community with a strong cultural press toward interpersonal openness and honesty coupled with a complementary press for shared social support and mutual help. Honesty and openness were encouraged if not "forced" on people by the Synanon Game, a variation of the confrontation group. Support and mutual help were given by a close knit residential life style. Synanon communities are now open to both addicts (for rehabilitation) and non-addicts who simply want the honesty encouraged by the Synanon Game as well as the support brought about by residential living.

Both Highlander and Synanon have a dual goal: to relate to the outer society in some obvious and constructive way as well as to maintain a sense of integrity within an inner community. The services one might render to a larger society fraught with a host of social diseases take no great imagination. Identifying minimal conditions required to build integrity for the inner community is a more difficult task. As a beginning we would list the following as necessary characteristics for communitarian reform institutions:

1. There must be a *common life*. This means they probably must be residential or quasi-residential and share some of the basic tasks of daily coping (preparing food, eating, housekeeping, etc.) commonly carried out in the nuclear family. The sharp separation between "home" and "work," between "family group" and "work group" must be reduced.

2. They must include a broad range of *human diversity* along such dimensions as age, sex, temperament, and talent to allow for the natural evolution of interdependent coalitions as well as leadership. The presence of diversity implies that the distinction between professional (or certified) elites and the common people must be minimized. Natural leadership within community must come from both sources.

3. There must be a substantial *reconnection or dealienation of the community with the basics of survival and human sociality* and a move away from living

"in one's head." Activities such as gardening, carpentry and mechanics have to be elevated to the same plane as the high arts or social science. Increased (and legitimate) satisfaction must come from simple and various human activities, such as gossip, storytelling, sports, singing, playing games. The present recreational habits of members of professional elites would have to go, e.g., ski weekends, jet trips, because they are too expensive and too exclusive.

4. Such communities would have to effect a fundamental shift in the modern attitude toward *religious and spiritual commitment.*

The problem of identifying minimum conditions for building community in a utilitarian society is actually *twofold.* One must ask, first, what conditions are necessary to provide the initial social cement to build sustained commitment; and second, what conditions are required to alter personality toward feeling comfortable with communitarian values and life styles. Fromm and Maccoby deal with the latter question in their study of an orphan community in Cuernavaca, Moreles, Mexico. They are interested in the conditions under which boys and girls coming from peasant villages might change their attitudes in essential areas, especially those of cooperation vs. selfishness and suspiciousness. They state:

Following are the most important principles which seem to us to be responsible for making this change possible:

1. *The principle of unconditional acceptance.* No child once accepted in the community is ever expelled, for whatever reason. . . . This situation expresses the principle of motherly love which is unconditional, and which never excludes a child, regardless of what he may have done. . . .

2. This motherly principle of unconditional acceptance is balanced by the paternal principle of demanding from the child *respect* for the rights of others and fulfillment of his obligations to the community in accordance with his age. . . .

3. Another principle which seems to us of great importance is that of the extensive participation of the children, especially the adolescents, in the *management of their own affairs.* Every two weeks a "house director" is appointed in the unit of boys who attend secondary school. . . .

The children cultivate their own vegetable garden and take care of the animals (chickens, cows, ducks, pigs). Aside from cooking, they also bake their own bread.

4. In relation to this, another factor must be mentioned which is crucially important. In spite of the fact that this is a rather large institution, it is conducted in a *nonbureaucratic spirit*. The children are not treated as "objects" to be managed by a bureaucracy, but are loved and cared for as individuals by Father Wasson and his assistants. . . .

5. Another factor of considerable importance is the *degree of stimulation* which the children receive. There is folkloric dance group, a mariachi band (string instruments and trumpets), and children play individual instruments too. . . . The children also learned to make their own costumes. . . . There is a carpentry shop, and there are classes in painting, sculpture, and ceramics. There are good soccer and baseball teams; a library of books and records is being developed.[19]

It should be noted that the orphanage fulfills a number of the conditions we have already cited above: It is residential; it has a broad range of diversity (with the exception that it is all-male); there are a range of dealienating conditions in the environment (e.g., cooking, gardening, carpentry, etc.); there is a rich religious and spiritual life.

Conclusion

The immediate question for individual educators who would take seriously the evolutionist-communitarian position is how to alter a life that is currently overspent coping with the utilitarian pressures of conventional schools. There are a variety of perspectives from which to view one's work in schooling. The utilitarian administrator uses a standard factory model. The school (the plant) produces or refines goods (students) for the community (consumers) using personnel (teachers) and tools (curriculum). Teachers who buy this model then focus on their own ability to administer standard curricula. More circumspect teachers who stand back and view the total institution as a human processing plant are prone to lunge forward and push toward the reform of the institution as a whole.

In this essay, we are suggesting that redoubling one's efforts to change the basic quality of life within schools as a whole is unlikely to achieve any substantial result. This is not to suggest that one should not try to correct the more obvious indecencies, e.g., requiring passes to go to the toilet. It simply means that schools, as other corporate institutions in the society, have a strong gravitational pull toward being highly managed directed settings. Schools no more have the potential for fulfilling man's basic communitarian needs than businesses or factories.

It is our guess that the most productive role for the teacher is in teaching an evolutionist or communitarian ideology as a basis for an alternate vision of society as well as creating opportunities for students to have positive experiences which would reinforce and be consistent with this vision. These experiences might include, for example, organizing or working in food cooperatives, helping in a parent-run day-care center, working in programs to integrate emotionally disturbed or mentally retarded children into settings with normal children.

Such a vision might be "fitted in" to the curriculum within a great number of standard courses. We might begin by teaching history as the history of the planet, rather than as the history of "civilized" or literate man. We might teach biology with as much awe and respect for the adaptive capacities of the honeybee as we have for man. Or in American history, we might stop glorifying the success of the Constitutional Convention and begin a sober reassessment of what the United States might have been had it remained a continent of small nations. In anthropology, we might stop talking in terms of cultural progress from primitive to modern man and begin to explore positive elements in quality of life for primitive people, peasants, and the people who inhabited pre-industrial cities. In sociology we might begin a serious assessment of the field commonly called "community." And perhaps most of all we should begin to face squarely, as teachers and in what we teach, the implicit and persistent distinction built into most societies between elites and common folk and ask: How can the two groups live among one another in a non-exploitative way, share a common life, and feel a mutual responsibility for a common welfare?

But this is clearly only a first step: to teach young people a different view of the planet, of man in a different kind of society, through words and drama and fragmentary experiences in more communitarian settings. The next step is the creation of fundamentally altered settings where humans can live at least part of their lives as neighbors. It is here that the Highlander Folk School or Synanon may be instructive.

What is presented here is an overall strategy for how a teacher who embraces an evolutionist or communitarian vision of society might spend one's life. The essence of that strategy is that educators not be seduced into attempting to change the overall tone or structure of the school as an institution (although this is usually the most direct road to "success" and mobility); that they spend their energy in three ways:

1. Revising curricular content so as to stop glorifying the utilitarian perfectionist view of nature, man, and society; and to create a new view of how man might inhabit this planet

2. Search for significant albeit fragmentary experiences for oneself and for students which would be consistent with the evolutionist-communitarian ideology

3. And finally, to participate in building "neighborhoods" or neighborly places quite apart from the school

While the creation of these "neighborly" institutions may seem increasingly unfeasible, even far-fetched, one should remember that large, centralized, highly managed, complex societies of the past did not last. They eventually experienced the fatal pains of alienation similar to our own. There is little reason, for example, to think that we shall escape the destiny of an Egypt or a Greece or a Rome. Nor is there any reason to think that there is not some broad historical dialectic in which man plays out the tower of Babel drama. His intelligence and arrogance lead him to the brink of a highly controlled managed society, a society in which the spontaneous roots of small, decentralized tribal cultures are all but snuffed out. And then it all comes crashing down.[20] The question is not whether we are on some linear track to cultural progress and perfection or whether we are caught up in a dialectical historical process. The evidence is substantially on the side of the latter conclusion. The basic question is how accurately we can identify the locus of historical transition; and whether or not enough of us have the intelligence, the courage, and the spiritual resources to prepare for that point in history.

NOTES

1. See Raymond Callahan, *Education and the Cult of Efficiency* (Chicago: University of Chicago Press, 1962), p. 180.

2. Michael Katz, *Class, Bureaucracy, and Schools* (New York: Praeger, 1971), p. 3.

3. Ibid., p. 7.

4. The reader is referred to Service for evidence on this point. See Elman Service, *Primitive Social Organization* (New York: Random House, 1971).

5. Stuart Hampshire, "Morality and Pessimism," *New York Review of Books*, 25 January 1973, p. 26.

6. Ibid.

7. Since this term is perhaps used in a novel way here, I would associate the position described generally with the writing of such men as G. Gaylord Simpson and Loren Eiseley. The specific position described is, of course, my own. The position is clearly not to be associated or confused with cultural evolutionists who construe human history as progressive development.

8. That some men have the capacity to place the interests of other forms of existence above their own is, of course, another paradox of the human condition.

9. Hampshire, "Morality and Pessimism," p. 26.

10. Note the behavior of animals in a zoo.

11. For example, in medieval Europe or colonial America.

12. Alvin Gouldner, *The Coming Crisis of Western Sociology* (New York: Basic Books, 1970), pp. 73–74.

13. Jurgen Habermas, *Toward a Rational Society: Student Protest, Science, and Politics*, trans. Jeremy Shapiro (Boston: Beacon Press, 1970), pp. 83–84.

14. Ibid.

15. The special historical and geographical conditions that have made the kibbutzim endure for two generations are probably not applicable to this country.

16. Frank Adams, "Highlander Folk School: Getting Information, Going Back and Teaching It," *Harvard Educational Review* 42, no. 4 (November 1972): 516–17.

17. Ibid., pp. 519–20.

18. For an introduction to Synanon, although somewhat dated, the reader is referred to Lewis Yablonsky, *Synanon: The Tunnel Back* (New York: Penguin, 1965).

19. Erich Fromm and Michael Maccoby, *Social Character in a Mexican Village* (Englewood Cliffs, N.J.: Prentice-Hall, 1970), pp. 214–16.

20. The dialectical vs. progressive linear themes as interpretations of history have a long and distinguished history. For more recent works supporting the nonlinear, nonprogressive view, the reader is referred to Robert A. Nisbet, *Social Change and History* (Oxford: Oxford University Press, 1969); and Malcolm Muggeridge, *Chronicles of Wasted Time* (New York: William Morrow, 1973).

10

URBAN EDUCATION:
THE ESTABLISHMENT'S LAST STAND

Gerry Rosenfeld

The development of urban education as a distinct and discrete social phenomenon in contemporary America seems to be the consequence of at least two related social forces. The first is the demographic shifts that have made the city increasingly the residence of the poor and the suburbs and exurbs the residence of the well-off. The second force might be seen at least initially in terms of the building-up of a massive bureaucracy, a bureaucracy which seemed the product of a dialectic involving, on the one hand, a traditionally entrenched central administration, and, on the other hand, a professional teacher cadre (union); both contend for autonomy and power in the determination and implementation of educational policy. (It might be noted that Gerald Moeller found a positive relationship between amount of bureaucracy and teacher sense of power.)

As the consequences (synthesis) of the forementioned dialectic have become more and more a matter of central control, the interests of urban clients, children and their families, seemed increasingly ineffectively represented, particularly when compared with the interests of their erstwhile neighbors now nestled in the suburbs. Thus, the consequences of teachers' union action can be regarded as the more thoroughgoing bureaucratization of the entire city system, carefully delineating (restricting) obligations and in a sense "freezing" the pattern in such a way that responsibility on the part of teachers for pupil success has looked increasingly attenuated.

As pupils' failures continued to pile up, as the bureaucracy became increasingly unmanageable, decentralization of administration—fostered in part by community-control advocates and opposed at least initially by teachers interested in protecting supra-unit-based investments and promotion opportunities (to say nothing of administrators protective of rights to let commercial contracts based on similar vested interests)—has become a central concern of urban educational life. In a new dialectical variation, notions of accountability, management-by-objectives, paraprofessional assistance, and other limited innovations aim to defrost the pattern. The basic structure, however, seems largely to remain in place. Ability grouping by grade level has been retained in an exponential scheme which allocates personnel and other resources in a way that constitutes a kind of compensatory education. In every case technological and technocratic innovations promise to assure enhanced efficiency of pupil learning while leaving the basic social structure of the school intact. For example, in New York City, what some call the "central group pattern," wherein teachers orchestrate student responses in a 1-to-30 or so set interaction pattern, looks to be a thoroughly institutionalized aspect of unchanging professional reality.

When seen in the context of the American experience of the past three decades, from postwar McCarthyism through the sputnik panic to the Nixon businessmen's government, such social-educational phenomena may perhaps be understood if not assented to.

Culture and Schooling

Cultures are forged by adults. And childhood, everywhere, is a function of what the parental generation defines it to be. Differences in definition exist across cultures, but there is essentially no variation from the pattern. If this were not the case, children would not grow up so identifiably like their elders. Of course, cultures shift and change with changing social circumstances, and what children were like in the last generation may seem different from what they are like in the next generation; yet they are unmistakably stamped by the procedures used to rear them. In short, Americans become Americans; Russians become Russians; Peruvians become Peruvians, etc.

When I speak of *education*, then, the reference will be to the individual's taking on his culture. *Schooling* will refer to that particular institution we have chosen in America to accomplish specific aspects of this societal task. In particular, the urban school will require our attention, for it is in this context that the playing out of significant social forces and culture patterns may be seen and examined. Moreover, the schools provide us with a stability of form over time that is truly remarkable, when we recognize the monumental changes that have taken place in technology, settlement pattern, and subcultural styles in little more than a generation. Schools may well be an index to the enduring American belief pattern. In any case, they remain the unchallenged medium for major aspects of child socialization and adult "becoming."

Every cultural system is adequate to the task. Namely, each human group succeeds in "apportioning the cultural baggage" as tradition has decreed it. This is done by withholding as well as transmitting certain kinds of information, to certain kinds of people, at certain times in their lives, by the use of certain procedures. Those who don't traverse the life cycle in the prescribed order are denied particular places and privileges in the social organizational scheme. The struggle for place and privilege becomes, to an extent, the prescribed meaning for learning. "In this way the spirit is pruned." [1] In this way individuals are made to feel vulnerable should they not participate in the reenactment of the social structure through schooling. Student status, itself, is an aspect of class distinction. So, in reality, while children are learning assent to America they are accorded low status, as if to verify for them the need to be acquiescent in this process. [2] The school, in the meantime, solidifies its own position by increased bureaucratization.

A bureaucracy is a hierarchically organized institution whose purpose is to carry on certain limited functions. Thus a school system, the army, a university, the government, are all bureaucracies. It is common knowledge, however, that bureaucracies have three functions, rather than one. Although, the first is ostensibly to carry out the tasks for which they are established, the definition of roles and the routinization of procedures in bureaucracies brings it about that an important function of the organization becomes that of preventing anything within it from changing. Even small change might make it necessary for the entire organization to change because each part is so interlocked with every other, that to alter any procedure in a bureaucracy without changing the rest is often like trying to increase the height of one wall of a house without modifying its entire configuration. A third function of a bureaucracy is to perpetuate itself, to prevent itself from disappearing. Given the functions of preventing internal change and struggling to survive, bureaucracies tend to devote much of their time to activities that will prevent change. Under these conditions it is difficult to introduce new knowledge into the system. Often only a general convulsion in the total society can compel a bureaucracy to change; and then it will do so only just enough to avoid going out of business. Obviously these are the conditions for incompetence: bureaucracies create the conditions for their own incompetence and hence for their own destruction.[3]

If we accept that the school is a bureaucratic institution, and that learners are persons striving for allowable places and statuses based on their learnings, we can begin to discern the processes, or *dialectics*, that depict urban education: the relationships and interconnectedness of events in and out of the school as these affect children's education. We can understand that education is itself a social problem in America and that both convergent and divergent social forces mark school functioning. Marshall McLuhan doubtless is correct: "Today in our cities, most learning occurs outside the classroom."[4] That world outside the classroom must also be examined. When we know the effects of something, we can usually find the causes (McLuhan again). We know the effects of education on the learner; let us find the causes, or the cultural meanings behind these phenomena.

CONVERGENT FORCES AND THE URBAN SCHOOL–Schools not only provide the answers to the problems we face as a people (though not the solutions), they also function to define the questions that will be asked. And it is instructive to look at World War II and the events leading therefrom to the present, to see how schools have been shaped by particular social forces. For the nation, World War II served as a rite of intensification; it forced a reassertion of national consciousness and purpose. Men and women fought and worked to preserve the world for democracy. Young men who went to war were genuine heroes. Blacks and Indians, for example, could take their places alongside whites as folk idols and historic figures (though discrimination by race and sex still pervaded the armed forces). And presently unlikely persons were major symbols in the moral fables presented to children in urban classrooms.

As an elementary school child, I remember planting "Victory" gardens and collecting paper and tinfoil for the war effort. Books like *The Races of Mankind*[5] (since then difficult to find on school library shelves) could be bought for five or ten cents. War bonds were paid for in installments by children in school. A favorite story was one about Paul Robeson, who was described as a great scholar, athlete, and theater artist. After his freshman year at Rutgers University, he brought a report home indicating seven *A*s and one *B* in eight classes. Anxiously, he showed this to his father who responded, "How come you received a *B*?" The moral was clear. All should strive for perfection. All could be like Paul Robeson if the effort was there. We all had to work together. No animosity was to exist along racial or ethnic lines. The United States was proving its belief in itself; it was the biggest, the best, the most-to-offer nation in the world. I later met Paul Robeson by chance. It was an emotional highlight of my youth. How ironic, then, that Paul Robeson would later be defined as an "enemy of the people"; his accomplishments belittled and the stories about him hidden from children's perceptions.

This schizophrenia in American life manifested itself more clearly in the aftermath of World War II.[6] In my own urban neighborhood the brothers of Jews and Italians who fought together as comrades in arms now engaged one another in gang fights and antagonisms borne of stereotypes and prejudices. Indeed, our stereotyped thinking about Germans and Japanese provided an easy carryover toward maintaining the real and covert prejudices Americans have always had about one another. After the war blacks were again "niggers" and Puerto Ricans immigrating to eastern urban centers were "spics." The Indians were still a "foreign" people; and we began now to worry about the Russians and the Chinese, who emerged from World War II as a political, social, and economic challenge to America (at least, that is what our leaders told us; and that is what the content of schooling would begin to suggest). The "cold" war succeeded the "hot" war and the "communists" were now the focus of national concern. The shift was not difficult. In order to rebuild materially and militarily, we needed enemies, foreign and domestic, to rally against. The schools were deemed a proper medium to assist in this job. They still do that job, as a matter of fact. "Post war hopes for better schools were not realized. In the schools, as in the country as a whole, the cold war brought restraints on civil liberties. War budgets rose year by year." [7]

One of the emergent social forces helping to shape school policy (curriculum, for example) was McCarthyism, a concomitant of the cold war and the striving to subdue communism, ideologically as well as militarily. There soon followed the Korean war. Let us put these in proper social context. The past generation has seen the rise of McCarthyism-Nixonism; the advent of the invasion of personal freedom; an era of character assassination and discouragement of dissent. Together with the ascendancy of a huge military-weapons technology, these impinged upon schools to make them places of noncontroversy. "Objective" learning became the watchword, particularly when the Russians put *Sputnik I* into space. Science and mathematics became the watchwords: disciplines that have no "judgmental" content. American educators and social scientists became preoccupied with learning in what Jules Henry has called the "culture of death." [8]

Turning to the contemporary school we see it as a place where children are drilled in cultural orientations, and where subject matter becomes to a very considerable extent the instrument for instilling them. This comes about, however, not only because school, as the heartbeat of the culture, naturally embodies and expresses the central preoccupations, but also because schools deal with masses of children, and can manage therefore only by reducing them all to a common definition. Since it is in the nature of things that the definition should be determined by the cultural preoccupations, school creates what I have called the *essential nightmare.* The nightmare must be dreamed in order to provide the fears necessary to drive people away from something (in our case, failure) and toward something (success). In this way children, instead of loving knowledge become embroiled in the nightmare.[9]

Schools, themselves, took on characteristics resembling the social institutions for which they were preparing students: factories, the military, and so on.

The organizational correspondence between the schools in metropolis and the other superstructures should by now have become increasingly apparent to those who know school operation. Bureaucratization, internal specialization, elaboration of a hierarchy of coordination, centralization of authority in a managerial elite, and expansion of activities are all characteristics resembling other corporate systems. Even some of the language and imagery of industrial organization has been taken up by educators who talk of packaged programs and view end results as products.[10]

Various forces thus converged to make urban schools the ground where the distribution of personnel (learners) would meet the needs of the culture. We have identified two of these culture patterns: (1) McCarthyism and the anticommunist syndrome it supported, along with the cold war and the Korean war, which helped to perpetuate this national world view; and (2) the launching of *Sputnik I*, which, coupled with the emergence of Russia and China as formidable political entities, spurred the United States on to an ever-expanding weapons technology and an ascendancy of the military in many aspects of American life and social policy. School subject matter and organization, particularly in metropolitan areas, was significantly influenced by these trends. Additional social forces, however, reinforced the pattern.

CLASS AND ETHNIC SEPARATION: THE NEW URBAN PATTERN–Despite the nation's concern with foreign nations and internal "enemies," the post-World War II years witnessed remarkable expansion in material goods and a definitive newer settlement pattern: suburbia. The proliferation of the automobile permitted persons to range farther from their places of work, giving workers, including urban schoolteachers now living in the suburbs, less of a commitment to the people they worked with. Rewards were sought on the back lawns of the many satellite towns springing up and not so much in the ethnic enclaves of the metropolis that heretofore had been the birthplace of all those aspirants to higher social status and material acquisition.

Personal striving was fantasized through the fantastic growth of television, so that whole new forms of recreation, group interaction, and even reality itself were matters of imposed definition by the media, rather than the sober assessment of the historic and neighborhood forces that had previously shaped the lives of inner-city dwellers. Social class was now a commodity to be safeguarded. Stickball in the streets of New York City, for example, gave way to Little League baseball on Levittown sandlots. Income, combined with ethnocentrism and formal educational attainment, was the index of success. The fences of the mind now had fences round the lawn to separate oneself from others.

More and more, children went to school with children who were more like themselves. The opportunity for significant cross-group experience was diminished. And the famous Supreme Court decision of 1954 soon prompted the marshalling of forces on the different sides of school integration. These were not disparate events dislocated in time and space; rather, they were the comprehensible occurrences of a nation still striving to define itself, still seeking to create an ethos out of a very brief history. It was soon to be realized that some folks were not making it in America, despite their sacrifices in World War II and Korea. Those who were privileged (safe homes, material goods, etc.) nevertheless were less intimate with their parents' work, the workings of gadgets that punctuated household life (dishwashers, airconditioners, and the like), or the political systems that governed their local communities. Paul Goodman said they were "growing up absurd." [11] Edgar Friedenberg depicted the "vanishing adolescent," caught up in the fears and preoccupations of the parental generation that had created social circumstances making it difficult for youth to identify with the larger cultural system.[12] We had all become part of "the lonely crowd." [13]

As the "flight" to the suburbs continued, the influx to the cities also continued, as ethnic minorities sought to gain work and a better share of life's circumstances. The makeup of the city was changing, and this was reflected in urban school population and procedure. While suburban schools built planetariums and football fields to accommodate their students, the nonwhite-majority schools of inner-city neighborhoods manifested material shortages, pupil underachievement, and an emergent mythology reflecting negatively on the alleged capacities of minority children and their families. Whereas schools had previously been the ground where immigrant children were made into proper Americans, and where many themselves learned to aspire to be teachers, the schools could now be recognized as places where children were spurned and rejected. We were told that the "new" children were different and "deprived";[14] that they brought incapacities to school that made it impossible to succeed. If this were true (it was not),[15] the arguments for desegregation of schools would suffer. Teachers would have to defend their status by increased allusion to their professional integrity. And advocates for the poor would be countered by apologists for the Establishment, as it sought to innovate in the schools in order to maintain the status quo; or at least not to deviate from it too much, even in the face of mounting militancy in the larger society.

In brief, these were the manifest culture patterns of the 1950s.

1. Marked suburbanization and the evolving life style now so familiar to us; the concomitants of neighborhood and community "centripetence" which still distinguishes both suburb and city; and the expansion of transportation means which allowed us to distribute ourselves farther in space from one another, so that for many the problems of the city (the problems of urban schooling, for example) were distant visages many sought to escape from.

2. Television became a major medium of cultural transmission which enabled us to fantasize our lives by indirect attachment to external happenings, while paradoxically making it difficult to avoid the major social problems of the day: poverty, inequality, political witch-hunting, and the general unevenness that still characterizes American culture.

The implications for the urban school were plain: children of ethnic minorities would have to be dealt with in some manner or another.

TWIN DISCOVERIES: POVERTY AND THE URBAN SCHOOL–The 1960s are known to us as the "civil rights decade"; in this period poverty was "discovered" [16] and grouphoods sought to redefine themselves in their own terms: Black Power, Black is Beautiful, Youth Culture, Red Power, Chicano Power, Peace, etc. Urban schools had previously functioned to strip children of their ethnic ties, to have them relinquish those ties to distant lands or different kin and ideology systems, so that they could give assent to America. Suddenly, people were saying in force that they valued their ethnicities and that schools had provoked them into submission to a system that ultimately denied and defaced them. They would no longer go along.

It was also a period when "intellectualizing" social problems was in vogue. President John Kennedy had around him college professors and social scientists. The tendency was to see the solution to critical social problems in the spheres of research and scientific simulation. The moral essence of these questions were raised by political disbelievers: the young, the disaffected, and the hitherto "complacent" victims. Powerful statements were made about growing up in the black ghetto,[17] the barrio,[18] and in jail.[19] Major figures emerged to give a definition to American life that few were previously willing to abide by, despite their compelling nature: Martin Luther King, Malcolm X, Cesar Chavez, and others. Schools in the city were described with literacy and passion as brutal places;[20] as places where teachers were estranged from children and knew very little about their real lives.[21] Freedom rides, boycotts, sit-ins, political disruption at national conventions, rent strikes, and antiwar sentiment were not tangential occurrences; instead, they were fundamental callings to a new social order. The urban classroom was now a focal point for social revision. Cries for school decentralization and community control would not be passing fancies. They were movements challenging some basic assumptions lodged in the nation's psyche.

These activist movements were not without their frustrations. The event that frustrated persons the most, perhaps, was the Vietnam war; its consequences are probably not yet fully realized. People began to see racism, unequal educational opportunities, war, economic inequality, and poverty as interrelated episodes of American culture. The generation gap was manifest in more than rock-'n'-roll music, drugs, and revitalized religious movements; it was seen as well in the moral and intellectual gap between teachers and students in urban schools. And just as the political establishment sought to be less vulnerable in its policies by deceit and the narrowest interpretation of law (even with respect to promulgating war against other nations), teachers clearly defined themselves as a political and interest group as they unionized and politicized their educational perceptions. Indeed, the urban school now aspired (its faculty and leadership) to maintain belief in the face of the contrary. Namely, the function of education was not to educate. In urban America the function of education for teachers was to maintain freedom from community pressure and responsibility for the products of their efforts (the achievements of children); for the educationally denied in the inner city, the school was the arena in the struggle for personal and political freedom.

Something else had transpired in this period: Third World peoples had shed the oppressor in Africa and Cuba. There was a pan-human identification by the oppressed in the United States with persons of color and economic disadvantage around the world. Cross-cultural research revealed educational systems in other parts of the world that permitted individual dignity and legitimate status for the learner. Alternatives to traditional schooling would be sought. The world was changing and information and knowledge needed redefining.[22]

In summary, the social forces that shaped America in the 1960s included:

1. The struggle for civil rights and the reassertion of group and ethnic identity by a variety of persons.

2. Third World independence was a spur to American revitalization movements.

3. The Vietnam war forced everyone to reassess his perceptions of the nation that claimed to be the leader of the free world while it waged war on a distant continent and fostered poverty and inequality at home. Persons began to doubt the wisdom and word of middle-class professors who had previously defined American life. Teachers' uninvolvement in the lives of their children in city schools forced a confrontation over school policy; and the establishment would have to respond.

4. Poverty was "discovered."

5. Youth culture was manifest even in the ways of the parental generation. For the first time, perhaps, cultural patterns were being promulgated by the young. The nature of cultural transmission had taken a small but noticeable shift. There were events in the world and items of information that came to all—irrespective of age or position—at the same time.

The orderly progression and apportionment of knowledge known to the past generation had been modified by shifting social forces. Soon some would call for the abolition of the school. The American value system was being laid bare. Assumptions were challenged more strenuously; retrenchment would take place in the schools. An era of "innovation" would be set in motion.

The Establishment's Defense: Cultural Deprivation

Certainly, it is difficult to summarize even the major events that transpire in a generation. In the period after World War II to the present much more happened than I have said. The Kennedys were assassinated; Martin Luther King and Malcolm X were killed. Students were shot down on the campuses of Kent State and Jackson State. Universities were in turmoil at Columbia, Berkeley, Wisconsin, and elsewhere. Cities were in minor revolt in Newark, New York, Detroit, Watts; Albany, Montgomery, Selma, and others now had their northern counterparts. Nonwhite athletes added new dimensions to national sport by their participation, and even the Olympic Games were marked by athletes' activism. Everyone had a transistor radio, and most had television sets; events and people could no longer go unnoticed. Groups like the Black Panthers, SDS, and the Young Lords were known to all via the media. Eldridge Cleaver,[23] Rap Brown,[24] and George Jackson[25] were as fluent in their declarations as were Harvard professors. Stokely Carmichael was a household word. And Vine Deloria even told the anthropologists that they didn't know what they were talking about.[26]

The baby boom of earlier years had increased the ratio of young to adults in the population, and the schools had larger numbers of children (of more diverse ethnic and economic backgrounds) to handle. The old questions and the old procedures of the urban classroom were pitted against new realities. While schools had previously fostered docility in children, events in the world outside the school prompted even the very young to be skeptical and resistant. Along with "giants in the washing machine" there were rats in the walls for many children; and they questioned the legitimacy of both. Parents of poor children, who before had been attacked as not interested in the education of their children, were now defined as too aggressive and unqualified to press for educational changes in city schools. Curiously, no one alleged this about suburban parents of white children, who ran for election on school boards and voted on school budgets as a matter of course.

What it all really meant was that America faced the dilemma a nation at cross purposes inevitably must face: how to bring the American experience in line with the American ethos. Belief had constituted the

American reality; now the American reality—poverty, militarism, inequality—rendered belief difficult. Dissenters, in some instances, were killed; others were exiled. Some were in jail. And some pressed on, often in the face of little or no support. Several times it seemed that the very vitality and viability of the American way was at issue. After all, who was right—the "hard hats" or the "long hairs"? Weren't both groups equally products of the same kinds of schools, the same social forces?

It was apparent that America—and schooling—had different meaning for different groups. And the difference in meaning was, to great extent, a matter of school practice itself. An elaborate mythology about children has pervaded the urban school designed to justify academic failures among children and to validate the apportionment of different social classes and ethnic groups in the public world of work and status. The school has been the establishment's most potent weapon in striving to ensure that each generation will take its designated place on the assembly line, in the military, or even in the pulpit. Previously, we had simply alleged that segments of the population were biologically inferior. Those arguments suffice less well now, so we attribute patterns of deprivation on alleged cultural bases to those the society must keep vulnerable and beholden: factory line workers, service personnel, and others. It could not be more plain, the urban schools (and other schools as well) have been the handmaiden of the political and economic structure. The urban classroom and school may well be the Establishment's last stand.

OF SELF-FULFILLING PROPHECIES: WHO ARE THE "DUMB" CLASS?–I have already suggested that one way of keeping persons dependent (for example, children) is to withhold information and knowledge from them. Particularly is this understandable when we realize that human status and achievement is grounded in learning. Though the urban school continues to employ this method, it is more difficult to do so when there are other means of cultural transmission: television, radio, magazines and newspapers, and so on. The steps that schools have taken as an alternative are the limiting of learning opportunities by selection of materials, teachers' classroom procedures, and most significant of all: tracking.

The urban school is a place where children are differentiated on bases of alleged capability. Sorting and selecting and packaging of children is done in much the same way as items are boxed on an assembly line. Some are discarded because they do not meet manufacturers' standards. On occasion some are sent back to be remade; in other instances, "faulty" commodities are junked. And a whole industry has grown up around an effort to prove that the underachieving have only themselves to blame. This is peculiar, to say the least, when we examine across cultures the tremendous variety of learnings transmitted to different children under varying conditions and circumstances. In every culture children are made to learn what it is thought they must learn. Indeed, it has been said that there is nothing that has been discovered that cannot be taught quite easily. What are we really saying, then, when we deny the learning capacities of some of our own children? Are we not saying that we know they in fact *can* learn, but that we do not want everyone to know the same things? If everyone was a doctor, would we have enough patients?

> Tracking is one of the educational system's major techniques for thrusting forward students with the necessary qualities of school-measured intelligence, docility, background, and the rest; and for channeling the others into "appropriate" slots. . . .
>
> But the real effects of tracking can better be seen in what happens to students in the academic high schools. A majority of blacks and Puerto Ricans fill lower tracks, which lead them—if they stay at all—to "general" rather than "academic" diplomas. Only 18 percent of academic-high-school graduates were black or Puerto Rican . . . and only one-fifth of that 18 percent went on to college, as compared with 63 percent of whites who graduated. In other words, only 7 percent of the graduates of New York's academic high schools who went on to college were black or Puerto Rican. The rest, for the most part tracked into non-college-preparatory programs, left school with what amounted to a ticket into the army.[27]

The Jensens, the Shockleys, and the Garretts have suggested that blacks may have genetic limitations to learning. Their arguments have received much attention elsewhere, and I do not want to take them up here, except to acknowledge that "inferiority" arguments have long been part of the school's mental repertoire. The important thing to realize, of course, is that when teachers regard their children as inferior, those children's learnings will indeed be limited, not so much by their imagined incapacities as by teachers' incapacities to teach well and overcome the stereotypes that seriously limit them as people.

> Over time, our educational policy question has changed from "who ought to be educated?" to "who is capable of being educated?" The ethical question has been traded in for the scientific question. For those children whose educability is in doubt there is a label. They are the educationally, or culturally, or socioeconomically, deprived children. . . . Quite inseparable from these differences between the advantaged and the disadvantaged are the differences in their

teachers' expectations for what they can achieve in school. There are no experiments to show that a change in pupils' skin color will lead to improved intellectual performance. There is, however [evidence] to show that change in teacher expectation can lead to improved intellectual performance.[28]

Most urban schools have their "dumb" classes. Most urban school systems have their "compensatory" programs. They may be called "opportunity" classes, "able" groups, "Higher Horizons" classes, or whatever. Their very existence lends undue credence to the belief that some kids need a "head start" in school because they are disadvantaged cognitively by their families, communities, and biologies. Rarely do we talk about the stupidities of formal schooling that make even the most alert and willing pretentious and detached. Perhaps it is those who unstintingly accept the inanities of schooling who are "inferior," for example: teachers. Are we (teachers), as Herndon says, the "dumb class"?

We are the dumb class because we cannot learn. Cannot achieve. Why not? Cannot concentrate, have a low attention span, are culturally deprived, brain-damaged, non-verbal, unmotivated, lack skills, are anxiety-ridden, have broken homes, can't risk failure, no study habits, won't try, are lazy . . . ? Those are the reasons *kids* are in the dumb class. . . . Even if . . . things are completely obvious, the dumb class cannot learn them or achieve them. . . .

Are the teachers a dumb class? Well, we are supposed to teach kids to "read, write, cipher and sing," according to an old phrase. Can we do it? Mostly not. Is it difficult? Not at all. We can't do it because we are a dumb class, which by definition can't do it, whatever it is. . . .

Yet, released from the dumb class to their private lives, teachers are marvelous gardeners, they work on ocean liners as engineers, they act in plays, win bets, go to art movies, build their own houses, they are opera fans, expert fishermen, champion skeet shooters, grand golfers, organ players, oratorio singers, hunters, mechanics . . . all just as if they were smart people. Of course it is more difficult to build a house or sing Bach than it is to teach kids to read. Of course if they operated in their lives outside of the dumb class the same way they do in it, their houses would fall down, their ships would sink, their flowers die, their cars blow up.[29]

What children need are persons who are confident that they can learn; teachers who feel students' accomplishments are teachers' accomplishments too. When one looks at small-scale societies, one can see the true nature of learning in the community, in all the grouphoods that constitute the total culture. In these societies the transmitting agent (the teacher) sees the child (learner) throughout the course of their natural lives. Failure or severe retardation in learning would be intolerable where persons interact and depend on one another, not merely in classrooms, but in all aspects of life. There is more than ample evidence that all children can learn,[30] in a variety of settings,[31] despite "handicaps" that are real or imagined.[32] We need simply to act on this evidence. Jerome Bruner suggested in 1960 that the fundamental structure of a discipline can be taught to children, but that children need the opportunity to be immersed in problems without the distortions or restraints normally imposed by schools.[33] The problem is whether schools in urban America can be restructured to permit such learning. It is really a question of determining what it is our schools ought to be doing.

THE UNMASKING OF DEPRIVATION THEORIES–Jules Feiffer once mused, in one of his pointed moral cartoons, that integration used to be so much fun until Negroes got into it (it was a white man talking to his black double). I suppose some feel the same way about urban schools; they would be fun if those kids weren't there to mess it up. And every time studies and programs try to put people in "their place," someone comes along to prick the mythological balloon.

When the Coleman Report[34] and the Moynihan Report[35] appeared, they reaffirmed for some that black children had family and subcultural deficiencies that precluded learning at levels achieved by white children. Implications were that money should not be wasted on special programs for minority kids because the roots of failure lay outside the school. However, the Coleman Report also acknowledged that such children fall further behind in school the longer they stay in school. Here, clearly, it could be seen that school, itself, has a detrimental effect on children, particularly those it defines as unprepared to be in tune with school demands. And Moynihan, whose report was not based on ethnographic research in poor or minority communities, was countered by studies that showed the presence or absence of fathers in the home had little to do, in the long run, with children's school achievements.[36]

Charles Valentine showed in his definitive work *Culture and Poverty*[37] that traditional conceptualizations about the poor were gross distortions of who they really were and what they were really capable of. Research by socially motivated and responsible social scientists revealed that children were enhanced or inhibited in their schooling by procedures and attitudes of teachers, rather than by their inherent attributes.[38] Universities, too, had been training teachers for ghetto schools on assumptions that clouded their understandings instead of clarifying them. With the best of intentions, as it were, college professors and students learned the hard way that they had a faulty understanding of urban schools and urban communities.[39] There was, to be sure, "quackery in the classroom," including the college classroom.[40]

Each time the "disadvantaged" child was pronounced vulnerable by yet another study (for example, the Jencks Report),[41] contrary evidence, perhaps less arbitrarily derived, could be found.[42] The issue, really, is no longer whether children in the urban school can learn; it is whether the schools are willing to have them learn—in ways befitting them, not in ways that make children casualties of a system that needs a subservient economic class. At present "much of what is taught is not worth knowing as a child, let alone as an adult, and little will be remembered. The banality and triviality of the curriculum in most schools has to be experienced to be believed." [43] As Jules Henry has asked, "Is Education Possible?" [44] And can we get "the schools off the backs of at least those students who want them off"? [45]

ESTABLISHMENT INNOVATION: MAINTENANCE OF THE PATTERN–In recent years several articulate spokesmen have called for the abolition of schools[46] or for drastic revision in them, so as to offer significantly different alternatives to those presently available to students.[47] Often, their arguments were compelling, if seemingly too distant in time to be realistic. Their reasoning suggests that innovation in the schools is merely more of the same; a catering to the very mythology that permits schooling to ritualize and validate the social order expressed in political and economic institutions. Yet, as attractive as this thesis may be, Herbert Gintis may be even more correct: "But negation . . . is not itself a form of liberation. . . . It is this act of overcoming (synthesis, consciousness) which is the critical and liberating aspect of dialectical thought. Action lies not in the act of negation . . . but in the act of overcoming." [48]

Only when urban schools are seen in the total urban context can school programs and reform have meaning. It is unlikely that revised forms of schooling, alone, can reshape societal life. Just as deprivation theories have in the main supplanted biological inferiority theories, opportunity on the basis of merit has replaced privilege by birth. Are these very much different from one another?

Even the changes occurring in urban schools are, in reality, geared to the already advantaged.

Among the new strata of workers, labor has become more technological, cerebral, and mobile, and has created more room for leisure. Not only must the training period of such a labor force be extended, but the kind of training must be changed. An emphasis on "creativity" replaces a pure emphasis on discipline. Play as an educational ideal becomes opposed to work, insofar as it encourages creativity.

Play is, then, closely linked to the changes in the character of urban middle- and upper-middle-income groups and the emergence of these new occupational strata as a cultural aristocracy. Schools organized to satisfy the educational values of these strata also have distinct "class" character: they often are exclusive, and more important, they represent an effort to escape or deny the ethos of the industrial system and its traditional asceticism. The free schools—like the styles of their pupils' parents—reflect not only differences in taste, but a freedom and a leisure that the distribution of wealth denies to the lower- and lower-middle-income groups.[49]

In other words, innovation of the Establishment provides us, still, with an emphasis on fitting persons to the dominant culture patterns: work, settlement pattern, and the distribution of power and status. Assimilation is even now the focus of the schools' efforts, even though ethnic integrity is the issue most clearly enunciated by minority communities in the cities. The educational system has consistently tried to make children over in the mold of the transmitting agency (the school's leadership: teachers, administrators, school boards, etc.). If this was not possible, and children could not be made diffident, they were described as difficult. The diffident are given comforts—for example, compensatory programs; the difficult are punished: rejected, failed, and demeaned. But after more than a decade of activism in many spheres of cultural life in the United States, many are unwilling to accept the pretensions of school people, and the convergent forces of schooling must face the divergent forces of aroused children and parents.

Consequence and Divergence: Bureaucratization and Community Context

Everyone knows the hackneyed phrase: "The more things change, the more they stay the same." In some ways, this typifies the schools. Kids are still hanging their coats on the same hooks, as it were. With all the "innovation" in urban classrooms, children are still an underclass in America; and they have virtually nothing to say about how their schooling will evolve nor at whose hands it will take place. They are, even more than their elders, "prisoners of culture."[50] When we innovate in the schools, then, we do so, not so much for our children, but to maintain our cultural compulsions with respect to jobs, the social order, and our moral strivings as a people. We provide no alternatives to school. What would a kid in the city do? If you don't go to school, you don't go anywhere. Open schools, individually prescribed instruction, micro-teaching, free schools, modular scheduling, deschooling, and accountability- or competency-based programs for teachers are all designed in the end to produce the same effect: to bind children to the culture. This is not to say that we ought not try new and more effective approaches to learning; it is to say that these should be seen for what they are: variations on a theme rather than fundamental changes in structure or essence.

Though these variations in some cases seem to be more comfortably played in some settings than others (free schools are a middle- and upper-class phenomenon), each "innovation" diffuses rapidly from its urban-technical point of origin to the suburban middle-class public and private schools whose clientele and personnel, operating in the mainstream of technocratic culture, know and want an establishment educational innovation when they see one. Thus, accountability-based programs, constructed originally as a response to a stereotype of time-serving urban teachers, seem to have found a more hospitable reception in the suburbs.

In a sense what has happened is that in terms of technique urban school bureaucracy has caught up with its suburban counterpart. Decentralization of urban schools has provided a bureaucracy which functions in place of one which did not. (Urban teachers report now, under decentralization, much less delay and difficulty getting supplies and materials.) The management-by-objectives or accountability doctrine is a natural correlate and outgrowth of bureaucratic development in our system oriented administrative stage. In-service courses in "open education" are given at district headquarters and their graduates are sent, formula in hand, to their classrooms. State departments of education bureaucratize and sponsor programs of "individually guided education." And the wave of "teacher-proof" curriculum materials (most of which carefully list their "behavorial" objectives) continues on its way carrying its summer teacher workshops with it. These bureaucratically and technocratically based programs constitute packaged responses to the problems of urban education today. The elements in the bureaucratic hierarchy seem more closely bound together than ever before reducing the freedom and autonomy necessary for an effective unit, and generating a sameness and resonance that prevents the achievement of genuinely divergent approaches.

The word "backlash" is widely used in our vocabulary for a reason. Though we accept change in technology, often matter-of-factly, we are wary of "radicals" who attack our morals and values. Principals don't want women teachers wearing slacks to class; and some women teachers don't want their kids wearing long hair to class.[51] Yet, they may all be for "individualized instruction," whatever that means.

Frankly, many teachers do not see a place for themselves in the "new" culture proposed by the young, the indigenous, the Spanish-speaking, the black, and the poor white. All their lives have been marked by a striving that was defined at the time they, themselves, were becoming Americans by doing well in schools. It's not fair, they think, to have the rules of the game changed now that they have attained their places. Too much has been invested in our schools as they are presently constituted for school people to even perceive giving it up for something different, or better. The New York City teachers' union (the UFT) is more a political power than it is an educational force. It argues against competency-based programs, unless it determines the competencies at issue. It opposes community control of schools because it feels job security will be undermined. (What about children's security and their right to a humane and competent education?) It fosters the inclusion of paraprofessionals in schools, perhaps only because those persons, no matter how contributing they may be to school functioning, are no professional threat to teachers. They are paid less, hold places of little authority, and pay their union dues. They virtually have no academic or reform role.

The fact is, technological innovation is something we casually accept—for example, talking typewriters in the classroom. This is in keeping with our collective world view. As consumers, we know that new products can be discarded for newer ones. We anticipate this. But if a Puerto Rican or a black gets on the school board, he is not so easily discarded or replaced. In fact, those who run schools in our cities have been deliberate in their failure to help create recipient leadership in local communities. There has rarely been a working through the existing social structure of the neighborhood. And urban teachers are not themselves part of those neighborhoods outside their function as teachers. The arguments and debates about education are really arguments about economic and political power. In all those graduate courses teachers take to polish their credentials everyone is for integration and better education. When these are issues on the job—in the urban school itself—another view is often acted out.

> Who controls the schools our children attend? Who *should* control
> them? And what is the appropriate relationship between a school and
> the surrounding community? . . .
> Much of the early controversy in New York centered on control
> of I.S. 201, a public intermediate school in Harlem. . . .

At first, the I.S. 201 activists attempted to elicit the agreement of the New York City Board of Education to conduct an experiment in community control of a school. The responses were evasive, perfunctory, or nonexistent. . . . (Until its recent expansion, only one member of the New York City Board of Education was Black and none were Puerto Rican, even though the student population was more than 50 per cent nonwhite.)

Failing to move the Board, I.S. 201 parents had also carried their integration fight to the Mayor's office. The Mayor, in measured and somewhat professorial tones, gave them a lecture on the tax base of the city, and told them that school integration might stimulate an escalation of the white exodus. . . .

Why do Black people seek control over their local schools? After watching the failures of the present school system, they have concluded that those in control of that system define its objectives in terms of white America. . . .

The minority-group student thus finds himself in the curious position of being miseducated by a system that represents everybody's interest but his.[52]

The drive toward community control of schools and the attempt to decentralize authority in the school systems of urban America is an attempt to answer the question: "Who speaks for the child?" In nonliterate societies around the world, it is indeed the total community that speaks for the child. Life in the community—within the group—*is* education. Parents in the cities here are merely reasserting what a comparative and holistic view of other educational systems has already revealed. It needs no proof of its social viability. It simply needs political acceptance. Those who make it solely an educational issue merely cover up that fact.

There are not simply two "cultures" at odds here; there are three—childhood and youth subculture, middle-class white subculture, and the subculture of the nonwhite poor. Having morality on your side is not enough. Youth and nonwhite, alike, need to align. If youth in college, including all those people preparing to be teachers in urban schools, identified with the children (and the children's parents) they will be working with, rather than the professors of the training institutions out of which they come, a true revolutionary force for better education would be created. Labor and youth have not combined efforts in our nation. Otherwise, teachers would not see children as antagonists, but as colleagues.

For education, more than any other process, is essential to the achievement of a society in which persons carve out their destiny according to their natures and their own deliberative choices. . . . But the prevailing rhetoric is not translated into educational policy. Quite the reverse; the actual trend of developments makes more and more difficult the achievement of promised goals. The Socratic ideal of the examined life gives way to an educational process that rewards academic imperialism, fits individuals to socially needed functional slots, and, by means of paternal manipulation, adapts students for that conformity to the conventional wisdom which a society devoted to consensus and minimal disturbance of the social order requires.[53]

I have always found it curious, to say the least, that second- and third-generation (sometimes first-generation) white teachers should be telling tenth-generation black children (not to mention American Indians) how to behave in order to be proper Americans. The movement toward community control of schools is only one manifestation of that same sense of outrage.

THE URBAN SCHOOL: ITS FAILURES, ITS PROSPECTS–Some have suggested that American culture is at "the breaking point." [54] I am not sure whether people would regard this as hopeful or not. As someone once said, we are "like other people—capable of the best and capable of the worst." How we resolve the very real issues of urban education will reveal to us exactly what we are capable of. We have asked blacks to step to the back of the bus, and whites to step to the head of the class. Similar mixups in our thinking occur with respect to still other children in America. Teachers' racism is called children's "retardation." And education is used to punish rather than reward.[55]

Many issues of policy and ethics must be faced; and these, as we said at the outset, are not unrelated to broader issues and culture patterns forming the larger American social configuration. How can the rights of Chicanos, Puerto Ricans, blacks, Indians, poor whites, and females be supported in urban classes, with respect to how they are portrayed as well as to their personal rights as individuals? Who will be accountable for the success or failure of children in schools? Can nontraditional procedures evoke from children and teachers the best of which they are capable, as contrasted with the deadening and demeaning procedures now widely in vogue? What functional place do quota systems, open-enrollment programs, voucher systems, and contracting procedures have in urban schools? Who will pay the cost of education? What autonomous subsystems will be permitted to exist within presently established school systems? Can teacher training be made more humane, as well as relevant to the urban setting? Can alternative images of the world external to the school be made viable in the school: hippies, fems, libs, gays—in short, all that is America? Can students, even in the urban public school, be given a voice in school procedures and governance? Can all these be done so that neither children nor their teachers feel threatened? As one young teacher candidly admitted recently, the teacher's union in his district, in its effort to discourage the imposition of state-mandated competency-based regulations for teachers, has taught him to dislike and fear the parents of the children he didn't like very much to begin with.

We have too many fears. Ocean Hill–Brownsville, Newark, Canarsie, busing, integration, bilingualism, even the way some children look, conjure up fears in our heads. It is, at least, an uncomfortable feeling, and an unseemly stance with respect to our culture's children. Schools were shut down for periods in New York City in 1966, 1968, and at other times. For children, for whom there is already too much schooling, these may have been periods of great potential learning about the schools. For others, these were moments to take sides in a continuing battle for ascendancy in the schools. We can label the issues "collective bargaining," "class size," "nonprofessional tasks," or whatever we want, but they are also issues of cultural self-analysis, which is always difficult and uncomfortable.

I have noted that the schools are among the most stable institutions in our culture. For that reason the problems that surround the schools remain with us also. More than ten years ago, I remember giving a talk at Hunter College about "ghetto" schools. It was part of their Project TRUE Program (Teachers and Resources for Urban Education). When I finished, a black woman rushed the stage, grabbed me, and said: "God bless you for saying what you did; and for having the courage to say so." She then left. A white woman just as eagerly approached me and said she thought she knew me. Suddenly, I recognized her too. She had been my seventh-grade social studies teacher. "I thought so," she said. "You didn't know what you were talking about then; and you don't know what you're talking about now." She then told me she was a principal of a ghetto school and that things were just fine in her school, unlike what I had described.

Well, the question is still the same. Which side are you on? Urban schooling is a success or a failure depending on the perspective we take in its examination. As an instrument and an agency of cultural stability, the school is a historical success. As a medium for the amalgamation of diverse cultures and acculturation, the school in the city has succeeded. As a funnel for fitting persons into the industrial segment of society (and keeping some out), it has done its job. As a reenactment of the social order of privilege and underprivilege, it has succeeded. In the need to make and keep each generation vulnerable to consumerism and technological expansion, it has accomplished the job, as well—in fact, too well.

M. S. Arnoni once said that America was like a burly man eating a bowl of spaghetti, and that what this man needed was a concert, not more spaghetti. Perhaps this is what Jules Henry meant by "enlightenment." Because in many ways the urban school has failed badly. It has failed to give the majority nonwhite school population in New York City, for example, the personal competence needed for status in political and economic spheres. It has failed, also, to give middle-class white students the sense of personal freedom and moral commitment to alter these circumstances as they enter the parental generation. And it has divided us along arbitrary lines as dominant culture persons, marginal culture persons, and culturally excluded persons—depending on our ethnic identities. It has made us take school so for granted that we simply accept that our children will always be, to some extent, at the whim of some other persons. School tells us how to use the calendar, how to dress, what to work at, where to live, and whom to be. It is not unfair to want to have a voice in those decisions. That is what urban education is all about, really.

Some people feel we expect too much from schools. They say that urban schools cannot solve the problems of urban areas. After all, can the schools prevent crime, political corruption and duplicity, bad housing, unequal job opportunity, bad health practice, and so on? Perhaps not. It is doubtful, in fact, whether the urban school can really educate children in a manner that we pretend. "The schools keep getting renewed calls for greatness from all sides. If we want schools to be brought down to human scale, we need to conceive a role for them that is also of human scale—a modest role that ordinary people can handle by themselves. To conceive of such a modest role is to conceive of schools without education." [56]

Though some would draw back in opposition to such an argument, it is worth considering. If we removed the pretenses and the educational-methods-searching and decided that we will use schools to make our children comfortable and cooperative, we would be getting more than we get now. But I am not sure we are capable of this, either. Parents who do not want their children to learn alongside "other" children, would not want their children to cooperate and be friendly with those children as well. In other words, the same issues might prevail, no matter how we seek to change the function of the school. People who dislike and distrust others on the bases of race and class usually carry those feelings over to all situations—work, play, neighborhood, church, and family. The rules of school need to be changed, but only secondarily to the need for rules changes in how we regard one another as people, and how we regard ourselves as a nation.

What then will correct these evils? The answer will not come from the school system, nor from the social scientists who serve society. It has . . . come from the victims themselves, the ghetto communities, the mothers and fathers, and from the students. Parents whose children have been arrested, beaten, or lost for days in juvenile centers have begun to question deeply whether they were wrong and their children right. Parents are now demanding the power to control the education of their children. They are demanding accountability from politicians, teachers, and researchers. The mood of the youth is new. They do not seek crevices in the strategies through which they can crawl to freedom. They challenge not just the strategies, but the education itself; not just the education, but the social system it is designed to perpetuate.[57]

We need such hopeful statements, and we need moral prophecy and exhortation; but we need, as Jonathan Kozol says: "The vision of men and women who can do things right; can start, continue, follow up and follow through; can instigate, promote, excite, inspire, and then can stick with that which we have helped inspire, promulgate, promote, long enough to bring it to at least a tentative level of completion." [58]

Passion, alone, is inadequate in building firm commitments. Competence is also required. A society that makes its children vulnerable, also makes its adults vulnerable by drawing them away from their children. This theme has been a recurrent one in this discussion. Bureaucracies, like the urban school systems we have been depicting, provide the reasons (and, sometimes, the means) for their own demise. Urban schools, allegedly the vehicles for opportunity, cannot continue to deny opportunity and survive intact. The first phase of renewal and revision in the schools has come upon us—parents, children, and others in the minority enclaves telling us they will have no more of it; no more of what has been a system of deliberate destruction of hope and fair chance for so many. Strategies are being shaped and refined. Competence is being gained.

Vested interests—political leaders, labor leaders, heads of institutions related to the schools (factories, etc.)—will exert their usual force to discourage change by control of media, hiring practices, appointments to office, and the like. Their actions have never been mysterious to those who understood their motivation. It is really that whole segment of persons in the middle who will make the difference: teachers, workers, parents, students. Those of us who characteristically belong in this group must learn to divest ourselves of our own fears and hangups that are parts of ourselves too long deceived. When we have learned to define one another, not merely as child or parent, pupil and teacher, layman and professional, but as persons sharing a similar right to a decent life, irrespective of personal or cultural style, the problem of education will appear in different perspective. I contend we need such a belief, and only serious effort will substantiate that belief.

We are really a society that uses its children. We like them when it is convenient. We even send them to war when it is convenient. As Dick Gregory observed, we would have less readily sent our pet dogs to Vietnam in place of our children. That may sound aggressive, for we know our intentions are better than that. Sometimes good intentions have bad results, however.

> I wonder . . . what kinds of loyalties can be constructed on a groundwork of desertion. There is a black child that I know in Boston who has now gone through four generations of white teachers, organizers, drifters, VISTAS, O.E.O.-supported revolutionaries and what he calls "The Hippie People," all in the course of six years. Peter can list the names of all the young white men and young white women he has known. They give him supper and they buy him shoes and take him out on hikes and sit down on the floor to play with the cuisenaire rods for one summer and one winter, and sometimes for one spring and for one summer once again. Then they switch gears, and they are into a New Thing. They cancel him out, or rather they do not "cancel" him—they cannot quite do that—but situate him in a slot of history or a place of pain known as "the race and conscience bag." They make new friends and read new books, and find a whole new set of slogans and bywords, and they are off to a new dedication.
>
> Peter, however, does not live within the "race and conscience bag." He lives on Columbus Avenue in the South End of Boston. He is a real person and, after they are gone, he is still there.[59]

I think the rest of us are real people, too. I see in my own children what is right and what is wrong with me. I see in other grouphoods the essence of our total humanity. The anthropological ethic is worthwhile: look at others, so that you may better understand yourself.

NOTES

1. Jules Henry, *Jules Henry on Education* (New York: Vintage Books, 1972), p. 10.

2. See Jerry Farber, *The Student As Nigger* (North Hollywood, Calif.: Contact Books, 1969).

3. Henry, *Jules Henry on Education*, p. 20.

4. Edmund Carpenter and Marshall McLuhan, eds., *Explorations in Communication* (Boston: Beacon Press, 1970), p. 1.

5. Ruth Benedict and Gene Weltfish, *The Races of Mankind* (New York: Public Affairs Committee, 1943).

6. See Robert Lynd, *Knowledge for What?* (New York: Grove Press, 1964). See especially chap. 3, "The Pattern of American Culture."

7. Celia Lewis Zitron, *The New York City Teachers Union 1916–1964* (New York: Humanities Press, 1968), p. 40.

8. See Jules Henry, *Culture Against Man* (New York: Random House, 1963), pp. 475–77.

9. Henry, *Culture Against Man*, pp. 320–21.

10. Solon T. Kimball and James E. McClellan, *Education and the New America* (New York: Random House, 1962), p. 211.

11. See Paul Goodman, *Growing Up Absurd* (New York: Vintage Books, 1960).

12. See Edgar Z. Friedenberg, *The Vanishing Adolescent* (New York: Dell, 1962).

13. See David Riesman, Nathan Glazer, and Reuel Denney, *The Lonely Crowd* (Garden City, N.Y.: Anchor Books, 1956).

14. See Frank Riessman, *The Culturally Deprived Child* (New York: Harper & Row, 1962).

15. See Gerry Rosenfeld, *"Shut Those Thick Lips!": A Study of Slum School Failure* (New York: Holt, Rinehart & Winston, 1971).

16. See Michael Harrington, *The Other America* (New York: Macmillan, 1963). It should be noted that American Indians were not included in this discussion. In a subsequent edition to his book Mr. Harrington acknowledged this significant omission.

17. See Claude Brown, *Manchild in the Promised Land* (New York: Macmillan, 1966).

18. See Piri Thomas, *Down These Mean Streets* (New York: Alfred A. Knopf, 1967).

19. See Alex Haley and Malcolm X, *The Autobiography of Malcolm X* (New York: Grove Press, 1966).

20. See Jonathan Kozol, *Death at an Early Age* (Boston: Houghton Mifflin, 1967).

21. See James Herndon, *The Way it Spozed to Be* (New York: Simon & Schuster, 1968).

22. See Margaret Mead, *Culture and Commitment* (Garden City, N.Y.: Natural History Press, 1970).

23. Eldridge Cleaver, *Soul on Ice* (New York: McGraw-Hill, 1968). A Ramparts Book.

24. H. Rap Brown, *Die Nigger Die!* (New York: Dial Press, 1969).

25. George Jackson, *Soledad Brother—The Prison Letters of George Jackson* (New York: Bantam Books, 1970).

26. Vine Deloria, Jr., *Custer Died for Your Sins* (New York: Macmillan, 1969).

27. Paul Louter and Florence Howe, *The Conspiracy of the Young* (New York: World, 1970), pp. 215–16.

28. Robert Rosenthal and Lenore Jacobson, *Pygmalion in the Classroom* (New York: Holt, Rinehart & Winston, 1968), p. 181.

29. James Herndon, *How to Survive in Your Native Land* (New York: Simon & Schuster, 1971), pp. 103, 106–7.

30. See Herbert Kohl, *36 Children* (New York: New American Library, 1967).

31. See Jules Henry, "A Cross-Cultural Outline of Education," *Current Anthropology* 1, no. 4 (July 1960): 267–305.

32. See George Dennison, *The Lives of Children* (New York: Random House, 1969).

33. Jerome Bruner, *The Process of Education* (Cambridge, Mass.: Harvard University Press, 1960), pp. 17–32.

34. James S. Coleman, *Equality of Educational Opportunity* (Washington, D.C.: U.S. Government Printing Office, 1966).

35. Daniel P. Moynihan and Paul Barton, "The Negro Family: The Case for National Action" (Washington, D.C.: U.S. Department of Labor, 1965).

36. See Rosenfeld, *"Shut Those Thick Lips!"*, especially chap. 8, "White Lies About Black Children," pp. 49–61.

37. Charles A. Valentine, *Culture and Poverty* (Chicago: University of Chicago Press, 1968).

38. See Eleanor Burke Leacock, *Teaching and Learning in City Schools* (New York: Basic Books, 1969).

39. See Gerry Rosenfeld, *A Study of the New York University Clinic for Learning Project: Whitelaw Reid Junior High School*, no. 57 (New York: Center for Urban Education, 1970).

40. See Samuel McCracken, "Quackery in the Classroom," *Commentary* 49 (June 1970): 45–58.

41. See Earl Lane, "The Jencks Report—Misunderstood or Mismanaged?" *Newsday*, 3 October 1972, pp. 3A–5A, 15A.

42. See David K. Cohen, "Does IQ Matter?" *Intellectual Digest* 2 (July 1972): 35–38.

43. Charles E. Silberman, "Crisis in the Classroom," *Intellectual Digest* 1 (March/April 1971): 106. Excerpted from *Crisis in the Classroom* (New York: Random House, 1970).

44. Jules Henry, "Is Education Possible?" in *Anthropological Perspectives on Education*, ed. Murray L. Wax, Stanley Diamond, and Fred O. Gearing (New York: Basic Books, 1971), pp. 156–62.

45. Edgar Z. Friedenberg, "What Are Our Schools Trying to Do?" *New York Times Book Review*, 14 September 1969, p. 57.

46. See Ivan Illich, *Deschooling Society* (New York: Harper & Row, 1970).

47. See Everett Reimer, *School Is Dead: Alternatives in Education* (Garden City, N.Y.: Doubleday, 1971).

48. Herbert Gintis, "Towards a Political Economy of Education: A Radical Critique of Ivan Illich's Deschooling Society," *Harvard Educational Review* 42, no. 1 (February 1972): 94.

49. David K. Cohen and Marvin Lazerson, "Education and the Corporate Order" (Andover, Mass.: Warner Module Publications, 1973), p. 62. Reprinted from *Socialist Revolution* (March/April 1972).

50. See George A. Pettitt, *Prisoners of Culture* (New York: Charles Scribner's Sons, 1970).

51. See Edgar Z. Friedenberg, "Contemptuous Hairdressers: Ceremonies of Humiliation in School" (Ann Arbor: Radical Education Project, n.d.), pp. 9–18. Reprint.

52. Preston R. Wilcox, "The Community-Centered School," in *Radical School Reform*, ed. Ronald Gross and Beatrice Gross (New York: Clarion Books, 1969), pp. 126–27.

53. Arnold S. Kaufman, *The Radical Liberal* (New York: Clarion Books, 1970), p. 19.

54. See Philip E. Slater, *The Pursuit of Loneliness* (Boston: Beacon Press, 1970).

55. See Annette T. Rubinstein, ed., *Schools Against Children* (New York: Monthly Review Press, 1970).

56. Carl Bereiter, "Schools Without Education," *Harvard Educational Review* 42, no. 3 (August 1972): 412.

57. Annie Stein, "Strategies for Failure," *Harvard Educational Review* 41, no. 2 (May 1971): 204.

58. Jonathan Kozol, "Politics, Rage and Motivation in the Free Schools," *Harvard Educational Review* 42, no. 3 (August 1972): 421.

59. Ibid., pp. 421–22.

PART FOUR

Divergence and Its Reflection in Schooling

11

PAUL GOODMAN AND
ANARCHISTIC EDUCATION

Maxine Greene

Paul Goodman saw the growing convergent forces of American society as an intolerable and unlivable reality. Anarchism was his approach to this unprecedented social and cultural reality. For Goodman viable life is possible not in convergent systems but in anarchist social groups and communities of least abstraction and minimal super-individual regulations where men, women, and children can live without the excessive artificiality of superorganic culture. Yet what is interesting is the fact that the anarchism of which Goodman speaks, primarily responds to those who have enjoyed benefits resulting from the development of the convergent forces. Undoubtedly he has been an articulate spokesman of anarchism in the past two decades to whom youth, educators, and men and women of various walks of life listened. It seems that his anarchist approach has somewhat lost its original appeal and vitality as we approach the mid-1970s. As an example of the divergent forces, it, however, exhibits its variations at present.

In this chapter I look critically at the character of Goodman's anarchist position and its shortcomings seen from the vantage point of the present time.

Anarchist Tradition

"The approach I took in *Growing Up Absurd* is the same I took 15 years earlier in a collection of essays called *Drawing the Line*. It is an old anarchist position. When you get an overcentralized society devoting itself to rather useless goods, empty power, statism and big corporations—the only way to stay alive is to draw the line." [1] This was Goodman in a 1971 interview, summing up the themes of his life's work: survival and independent action and being in the world. And indeed he was right to link them to the anarchist position; since the writing he did in the fields of psychology, social criticism, and education can be understood only when viewed within an anarchist frame. At the same time, however, he stood squarely in the tradition of Romantic individualism that reached its peak in the nineteenth century. Its roots were in Jeffersonianism and the belief that the individual was above the state, with the best government being the one that governed least.

In the background, too, hung the literature of American romanticism and its renderings of felt disparities between the person and the institutions among which he lived. From the early days of Transcendentalism through the founding of the utopian communities, from Thoreau's experiments at Walden Pond through Huck Finn's and Jim's community on the raft, there was a preoccupation with autonomy and self-regeneration; over and over, individuals—actual and fictional—felt compelled to "draw the line." Emerson's words still resound: "Society everywhere is in conspiracy against the manhood of every one of its members. Society is a joint-stock company. . . . Whoso would be a man must be a nonconformist." [2] Melville's great novel *Moby Dick* begins with a description of New Yorkers coming on Sundays to look at the sea, landsmen "of week days pent up in lath and plaster—tied to counters, nailed to benches, clinched to desks. How then is this? Are the green fields gone? What do they here?" [3] The metaphor suggests a crucifixion: individuals, purportedly free, are being sacrificed to a system. Later, Melville wrote of "Man disennobled—brutalized" [4] by science and by industry. Thoreau, long concerned with his own "economy," wrote in *Civil Disobedience* of how he refused allegiance to an unjust, brutal state, of how he would not acquiesce. "Let your life be a counter friction to stop the machine," he said. "I came into this world, not chiefly to make this a good place to live in, but to live in it, be it good or bad." [5]

The romantic individualist, civil disobedient or not, was neither reformer nor philanthropist. Usually a middle-class intellectual, he was not concerned with transforming social reality for the many. Most often, he was committed to arousing other individuals to self-identification and awareness; he had little influence on the shape of institutions or the direction of social change. The same must be said about anarchism in America: it has had a relatively minor impact on political and educational thought.

Paul Goodman, generally unheeded, spent twenty-five years questioning the "game of conformity" [6] and the possibilities of being "thought-free, fancy-free, imagination-free" [7] in the modern world. Whether he was writing philosophy, fiction, or social theory, he was exposing depersonalization, manipulation, and centralism; but he began achieving popular success only at the start of the last decade. The success was due to the overlap between the assertions of a just-burgeoning counterculture and Goodman's reaffirmation of the anarchist counter-ideal to affluence and "top-down" control. Today, when the sense of powerlessness has been exacerbated, when confidence in the "revolution of consciousness" [8] has drained away, the matter of his relevance must be dealt with from a new perspective, with different perceptions of context and possibility.

In *Growing Up Absurd*, Goodman discerned intimations of the future in the Beat Generation's rebellions; because he saw the Beats acting out a "critique of the organized system that everybody in some sense agrees with" and providing a "pilot study of the use of leisure in an economy of abundance." [9] Nine years earlier, he had written in *Gestalt Therapy* about the dangers to personality in adjustment to "a dubiously valuable workaday society." [10] Although he saw the weaknesses in the Beat preoccupation with cool beatitude and heightened consciousness, he saw in their dissent intimations of what might happen when the American people recognized that they could "go it on their own." There seemed to him to be a fundamental soundness in individuals who could throw off unnatural repressions and resentments. Moreover, the Beats were pacifist and were inventing a "community creativity" that seemed to him unique. They were *grounded* in experience, and they were rejecting the tight maturity demanded by a Puritan society that "does not let one be." Goodman's overriding concern at the time was with the throwing off of the restrictions that hampered personal growth—with possibilities of becoming spontaneous, somehow primitive, and free.

Two years later, in 1962, Students for a Democratic Society was founded; and Thomas Hayden and others wrote what was called the Port Huron Statement. The students (some of them veterans of civil rights marches and sit-ins in the South) were reacting against a generalized apathy, against "the actual separation of people from power, from relevant knowledge, from pinnacles of decision-making." [11] Their feelings of outrage occasionally moved them to social reform, which was carried out initially in the mode of civil rights protest and community organization. A few of them saw themselves as "spiritual, if not philosophical anarchists," [12] others as socialists, some as liberal intellectuals; almost all were white and middle class.

There is no evidence that their early statements were influenced by Goodman's writings, nor that they directly influenced him. But it is interesting to discover that the essays in *People or Personnel* (written between 1963 and 1965) specifically discuss the issues facing the founders of SDS: powerlessness, estrangement, the impacts of the "present centralized style of social organization." [13] Developing his notions of authority, surplus productivity, and "getting into power," Goodman was reporting increasingly on encounters with students; but, in effect, he was continuing to elaborate on his own tradition, the "old anarchist position." Only now he believed he could see it in practice; and he talked optimistically of the way "poor Negroes and Puerto Ricans, bearded students, and Bohemian artists exercise citizenly initiative and engage in reform politics." [14]

Simultaneously, he began exploring what it actually meant to be a full and serious human being within a society still characterized by "meaningless management" and a "showy style of life." [15] When young dissenters began living lives of voluntary poverty, defying militarism, IBM cards, roles, perquisites, and the rest, it was as if Goodman's was an idea whose time had come. He wrote ever more persuasively, in consequence, about "meaningless enterprise," the need for *Lernfreiheit*, the search for new forms of community.[16]

The matter of his influence, like the larger issue of the counter-culture's rise and fall, remains to be explored; but Goodman's language obviously assisted young people in their efforts to articulate what they were convinced was wrong. In *Speaking and Language*, Goodman insisted that speaking is a mode of action and that language functions primarily to create meanings—that it "shapes how people think, feel, and judge what is functional." [17] His language did not launch the protest movements; but his writings played some part in focusing those movements and shaping judgments of what was possible. In the same fashion, they eventually helped to shape a radical critique of the schools, especially when that critique focused upon social structures, coercion of the young, and the evils of compulsory education. It was Goodman, with his anarchist hopes, who first proposed the "deschooling" Ivan Illich so effectively popularized.[18] There was, unquestionably, an overlap between Illich's disestablishmentarianism where the Catholic Church was concerned and Goodman's vision of the school system as a "compulsory trap." Again, the direct, cranky Goodman voice helped to shape how diverse individuals came to feel about the peculiar institution of schooling. No matter how wrongheaded he might turn out to be, Goodman had a great gift for defining alternatives in situations where structures seemed in some manner God-given, "natural," unchangeable by human hands.

The alternatives Goodman saw depended upon self-motivated individuals willing to take small, independent actions, willing to take risks and perform experiments without concern for official strictures or the official tests of validity. The consciousness behind all this was clearly steeped in anarchist and romantic tradition: the objects of Goodman's perceiving and judging were particular individuals and arrangements; human beings who were rational and capable of autonomy.

In an essay called "The Black Flag of Anarchism," he ascribed to militant young people the anarchist feelings that had sustained him throughout his life and, in so doing, explained what anarchism meant to him: "They believe," he wrote, "in local power, community development, rural reconstruction, decentralist organization, so they can have a say. They prefer a simpler standard of living. Though their protests generate violence, they themselves tend to non-violence and are internationally pacifist. But they do not trust the due process of administrators and are quick to resort to direct action and civil disobedience." [19]

This is clearly a latter-day expression of one of the more pacific strands in the anarchist tradition. It evokes Peter Kropotkin's view that anarchism was simply a theory of life under which society was conceived without government. Harmony in such a society, he said, would be achieved through "free agreements concluded between various groups, territorial and professional, freely constituted for the sake of production and consumption, as also for the satisfaction of the infinite variety of needs and aspirations of a civilized being." [20] It evokes, also, Alexander Berkman's affirmation that anarchism meant "a condition of society where all men and women are free and where all enjoy equally the benefits of an ordered and sensible life." [21] It raises the echoes of Emma Goldman's call for liberation of mind and body, for a social order "based on the free grouping of individuals for the purpose of producing real social wealth." [22]

There is no serious talk here about collective consciousness or revolutionary classes. The ownership of the means of production is not a prime issue, nor is any theory of surplus value or of alienation caused by separation of the worker from the product of his work. Freedom and self-determination are both presumed. Through the acts of free men, exploitative systems can be made to give way to simpler and more economical ways of doing things. Production, freed of "top-down" regulations and busywork, can be geared to function and utility. The authoritative state, under such conditions, will not be necessary. Action will at last be self-chosen and voluntary; persons, each one fundamentally decent (when not pressed out of shape by rulers and organizers), will be able to determine the course of their own lives.

Goodman's Vision as an Anarchist

Goodman put his stress on what he called the "system" rather than government or state. It is not always easy to discover what he meant by the "system," although he identified it with the dominant mode of organization in the United States. He did not see it in economic terms, as the Marxists do; he did not take Jacques Ellul's view that a self-generating "technique" lies behind the managerial organization.[23] He did not even see it as primarily exploitative; and this fact helps to explain his view that individuals, creating themselves as persons rather than agreeing to be personnel, could make a significant difference. It also helps to explain why he believed that the youth movement could be such an effective counter-force.

In *Like a Conquered Province*, Goodman wrote that the major trends in the dominant organization were "its tendency to expand meaninglessly for its own sake, and its tendency to exclude human beings as useless." [24] What he saw was an empty society rather than an affluent one; and he objected to monopolies, advertising, pollution, the neglect of public services, and the predominance of "made-work (or war)" primarily on the grounds that they all led to meaninglessness. Young people, deprived of useful functions and prevented from playing significant parts in the world, became (for him) the exemplary exploited class, largely because they were excluded and nothing meaningful was offered for them to do. He found among them the seeds of responsibility, moral courage, and communal feeling that might lead to the restoration of a kind of Jeffersonian, town-meeting democracy—a creative involvement, a sense of efficacy. This, rather than deliberate or "liberal" reform; this, rather than outright revolution on the part of the oppressed, would counteract the emptiness and open the way to a decent world.

Meanwhile, Goodman saw the system working through a monolithic school system and effectively flouting "independence, initiative, scrupulous honesty, earnestness, utility, respect for thorough scholarship." [25] He saw it working through "military industrial structures" to eradicate ordinary human purposes along with "manly" work. He saw it laid out before him in deadly, unplanned urban centers that made unthinkable the development of viable community life. The remedy was to chip away at it, to engage in "creative disorder" when necessary, to create alternative forms of grouping and producing and being in the world. Individuals, especially young middle-class individuals, had the capacity to understand that the system was man-made and could be undone by people resolutely refusing to be personnel.

In all his many roles, with all his many *personae,* Goodman worked in a nondiscursive, unabashedly "poetic" way to arouse people to integration as mindful, sensual, emotional, and sexual beings destined to create themselves in a concrete, often inhospitable world. Always, there was a concern to work with what he saw to be the decentralizing tendencies in mass society and to build upon the growing discontent with life in the collectivity, in what Kierkegaard had called "the Crowd." [26]

Goodman wrote continuously about alternative ways of living and being together—in rural communities, in the therapeutic atmospheres of mini-schools, in work camps for adolescents, in urban radio stations, in neighborhood theaters, in decentralized school boards, in free universities, in action organizations functioning in the spirit of participatory democracy. Theodore Roszak wrote that Goodman's communitarianism was "his greatest and most directly appreciated contribution to contemporary youth culture." He went on (and there is a pathos now in reading it): "The pseudo-Indian tribes that now camp in our cities, the psychedelic communities in the California hinterlands or the wilds of Colorado, the Diggers with their hazy ideas about free stores and cooperative farms . . . whatever their failings, these are part of that Utopian anarchist tradition which has always bravely refused to knuckle under to the proposition that life must be a bad, sad compromise with Old Corruption." [27]

Goodman, it is believed, had much to do with the *shape* of some of these communities, for all his "neolithic" objections to some of their extremes. Surely, they were responses to his repeated suggestions that people take the initiative themselves and, if they could not tolerate the mass society, invent their own ways of life. Of the first importance was a communal atmosphere: hierarchies were to be abolished, along with rulebooks and expertise. The new communities were to be (and often were) improvisational, easy, open, involving all participants in direct and spontaneous ways.

In *Communitas,* when Goodman and his brother wrote about intentional communities, they made the point that their principal motivation was the achievement of "a well-rounded life in a free community." Significantly, they went on:

Such an attitude belongs not to backward but precisely to avant-garde groups, who are sensitive and more thoughtful than the average, and who react against the extant condition of society as fragmented, insecure, lonely, superficial, or wicked. They are willing to sacrifice social advantages to live in a community of the like-minded.[28]

With tense, urbanized individuals in mind, Goodman later found his paradigm in the Israeli kibbutz and called it "the conflictful community." [29] He was responding to sceptics who doubted Americans could live peacefully together; and he spoke optimistically of "excellent sociological and psychological techniques for maintaining and increasing contact in conflicts." [30] His point was that stereotypes and even stupidity would disappear as give-and-take relationships arose out of conflicts that were therapeutically resolved. Through such means, "thoughtful" people would learn to live together fraternally and peaceably; they would devote themselves to inventing a new, face-to-face style of life. This was the point in coming together, not the political action so many young people preferred. In Goodman's many discussions of community, there are hints of incipient disorder and "acting out"; but there are no explicit anticipations of the Weathermen, nor of the affinity groups who later organized such actions as the one called Mayday and the one celebrated as "Days of Rage."

He seemed truly to believe that the establishment of alternative communities would eventually undermine the centralism and the intricacy of the system. The system, before long, would find itself unable to tolerate the tensions set up and the refusal of increasing numbers to resign themselves to the status quo; and controls would therefore loosen, while organizations decentralized, and more and more people claimed the right to "go it on their own." It was not the implacable rationality of the corporate system that disturbed Goodman, nor the "total mobilization" Herbert Marcuse dramatically described.[31] It was, rather, the closed-in, confining character of the lives people lived within their institutions.

Sterling Fishman,[32] reminding us that Goodman wrote a book called *Kafka's Prayer* in 1947, has laid stress on the parable he presents in *Growing Up Absurd*, a Kafkaesque parable:

So imagine as a model of our Organized Society: *An apparently closed room in which there is a large rat race as the dominant center of attention.* And let us consider the human relations possible in such a place. This will give you a fair survey of what disturbed youth is indeed doing: some running that race, some disqualified from running it and hanging around because there is nowhere else, some balking in the race, some attacking the machine, etc.[33]

The room, of course, was only "apparently closed"; there was a way out for those healthy and articulate enough to create another place to live.

The response on the part of those in the room is more likely to be boredom and a sense of meaninglessness than rage or revolutionary fervor. In addition there is shame, and there is a sick awareness of the artificiality of roles; but there is little anger at inequities or injustice or the ways in which people *in general* are oppressed. It appears unlikely, therefore, that Goodman could conceptualize a society so brutal and inhuman as to arouse (perhaps justifiably) violent outrage in certain youth. And this may account for his overarching interest in doing away with traps and compulsions; if the doors were opened, if the young were freed, there would be no need for revolutionary action. The closed room, the system, would simply be *replaced* by "individualist community cooperation."

In *Compulsory Mis-Education*, Goodman concentrated on the "trap" set by the schools. He wrote (beginning to fashion the language of what would soon be called the "romantic" critique):

> The advance guard problem is that the compulsory school system, like the whole of our economy, politics, and standard of living, has become a lockstep. It is no longer designed for the maximum growth and future practical utility of the children into a changing world, but is inept social engineering for extrinsic goals, pitifully short-range. Even when it is benevolent, it is in the bureaucratic death-grip of a uniformity of conception, from the universities down, that cannot possibly suit the multitude of dispositions and conditions.[34]

And he proceeded to call, as is well known, for the end of compulsory schooling.

Doing so, however, he neglected to discuss the historical role of the schools in serving the requirements of a developing industrial order; nor did he touch upon the "legend" of the public schools where the equalization of opportunity was concerned. The school system "has *become*," he said, "a lockstep. It is *no longer* designed for the maximum growth." The implication is that, having originated in earlier times, the schools somehow embodied the Jeffersonian spirit of participant democracy or, at the very least, did not interfere with the spontaneous education Goodman believed went on in any human society. He knew that what he called "the social machine" demanded conformity and specialized aptitudes from the young, and that this was largely why children were compelled to go to school. But he did not appear to see the complex interrelations between a school system and a social class system.

Bowles and Gintis argue, for instance, that "the emphasis on intelligence as the basis for economic success serves to legitimize an authoritarian, hierarchical, stratified, and unequal economic system of production, and to reconcile the individual to his or her objective position within this system." [35] As they see it, it will be necessary for the hierarchical division of labor to be eliminated by organized social movements if self-realization is to become possible on any large scale. Theirs is a view of the system that is much more multifaceted than Goodman's and far less romantic. It is a view that renders the apolitical, fundamentally negative approach wholly insufficient.

Goodman recommended "real apprenticeships," workshops created by industrial designers, studies of urbanism "in the field," deliberate secession by scholars from the system. All these proposals have intrinsic value; many of them may diversify educational opportunities and counter alinenation. But, from the present vantage point, his hopes that these would shake the system and lead to its transformation seem ill-founded— as ill-founded as his belief, at the end of the 1960s, that Summerhill schools were appearing in slum areas and in the suburbs, that "a combination of education and direct social action is springing up on all sides," and that "the new advance of progressive education is a good index of what the real situation is."

None of this means that Goodman did not present some concrete and serious ideas respecting education, ideas that ought to be heeded even by those who take quite another view of the corporate society. Some of his notions are clearly attributable to the influence of John Dewey and A. S. Neill; some, to the anarchist centering on the individual and his private concerns. But the uniqueness of his proposals seems to have been a function of his ability to see the anxiety of young people trying to cope with structures that have gone beyond human scale. He could describe the frustration of a boy unable to use a hammer, the insistence on "doing the forbidden" among twelve-year-olds, the sexless climate in the classrooms, the "Sunday-afternoon" neurosis of chronic boredom. He could talk about delinquent behavior as a response to lack of opportunities, of causes to believe in. Young delinquents, he said, wanted manly jobs and self-esteem, better schools, "sex without fear or shame . . . a community and a country to be loyal to; to claim attention and have a voice." Middle-class youth resisted being groomed for slots in the system, and so they looked for jobs ambivalently and without commitment or hope.

McClellan has remarked on Goodman's capacity to see "rage" and "grief" and other violent emotions when he visited classrooms.[36] He wanted his readers to feel concern and compassion; he wanted to extend their sensibilities so they could feel the suffering of children. It is perfectly true, as McClellan points out, that such an extension of sensibility cannot provide adequate justifications for policy changes. Nor can it resolve the conflict between the educational needs of the person and the educational needs of the society. Nevertheless, his particular form of anarchy focused on the proposition that "The demands which others put upon a person are always limited by that person's legitimate drive to unify his thoughts, feelings, and actions." It may follow from this idea that "the anarchical community is the ideal educational environment," that the anarchist's "non-System will achieve those genuinely educative values to which even the System is, in principle, dedicated." [37]

Indeed this may be one of the central ironies in American education: so many of our values and commitments stem from the tradition of romantic individualism, which is the stuff of the American dream; yet the requirements of an increasingly technological society have led to practices that explicitly deny such values. Goodman's self-chosen task was to reaffirm them, to find some embodiment for them, to seek out ways in which individuals—free at last—would be empowered to abandon the system, leaving it to destroy itself. Projecting, looking with a novelistic eye within the "apparently closed room," he was able to penetrate the phenomenology of schooling, the actual experiences of young people struggling somehow to be. Doing so, he made it possible for readers and (after a time) reformers to ask questions of a sort never framed before. Even today, the concreteness of his vision serves many people as a corrective for abstract formulations of what happens in classrooms and for the language of management science that makes so explicit the schools' roles as factories.

Goodman's conception of mini-schools, for example, has touched the imagination of many teachers, perhaps especially the teachers of the poor. He proposed for each neighborhood a "tiny school" with four teachers for twenty-eight children in, preferably, found space. The space might be a store front; a housing project room that could be transformed, when needed, into a clubhouse; the basement of a church. "Top-down" administration would not be needed because of the small scale; there would be neither principal nor secretary.

He went on to talk about the appropriateness of such a model for the natural learning of reading; the opportunities for exposure to neighborhood activities; the provisions for flexibility in approach. "Given so many contexts," he said wisely, "the teacher can easily strike when the iron is hot, whether reading the destination of a bus or the label on a can of soup. When some children catch on quickly and forge ahead on their own, the teacher need not waste their time and can concentrate on those who are more confused." [38] This, along with his insistence on the need to combat blandness and verbiage, and on the importance of making people understand that reading is "a special useful art with a proper subject matter, imagination and truth, rather than a means of communicating top-down decisions and advertising," can be very suggestive—perhaps particularly in a time of Watergate Newspeak.

Goodman testified in this manner to the New York City Board of Education in the hope that awareness of failure where the teaching of reading was concerned would move the administrators to try a different way. At once, he nourished hopes of breaking down the system represented by "110 Livingston Street" and the bureaucratic centralism that dominated the work of the schools.[39] He was proposing a series of alternative school systems or alternative educational communities geared to therapy and the achievement of something resembling a real world. Children allowed to be "natural," spontaneous, interested, free, were children who would learn.

He was convinced that "any literate and well-intentioned grown-up" could teach and that the usual teacher-training was of little value, since "the relevant art is psychotherapy." Most important was concern for children and an ability to be inventive with them. Professionalism, he believed, tended to destroy the needed authenticity. Like the historian Michael Katz (who warmly acknowledged his debt to Paul Goodman), he saw connections between professionalism, bureaucratization, and scepticism with regard to "integration, small size, and community involvement." [40] Goodman was quite aware, in consequence, that the United Federation of Teachers would join with the bureaucracy in opposing his idea. At once, he recognized that the poor would be opposed to it, because of their suspicion of unstructured education. Katz, indeed, wrote that Paul Goodman did *not* represent the attitudes of poor people:

> In fact, I suspect that what the poor want for their children is affluence, status, and a house in the suburbs rather than community, a guitar, and soul. They may prefer schools that teach their children to read and write and cipher rather than to feel and to be. If this is the case, then an uncomfortable piece of reality must be confronted: Educational radicalism is itself a species of class activity.[41]

George Dennison, influenced by Paul Goodman as well as John Dewey, set up his First Street School as a mini-school for poor children on New York's lower East Side. There was freedom there; there were vital encounters between teachers and students; there was deliberate guidance where learning was concerned; there were projects, games, a great deal of play. Dennison knew well that the children's parents were in no way libertarian; but somehow he involved them as participant and overcame distrust.

> They thought they believed in compulsion, and rewards and punish-
> ments, and formal discipline, and report cards, and homework, and
> elaborate school facilities. They looked rather askance at our noisy
> classrooms and informal relations. If they persisted in sending us their
> children, it was not because they agreed with our methods, but
> because they were desperate. As the months went by, however, and
> the children who had been truants now attended eagerly, and those
> who had been failing now began to learn, the parents drew their own
> conclusions.[42]

Within two years, of course, the First Street School failed—for want of money, for lack of motivation on the part of the dedicated teachers.

Dennison said it was at best a stopgap, that the long-range effects—"poverty, neglect, abuse, racism, barrenness of environment" [43]— all continued. Like Paul Goodman, however, he believed that whatever hope there was for a new spirit in education lay "outside the present establishment . . . among parents themselves, and in revitalized com-munities, and among younger teachers." [44] Like Goodman, too, he thought school professionals were incompetent, that centralized institutions (even expert ones) corrupted and destroyed individual competence.

Still, the question of the "long-range" remains open. It seemed indeed likely, at least for a moment, that parent desperation and professional frustration would make experiment possible in education, might even permit the workings of love. What of poverty, neglect, abuse, rac-ism . . . ? Will increasing humaneness in the classroom cut into these in any significant way? If it makes a difference in the lives of children, will that make a difference in the larger society? If schools are eradicated, will that make a difference? Will the social pathology be cured?

In *The Community of Scholars*, Goodman had an optimistic answer. Objecting to the relations presently obtaining between school and society, he wrote:

> If the schools are used for free growth, criticism and social experi-
> ment, the socializing of the young becomes a two-way transaction: the
> young grow up into society, and society is regularly enlivened, made
> sensible, and altered by the fact that the young must grow up into it.
> Such social purposes preserve the community of scholars from
> becoming incestuous and merely academic. . . . Perhaps this is what

Jefferson meant by the need of a revolution every twenty years, every new generation.[45]

He did not think this could happen if education were made subservient to "national goals"; nor did he think it could happen if young people were not freed from continuous tutelage, so that they could choose what they wanted to learn. He thought they were earnest enough and confident enough; it was the Organization that persisted in making them into personnel. The rigid managerial aims of the society were continually being imposed upon them, because the system needed replacement and labor; and it was this imposition that made youth into an "exploited class."

It is clear enough that he had middle-class college students in mind when he made that point, not the sons of workingmen. He justified the claim by identifying contemporary youth with the French Romantics after the Congress of Vienna, with the bohemians who supported Mazzini and Garibaldi, and even with the supporters of Castro (who may have been, he said, "just the youth . . . with the complaisance of the disgusted elders"). None of these groups, in any traditional economic sense, were members of an exploited class; but Goodman saw them as people managing to resist preformation and becoming "class-conscious of themselves as exploited."

He had problems with them, of course. They had no sense of history, he realized; they had no tolerance for objective subject matter. He himself would have liked to teach, he said, the culture of the Western tradition: "the values of Greece, the Bible, Christianity, Chivalry, the Free Cities of the twelfth century, the Renaissance, the heroic age of Science, the Enlightenment, the French Revolution, early nineteenth century Utilitarianism, late nineteenth century Naturalism." [46] But he knew that the youth who so attracted him would have no patience with such a curriculum. He blamed it on the ways in which they had been socialized, on the ways in which the elite had imposed upon itself "a morale fit for slaves." As a result, youth compensated for felt powerlessness by nourishing "astonishing private conceits," by taking drugs, by groundless and frequently unreasonable commitments. Somehow or other, he kept musing, education "must unmake *anomie* and anxiety."

Education? He did not appear to appreciate the significance of what Herbert Marcuse had been describing as "false consciousness," signifying a "factual ingression of society into the data of experience—an academic confinement of experience, a restriction of meaning." [47] Due to the continual manipulations of the media, of rhetoric and advertising, people come to think they *require* styles of life, values, consumer goods, particular attitudes toward work, particular political candidates. After the antiwar struggles, the civil rights campaigns, the inventions of the counterculture in the last decade, there followed violence and frustration and despair. The opposition to the system that had been so heartening to Goodman was somehow neutralized. Young people in many places stopped experiencing what Marcuse called their "servitude." They were no longer "class-conscious" in Goodman's sense; but this was not solely or even largely due to education—nor to continuous tutelage, nor to the imposition of managerial aims. It was the result of the fundamental structures of a meritocratic, acquisitive, inequitable society which could neither be defied nor denied by people going it on their own, by individuals simply set free (within the structures) to *be*.

Goodman was not very hopeful at the end. First there were the doubts occasioned by the authoritarianism of certain young people, by their presumptuous choosing *for* other people, by an arrogance and hotheadedness he found so venal. He was troubled, too, by the activities of the neo-Leninist wing of the New Left.

> It is that the abortive manipulation of lively energy and moral fervor for a political revolution that will not be, and ought not to be, confuses the piecemeal social revolution that is brightly possible. This puts me off—of course they have to do it their own way. . . . Everything should be done for its own sake.[48]

Certain young people antagonized him by seriously talking about a future they would live without meaningful work. The hipsters irritated him, and the anti-intellectuals and the hecklers and the ideologues. Soon he was presenting himself ironically as "neolithic conservative" and (like the characters in his 1963 novel) bitterly concluding that all there was was "making do." Somehow the anarchist dream seemed unattainable; the door to the room seemed to be marked "No Exit" after all.

Perhaps piecemeal social revolutions have become futile in our time. Reading Goodman, responding to his passion and his disclosures, one cannot but wish for more. In *Growing Up Absurd*, he recalled the emergence of progressive education as a challenge to "boredom, lack of personal engagement, cultural irrelevance, and ineptitude, in conditions of mass industry and mass education." [49] He talked of James, Dewey, and Veblen and their war against leisure-class culture, waste, and greed. Populism had influenced them, he said, before its lapse into progressivism and modern liberalism. Regulatory agencies, progressive income taxes, women's suffrage, planning, welfare legislation, extended schooling—all these, he said, "have cumulatively added up to the one interlocked system of big government, big corporations, big municipalities, big labor, big education, and big communications, in which all of us are pretty regimented and brainwashed, and in which direct initiative and deciding have become difficult or impossible." [50]

In effect, he was saying, the pragmatists—because of their stress upon cooperative intelligence, planning, and social harmony—had prepared the way for the managerial society, for the system with which he was at war. His argument, however, was a peculiar one: fact, inference, guesswork, metaphor, and heuristic are all linked inextricably together. It may indeed be the case that regulatory agencies, welfare legislation, and the rest have led to the establishment of big government; but they have not necessarily caused the establishment of big corporations or big cities or big labor. And women's suffrage? Planning? Have these inexorably led to an inhuman environment, a sterile managerial system, a closed room?

Explaining the rise of the corporate state in this fashion, he was revealing his own dislike of a government that governs too much; but he was also revealing an incapacity or unwillingness to perceive the culture from a social point of view. He had a libertarian scorn for welfare, even though welfare legislation (before the advent of guaranteed incomes and negative income taxes) at least made it possible for the once invisible poor to survive. He rejected the idea of planning (even though he had been a city planner) because planning had to do with centralism in his mind. In *Communitas*, he talked about physical community planning to meet "economic, ecological, or strategic needs"; and there is no evidence that he had anything but a "piecemeal" revolution in mind. It is almost ironic now to read his comment on progressive education in the 1920s ("midway in this transition from the old tycoon-and-clergyman culture to the new managerial organization"):

> Progressive education drew on every radical idea since the middle of the eighteenth century, in pedagogy, politics, socialist and communitarian theory, epistemology, esthetics, anthropology, and psychiatry. It was as if progressive education resolved that *in the education of the children there should be no missed revolutions and no unfinished situations.*[51]

He said, however, that it soon became moribund as it gave way to the ruling class demand for an emphasis on "adjustment." People within the movement itself, he believed, betrayed it: concerned about socializing the young within the organized system, they compromised through "life adjustment." Dewey's theory "of continual scientific experiment and orderly, nonviolent social revolution"[52] was perverted once it was applied; and the only authentic progressive education (because it more directly challenged the Organization Men) was "Summerhill," modeled on Neill's

English school. Deweyanism, as Goodman understood it, was another "missed revolution." And so he abandoned what he conceived it to be; and, Dewey would have said, fell prey to an either/or.

Dewey had written in *Experience and Education*:

> When external authority is rejected, it does not follow that all authority should be rejected, but rather that there is need to search for a more effective source of authority. Because the older education imposed the knowledge, methods, and the rules of conduct of the mature person upon the young, it does not follow, except upon the basis of the extreme *Either-Or* philosophy, that the knowledge and skill of the mature person has no directive value for the experience of the immature.

He talked about the need for multiple contacts between the mature and the immature and said that the problem was how they could be established without violating the principle of learning through personal experience. "The solution of this problem requires a well thought-out philosophy of the social factors that operate in the constitution of individual experience." [53]

Goodman was, of course, disillusioned by what he conceived to be the appropriation of progressive education by the ruling class, and by the inability of the progressives to challenge the managerial system pragmatism (as he viewed it) had unintentionally helped to create. He did not find in Dewey's initial theories and proposals a mere continuation of the effort to impose middle-class values upon the young; he did not (as Michael Katz and his fellow revisionists were to do) find anything inherently "conservative" in progressivism, for all its failure to challenge the structures of the schools. He did not even isolate and criticize (as well he might have) Dewey's conception of "social control." Having viewed Dewey as a kind of latter-day Jeffersonian, he was able to adapt many of the things he had said, in addition to the emphasis on learning through personal experience. Then, with a type of *post hoc propter hoc* reasoning, when the progressives struck him as being less than Jeffersonian, certainly less than anarchist (if not "mental hygienic," behavioristic, or manipulative), he rejected progressivism in its transactional mode and turned toward a version stressing "free animal expression, learning by doing, and *very* democratic community processes."

The most serious oversight may well be the neglect of the "social factors that operate in the constitution of individual experience," since this seems to have been the source of many of Goodman's miscalculations and perhaps finally the source of his "neolithic" discontent. Opposed as he was to centralized planning and coalition politics, he did not concern himself, as Dewey did, with the emergence of an articulate democratic public; nor did he perceive education as being relevant to the growth of persons who would be socially conscious in a large sense, finding their own fulfillments through contributions made to a differentiated societal world. Dewey was also committed to face-to-face relationships and to the restoration of the spirit of the Jeffersonian community. He was also opposed to monopolies of knowledge by experts, to boredom and empty talk; but he believed that deliberate planning was needed to make local communities "genuine centers of the attention, interest, and devotion for their constituent members." Being a democratic socialist, he did not mean merely psychotherapeutic conflict resolution within the given community; nor did he mean merely planning physical settings in response to distinctive styles of life.

In *The Public and Its Problems*, he wrote that some day (after such planning) "organization may cease to be taken as an end in itself. Then it will no longer be mechanical and external, hampering the free play of artistic gifts, fettering men and women with chains of conformity, conducing to abdication of all which does not fit into the automatic movement of organization as a self-sufficing thing. Organization as a means to an end would reenforce individuality and enable it to be securely itself by enduing it with resources beyond its unaided reach." [54] The problem was not, according to Dewey, for men to separate themselves from society or the system. It was not to go in search of alternative communities, thus creating centripetal forces that would destroy the Organization. The problem, rather, was to discover ways of adjudicating differences, of shaping flexible social policies of a kind that would sustain individuality and nurture personal growth. He knew well enough about those conducting business for pecuniary profit and finding ways in which the "governmental machinery could be made to serve their ends." He understood the degree to which free communication was limited and the degree to which "hidden entrenchments" permitted exploitation of the mass of men. He said, "No man and no mind was ever emancipated by being left alone. Removal of formal limitations is but a negative condition; positive freedom is not a state but an act which involves methods and instrumentalities for control of conditions." [55] Unlike Goodman, he was not as interested in the invention of small conflictful communities as he was in the creation of a "Great Community: a society in which the ever-expanding and intricately ramifying consequences of associated activities shall be known in the full sense of that word, so that an organized, articulate Public comes into being." [56]

Unlike Goodman, too, Dewey was not inclined to celebrate "voluntary poverty"; nor was he as likely to discover a healthy significance and simplicity in the lives of the poor. Goodman, in his preoccupation with the anomie and anxiety of the sensitive middle class, believed that profit making could be benign. A "decent poverty," he wrote, could be made possible with increases in minimum wages, expanding unionization, and "a guaranteed minimum income, which would be far preferable in the United States to the present system of welfare payments and social services." The implication, again, was that far-ranging revolutionary change was neither necessary nor possible, that it might do more damage to persons than a maintenance of the present economic system, assuming that "counter-forces" were permitted to work. Libertarianism and the quest for personal authenticity, he continued to argue, would constitute sufficient opposition to the "overcentralized, interlocking, and empty society."

His opposition to Marxism and to dialectical explanations of what was occurring was intense, as we have seen. Marx's notion was that "the human essence is no abstraction inherent in each single individual. In its reality it is the ensemble of the social relations." [57] This, clearly, was anathema to Goodman, as was the idea that consciousness was culturally determined. He believed that individual choosing and individual thinking could transcend both economic determinism *and* the dialectical movement of history, if people could (through their own private actions) liberate themselves from control. In addition, his conception of social class and exploitation was totally at odds with any view focusing on economic relationships.

Like Dewey, however, he shared the Marxist concern for "demystification," in the sense that he spent much of his life challenging the idols and superstitions used to lull people into acquiescence. He expressed occasional dismay at "the Iron Law of Wages," at the military-industrial complex, at "the scientific war corporations, the blimps, the horses' asses, the police, the administrative bureaucracy, the career diplomats; the lobbies, the corporations that contribute Party funds." [58] Because he was so preoccupied with finding alternative ways of living, he was often more eloquent than Dewey or Marx in pointing to the man-made and *alterable* nature of institutions. Nevertheless, his major effort was not to transform those institutions by marching through them, attacking them directly, or deliberate social planning; it was clearly not to develop programs for long-range reconstruction over time. It was—and remained—a commitment to moving persons to concern themselves with private business, "to live communally and without authority, to work usefully and feel friendly, and so *positively to replace an area of power with peaceful functioning.*" [59]

Epilogue: Beyond Goodman

What does Goodman's critique of the system mean today? There are terrible realities in the present decade, and there are few illusions left. We know more than we admitted in earlier years about the inequities in our society and the injustices. We understand better than we did the corruptions and deceptions in high places; and we know that it is not enough for the sensitive and the restless to withdraw. Moreover, simply to call for freedom and doing things on one's own is to be in some manner elitist, since the call can only be heeded by those who have the living space for choice.

A Marxist novel, *Antoine Bloye* by Paul Nizan, makes this point. Antoine is the son of a peasant turned railroad worker. He receives a prize book when he graduates from school, and he opens it at random.

"Man is free" he reads, "he is ever aware of his power not to do what he does do and to do what he does not do."

Antoine reflects on these words and on some others besides. He ill understands them. Is his father free not to be poor, not to work nights, not to go where he does go? Is his mother free not to have her back ache from work, not to be tired out and old before her time? He himself—in what way is he free? To be free means simply not to be poor and not always ordered about. The rich enjoy a form of freedom. People with an income. So M. Jules Simon's words, too exalted for a worker's son, are understood by him in a way the author never intended. He is not refined, he does not grasp thoughts that are too noble, he is endowed with a simplicity he will find hard to lose. He shuts M. Jules Simon's gilt-edged book never to open it again.[60]

There is no question but that a pursuit of libertarian values makes sense in classrooms, since it is that pursuit that sustains the cause of individual growth. We have already suggested that the community envisaged by the anarchist may make the ideal educational community; and we have talked about the way in which the anarchist and the romantic individualist define precisely the ends to which public education has *explicitly* dedicated itself. The crucial problem, however, is and has been that those ends are unattainable in an industrialized, technologized, bureaucratized system, particularly when that system utilizes the schools to serve *its* needs.

F. Scott Fitzgerald's novel *The Great Gatsby* presents the dilemma in an appalling fashion; because Jay Gatsby began his quest with a dream of freedom much like the individualist dream. He was the son of God, he thought; in pursuing his personal Grail, he was going about his Father's business. The trouble was that what was once a Garden had become a Valley of Ashes; there was a "foul dust" in the air that corrupted the dream and made it into a search for "a vast, raw, and meretricious beauty" [61] rather than a Jeffersonian community and a harmonious life. Like Goodman, in a sense, Gatsby believed he could repeat the past, that he could "fix everything just the way it was before." At the end, the narrator muses: "He did not know that it was already behind him, somewhere back in that vast obscurity beyond the city, where the dark fields of the republic rolled on under the night. Gatsby believed in the green light, the orgiastic future that year by year recedes before us. It eluded us then, but that's no matter—tomorrow we will run faster, stretch out our arms farther." [62]

It is too late for that. This is a moment for the deliberate nurture of critical consciousness on all levels of society, on all levels of the school. Persons of all classes, of all heritages, have to be enabled to question what has so long been taken for granted; they have to be enabled to engage in cognitive and critical inquiry into their own social realities, to the end of transforming them.

This is quite different from simply "drawing the line." It is a larger and more rigorous effort than the one involved in inventing a new way of life. The reason for this is that it demands a struggle against oppression— against the "false consciousness" that submerges, against the powerlessness that silences, against the illusions that paralyze. Only when individuals themselves learn to explore the themes of their own lives and pose the questions these suggest, only when they launch themselves into the inquiry that is praxis, will they be in a position to transform their worlds.

For Goodman, it was enough to break with the overwhelming system and with the imposition of others' aims. But it is not enough simply to say No, to break away. Negative freedom and wide-awakeness are beginnings, not endings in these times. There must be social action, deliberate cooperative action to the end of creating a new society, perhaps a "Great Community," in which human beings—in new alignments, with new possibilities of control—can at last begin to be themselves.

Goodman said nothing about justice. He paid no heed to the fundamental inequalities that limit expectations and reduce the sense of worth. Concerned as he was for self-fulfillment and being in the world, he did not raise the question of how individual lives can be enriched by engaging in praxis cooperatively to the end of remaking the world. He must be remembered for his refusals and his visions; he must be cherished for his reminders of the absurdities men have made.

But there are new problems on the agenda now and new exploited classes demanding recognition and release. The concern of the educator today must be with equipping those he encounters to act *upon* their freedom, to move to realize possibilities they themselves can define. Goodman helped to show how unbearable it can be to live submerged; but nothing is truly recognized as intolerable until the sense of a new order emerges. Educators will be guilty of cultural imposition if they impose on students their sense of what the future ought to be; they will go the way of the Great Gatsby if they try to fix things as they were. "There is no distinction," wrote Paulo Freire, "between cultural action for freedom and cultural revolution." [63] The problem is to create a mode of education for liberation—a mode of education that will enable persons to combat domination and to transform their inhabited world.

NOTES

1. "Paul Goodman, A Conversation" by Robert W. Glasgow, *Psychology Today* 5 (November 1971): 62.

2. Ralph Waldo Emerson, "Self-Reliance," in *Emerson on Education*, ed. Howard Mumford Jones (New York: Teachers College Press, 1966), p. 106.

3. Herman Melville, *Moby Dick* (New York: New American Library, 1962), p. 22.

4. Melville, "Clarel," in *The Portable Melville*, ed. Jay Leyda (New York: Viking Press, 1962).

5. Henry David Thoreau, "Civil Disobedience," in *Political Man and Social Man*, ed. Robert Paul Wolff (New York: Random House, 1966), p. 136.

6. Emerson, "Self-Reliance," p. 109.

7. Thoreau, "Civil Disobedience," p. 146.

8. Charles A. Reich, *The Greening of America* (New York: Random House, 1970), p. 226.

9. Paul Goodman, *Growing Up Absurd* (New York: Vintage Books, 1962), p. 170.

10. Frederick Perls, Ralph Hefferline, Paul Goodman, *Gestalt Therapy* (New York: Delta Books, 1951), p. 297.

11. "From the Port Huron Statement," in *The New Student Left*, ed. Mitchell Cohen and Dennis Hale (Boston: Beacon Press, 1967), p. 15.

12. Jack Newfield, *A Prophetic Minority* (New York: New American Library, 1967), p. 87.

13. Paul Goodman, *People or Personnel* (New York: Vintage Books, 1968), p. 75.

14. Ibid., p. 49.

15. Paul Goodman, *Like a Conquered Province* (New York: Vintage Books, 1968), p. 257.

16. Ibid., pp. 279–91.

17. Goodman, *Speaking and Language* (New York: Vintage Books, 1971), p. 26.

18. Ivan Illich, *Deschooling Society* (New York: Harper & Row, 1971).

19. Goodman, "The Black Flag of Anarchism," in *Anarchism*, ed. Robert Hoffman (New York: Atherton Press, 1970), p. 151.

20. Peter Kropotkin, "Anarchism," *Encyclopedia Britannica* (1947), I: 873.

21. *Now and After: The ABC of Communist Anarchism* (New York: Vanguard Press, 1929), p. xi.

22. Emma Goldman, "Anarchism: What It Really Stands For," in Hoffman, *Anarchism*, p. 45.

23. Goodman, *People or Personnel*, p. 73; *Like a Conquered Province*, pp. 297–98.

24. *Like a Conquered Province*, p. 265.

25. Goodman, *Compulsory Mis-Education* (New York: Vintage Books, 1964), p. 26.

26. Soren Kierkegaard, "The Individual," in *The Point of View for My Work as An Author* (New York: Harper Torchbooks, 1962), p. 119.

27. Theodore Roszak, *The Making of a Counter Culture* (Garden City, N.Y.: Anchor Books, 1969), p. 201.

28. Paul and Percival Goodman, *Communitas* (New York: Vintage Books, 1960), p. 104.

29. Paul Goodman, *Utopian Essays and Practical Proposals* (New York: Vintage Books, 1962), p. 20.

30. Ibid., p. 21.

31. Herbert Marcuse, *One-Dimensional Man* (Boston: Beacon Press, 1964), pp. 3 et seq.

32. Sterling Fishman, "The Paul Goodman Problem and The Cult of Youth" (Paper read at AERA, April 1974). Mimeographed.

33. Goodman, *Growing Up Absurd*, pp. 159–60.

34. *Compulsory Mis-Education*, pp. 45–46.

35. Samuel Bowles and Herbert Gintis, "I.Q. in the U.S. Class Structure," *Social Policy* 3 (November/December 1972 and January/February 1973): 66.

36. James E. McClellan, *Toward an Effective Critique of American Education* (Philadelphia: J. B. Lippincott, 1968), p. 270.

37. Ibid., p. 297.

38. Goodman, "Mini-Schools: A Prescription for the Reading Problem," *New York Review*, 4 January 1968, p. 71.

39. David Rogers, *110 Livingston Street* (New York: Random House, 1968).

40. Michael B. Katz, *Class, Bureaucracy, & Schools* (New York: Praeger, 1971), pp. 108–10.

41. Ibid., p. 139.

42. George Dennison, *The Lives of Children* (New York: Random House, 1969), p. 7.

43. Ibid., p. 269.

44. Ibid., p. 275.

45. Paul Goodman, *The Community of Scholars* (New York: Vintage Books, 1964), p. 216.

46. Goodman, *Compulsory Mis-Education*, p. 114.

47. Marcuse, *One-Dimensional Man*, p. 208.

48. Goodman, "The Black Flag of Anarchism," p. 157.

49. Goodman, *Growing Up Absurd*, p. 80.

50. Goodman, *People or Personnel*, p. 44.

51. Goodman, *Growing Up Absurd*, p. 81.

52. Goodman, *Compulsory Mis-Education*, p. 42.

53. John Dewey, *Experience and Education* (New York: Collier Books, 1963), p. 21.

54. John Dewey, *The Public and Its Problems* (Chicago: Swallow Press, 1954), p. 216.

55. Ibid., p. 168.

56. Ibid., p. 184.

57. Karl Marx, "Theses on Feuerbach," in *Marx and Engels: Basic Writings on Politics and Philosophy*, ed. Lewis S. Feuer (Garden City, N.Y.: Anchor Books, 1959), p. 244.

58. Goodman, *People or Personnel*, p. 188.

59. Ibid., pp. 188–89.

60. Paul Nizan, *Antoine Bloyé* (New York: Monthly Review Press, 1973), p. 54.

61. F. Scott Fitzgerald, *The Great Gatsby* (New York: Charles Scribner's Sons, 1953), p. 99.

62. Ibid., p. 182.

63. Paulo Freire, *Cultural Action for Freedom* (Baltimore: Penguin Books, 1972), p. 83.

12

IVAN ILLICH AND DESCHOOLING SOCIETY: THE POLITICS OF SLOGAN SYSTEMS

Michael W. Apple

One contradiction that seems so odd at first glance is the fact that people who are being so thoroughly challenged by others often read them, teach them, and thus sometimes are even converted by them. Perhaps the best current example of this phenomenon is the work of Ivan Illich. His interest is in abolishing schools, yet his books consistently find their way onto book lists in classes within schools of education. Courses containing present and future teachers for the very schools he wants to eliminate discuss (and even get tested on) his ideas. It is hard not to see the paradox here. It could be explained by Marcuse's provocative notions of repressive tolerance and cooptation, where an institution opens its doors to radical ideas only to discuss them to death within the framework these radical ideas want to criticize. Or, it could be that educators themselves are riddled with self-doubt and are seriously questioning the role they play in society. Any explanation would probably need pieces of both interpretations of Illich's "popularity" among schoolpeople. However, explaining the paradox is less important for our own analysis here than seeing what Illich himself is actually about, exploring his strengths and weaknesses, and pointing to some possibilities for action.

In this chapter I have tried to provide a basic outline of Illich's educational criticisms that would represent the more extensive treatment found in his many (though often repetitious) writings on deschooling. Thus, the reader should not assume that this analysis deals with all Illich's points. In fact such a treatment would be impossible in an essay of this size. Rather, what I shall do is to point out the major aspects of his arguments and at the same time raise a number of criticisms of him, ones that may seriously detract from his potency. While Illich is provocative, he is also sometimes wrong. For example, in parts of this analysis it will be necessary to compare Illich's position to the Marxist tradition; he is seemingly indebted to it, yet he oddly misappropriates parts of it. He thereby weakens his arguments and runs the risk of making complex dilemmas seem easy to solve.

In a number of places throughout this essay, I have specifically chosen to let Illich speak for himself. This is done for two reasons. In the first place, it is helpful to get the style of an argument. In Illich's case this is actually quite important since style and content blend together, each complementing the other. Secondly, by letting Illich speak, the systematic ambiguity of his writings will be evident. As we shall see, this ambiguity is of no small moment in enabling various groups of people, people who might otherwise disagree, tune into certain aspects of his critique of the process of schooling and his suggestions for deschooling society. The ambiguity also has the opposing tendency, however, of being less than efficacious in leading to effective action by these groups.

At the outset let me note that Illich is not talking about schools in advanced industrial societies, but about schools universally as they are found in capitalist, socialist, and Third World countries as well. The roots of evil lie in the phenomenon of formal schooling, not in any particular economic form. Furthermore, he is not talking about increasing public expenditure to create alternatives to our dependence on schools. The answer is not new and more costly devices that will make people learn. Instead, what Illich envisions is a new type of relationship, but still an educational one, between men and women and their environment. But this requires some fairly radical rethinking not just about schools, but also about such deep-seated things as our dominant attitudes toward growing up, our perception of the types of tools available for learning, and the quality and structure of our day to day lives.[1]

For Illich, the fundamental choice we must ultimately make is that between "more efficient education fit for an increasingly efficient society and a new society in which education ceases to be the task of some special agency." [2] Now this is somewhat different from what educators and the general public are used to hearing, to say the least. Because of this it is easy to dismiss the notion of deschooling as patently absurd in the face of the way life really is. Yet, as I shall argue, Illich's fundamental weakness does not lie in his being totally unrealistic—he very consciously wants *not* to accept reality—but rather in his inability to deal with the complexity of changing what he perceives are the problems themselves. We shall look more closely at this in the next section.

Deschooling as Vision and Slogan System

It is wrong, I think, to argue against Illich because he is unrealistic. That is not what he is about. That is, Illich wishes to create a *vision* of different educational relationships, to posit a new reality based on trust and overt interpersonal need. In so doing, he must ignore current institutional practices as a basis for future educational ones. By creating a distinctly different picture, one that is at times nearly maddeningly vague, he hopes to enable people to disclose possibilities for educating themselves and others that go beyond what currently exists.[3] In essence, that almost seems to be Illich's plan, to show that there are alternatives to those basic practices now dominating the educational process so that individuals and groups of people can engage in self-conscious reflection and action on these "unreal" possibilities. One test of Illich's notions, hence, becomes their fruitfulness in stimulating our imagination, in forcing us to reflect on the taken-for-granted nature of a good deal that educators do. Here it is important to remember his priestly background and the critical place vision plays in religious thought, for in this tradition utopian prospects precede (and unfortunately too often take the place of) political action and argumentation.

In order to give power to any imaginative vision of alternative social relationships, it is important to illuminate the problems of current institutional practices. In more philosophical terms, one *bears witness to the negativity* of current relationships. This is close to a dialectical method of inquiry. One must call forth the contradictions, the antithesis, the negativity *within* any existing position so that these contradictions can stand against the common sense of that position. Only through the interaction of the negative and the taken-for-granted elements of an accepted position can a radically different alternative arise. Only when the negative characteristics of schooling—and here he means the very basic and fundamental structures of the institution—are used as lenses to focus on the supposedly positive elements of schooling, only through the contradictions of what schools are supposed to accomplish and what they actually do accomplish, can progress toward "true" education arise.

The notion of "true" education is obviously the key here. For Illich, education involves the conscious choice by an individual or group to learn something, to "school" oneself. As such it is a self-determining process, not a compulsory activity that is forced upon an unwilling or unknowing student.

I believe that only actual participation constitutes socially valuable learning, a participation by the learner in every stage of the learning process, including not only a free choice of what is to be learned and how it is to be learned, but also a free determination by each learner of his own reason for living and learning—the part that his knowledge is to play in his life.[4]

Based on this position, in Illich's view a good system of education must fulfill at least three purposes. Those individuals or groups who desire to learn must have access to adequate resources at any time during their lives, not just during the years usually set aside for formal schooling. Thus, technology must play a crucial place in the process of deschooled education. Quality education must also challenge the ideas of institutional certification by providing access for those people who want to share their wisdom with others who might want to learn it from them. Obligatory curricula become unnecessary. Finally, a system of education that proposes to be excellent must furnish an opportunity and the means for individuals to make public any issues or challenges they wish to make before the body politic.[5]

But how is one to deal with the complex problem of organizing people and recreating institutions (or creating new institutions) to fulfill these three purposes? Starting from the stance that the proper question to ask about education is not "What shall someone learn?", but rather "What kinds of things and people might learners want to be in contact with in order to learn which may enable them to define and achieve their own goals?",[6] he proposes four networks. Each of these grows out of his conception of "left-convivial institutions," networks of individuals or groups that "facilitate client initiated communication or cooperation." These networks of educational resources are ideal types that are more visionary than made to fit existing social arrangements. They include the following:

1. Reference Services to Educational Objects—which facilitate access to things or processes used for formal learning. Some of these things can be reserved for this purpose, stored in libraries, rental agencies, laboratories, and showrooms like museums and theaters; others can be in daily use in factories, airports, or on farms, but made available to students as apprentices or on off hours.

2. Skill Exchanges—which permit persons to list their skills, the conditions under which they are willing to serve as models for others who want to learn these skills, and the addresses at which they can be reached.

3. Peer-Matching—a communications network which permits persons to describe the learning activity in which they wish to engage, in the hope of finding a partner for the inquiry.

4. Reference Services to Educators-at-Large—who can be listed in a directory giving the addresses and self-descriptions of professionals, paraprofessionals, and free-lancers, along with conditions of access to their services. Such educators could be chosen by polling or consulting their former clients.[7]

Illich has little desire to make these proposals into recipes that would give a step-by-step syllabus for deschooling and establishing such networks. Once the vision is established, given his underlying faith in the nature of individuals as striving for "self-realization," [8] there will be a growing motivation to fulfill the possibilities inherent in the alternatives he proposes. This overly confident view, as we shall see, may provide some decided difficulties in Illich and his even more optimistic followers. However, the broadness itself that this view embodies may be helpful in a variety of ways.

Most proposals that have sought to change the nature of schooling, be they curricular proposals or those aimed at even more substantive alterations, are slogan systems. By calling these proposals slogan systems, I do not mean to denigrate them; rather, it is important to note that these systems of ideas are not usually "scientific" or "provable" in the way we usually talk about science or proof. Instead, slogan systems are founded on strong social and valuative commitments and have certain characteristics that may make them successful in changing every day practices in schools.[9] They do not aim essentially at producing new information or explaining social interaction as much as they aim at altering (often substantially) the usual patterns of things that had up to that time been accepted as given in schools.

Logically the difference might look like this:

scientific: If X, then Y.

   proposal from a slogan system: If you want Y, then do X.

The imperative, the commitment (Y), must be acceptable if the proposal is to be effective. But the effectiveness of a slogan system is even more complex than simply a viable social commitment.

To be effective in moving people to action a slogan system must have certain specific aspects.[10] It must be broad enough to encompass a wide variety of people who might otherwise hold disparate views. In this way, it acts as an umbrella to cover a diversity of social, political, and educational interests and enables people who have these interests to work together. But broadness is not sufficient. The slogan system must also be specific enough to give concrete suggestions for action to these committed groups and individuals so that the broad proposal "makes sense" in terms of their modes of operating in day-to-day life. This is a tenuous balance, obviously. If it is too broad, it has little power to give tactical guidance to the people who fit under it. If it is too specific, it risks alienating a large portion of its original adherents who disagree with some of the concrete suggestions.

Yet another characteristic of a successful slogan system is its ability to stimulate the imagination, to provide a means for going further than what is given. In essence, it needs what might be called "the power to charm," the imaginative capacity to attract both disciples and opponents.[11] Given the immense amount of space devoted to discussion, both pro and con, of Illich's thought on deschooling in books, journals, and elsewhere, it is difficult to find fault with him here.

A good example of a relatively successful slogan system in the recent past was Bruner's articulation of the structure of disciplines movement.[12] It was open enough to draw upon both advocates of "child-centered" education and those who felt that some aspects of the progressive movement debased the importance of sophisticated and disciplined inquiry into the disciplines of knowledge. By combining a discovery emphasis with subject matter specialization, it was able to give concrete suggestions for changing educational practice without eroding a significant extent of its support within a broad-based movement. As an aside, however, it is interesting to note that even with its success as a slogan system, it is possible to argue that the discipline centered movement was much less effective than most educators suppose in actually bringing about significant change in the patterns which dominate classroom life.[13] Thus, even if a proposal meets all these characteristics there is no guarantee of its success in altering social or educational practice. This is at least partly due to the inability of the field of education, and perhaps especially the curriculum field, in dealing with the political and economic complexity of institutional innovation.[14]

The "failure" of the discipline-centered movement substantially to transform the process of schooling, however, can at least partially explain why the notion of deschooling has found a number of adherents even among educators. If these ameliorative curricular and educational reforms continually do not live up to their promise, then the questions might be asked "Is it the very nature of the institution that must be changed?" or "What alternative frameworks can be designed that are more effective in enabling significant educational dialogue to emerge?" These are questions that Illich wants to take seriously.

This process of questioning is complemented today by the existence of significant groups of people whose appraisal of most if not all the dominant institutions of advanced industrial society is quite critical. Not only do these institutions—and schools among them—perform in a manner that does not alter the relative distribution of knowledge, power, and economic resources that exists now, but they are linked together in such a way that cultural, economic, and political challenges to prevailing institutional structures logically must include the school. It is difficult to censure, say, economic structures in a society, structures that seem to keep millions of people in poverty or in a state of anomie and alienation, without at the same time transferring these feelings to a rather immediate institution, the school. Thus, a coalescence of forces combining serious and often warranted questioning of nearly all of the major institutions of a society and the perceived inability to make schools significantly more "humanized" makes for more fertile ground than usual for a proposal such as deschooling and the slogan system in which it is encased. These conditions could cause a number of people to reject the current "reality" of schools and search for ways to find a new one based on someone like Illich.

While one should not carp about the "reality" of Illich's vision, it is quite possible to point to decided weaknesses in his program—that is, if Illich has put forward his alternative as a serious proposal for action rather than *only* as a model or mirror against which we are to see the decided problems of current educational practices. If the idea of deschooling society is "merely" a notion that enables us to reflect upon the differences between what we think education should ideally be like and our inability to come close to that ideal, then the test of its usefulness would be its ability to stimulate our thought. However, if the idea is intended to be more than this, to provide ways in which self-conscious agents can begin acting differently, then its fruitfulness must also be determined by its success as a *political* program.

Here, one of Illich's major weaknesses can be found. He provides a slogan system that can enable a number of disparate groups to come together and perhaps begin to talk and clarify their goals. This is primarily due to his description of the contradictions of industrial society—the possibilities to feed, clothe, educate, and make life fulfilling because of a society's wealth and technological power on the one hand, while there are such things as the deterioration of life in cities and our environment, massive poverty and inequality, and alienating and unfulfilling work on the other. However, while this illumination of the contradictions of a modern industrial order is relatively accurate, he does not provide specifics, an effective program that can be employed by these individuals and groups once these goals have actually been classified. In fact, it may well be the case, as Gintis has argued, that Illich's rather broad and ethereal program is a "diversion" from the rigorous conceptual, organizational, political, and ultimately personal analyses and commitment that may be necessary to effectively modify the conditions to which Illich points.[15] I shall have more to say about this later in our discussion.

Consumption, Reality, and the Hidden Curriculum

But what are the conditions of a modern industrial order that Illich points to and how does formal schooling in bureaucratic institutions fit in? Central to his argument is his analysis of the hidden curriculum of schools, the tacit teaching of certain social norms, values, and dispositions that are "guaranteed to produce a universal bourgeoisie," [16] a class of consumers who treat all aspects of knowledge as commodities. It is not the subject matter, per se, the overt curriculum, that teaches these things; instead, it is the very structure of the school as an agency that certifies competence which communicates these hidden perspectives. This is perhaps best stated in a quote from Illich himself.

> The hidden curriculum teaches all children that economically valuable knowledge is the result of professional teaching and that social entitlements depend on the rank achieved in a bureaucratic process. The hidden curriculum transforms the explicit curriculum into a commodity and makes its acquisition the securest form of wealth. Knowledge certificates—unlike property rights, corporate stock, or family inheritance—are free from challenge. They withstand sudden changes of fortune. That high accumulation of knowledge should convert to high personal consumption might be challenged in North Vietnam or Cuba, but school is universally accepted as the avenue to greater power, to increased legitimacy as a producer, and to further learning resources. . . . The hidden curriculum makes social role dependent on the process of acquiring knowledge, thus legitimizing stratification. [It] also ties the learning process to full-time attendance, thus illegitimizing the educational entrepreneur.[17]

Illich goes on:

> Everywhere the hidden curriculum of schooling initiates the citizen to the myth that bureaucracies guided by scientific knowledge are efficient and benevolent. Everywhere this same curriculum instills in the pupil the myth that increased production will provide a better life. And everywhere it develops the habit of self-defeating consumerism of services and alienating production, the tolerance of institutional dependence, and the recognition of institutional rankings. The hidden curriculum of school does all this in spite of contrary efforts undertaken by teachers and no matter what ideology prevails.[18]

Thus a consumer consciousness is effectively taught to students in schools. But that is not all, for, according to Illich, the very real human need for further learning is translated by this hidden curriculum into a demand for further *schooling* instead. Knowledge, a term that should signify intimacy with others and shared life experiences, is remade by the school into professionally packaged products and marketable credentials. Here, then, personal knowledge is (and must be) discredited, since students must be taught to consume ever more packages of official "public" wisdom. In this way, students learn not to trust their own judgment and to turn themselves completely over to the hands of therapeutic institutions, institutions which may actually cause many of the social problems modern society faces. That is, the hidden curriculum, and the attitude toward knowledge that coheres with it, produces disciplined consumers of bureaucratic instructions ready to consume other kinds of services and treatments from institutions other than the school that students are told are good for them.[19]

It is important, as well, that modern techniques of persuasion be used to make the individual consume "packaged" learning in a self-motivated fashion.[20] Thus, many reforms of schooling are really devices that condition students to be happy in institutions that prevent them from clarifying their actual educational, economic, and social situations.

The internalization of the hidden curriculum by students has important social and political consequences other than those noted so far. First, by learning to be a "consumer of pre-cooked knowledge," the individual also learns not to react to "actual" reality but to the reality that teams of certified experts have seen fit to distribute as a commodity. The student becomes politically powerless because the avenues of access to reality are controlled by the therapeutic institution, and the world behind the packaged recipes becomes what Illich calls neutral and hygienic, devoid of significant conflict and drama. The role of the school is to make certain that the process itself is accepted as natural, as the world *tout court*, by students.[21]

The second major consequence concerns the nature of schooling as a mechanism of social and economic control. Schools actually contribute to the maintenance of an already unequal society; they "conspire against the poor and disenfranchised." [22] Schools provide through their sorting and channeling functions a labor force that is differentiated according to existing economic needs and social stratification.[23] And this very economic model and the system of social stratification which arises out of it completes the circle by confirming individuals and groups in the slots they have been "trained" for. Thus, schools provide the fundamental mechanism for maintaining an unequal and oppressive economic and social order. They control people and they are ultimately central to the control of an economy.

Now Illich is certainly not alone in seeing schools as primarily institutions of social control. While Illich is a bit too reductive himself in perceiving schools as only agents of social control, the position that the educational structures of, say, the United States as they grew and developed represented conscious attempts to socialize (and ultimately control) large groups of people, and especially the masses of immigrants, has been articulated by several revisionist historians of education.[24]

There is a paradox here, though. While Illich obviously is against schooling as a formal mechanism of education—and this is his "radical" aspect—he can be interpreted as really part of a long line of *liberal* reformers who believe that education is *the* fundamental avenue for changing society. That is, while schooling itself is condemned by Illich as a means of education, the faith that education offers the basic strategy for institutional and cultural change is even stronger than in most of the past progressive educational reformers. This enables a number of people, who would not otherwise look twice at his proposals, to feel more comfortable with them since the problems of our society are still perceived as profoundly educational. However, this is still a relatively small percentage compared to the others who reject him outright.

Perhaps one of the major reasons many individuals feel uncomfortable with Illich's *approach* as well as his conclusions is something I mentioned earlier in this discussion, the fact that behind most of the questions educators ask is a model of how thinking should be carried on.[25] This involves two things. First, the model inclines us to ask ameliorative questions and to accept only those answers that fit existing conditions and assumptions. This is something of a normative framework that looks askance at basic research, at investigations that do not seem to have some visible relationship to current classroom problems. Thus, difficult conceptual issues such as whether the concept of, say, "learning" itself is really as useful as we believe are shunted aside or not even considered.[26]

Second, and for our interpretation of Illich quite important, is our tendency to neglect the contradictions and negativity built into each of the accepted ways we usually go about schooling children or valuing that schooling. That is, for Illich (and here he has borrowed a bit from Marx, though he could have made it more powerful) each intellectual and social institution has its contradictions, its negative elements, already built into it and as the process of the institution unfolds these contradictions get larger and larger. Therefore, as formal schooling reaches more people (supposedly a positive element), more people are turned into passive consumers who can be manipulated and the more schools reinforce existing social and economic distinctions that are generated out of the economic structure of a society (the contradiction and negativity).[27] Unfortunately, while Illich's approach is an interesting beginning and is perceptive in describing some of the very real problematics of current institutional practices, it fails where it needs to be strongest. This failure is twofold. First, it does not offer significant hope for more than individual action. Second, it tends to be naïve in what is really required to change widespread conditions in advanced industrial societies like our own.

On the Dialectic of Individual and Group

The vision of men and women that Illich seems to hold is obviously an optimistic one. Not only are people ("Man") self-creating and capable of self-direction, but any institution that fetters man, that prevents this potential from evolving, must be explained and either reconstructed or eliminated. Thus, schools act as barriers to this self-directing and creative process. They prevent individuals from realizing their human potential and actually work against a person even perceiving the need to fulfill these constitutive properties of man. This optimistic view of man is shared by many radical critics and in fact is the initial grounding of some of Marx's own early work. This confident stance, though, presents a weakness in Illich's analysis, one that poses much less of a problem in the Marxist tradition due to its complementary focus on the complex relationship between the individual and the group. Illich looks to each individual on his or her own to engage in the sort of questioning and institutional recreation he advocates. Each separate person is responsible for his or her own enlightenment.[28] What is missing here is any real sense of the importance of collective commitment, of the possibility that historical change may be the result of mass movements which embody the creative potential of each individual.[29]

This absence is evident in his proposal for left-convivial learning webs as well; for his suggestion actually substitutes an entrepreneurial relationship for the existing schooling process. It is the ethic of the small businessman able to sell his wares on an open and competing market. This in itself is rather dispersive and fragmenting of community. It also does little to account for the fact that the structure of the open and competing market may have had a strong impact on why schools are as Illich sees them.[30] This is one of the many paradoxes in the notion of deschooling. Its analysis of what may be taught through the hidden curriculum in schools is insightful, yet its suggestions for change may in fact lead one back to the very elements that could have caused the problems in the first place.

It is interesting to note here that the United States has had an extensive history of what could be called "entrepreneurial radicalism." From the Jacksonian to the Populist era, for example, a number of militant groups—among them the wheat farmers of the plains, metal miners in the West, and poor whites and blacks in the South—fought against the domination of society by business. However, they struggled to find mechanisms to provide the economic foundation for a society of small producers.[31] Illich, a person who begins his arguments by censuring a society which produces a universal class of petty bourgeoisie, finds himself in odd ideological company, then, if he is serious about the changes he advocates.

All this is not to say that individuals have no part in any realistic scheme for changing institutional arrangements. Quite the contrary is the case. In fact it is ultimately a question of individual responsibility to begin the questioning. However, what gives this critical process potency is the linking of individuals with others who are also engaged in similar activity. Now the broadness of Illich's slogan system does this to some extent. But this is not merely a strategy of finding people in the here and now who share like commitments. It also includes *a search for traditions* in the past that have struggled with the questions now before these people. In Illich's case, this tradition lies in something akin to the Marxist Humanism movement.[32] Unfortunately, the ties to this tradition are missing in his analysis. I say unfortunately for the reason that critical potency is enhanced when a group can find its roots and hence can identify with a movement that is and has been larger than itself. A struggle against, say, repression is made legitimate and at the same time the pressure for immediate "victory" is tempered by a historical perspective that illuminates the arena in which painfully slow progress can be made. A reader of Illich has no sense of this tradition and, thus, he or she has difficulty using him as an entry point into present or past groups that have been and are now confronting the basic institutional structures of, say, advanced industrial economic orders like our own. Here again Illich does not provide a mechanism by which individual *and* collective commitment can evolve. In saying this, I do not mean that one should appropriate a tradition whole, without criticism, without questioning. The act of criticism is especially important in dealing with any of the number of extant "Marxist" and "Neo-Marxist" positions. Rather, one grounds oneself in it and goes beyond the parts that are not utile; but it is impossible to go beyond what one does not know and Illich does not help one know.

Should Schooling Be the Central Focus?

Another problem arises with the idea that schooling provides the fundamental place for changing a given social order. The central role given to schooling by Illich is shown in his argument that any political program to change society that does not explicitly see the necessity for deschooling as well is simply not revolutionary. In his eyes, a political program must be evaluated primarily according to the following criteria: "How clearly does it state the need for deschooling, and how clearly does it provide guidelines for the educational quality of the society for which it aims?" [33] This is the case because schools are not merely dependent variables, but instead are the "major reproductive organs of a consumer society"; they are the essential mechanisms for producing institutional dependence and the habits and expectations of a "managed consumer society." [34]

To the criticism that schools are reflections of other social structures and that conditions in schools are symptomatic of other social ills, not strong constitutive elements themselves, Illich answers that schooling is actually the largest single "employer" in this society. If one counts students within the varied institutions of education and people employed or affiliated with educational, teaching, or other cultural structures, then one comes up with the rather startling figure that 62 million people are "employed" in schools (again including students in the category of school related workers), while only a slightly higher figure, 80 million, work elsewhere. Hence, the theory of deschooling merely recognizes the fact that a large proportion of work in this society is engaged in producing demands for goods and services that are necessary to keep an economy growing. Since the schools perform the most important role in producing these demands and are such significant institutions economically in terms of employment, then, according to the theory's proponents, disestablishing them is a truly revolutionary act in changing these other social structures as well.[35]

While there is a danger in reducing the argument over the role of the school in an industrial order to a chicken-and-egg debate, the question of the *roots* of the problem is critical. It is possible to argue that the conditions to which Illich points—the increase in bureaucratic consciousness and the growth of social welfare institutions and therapeutic conceptual models, the alienation and compulsive consumption, the "universal bourgeoisie"— are *not dependent* on the schools. While Illich never quite states that schools are the originating cause of social ills (and in fact occasionally points to economic roots) he comes quite close to this position by implication given his focus on the school as a central agency in advanced society. This places formal education and the bureaucratizing consciousness which dominates it in too much of a vacuum. It neglects the economic nexus that at least partially explains *why* such symptoms emerge. It also places unwarranted limits on appropriate avenues for action.

While educational, social, and political ideologies and institutions cannot totally be explained by economic analysis (and this is one of the misinterpretations of Marx by all too many individuals),[36] to ignore it as a major factor in analyzing the dynamics of these ideologies and institutions of a society is questionable. Without it, there is a tendency to see the educational mechanisms of a society as underlying causes as opposed to actually being symptomatic of much larger economic and cultural configurations. Parts of this economic explanation of the growth of alienation, "oppressive institutions," welfare, etc., are set out by Schroyer.

All advanced industrial societies are committed to the stimulation of economic growth (indicated by GNP, per capita income, and levels of investment) which creates social dislocations that increase the need for social amelioration. Societal planning and organization to increase economic growth has conflicting consequences because the revolutionizing of production deepens the collectivizing trends that uproot communities, individuals, and the environment. In this general sense, the dynamic of all advanced industrial societies recurrently results in a contradiction between the priority of economic growth and its social costs and consequences. It is this contradicting tendency that promotes the extension of bureaucratic organizations to deliver goods and services to those groups that suffer from rapid economic development, e.g., occupational and regional obsolescense. This generally results in the increasing integration of the individual into the web of bureaucratized organizations, concerned with work, education, government services, and so forth, and the resultant growth of "dependent participation" and manipulated consumerism. . . . [This interpretation stresses] the sociocultural consequences of stimulated economic growth that makes the work experience and everyday life less intelligible, transforms the human milieu into a technologically determined system, and systematically blocks symbolic communication by the superimposition of more and more technical rule and constraints derived from rationalizing processes.[37]

Even if Illich is correct about the importance of schools in the process of instilling ideological rules of action in students—and here he is probably more correct than in some of his other points—he does not go far enough in seeing the relationship among economic institutions, ideological production, and social agencies such as the schools. A more appropriate appraisal of the nexus between "repressive" educational institutions and a larger society, between knowledge production and economic production, could be found in the work of the critical social theorist Jurgen Habermas.[38] Starting out with a utopian concept of nonrepressive interpersonal communication—the ideal speech situation—Habermas constructs a framework for analyzing modern society and the ways in which scientific, therapeutic, and rational/bureaucratic ideologies are related to existing institutions, ways that prevent significant social change from arising. What makes it more interesting than Illich (though more difficult to read as well) is his combination of Wittgenstein's later work in linguistic philosophy with the reconstructed Marxism of Adorno and Horkheimer.[39] This is done in such a way as to illuminate the close connections between the styles of personal action, interpersonal communication, and economic relationships of a society on the one hand and the interest structures of the knowledge producing sciences and institutions on the other.

In essence, by showing the control orientation of modern institutions (something Illich certainly recognizes) and dialectically relating it to the rationality of control in the modern physical and behavioral sciences *which provide the technical expertise for policy making based upon and within these institutions,* Habermas is able to get much closer than Illich can to the problem of institutional reification.[40] In so doing, he also gives a clearer picture of the possible steps specific groups can take toward emancipation from these widespread rubrics of control. Furthermore, he does not shy away from pointing to the complexity of any serious analysis of advanced industrial society and the factors that must be considered in changing it. Illich's own analysis seems rather weak in comparison. Ignoring complexity is beneficial in stating positions in a broad enough fashion to gain support; it is less so if one wants to engage in knowledgeable action.

Etzioni's argument is instructive in regard to this complexity. He argues that many of the institutional forces of our society may tend to make children passive, dependent, and alienated. However, he raises serious questions about the reliance on deschooling for social change. In essence, in contradistinction to Illich's tacit espousal of a position that holds that by "changing children" one sets in motion major forces that will also change society, Etzioni asks if it is realistic to assume that the institutional forces that act to support the existing economically and politically stratified structure of our society will sit back and allow educational resources to be used against them. Furthermore, he raises the interesting and potent issue that deschooling, the eradication of formal educational institutions, serves to turn children over to a number of other problematic institutions including the authoritarian family and an exploitative labor market. It thus ignores the magnitude of the problem of changing a given social order.[41]

These points are rather telling. Nevertheless, there may be political and practical reasons for focusing on schools, not the reasons Illich gives, but reasons of another sort. Granted the problems are much deeper than even Illich himself realizes, but schools can be a proper focus for change for at least three reasons of another sort. First, they provide a testing ground, though not always a conscious one, for tactics and strategies that enable people to see the possibility of reasserting their role in the crucial argumentation over the means and ends of the institutions that distribute goods and services to them. Second, by often dealing with issues piecemeal, one structure at a time, concrete progress toward creating more economically, educationally, and socially responsive institutions can be effected. After all, there are children "living" in these schools now, and they must not be forgotten in Illich's or anyone else's attempt to create conditions for long-range institutional change. Third, focusing on the schools may lead to the clarification of where the real problems may lie. That is, our attempts and failures at making significant and lasting changes in schools may lead people to ask even more basic questions about the generally unresponsive nature of other organized structures in advanced industrial societies, and, hence, these attempts can be educative acts in the best sense of the term.

I do not mean in this section, however, to be totally negative concerning Illich. After all, if his goal is to stimulate imagination and argumentation through his vision, then he has found some measure of success. He also provides what is at times a telling appraisal of certain conditions which are found in schools and this, combined with suggestions growing out of an analysis of his weaknesses, as we shall see can lead to some possibilities for action on the part of educators and others.

Critical Scholarship and Critical Action

A major point, and one that Illich does expressly recognize, is the potential for social control in the *knowledge* that is taught in schools. This occurs in two types of knowledge. First, as we saw in Illich's treatment of the hidden curriculum, the social norms and values expressed in and by the basic structural properties of schools communicate to students "the way life really is" in a society, though this may in fact be a distorted picture of reality. Children internalize these knowledge forms simply by being in the school for a number of years. The knowledge is learned "merely" by participating in the activity of school life.[42] Second, and here Illich is weaker than he should be, the selection of "cognitive" knowledge in the school curriculum also effectively communicates a somewhat distorted view of reality,[43] a view that often supports political and intellectual quiescence rather than conflict and serious questioning by students. For example, investigations into the forms of knowledge found in science and social studies curricula indicate that there is a massive presentation of an ideology that ignores the importance of conflict and basic argumentation in these fields and social life in general. Assumptions of consensus—both intellectual and normative—seem to dominate the knowledge itself.[44] Not only is this an unrealistic presentation, but it embodies the interests and world views of only a limited representation of society and may cause students to have negative perceptions on the uses of conflict in making needed changes in society.

Investigations like these and many of the arguments offered by Illich can be better understood by again referring to the similarities they have to Marxist perspectives. According to this position, basic forms of knowledge and the criteria of selection and organization of this knowledge are not necessarily neutral, but are valuative in nature. They may, in fact, contribute to and be a mechanism of political domination. Apparently "objective" knowledge is often only partial knowledge, meaning structures that come from and legitimate the most powerful elements of a society.[45] The Marxist notion of "false consciousness" is helpful here.

The dominant consciousness of social groups is thought to be a reflection of their place in the economic and political structure of a society. The oppressed and minorities (in traditional Marxist theory, the proletariat and even the bourgeoisie) have views of the world—of what is important to know and to do, to produce and consume—that are "untrue." These views are distortions of reality that support the economically and politically powerful classes and groups of society. They are taught to the less powerful groups through these people's participation in the major institutions of society from economic structures to the family to the schools.[46] For Illich obviously and to a lesser extent for the investigators of the relationship between ideology and curricular knowledge, it is the school that is the central institution in effectively communicating this ideologically ridden false consciousness.

One thing that does arise from a serious treatment of these ideas is the necessity of seeing many educational problems in a larger context. Not all (or perhaps even most) our questions can be solved or even adequately posed in a "learning" framework. By the very fact that learning language is apolitical, it covers the relationships of power, expertise, and money that control a good deal of the process of schooling in the United States. Once this larger political and economic context is revealed, then *part* of the task of committed educators is to engage in the rigorous historical, analytic, and empirical scholarship necessary to show how many of the tools, categories, perspectives, and ideologies of education provide unquestioned support for this sociopolitical framework.[47] Models of what might be called critical scholarship need to be developed that take as one of their fundamental tasks the illumination of the concrete mechanisms by which this support for existing and often problematic institutional structures is marshalled in education.

This points to a problem with Illich. One of the dangers of someone like Illich writing about education is his lack of insight into the fact that many committed individuals are and have been delving rather deeply into the issues he raises. For example, he argues that an educational revolution requires as one of its facets a totally new orientation to educational research, one that does not merely seek to optimize the quest for efficiency within the existing institutional framework.[48] Now many people will agree with this, and in fact that is exactly the point. There are and have been numbers of committed educators who are seeking to establish a critical framework for educational scholarship, who are proposing new models of educational research and activity based on in-depth analysis of the strengths and very evident limitations to those models now in use.[49] This also points to the need for historical insight in the field so that the roots of this critical tradition (in people such as Counts, Rugg, and others) are not lost.

This is not to say that Illich is always wrong in making these arguments. Rather, if Illich's assertions are to go beyond mere stipulations, a good deal of further investigation is required in a number of areas. Perhaps one of the most important places to begin would be in what might be called the sociology of school knowledge. This type of study has important implications for curriculum thought, for example. We need to examine critically not just "how a student acquires more knowledge" (the dominant question in our efficiency minded field), but "why and how particular aspects of the collective culture are presented in school as being objective, factual knowledge." How, *concretely*, may official knowledge represent ideological configurations of the dominant interests in a society? How do schools legitimate these limited and partial standards of knowing as unquestioned truths? [50] These questions must be asked of at least three areas of school life: (1) how the basic day-to-day regularities of schools contribute to these ideologies; (2) how the specific forms of curricular knowledge reflect these configurations; and (3) how these ideologies are reflected in the fundamental perspectives educators themselves employ to order, guide, and give meaning to their own activity.[51]

But besides these important areas of scholarly investigation there are concrete and practical arenas for action on the part of committed educators to which Illich (usually unconsciously) points. For instance, an issue that Illich raises but does not go deeply into is the necessity of a change in our attitudes toward growing up. He very much wants to argue that the possibilities of choice and responsibility that students have today are conditioned by the economic needs of our society. The capacity for significant choice and the process of taking responsibility for one's own growth have atrophied in "schooled societies." One of the tasks of concerned individuals, then, is to expand both the range of choices available and, if I may go further than Illich, the *right* of students to make these choices.

Historically, childhood has become more and more a protected status and has expanded upward in age to include individuals who in previous times would have been accorded all the rights of adults. Aries'[52] excellent treatment of the history of childhood documents the interaction of economic and social necessity with the increasing contraction of the range of options "children" are entitled to have and the situations they may honestly confront without total simplification by "adults." That is, it is not naturally preordained that students should be protected from choice and should have few rights. This is very much a historical condition. It is also interesting to note that at the end of the nineteenth century many of the people in the United States who attempted to create institutions such as more "humane" schools and juvenile homes ultimately provided mechanisms that abridged already existing rights of children. They thereby contributed to the trend to which Illich accurately points.[53]

These facts, though, open up an area of action where considerable progress can be effected—that of *student rights*. The Supreme Court has ruled that schools are not places where constitutional guarantees are lost. The student does not leave his or her rights at the door when entering the schoolhouse. Exactly the opposite is the case. If education is to be more than mere training or indoctrination, then controversy, argumentation, and conflict must be an integral part of it.[54] Because of this, it is all the more imperative that the constitutional rights of students concerning freedom of speech, of access to information, or procedural and disciplinary activity, be upheld, reestablished, and strengthened wherever possible.

Action by educators can be centered around several concrete proposals here which while focusing on schools (something Illich might feel somewhat uncomfortable about) can lead to the significant expansion of the rights of students and on alteration of our common-sense attitudes toward growing up. Bills of student rights can be established in schools. Educators can help students clarify the causes of their discontent and help them focus on strategies for dealing with these problems. They can teach students their rights in as honest a fashion as possible. Furthermore, through their professional organizations, educators can lobby for organizational backing and monetary support for student rights advocacy and the judicial proceedings that may arise from the conflict over them.[55]

This can be taken even further if one treats seriously the question of the role of an educator in what is to some degree a political struggle. The work of John S. Mann is exceptionally important in this regard. He argues that part of the task of politically oriented educators (and we all are since it is exceptionally difficult for education to be neutral activity) is to affiliate with political movements and use the educational expertise they possess in programs that will assist these movements in the political education of workers, youth, and others who are oppressed. In this way, one goes beyond Illich in linking oneself with those concrete traditions that I discussed earlier in this essay.

It is possible to argue based on the analysis of Illich presented here that what is needed is a twofold or at least a dialectical outlook on the process of social and educational change. The primary focus of economistic Marxists is upon changing the material forces of society so that the distribution and control of goods and services is more just and equitable. This is rather reductive in that all economic, educational, and social problems are reduced to their basis in the modes of production of a given collectivity—e.g., what social class controls the wealth of a country and lives off the surplus value produced by the labor of a larger, poorer group.

Now this may or may not be an accurate explanation of social and economic stagnation and crisis in modern capitalist societies. However, even if it is accurate, its fundamental weakness lies in its lack of any coherent treatment of both character structure and the specific means or *mechanisms* by which individuals and groups of people are socialized into accepting as given, and indeed even yearning for, the ways in which goods and services are produced and distributed. That is, an examination of the economic roots of how a social order operates is incomplete without at the same time engaging in an investigation of the institutions whose job it is to instill and reinforce in the young the dispositions and propensities, the hopes, fears, and anxieties, that enable the economic roots to keep functioning.[56] And here is where Illich in his admittedly vague, "unreal," and even sometimes wrong way, can at least stimulate the questions that might profitably be asked in a more specific and disciplined approach. The "economic" and the "characterological" are complexly intertwined with the former still probably more fundamental than the latter, and educators need much greater sophistication in their analyses than has heretofore been the case. If Illich does not offer the sophistication, he at least offers an interesting problem both in refuting where he is wrong and going beyond where he is too simple.

One idea should be kept in mind in the future. If it is the case that schooling is dialectically linked to other more fundamental institutions of a modern industrial society, then attempts at making more permanent changes in the formal mechanisms of education (even toward Illich's own proposals) may require substantive critique and change of the institutions which surround the school. Therefore, educational commitment must go hand in hand with political, social, and even aesthetic commitment. Obviously such a realization makes it even harder to deal with; but then honest appraisals need to accompany knowledgeable action. Perhaps Illich is oddly correct here. One starts by taking responsibility for making oneself knowledgeable. Then, it will be possible for knowledge and action to be joined.

Conclusion

As discussed in the introductory chapter of this volume, Illich reflects the divergent forces of American culture. Like Charles Reich, Illich points out the need of sophisticated technology, but both of them are highly critical of the function of technological rationality as it is related to the central structure of the convergent forces. They seem to have relatively simplistic notions of consciousness and individual self, and their structure and functions. The dialectic of individual and group is treated in their works but it fails to address itself critically to economic, political, ideological, and characterological questions. Illich and Paul Goodman employ effectively a "negativity" approach (as discussed above) to their critical analyses of schooling. Yet their shortcomings, particularly Illich's, lie in the relative absence of their attention to the complexity of the relationship between schooling, on the one hand, and economically and politically determined structural conditions of society, on the other. This relative absence of attention to such complexity of the relationship among these variables, however, is very much reflective of the divergent forces, as we have seen.

NOTES

1. Ivan Illich, "Education Without School: How It Can Be Done," in *Farewell to Schools???*, ed. Danuel U. Levine and Robert J. Havighurst (Worthington, Ohio: Charles A. Jones, 1971), pp. 35–36.

2. Ivan Illich, "After Deschooling, What?", in *After Deschooling, What?*, ed. Alan Gartner, Colin Greer, and Frank Riessman (New York: Harper & Row, 1973), p. 2.

3. The concept of *disclosure models* is critical here. While these models do not seek to be pictorial representations of reality, they do seek to consciously bracket taken-for-granted perceptions and to create new "paradigms" that will enable more fruitful descriptions and possibilities to emerge. See, e.g., Ian Ramsey, *Models and Mystery* (New York: Oxford, 1964).

4. Ivan Illich, "The Breakdown of Schools: A Problem or A Sympton," *Interchange* 2, no. 4 (Spring 1971): 3–5.

5. Illich, "Education Without School," p. 37.

6. Ivan Illich, *Deschooling Society* (New York: Harper & Row, 1971), pp. 111–12.

7. Ibid., pp. 112–13.

8. Ignacio L. Götz, "On Man and His Schooling," *Educational Theory* 24, no. 1 (Winter 1974): 85–98.

9. I do *not* mean to infer here that science itself is not committed (though this may be tacit in science rather than overt) to social and valuative interests. As I have argued elsewhere, these interests may be quite strong in scientific rationality in advanced industrial societies. See Michael W. Apple, "Scientific Interests and the Nature of Educational Institutions," in *Curriculum Theorizing: The Reconceptualists*, ed. William Pinar and Paul Klohr (Berkeley: McCutchan, 1974); and Trent Schroyer, "Towards a Critical Theory for Advanced Industrial Society," in *Recent Sociology Number 2*, ed. Hans Peter Dreitzel (New York: Macmillan, 1970), pp. 210–34.

10. Here I am drawing upon the lucid analysis of slogan systems found in B. Paul Komisar and James McClellan "The Logic of Slogans," in *Language and Concepts in Education*, ed. B. Othanel Smith and Robert H. Ennis (Chicago: Rand McNally, 1961), pp. 195–214.

11. Ibid., p. 211.

12. Jerome Bruner, *The Process of Education* (Cambridge, Mass.: Harvard University Press, 1960).

13. Seymour Sarason, *The Culture of the School and the Problem of Change* (Boston: Allyn & Bacon, 1971). There are, of course, analytic and programmatic problems with the structure of disciplines approach besides this lack of effect. See, e.g., the work of Fred Newmann and Herbert M. Kliebard.

14. For a comprehensive treatment of the problem of curricular innovation, which unfortunately limits itself to only educational issues, see the entire issue of *Interchange* 3, No. 2/3 (Winter 1972).

15. Herbert Gintis, "Toward a Political Economy of Education: A Radical

Critique of Ivan Illich's *Deschooling Society*," in Gartner, Greer and Riesman, *After Deschooling, What?*, pp. 30–31.

16. Illich, "After Deschooling, What?", p. 5.

17. Ibid., pp. 8–9.

18. Illich, *Deschooling Society*, p. 106.

19. Illich, "The Breakdown of Schools," pp. 3–5.

20. Ibid., p. 4.

21. Ibid., p. 7. On the notion of the world *tout court*, see Peter L. Berger and Thomas Luckmann, *The Social Construction of Reality* (Garden City, N.Y.: Doubleday, 1966).

22. Neil Postman, "My Ivan Illich Problem," in Gartner, Greer, and Riesman, *After Deschooling, What?*, p. 144.

23. Cf. Gintis, "Towards a Political Economy of Education," pp. 57–62.

24. Cf. Clarence Karier, Paul Violas and Joel Spring, *Roots of Crisis: American Education in the Twentieth Century* (Chicago: Rand McNally, 1973).

25. Karl Mannheim, "The Sociology of Knowledge," in *The Sociology of Knowledge*, ed. James E. Curtis and John W. Petras (New York: Praeger, 1970), p. 118.

26. See Michael W. Apple, "Curricular Design and Cultural Order," in *Educational Reconstruction: Promise and Challenge*, ed. Nobuo Shimahara (Columbus, Ohio: Charles Merrill, 1973), pp. 157–83.

27. Merton's notion of "latent dysfunction" is similar here, except that structural functionalism tends to see society in static terms, while, say, Marxist positions see social flux and conflict as the usual occurrences. See Robert K. Merton, *Social Theory and Social Structure* (New York: Free Press, 1968), pp. 73–138. For the Marxian emphasis on social flux and change, see Bertell Ollman, *Alienation: Marx's Conception of Man in Capitalist Society* (New York: Cambridge, 1971), p. 233; and Michael W. Apple, "The Hidden Curriculum and the Nature of Conflict," *Interchange* 2, no. 4 (Spring 1971): 27–40.

28. Gintis, "Towards a Political Economy of Education," p. 35.

29. Ollman, *Alienation*, pp. 126–27.

30. The best treatment of Illich's acceptance of an entrepreneurial (but small-scale rather than corporate) society can be found in Gintis, "Toward a Political Economy of Education."

31. Michael Harrington, *Socialism* (New York: Bantam Books, 1972), p. 139.

32. Ludwig Kolakowski, *Toward a Marxist Humanism* (New York: Grove Press, 1968).

33. Illich, "Education Without School," p. 37.

34. Ibid.

35. Götz, "On Man and His Schooling," p. 93.

36. Marx, himself, was not an economic determinist in the strict sense of the word. See Ollman, *Alienation*, p. 9.

37. Trent Schroyer, *The Critique of Domination* (New York: George Braziller, 1973), p. 225.

38. There are exceptional problems in translating Habermas' analyses into English. The most accessible (in terms of readability) work is Jurgen Habermas, *Toward a Rational Society* (Boston: Beacon Press, 1970).

39. Cf. Theodore Adorno and Max Horkheimer, *Dialectics of Enlightenment*

(New York: Herder & Herder, 1972); and Martin Jay, *The Dialectical Imagination* (Boston: Little, Brown, 1973).

40. Schroyer, *The Critique of Domination*, pp. 132–67, 216–20.

41. Amitai Etzioni, "The Educational Mission," in Levine and Havighurst, *Farewell to Schools???*, pp. 95–97.

42. Philip Jackson, *Life In Classrooms* (New York: Holt, Rinehart & Winston, 1968).

43. Pierre Bourdieu, "Systems of Education and Systems of Thought," in *Knowledge and Control*, ed. Michael F. D. Young (London: Collier-Macmillan, 1971), pp. 189–207.

44. Apple, "The Hidden Curriculum and the Nature of Conflict."

45. Philip Wexler, *The Sociology of Education: Beyond Equality* (Indianapolis: Bobbs-Merrill, 1975), p. 50.

46. For a detailed treatment of "false consciousness," see Herbert Marcuse, *One-Dimensional Man* (Boston: Beacon Press, 1964) and the exceptionally well written portrayal of the ideas of "estrangement," "alienation," and "class interests" in Ollman, *Alienation*, pp. 121–36.

47. Michael W. Apple, "Common-Sense Categories and Curriculum Thought," in *Schools in Search of Meaning*, ed. James B. Macdonald et al. (Washington, D.C.: Association for Supervision and Curriculum Development, 1975).

48. Illich, *Deschooling Society*, pp. 101–2.

49. See, for example, the work of Huebner, Mann, Kliebard, and others. Much of this perspective can be found in Pinar and Klohr, eds., *Curriculum Theorizing: The Reconceptualists*.

50. Wexler, *The Sociology of Education*, p. 7.

51. Cf. Michael W. Apple, "The Adequacy of Systems Management Procedures in Education," in *Perspectives on Management Systems Approaches in Education*, ed. Albert H. Yee (Englewood Cliffs, N.J.: Educational Technology, 1973), pp. 3–31; Michael W. Apple, "The Process and Ideology of Valuing in Educational Settings," in *Educational Evaluation: Analysis and Responsibility*, ed. Michael W. Apple, Michael J. Subkoviak, and Henry S. Lufler, Jr. (Berkeley: McCutchan, 1974), pp. 3–34; and Apple, "Common-Sense Categories and Curriculum Thought."

52. Philippe Aries, *Centuries of Childhood* (New York: Random House, 1962).

53. Anthony M. Platt, *The Child Savers* (Chicago: University of Chicago Press, 1969).

54. Cf. the decision written by Supreme Court Justice Fortas in *Tinker* v. *Des Moines Independent Community School District*, 393 U.S. 503, 511 (1969).

55. Michael W. Apple and Thomas Brady, "Towards Increasing the Potency of Student Rights Claims," in *Schooling and the Rights of Children*, ed. Vernon F. Haubrich and Michael W. Apple (Berkeley: McCutchan, for the National Society for the Study of Education, 1975). See also John S. Mann, "The Student Rights Strategy," *Theory Into Practice* 10, no. 5 (December 1971): 353–62.

56. Bruce Brown, *Marx, Freud, and The Critique of Everyday Life* (New York: Monthly Review, 1973), p. 138.

13

EDUCATIONAL HORIZON: PROMISE, CHALLENGE, VULNERABILITY

Adam Scrupski

Standing as ideological and empirical models between Goodman's new reformation in education and Illich's deschooled society on the one hand and Establishment education on the other is what has been referred to earlier as the new school movement. The movement and the generally short-lived experiments that issue from it, popularly called "free" schools or "alternative" schools, is in large part a reflection of the countercultural thrust in American society. The movement's guiding implicit educational theory includes a relatively asocial or at least socially neutral neoromantic concern for the inviolability of the "individual" personality, what Nobuo Shimahara calls a "personalistic orientation."

Though some of these new schools have been successful at student self-governance,[1] the typical free school seems to be similar to that encountered by Sylvia Ashton-Warner in Colorado, where she served a year as a visiting teacher.[2] Having first been told that the parceling out of "jobs" (chalk caretaker, eraser clapper, paper collector, etc.) was not in keeping with the spirit of the school, though a thorough adaptation to the immediate predisposition of its pupils, two of whom replied in succession to a request to pick up some pencils, "They're not mine" and "I didn't use them." [3]

Warner went on to suggest child helpers for the teacher. This suggestion was denied because it would set up children as authorities intervening between teachers and the rest of the children; some conception of equality of status was by informing the cadre; however, it seemed not to be associated with a sense of interdependency. As Warner notes,

> Authority, Equality, Freedom. Yet someone did use the word "Responsible" one day . . . each is responsible for his own possessions. Not: each is responsible for all possessions, which is too collective.[4]
>
> Cooperation, that's what's missing, the desire to do, to help one another.[5]

Apparently the structure and external system sentiments of free schools are productive of a certain "I'm all right, Jack" temperament, despite general countercultural protestations of a sense of love and brotherhood. Difficulties that free schools have in establishing authentic self-governing student activities have been recently demonstrated.[6]

Warner's easy and individualized method of teaching reading developed among Maori children in New Zealand and publicized in her book *Teacher*[7] has been widely applauded by many free-school advocates and radical educational theorists, among them Paul Goodman.[8] Operating with a method which produces for each child his own collection of words, called a "Key Vocabulary," Warner finds support for her description of her American pupils as a *Spearpoint*, "The post-industrial; advance-guard of the society," [9] in the nature of the children's words. They are "outside" words, waving about "independent of emotion's origin."

> . . . the inside words have been covered before they came to school . . . so that some of the children are a dimension short.[10]
>
> There is little flow . . . from the inner man out. . . . The large percentage of their words have little instinctive meaning: fears, loves, desires, hates or reeling disappointment. They cannot be two-dimensional only, but it does look something like it.[11]

Warner's observations are curious and disappointing. Though no claim is made here or in *Spearpoint* that the Colorado school at which Warner worked was a typical free school, nevertheless the teachers are representative of free-school teachers; they are reported as saying the things we expect free-school teachers to do, and the structure of activities reported rings true as a free-school typification. One would expect more "inside" words from clients of a school whose link with the counterculture as well as its explicit principles imply a consideration of the individual self as sacred. One gets the impression as their New Zealand visitor writes about them, and is treated frequently with a certain callousness, that these children are deficient in role-taking propensity and therefore deficient in a sense of interdependence and sensitivity to others' plight (are the brotherhood-embracing protestations of their countercultural older brothers and sisters a huge overcompensation?). In any case, recognizable social purpose was missing. Is it because convergent social forces have already worked their way with these children, hiding and covering the precious "inside" self so thoroughly that even the nurturant atmosphere of a free school is not able to release it? Or is there a sense in which the free school itself is a convergent phenomenon, a newer version of the private school for a new elite?

The hope that free schools or alternative schools might attain a prominence that would enable them to be models and agents of diffusion for conventional public schools is not very promising. Schoolteachers and administrators are not a part of the public for the works of Neill, Holt, Kohl, Friedenberg, and Illich and appear relatively oblivious to the free-school movement. For divergent trends to be made manifest in public schools may require an alliance with emerging forces which are rooted perhaps in the changing general expectations and orientations of parent clientele, students, teachers and administrators, who constitute a significant institutional tributary to the mainstream of American society.

For one thing, the extent to which structural differentiation and specialization have multiplied identities available to teachers and students should be noted. Thus, there is an increasing amount of specialization among faculty personnel. Counseling itself is a new role, taking over responsibilities formerly performed by teachers and administrators. Increasingly there are created such positions as learning disabilities specialist, reading specialist, and audio-visual coordinator. Specialization by subject matter or discipline is on the increase. Greater opportunities for a special and therefore more secure identity for individual teachers have become available; as such, given the tradition of teacher isolation along with the added interaction made available by a "team" approach, teacher equality as an element in teacher belief-structure can be seen as strengthened and with it, as Dan Lortie observes, the autonomy of teachers in their dealings with the administration.[12]

Mini-courses, growing in popularity constitute both further specialization and individualization; History teachers teach courses on the frontier or the Great Depression while English teachers teach courses in Poe's short stories or a single novel. A history teacher who is peculiarly interested in the reconstruction period may teach a course in the period; one who is "into" rock culture may offer a course in the area; their identities as teachers among students can be further individualized as they deal more with the "sacred" and less with the profane, i.e., the curriculum specified by the board. As teachers find students who share these relatively idiosyncratic interests, bonds of particularism and affectivity are more likely to develop.

As noted, the normative upgrading that constitutes the necessity for teachers to play a more intensive, affective, personal "subordinate subsystem" role requires greater autonomy on the part of teachers; there are no clear guidelines in this area of teacher-pupil relationship; here bureaucratic routinization of decision-making may not enter. What appears to be an increasing difficulty in maintaining pupil discipline based on bureaucratic authority seems related. Children are no longer "good," because the adult at the front of the room has been given the title of teacher for a year or, in the case of substitute teachers, for a day. Increasingly, each teacher must *personally* legitimize whatever authority he presumes to. Despite the "solid front" that the teacher group attempts to maintain, authority for teachers is more now than ever a personally won affair. As such it may constitute an element of particularism within the basic universalistic orientation the school promotes. The existence of mini-courses, as it multiplies offerings and accounts for a set of narrower interests to be elected and shared by students and teachers, exhibits a trend toward the fusion of formal teaching and subordinate subsystem interaction.

More significantly individuated in terms of their teaching and nonteaching functions, divested of their "guidance" functions, less distanced socially from students, teachers are perhaps being divested of their general societal socialization responsibilities in favor of their teaching functions, the counter-cyclical action favored by David Riesman in the fifties, and perhaps a manifestation of structural differentiation and adaptive upgrading.[13]

That divergent forces should be reflected in students' behavior should be expected. Melvin Kohn has demonstrated that child rearing for self-direction, consideration, and responsibility rather than for obedience and neatness is related to occupational position.[14] As the occupational structure shifts, increasing the proportion of jobs involving work with people or data rather than things, involving a variety of approaches rather than a single routine operation, and involving loose rather than close supervision (Kohn's three indicants of occupational self-direction),[15] and census data tells us the labor force composition is moving in such a direction, the proportion of children reared for self-direction, curiosity, and consideration may also be expected to increase. Such children, it is suggested, are more highly individuated and more personally autonomous. Their individuality should be reflected in a greater demand to be treated as an individual within the social world of the school.

In this respect one gains the impression that except in working-class schools, the variety of extracurricular activities has been increasing along with the variety of curricular activities. The latter, involving nonvoluntary participation and therefore less susceptible to control by leading crowd groups perhaps constitutes a thrust toward a more egalitarian or democratic student social structure. Some of these "new" activities and identities are competing successfully with athletics and cheer leading for prestige and esteem within the student group. A significant unanswered empirical question is: Is a greater variety of activities manifesting itself in larger schools, as Conant predicted, or in smaller schools?

The thrust for autonomy among children reared for self-direction, consideration, curiosity, and happiness has been exhibited in recent years in student movements on elite college campuses. While there has been some diffusion to high school situations, by and large high schools generally have not experienced such politically motivated movements and high school administrators and staff have not been forced or even asked to any great extent to share their decision-making activity with students. On the other hand, recent years have seen the advent of "modular" scheduling with its varying time allotments making rigid control of student movements a virtual impossibility. More and more high schools are releasing students on their own recognizance (the analogy with penal-system terminology is probably not accidental) during study period, lunch period, or other academically unassigned time. And, as David Matza suggests, the amelioration of child dependency of the past several years constitutes a kind of revolution of expectations among youth and is likely to lead to demands for greater amelioration.[16]

One even notes informally, as perhaps a reflection of divergent forces, some amelioration of the rigid tracking system in the schools. In the more "cultural" kinds of courses, specifically English and social studies, increasing numbers of high schools appear to be "mixing" their students. In Meadowbrook Junior High School in Newton, Massachusetts, curricular placement is almost exclusively a student-elected matter, though, of course, in the absence of other class-counteracting agencies, such individual student elections may not affect very strongly the stratification of student groups. Of course, at the elementary school level evidence of the individuation of pupil clientele may be seen in "open classroom" approaches and "individual guided education."

Already noted has been a trend in school organization to a "house plan" or "school-within-a-school" structure, wherein relatively small collectivities of students are assigned to a relatively small cadre of teachers, who presumably are able to fashion a more enduring and diffuse relationship with their students over their career in the school. Open-plan architecture has broken down the barriers that have so long separated teachers at work; in such schools it is possible for colleagues to confer with one another, professionally or informally, just as colleagues in other professions do. As a result, perhaps the "specter of fear of loss of control" will fade for the teacher, who is now in a more immediately socially supported position, a position in which his "humanity" may become more visible to students. A second consequence may be the greater diffusion of successful teaching practices, as they become more visible to teachers, thus enhancing a thrust toward genuine professional colleague control. A trend toward a more sane physical education, one which does not require huge gymnasia (which constitute one of the facilities supposedly necessitating larger schools; one cannot build a gymnasium for only two or three hundred students), may be emerging.[17] Hopefully, creative administration may yet deal effectively with the other such centralizing and aggregate-izing facilities like libraries and science laboratories.

In *Life in Classrooms* Philip Jackson was able to examine fifty teachers identified for him as superior by administrators. (Some anti-administrative cynics might protest that such identification is Establishment-biased and therefore suspect. Experience suggests, however, that such identifications would be confirmed by pupils and their sponsors; there is a sense in which administrators are the only official personnel in a position to judge the receptions teachers get from the school's clients and tend to know who is really teaching and who is not.) In a series of interviews Jackson was able to identify four characteristics of these teachers.[18] The first was a sense of immediacy concerning their work with children. Jackson uses the word "spontaneity" to describe it. These were teachers who gave little emphasis to testing of any sort; not the type who, when asked how a particular child is doing reply, "Wait till tomorrow when I give the test; then I can tell you."

A second theme arising from Jackson's interviews was informality. These teachers reported being "casual" with children; a "lot of jumping around," and being as much as possible "like a family group sitting around a fireplace or around a table when some question has come up and they're discussing it." [19]

A third characteristic of the successful teacher was professional autonomy. Jackson's interviewees rejected curriculum guides, mandated lesson plans, restrictions on choice of teaching materials, and close supervision.

The fourth theme discerned in the interviews was individuality, indicating a concern on the teacher's part for children as individuals. Although these teachers confront an entire class, "it is what happens to individuals that really counts." [20]

Without laboring these characteristics of teacher personal behavior, we might note that they are consistent with the emerging structural phenomena noted above. The multiplication of identities making a more thorough individuality possible for both teacher and student, the spontaneity and autonomy demanded by normative upgrading, the diffuseness or informality implied in curricular departures in the form of mini-courses and scaled-down organizational structures, and the autonomy developed through enhanced pluralist and professional solidarity have all been outlined. While nowhere is seen anything approaching a deschooling of society, or a new reformation in education, what is taking place in some quarters is a certain de-bureaucratization or de-institutionalization of schooling, and if not a reformation, at least a certain clearing away of dogma and myth. Such movements have a way of growing.

NOTES

1. Independence High School, which serves a working-class clientele in the "Down Neck" section of Newark is one.

2. Sylvia Ashton-Warner, *Spearpoint: "Teacher" in America* (New York: Alfred A. Knopf, 1972).

3. Ibid., pp. 24–25.

4. Ibid., p. 52.

5. Ibid., p. 85.

6. See Center for New Schools," Strengthening Alternative High Schools." *Harvard Educational Review*, 42, no. 3 (August 1972): 313–50.

7. Sylvia Ashton-Warner, *Teacher* (New York: Alfred A. Knopf, 1963).

8. Paul Goodman, *New Reformation* (New York: Random House, 1970) pp. 99–100.

9. Ashton-Warner, *Spearpoint*, p. 97.

10. Ibid., p. 9.

11. Ibid., pp. 101–2.

12. Dan Lortie, "The Balance of Control and Autonomy in Elementary School Teaching," in *The Semi-Professions and Their Organization*, ed. Amitai Etzioni (New York: Free Press, 1969).

13. David Riesman, "Thoughts on Teachers and Schools," in *The Anchor Review*, no. 1 (Garden City, N.Y.: Anchor Books, 1955).

14. Melvin L. Kohn and Carmi Schooler, "Class, Occupation, and Orientation," *American Sociological Review* 34, no. 5 (October 1969): 659–78.

15. Ibid., pp. 671–73.

16. David Matza, "Position and Behavior Patterns, of Youth," in *Handbook of Modern Sociology*, ed. Robert E. L. Faris (Chicago: Rand, McNally, 1965).

17. See Muska Mosston, *Developmental Movement* (Columbus, Ohio: C. E. Merrill Books, 1965), and *Teaching Physical Education: From Command to Discovery* (Columbus, Ohio: C. E. Merrill Books, 1966).

18. Philip Jackson, *Life in Classrooms* (New York: Holt, Rinehart & Winston, Inc., 1968), pp. 115–43.

19. Ibid., p. 127.

20. Ibid., p. 133.